A MIDSHIPMAN'S ODYSSEY

EXCERPTS FROM

"LETTERS TO LOU"

THE SEQUEL

Jim
ENJOY!!

Donald "Ben" Hogan
2/2003

A THREE YEAR JOURNAL OF LIFE AT THE MASSACHUSETTS MARITIME ACADEMY

1954 -1957

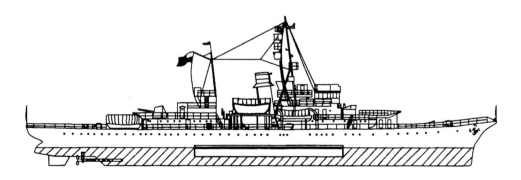

Donald "Ben" Hogan

Copyright © 2002 by Donald Hogan

ORIGINAL COPYRIGHT 1998

Written for the men and women, past, present, and future of the
Massachusetts Maritime Academy

Proceeds to
MMA Emery Rice Scholarship Fund

ISBN 0-7414-1248-9

Published by:

INFINITY
PUBLISHING.COM
519 West Lancaster Avenue
Haverford, PA 19041-1413
Info@buybooksontheweb.com
www.buybooksontheweb.com
Toll-free (877) BUY BOOK
Local Phone (610) 520-2500
Fax (610) 519-0261

Library of Congress Control Number: 2002113784

Printed in the United States of America
Printed on Recycled Paper
Published October, 2002

DEDICATED TO THE CLASS OF 1957
AND IN MEMORY
OF OUR DEPARTED SHIPMATES

Charles Broadbent

Guillo Cialdea

Joseph Fee

James Gillen

Forbes Graham

Richard Greer

David Lacaire

Robert Stickney

Robert Taylor

Robert Anderson

Edward Ascollio

Joseph Lach

Neil Duffley

Frederick Ferguson

James McKenna

John Flaherty

Robert Strautman

June 2002

Moored at Buzzards Bay, Massachusetts

CONTENTS

Officer Of the Watch - Dave Lacaire

"RACKS"
- Four High -

INTRODUCTION

Lou   November 1954   Ben

"LETTERS TO LOU" ©
THE SEQUEL

This is not a narrative but rather a daily journal (logbook style) of stories, historical notes, and interesting facts of life at the Massachusetts Maritime Academy. Events, **_all true_**, are both funny and tragic. Occasionally names have been omitted to protect the guilty and to prevent embarrassment to those involved. Most of these "sea stories" are "excerpts" from letters written to my future wife while I struggled to survive. Tales and documents were also contributed by classmates, shipmates and others.

Credits to contributors are noted in brackets, i.e. [Charlie Nobel], on the following Contributors page. A special thanks goes to Mr. Richard Boles, who proof read, edited, and advised me on this project.

Very little has been written about life at the Academy. This journal is an attempt to fill that gap. The text or other documents have been **copied as written** with very few exceptions. It may also answer the question "What was school like back in the **_olden days,_** Grampa?"

I apologize in advance for some of the terminology or phrases used. To attempt substitutions would not be *"telling it as it was"!*

July, 2002

Engine Room

CONTRIBUTORS

Louise (Lou) Hogan	Major source. Three year letter collection.
Jane Stickney '57' '58'	*Many pages "Excerpted" from Bob's letters shown in Italic text*
James McCluskey '57'	Pot-Pourrri of "Good Old Days", Academy Documents
Admiral Maurice Bresnahan '59'	"Once There Was A Youngie" and a "Youngie Cruise Letter."
Richard Boles '57'	Fez, Brookline Bar, and Hurricane Capers
Admiral John Aylmer '57'	Charleston Ship History, and Academy Documents
Henry Billings '57'	Several Funny Sea Stories
Peter Readel '57'	More Sea and "Hop" Stories
Anthony Scarlata '57'	Bus, Hop, Genoa Stories
John Sweet '57'	Bird Poem
Lincoln Kennedy '57'	Old "Muster" Photographs and Newspaper Articles
John Dalton '58'	Aug.-Sept. 1998 Alumni Bulletin Articles
Robert Roffey '57'	Cracked Corn, Feathers and Sid Story
Evan James Pilavis '82'	Accident Report from Alumni Bulletin Aug.-Sept. 1998
Lincoln Kennedy '57'	
and Peter Readel '57'	Co-Editors of 1957 "Muster" Yearbook
'57' - "Muster" Yearbook Staff	Anthony Scarlata, James Gillen, Robert Taylor, John McGrath, Frank Southworth Robert Young
Captain Thomas Bushy '74'	"Rwetheryet" taken from the Captain's Log of the Schoolship 'Patriot State' MMA Web Page. Arrival Feb 20,1998
Joel Tanner	Computer/Scanner Assistance McGee Ranch, Sahuarita, Arizona
Sandy Parker	Computer Expertise, Arivaca, Arizona
David Hogan	Second Edition Assistant
Various MMA Yearbooks	Several interesting items and ideas purloined
Richard Boles '57'	"Letters from Lou" - Editor and Advisor and "The Hurricane Caper."
Donald (Ben) Hogan	Author and Illustrator. Several stories and Historical Notes

PART 5 REPLIES, ETC. CONTRIBUTORS

E-mail replies in the order presented	Maurice Bresnahan '59, Richard Volkin '63, Kevin Seaver '63, Rob Tryon '99, Stan Suza '85, Peter Galanis '55, Frank Johnson '59 Bob Hillary '75, Tricia Kelly '94, Richard Phelan '54, Janice Walton, Carl Megonigle '57, Don Flynn '52 , Paul Berry '55 & '56, Lee Cueroni '55.5 Neil A. Daboul '88, Robert Vaughn '49, Don Leach '49, Paul Driscoll '62 thru '65, Tony Scarlata '57, Mat Cleary '94, Jack A. Butler '47, Larry Marsden, David Anderson '91, Chuck Sweet '59, Josh Hill ?, Al Wilson '59.

A SPECIAL THANK YOU TO...

George Stewart '56	For his extensive verification and amplification of life at MMA.
Jane Stickney	*Research of the Doyen/Bay State's first year and cruise information.*
Sandy Parker	Once again, for her patience and assistance with "MS Word."
Unknown Artist	For the ships drawing on the cover taken from a '57 Yearbook.
Numerous Others	For your Email messages expressing how much you enjoyed the first edition of "Letters to Lou."

HISTORY OF THE ACADEMY

In 1891, the Massachusetts Nautical School, forerunner of the Massachusetts Maritime Academy, was established. At that time, the bark "Enterprise" served as the training ship for young men aspiring to follow the sea. Many of these men have gone on to become leaders in the maritime field.

A new training ship, the barkentine "Ranger", was acquired from the U.S. Navy in 1909. This vessel, later renamed the "Nantucket", carried the cadets of the Massachusetts Nautical School to the four corners of the world as good will ambassadors of their country.

After World War I, the Nautical School began to find itself getting behind the times, but the proud "Nancy", as she was called, continued to traverse the oceans of the world for two more decades, despite numerous attempts to abolish the school during the depression.

But once again as the dark clouds of war began to gather, Massachusetts was called upon to supply the sea with the men who make our Merchant Marine and Navy the greatest in the world. To keep pace with this ever increasing demand, the buildings and the facilities of the shore base were established. The course was necessarily shortened, and every eighteen months a new group of young officers took their places in the U.S. Merchant Marine as graduates of the Massachusetts Maritime Academy.

At the end of the war, the course was lengthened to three years, and additional subjects were introduced so that the graduates could take with them a college degree, in addition to their Naval Reserve commissions and Merchant Marine licenses.

In 1948 the gunboat "Charleston" was acquired and, in an effort to bring ship and school closer together, the Academy was moved to the State Pier in Buzzards Bay where the ship could be berthed. Shore facilities were improved, but whether this will become a permanent base or not is something that time alone will determine.

Whatever the future holds for our Academy, it is the sincere belief of every young man who has had the good fortune to be one of her graduates that she will continue to uphold the traditions of the state of Massachusetts by producing many of the finest seafarers in the world.

Quoted from the 1953 " Muster" (Yearbook)

The Academy remains at Buzzards Bay situated on 55 acres overlooking the Cape Cod Canal. Surrounded by water, this beautiful campus includes specialized labs, dock facilities, dormitories, and the modern training ship, Patriot State. The student body of about 750, male and female cadets, attend for four years with the annual Sea Term Semester taking them to many foreign ports of call.

June 1998

HISTORY OF A TRAINING SHIP

U.S.T.S. CHARLESTON

TRAINING SHIP OF THE MASSACHUSETTS MARITIME ACADEMY 1948 - 1957

The fourth **Charleston** (PG-51) was launched 26 February 1936 by Charleston Navy Yard; sponsored by Mrs. C.L.B. Rivers; commissioned 8 July 1936, Captain R.K. Awtrey in command; and reported to the Atlantic Fleet.

Charleston sailed from Norfolk, Va. 24 February 1937 to join Squadron 40T, the special force in the Mediterranean created during the Spanish Civil War to patrol and guard American interests. With this squadron she visited Dubrovinik, Yugoslavia; Trieste and Naples, Italy; and Algiers before returning to Charleston, S.C. for overhaul 24 April. On 9 July, she left Charleston for Balboa, C.Z. where she became flagship of the Special Service Squadron, carrying out a varied program of exercises and battle practice in the Panama area until 1 March 1938, when she stood north for Charleston.

Returning to the Caribbean again between 21 April and 3 October 1938, and between 4 January 1939 and June 1940, **Charleston** joined in Army-Navy maneuvers, conducted offshore patrols, and created good will by visits to Central American and Mexican ports. During the second of these cruises, she again served as flagship. On 8 September 1940 **Charleston** cleared Norfolk, Va. for Seattle, Wash., and duty as flagship for Commander Alaskan Sector, 13th Naval District. From 6 November 1940 to 27 November 1941, she made five cruises from Seattle north to Aleutian and Alaskan waters to guard this long section of American coastline.

Upon entry of the United States into World War II, **Charleston** intensified the schedule of patrol and convoy escort duties necessary to protect this far-north region and, except for four voyages to west coast ports for maintenance, she operated from Dutch Harbor or Kodiak throughout the war. Along with her escort and patrol duties, she carried out such missions as landing reconnaissance parties, aiding stricken ships, and taking part in the operations at Attu, which was assaulted 11 May 1943. Two days later, **Charleston** arrived to bring her firepower to support Army troops ashore, bombarding Chichagof Harbor, and screening the transports lying off the island. During the attack of Japanese bombers on 22 May, she evaded aerial torpedoes by radical maneuvering, while splashing one enemy plane and helping to drive off others. She provided call fire until the island was secured, and supported its occupation through convoy escort runs between Attu and Adak.

At the close of the war, **Charleston** prepared for Far Eastern duty, and on 25 November 1945 arrived at Hong Kong. She also visited Shanghai before returning to San Francisco 4 March 1946. Here she was decommissioned 10 May 1946 and **transferred to the Massachusetts Maritime Academy 25 March 1948.**

Charleston received one battle star for World War II service.

"A COMMEMORATIVE REVIEW OF A TRAINING SHIP"

In 1948 the officers and cadets of the Massachusetts Maritime Academy traveled to San Francisco and boarded a new training ship, the **USS Charleston**.

Returning to Cape Cod via the Panama Canal, the "Chun", as she was fondly nicknamed, was berthed at the State Pier in Buzzards Bay, now the permanent home of our school. While there would no longer be sail drills on the "Chun", she was no less successful than Enterprise and the "Nancy" in churning out seafarers of the finest order. Life was virtually the same as on earlier schoolships. She had a long easy roll and with her low freeboard and armored belt an uncanny inclination to smash straight through the big ones. The Navy built two of this class; her sister, Erie, was torpedoed and later sank off Curacao. The design was highly successful and provided a prototype for the earlier Hamilton class cutters.

The **Charleston** was 328 feet in length with a 41-foot beam. Her draft was 13 feet. She had oil-fired boilers driving twin-geared turbines, developing 6,000 shaft horsepower at a speed of 20 knots. The "Chun" was able to accommodate 275 officers, cadets, and crew in very tight quarters. She cruised the waters of the Pacific, Atlantic, South America, Caribbean and Mediterranean for a decade until age and a growing enrollment necessitated a larger and newer vessel. She was a fine ship in every sense of the word.

In the fall of 1957 the **Charleston** was retired and relieved by the Navy's Attack Troop Transport USS Doyen(APA-1) which was later renamed the Bay State.

"STAND BY TO GIVE WAY, LADS - GIVE WAY TOGETHER!"

Lee Harrington
Rear Admiral, USMS
President

(1974)

THIRD CLASS YEAR

PART 1 - YEAR 1

August 17, 1954 Report date for those appointed to the Class of 1957 of the Massachusetts Maritime Academy, "The Cape Cod College of Nautical Knowledge", and the good ship "Charleston", otherwise known as the "Chun"(or CHN). Our home for the next three years.

This was the first day of my nautical career. Eager, excited, and ready to go! I am not alone, about a hundred other guys have been "**delivered**" to this site. Some are fresh out of high school, others are military veterans. All quickly learned to respond to the cry of **"young man"**. All agreed to the fact that they are lower than whale excrement on the bottom of the ocean. All have also agreed to three years of voluntary confinement and to play the game of **"You Bet Your Weekend"**.

The first week of a **"youngie's"** experience is eloquently described in the third part of this journal by one of our youngies (Bresnahan). I won't even attempt to compete with such an outstanding composition here.

Prior to my arrival I met a beautiful young lady named Sandra *Something* at the Stoneham Community Swimming Pool. She learned of my acceptance by MMA and told me about this really nice guy she knew that also went to MMA. When you get down there look him up, tell him we are friends. I'm sure "he will take care of you." He was waiting for me, assumed I was responsible for their break-up, and really did "*take care of me*." I became the servant of the "Pink Bubble".

We all took a tough entrance exam for admission several months earlier. It turns out that for the first week all we really had to know was our numbers, letters, colors and the ability to walk upright. To confirm our identity we stenciled our name on everything we were issued. One of the items was a strange knife that we wore on a heavy string around our neck. Months later we were allowed to clip it and our keys on a belt loop. The pointed instrument is called a marlinspike which is used to untie bad knots and other things.

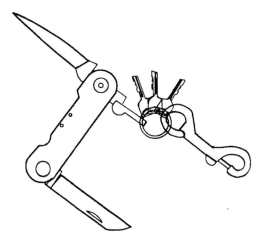

In addition to the knife, youngies were required to act as "Butt Machines" and to always have cigarettes and matches available to dispense to the upper (superior) class.

August 18, 1954

Dear Lou,

This is my first of, probably, many letters to you.

I'm trying to figure out what the hell is going on around me. This place is a madhouse!

**MMA CAMPUS 1954 – AFTER HURRICANE
TAYLOR'S POINT   BUZZARDS BAY, MASS.**

The campus consisted of a classroom building, a parking lot, a long wooden finger pier, a garbage battery, and the patrol gunboat "Charleston". The ship was an old Navy cast-off used to train merchant mariners. The sandlot west of the parking lot was used for playing or practicing outdoor sports. All of the above was isolated on the southern end of the Cape Cod Canal, Buzzards Bay, Massachusetts. It's truly "God's Country" ... nobody else would claim it! The weather was consistent, always windy and cool or foggy and damp. A rare warm sunny day was justification for a celebration.

I had a cold for three years!

"THE QUARTERDECK"
M.T.S., CHARLESTON, MASS. MARITIME ACADEMY

A simple but memorable scene, especially when one considers how many times in the course of three years midshipmen crossed this gangway.

Remember the Captain's masts and check musters held here?

Many a frigid or steaming watch was stood here over the years. The gangway represents conventional boarding and disembarking methodology, a sometimes boring substitute for bow and stern lines which, as we know, presented risk, excitement, and demerits.

[Jack Aylmer]

Letters to Lou...

August 25, 1954 They've had me chipping paint all week and giving me all the dirty details they can think of. The underclass around here are planning a revolution. A lot of good it will do them!

August 30, 1954 There's a lot of excitement down here now. The hurricane is only about two hours away. The officers have confined us to the building. The ship has been secured to the dock but they are afraid that it's going to break free.

The officers are in conference now. The grapevine says that they might move the ship to Martha's Vineyard and take cover in a small cove. The engineers have had the ship ready with a full head of steam for about an hour.

If they move the ship we will go with it.

It's only ten o'clock and the storm won't hit with full force until twelve. They expect more than seventy miles per hour winds at eleven.

All classes have been canceled. The under-classmen are confined to the building. The upper jobs have been snaring some of the small craft that's drifting alongside. Every so often a small sailboat will drift across the canal and smash against the rocks.

One kid no longer has a roof on his car.

I was over to the restaurant (snack shack) about fifteen minutes ago. On my way back, while I was running full speed for the building, the wind caught me and held me fast for about five seconds. I never felt so helpless in my life.

The small finger pier that we have to cross to get to the ship is swaying badly.

August 31, 1954 They are still raising hell down here. The food is getting better but I'm still not getting much sleep.

Only sixty-five miles from home. It might as well be a million.

As I write this the upper jobs think I'm studying. If I get caught I'll have to write this about ten times and read it before the class as another youngie has done earlier tonight.

September 1, 1954 The hurricane left us with a huge mess. We are still tied up at the State Pier. They did not move the ship. We are not allowed to go more than two hundred yards from the ship. The National Guard is out in full force to prevent looting. We worked until 1 AM mopping the water out of the building. There was 6 to 20 inches of water covering the floors. The doors are warped and off some hinges.

Up at 5 AM to continue the clean-up. The Captain, chief mate, and a few students lost their cars to the sea. Some of them were swept into the canal. The Captain's car, driven by the wind, rolled across the parking lot, bounced over the log barrier, floated about 20 yards further and then slowly sank into the canal. At that point a cheer went up! At the height of the storm most of us were standing on the leeside of the main deck. The ship was rolling and riding above the finger pier. Usually we ride level with the pier. We could only see about half a mile due to the heavy rain. The cars in the parking lot were covered by the tide and the spray of the high winds.

The snack shack across from the building is now about fifty yards northeast of its original position and five yards from the canal. Most of the cottages in the area were smashed and off their foundations. The guy that owned the snack shack also lost his home and car. Someone said his property was worth twenty-seven thousand dollars....all gone. He said he had enough and was moving to Colorado.

We saw a lot of real nice boats drift by. One of then rammed the ship and sunk thirty yards off the port bow.
Port = Left side...Starboard = Right Side

Never saw such a mess in my life. The only thing not damaged was the ship. We have water and the ship makes its own electricity. The food has been rotten. If you like boiled eggs, lettuce, and tea you'd love it here.

Third Class Year

...this place is a madhouse!

As I write this I'm hiding in a corner in the locker room below decks. The upper jobs have slacked off as far as the hazing is concerned, but the work parties have gotten worse.

I was topside a few minutes ago and saw a few land owners estimating the damage. All the time, work, and money that they have put into their camps is now nothing but a pile of lumber. Really sad!

The most terrible part of the storm was the loss of life. A body was sighted off the port side of the ship about one o'clock, but they couldn't snare it. It drifted into the bay. There are several known dead here at Taylor's Point, but we haven't heard any more since last night.

We don't have a radio, telephone, or contact with the mainland. The only people allowed to leave the ship are the officers and the unlucky kids that have lost their homes on the Cape.

As I write this I can hear some upper job yelling at a group of guys that were caught hiding in the gear locker. Oh well!

We went on a hike today looking for our small boats. The upper-job in charge, of course, marched us through the biggest puddles he could find.

I've been writing this all day (off and on). I'll write about five lines and some upper job will find something for me to do. I'm writing this on the side of a locker. Every time someone slams a door the paper, pen or both get jarred around.

Supper was hot tonight but the food was lousy! It looked like snails mixed in gravy and flavored with seaweed. I had four slices of "bunny" bread and a glass of milk. I won't eat anything I can't identify.

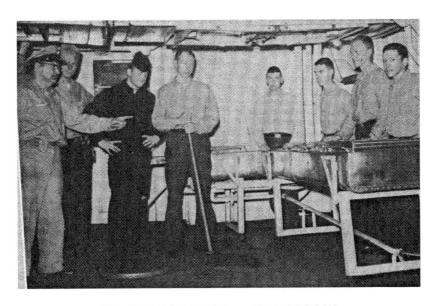

SID, STEAM TABLES, and MESSCOOKS

THE HURRICANE CAPER

The hurricane had blown across Buzzards Bay that day. The finger pier was underwater and cars were floating off the pier. Almost every house on Taylor's Point had been destroyed or severely damaged. The water level was two or three feet deep in the main school building. Taylor's Point was underwater and the devastation manifested itself in all directions. The Governor of Massachusetts had declared marshal law and ordered the National Guard into Buzzards Bay. The road leading into Taylor's Point was cut off by water and patrolled by the National Guard. There was no power, no lights, just penetrating blackness and silence.

The sight of all this chaos and devastation inspired three or four of the more civic minded first classmen to think about refurbishing and redecorating the "junior officers" wardroom which was located in the forward compartment of the Charleston. The collective mind of these first classmen resembled that of a ship with its rudder stuck hard over. The conditions for such a venture were auspicious in that Mr. Wickander had the deck and it was a very dark and moonless night. Accordingly, sometime after midnight, six or eight youngies were roused from their otherwise fitful sleep and ordered to report to the lifeboat on the port side of the main deck. Quietly, under the guidance and leadership of the first classmen, the lifeboat was lowered over the side without awakening Mr. Wickander. The youngies leaned their backs into the oars while a first classman at the tiller guided the lifeboat around the bow of the Charleston. The rowing was accompanied by the singing of an appropriate rum drinking song which all hands were directed to participate in. Undoubtedly this provided inspiration to one and all. The logic was as tortured as a position from Kama Sutra. As they rowed onto Taylor's Point, which was still under several feet of water, silence was ordered about the boat. Slowly, patiently, they drifted in and around what was left of the houses on Taylor's Point. A feeding frenzy ensued as couches, stuffed chairs, and lamps were quickly salvaged and stored in the boat. The order was given to lean into the oars once again as slowly they maneuvered their way back to the Chung. Silence was ordered as the lifeboat pulled up along the port side of the ship and slowly and quietly was hoisted aboard and secured in its davits, like a sacrificial goat tethered to a post. The salvaged items were unloaded and taken to the forward compartment to furnish an otherwise empty "junior officer's wardroom." Here, those high and mighties who had become the object of their own adoration could relax and reflect at the end of the day. This civic mindedness on the part of the first classmen has been a continuing source of inspiration for all the youngies involved.

[Dick Boles]

September 3,1954   A youngie was directed to steal a box of oranges from the galley this morning. He then spent the afternoon making juice!

There is a letter waiting for me in the mail bag. I missed mail call yesterday due to Mr. Berry. I'll get it later today.

I finally got a night's sleep. They didn't pay attention to me last night. It's just the lull before the storm. I understand (from the grapevine) that the choir just can't do without me and that I'll be back in the show tonight. They salvaged a book of 250 favorite and modern songs from one of the cottages down here. I bet we sing everyone of them at least

BUZZARDS BAY
DEC 5
6 PM
1954
MASS.

3 CENT STAMP

Miss Louise Moldt
Lawrence Memorial Hospital
Nurses Home
170 Governors Ave.
Medford, Mass.

…this place is a madhouse!

I thought I would send you a rough idea of what we do with all our spare time (ha-ha). "Turn-to" means to clean up the living quarters and the heads. This we do every time we turn around.

5:55 AM	I get up early to turn soft music on for the upper jobs. They like a soothing atmosphere in the compartment. I also provide coffee for several upper jobs.
6 - 6:10	Dress, wash, and muster on the pier.
6 - 7:45	Turn-to.
7:45 – 8	Breakfast.
8 - 9:45	Classes. Before class we march around, drill and present colors.
9:45-10	Mid morning break. Mild hazing period.
10-12:45	Classes.
12:45-1	Lunch formation.
1 - 1:15	Lunch.
1:15-1:30	Turn-to.
1:30-3:30	Sea maintenance (chipping paint) or seamanship (rowing whale boats).
3:30-4	Turn-to.
4 - 5 PM	Usually washing, steel wooling brass or the *floors* of the head.
5:00-5:00	Rest period.
5 - 5:15	Supper formation.
5:15-5:30	Supper.
5:30 – 6	Work and play (ha) formation.
6 - 6:15	Turn-to.
6 - 8:45	Study period. Usually the upper jobs set us up as an **"86"** (look out) watch and have a little fun.
8:45-9:40	Turn-to. I've joined the band so I usually miss this one.
9:40-10PM	Shower, wash, shave(with three sinks and sixty guys) and get into your rack before 10 PM. Taps.
10 - 6 AM	The usual evening ceremonies start about 10:30. Normally we have evening concerts, miscellaneous talent shows, and a few dance hall routines. If you saw Stalag 17 and remember the Christmas scene, you'll have a pretty good idea of the type of ballroom dancing we have here.

If we're lucky we'll get two or three hours of real sleep.

A couple of great guys would like to be fixed up for the ring dance. Know anyone that would like to go to the dance?

We are gonna have a "field day" this afternoon. That means we'll wash, polish, shine, and steel wool every corner of the ship and building. It usually runs all day, most of the night, and all of tomorrow morning.

September 4, 1954   I'm writing this in the building between classes. As I look around I can count nine guys that are asleep at their desks. If they get caught they'll get 10 demerits and lose a weekend.

Last night was hell around here, no one got any sleep. The upper jobs went out and got blind. They came back around 3 AM, got all of us up, and had a concert on the mess deck. If I told you everything that happened you wouldn't believe it.

This morning we had a general appearance inspection. We all failed. They made sure that there was something wrong with us. I'm on report for not shaving, dirty fingernails, uncombed hair, dirty shoes, and un-pressed pants. I was lucky some guys will never get their things or themselves together. They expect us to be perfect but they don't give us time to do things that are required.

We're back in class this morning without electricity. No study period tonight in the building.

I was caught above decks yesterday without my hat. I had to write "I will not go above the decks without my hat" 300 times before I could go to bed. Turned in about 1 AM.

Letters to Lou…

The youngie class drag themselves back and forth and look like a bunch of dope fiends. Everyone in the class has bags under their eyes. Even with all the comforts and luxury we have, I wouldn't give it up for the world. In fact sometimes I enjoy this place. Weird, huh? When we get together and talk over what's happened its always good for a few laughs.

I received your letter yesterday at lunch but didn't get to read it until supper. I can spot your blue envelopes long before they call my name. It sure helps to take my mind off this place.

Tell Kay that I've got her fixed up with a guy from Quincy. He's a great guy. I'll tell you more when I get home. Say hello to everyone at the nurses home for me. I can fix up Elaine if she wants. Also, give my regards to Miss Tate the next time you see her.

September 7, 1954   I've been standing watches with my good friend Mr. Berry all week. I'm his messenger eight hours a day every day this week. We stand four hours watch and have eight hours off. It's not too bad. The hard part is when your off watch you have to work with everyone else. This without a doubt will be my worst week. After this week the rest will be a push-over. Can't wait to get home Friday. The problem is that the weekends go by too fast.

Saturday let's go to the drive-in with a few cokes and cold beer. OK!

September 13, 1954   Things are about the same down here. I think I've shined every pair of shoes in the compartment. Two pair belonged to my buddy, Mr. Berry.

We had a couple of surprise tests today. The studies are getting a little stiffer everyday. I suppose you can't expect them to get easier.

I'll call Thursday night at 7:50. I'll let you know what's going on. I'm not sure about a ride. Probably have to hitch-hike in my job suit with the sea bag of laundry.

September 14, 1954   Well this place is in an uproar now. The officer of the deck has left the ship and there are no officers aboard. The 1st jobs are having a ball. We have a loud speaker aboard and they are sure putting it to use. *"Now hear this....* All those forward run aft ... all those aft run forward...etc."* Guys were running into each other, around each other, and jumping over everything. I just hid and watched. Stupid but kinda funny! *"Now hear this... All those that have not done so, do so now"* was just piped.

They had Greer on the beach in his skivvies this afternoon. I don't know why, but he is still cold and trying to thaw-out.

We have been invited to a party in Brookline after the Ring Dance. Sounds great! Lets go and have a ball! OK!

September 15, 1954   Just returned from kangaroo court. I was the assistant defense council for Dick Greer. He was charged with laughing in class. Joe Lach was the district attorney. We pleaded our case since 10 PM. They, of course, returned with a guilty verdict. We haven't been sentenced yet but I bet we pull some real deals!

…no eraser!

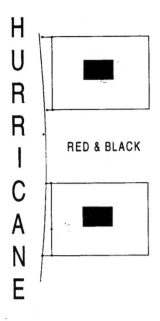

RED & BLACK

The upper class have posted storm warnings. Expect another hurricane tonight. They call it **"Hurricane Charleston"**. We were hosed down pretty well. They ran the youngies through the cold hose spray. They came out soaking wet, cold and damn mad. Slept in wet skivvies that night. One 3rd job emptied a bucket of water on a 1st job's head. They sat the youngie in a stream of cold salt water and threw water at him for fifteen minutes.

I've never worked harder, studied less and laughed more in my life. Some day someone should write a day-by-day account about what goes on down here. It could be a best seller. There are more characters collected here than in a circus. I never stop laughing. There are times when I really love this place. Weird huh!

Lt. Harrington (our math teacher) entered the classroom this morning. Our poor unfortunate deckie section leader, Eddie Ascolillo, called us to attention. We rose to attention. *"Be seated"*. We did so! He wrote several equations on the blackboard and looked around for the eraser. *"No Eraser!" "Where is the eraser?" "I don't know, Sir."* He slowly took off his Navy suit coat, slowly removed his black neck tie, and placed them on the desk. He then un-buttoned the top three buttons on his white shirt, grabbed the top, and tore it off, popping off the remaining buttons. He then slowly, silently, methodically erased the board with the shirt. On his way out he threw the shirt at Eddie and stated *"Be prepared!" "Report to me when the class is ready!"* The class sat silent for the remainder of the period. Eddie, in shock, shook nervously until we left the room.

September 17, 1954 I'm writing this in hope that you get it Friday. The telephone is out of order at the snack shack. I couldn't call you as promised. Can you fix up Bob Strautman with Les? Joe Lach and Dick Greer can't go. The Admiral did not approve their special request for a watch change to go to the ring dance.

We get more to study and less time to do it everyday. Right now we are studying Morse code, compass readings(boxing the compass) and rules of the road.

RING DANCE WEEKEND

Our first ring dance. We had a great time but I don't have any notes on the subject. Bob Strautman mentioned that he thought Leslie was terrific and also had a great time.

The social highlight of a Midshipman's career is of course his senior ring dance. The Greatest care and preparation are employed to make it a most memorable affair. The dance is usually held in a large Ballroom in a Boston Hotel. Always an impressive sight, the guard of honor with their white gloves, spats and web belts provide a military air to the ceremony.

Admiral Wilson eased any tension at the commencement of the rite with his anecdote about the origination of the ceremony. He reminded the Midshipmen that previously there had been no such affair but instead the boys threw each other into the brig. This was abruptly discontinued when one of them failed to come up. Immediately the Commissioners discontinued this dangerous ritual and for it they substituted the somewhat milder and much more desirable Ring Dance. The midshipman and his date walk to a binnacle placed under a splendid wreath of carnations in the form of a ring and the girl places the middies ring upon his finger and seals it with a kiss signifying that he is married to the sea. They step through and dance until the last man has passed through the ring. Our thanks go to the Dance Committee for their untiring efforts which made this the most outstanding ring dance ever to be held at the academy and one never to be forgotten by those in attendance.

[19 **M**uster 54 (yearbook)]

Letters to Lou...

September 20, 1954   I got aboard five minutes before ten last night. Just made it! It was raining and a cold fog was coming across the canal. Tom drove me down to see the ship. He did not see much due to the weather.

A lot of guys did not come back Sunday. Don't know why, but another youngie quit today. He probably had enough! One poor kid - everything he did or touched turned soft, brown and smelled bad. He's gone! He's out of here!

We'll go to the Boston shipyard October 18th for three weeks. I hope we never come back to Buzzards Bay!

September 21, 1954   The upper jobs got chewed out yesterday. It seems that the Commissioners have received 15 letters from angry parents about hazing. The four striper (Leader of the first class) has to go before the board today. He and others may lose their stripes? We shall wait and see! There shall be **"NO MORE HAZING"**.

Berry was standing over me yesterday while I was painting a bulkhead (wall). As I dipped my brush into the bucket of red lead and took it out, I ran a stripe of red dots across his new well-polished shoes. He blew his stack! He cursed me up and down as I stood there with a sober straight face and said I was sorry. The guy I was working with almost fell over the side laughing.

I spent the remainder of the day polishing brass portholes. Later, while I was polishing (with steel wool and Brasso), one of the officers came by and asked me why I wasn't getting ready for supper. I told him I was working for Mr. Berry. He told me to go eat and went looking for Mr. Berry. When he found him he blasted him for ten minutes and threatened to put him on report. Berry won't speak to me any more. I was just getting to like him too!

"The Pink Bubble" had me painting again today. He thinks I hate it so he sees to it that I get to paint everyday. If he only knew! I was told that Mr. Berry was labeled as a youngie by his upper jobs. He's average size with red hair and a pink complexion. When excited or angry he glows! The name fits perfectly!

We started getting our shots yesterday. I've had better from student nurses. The guy down here is a real horse doctor. We got hit in both arms. Most of the guys were sore this morning.

I'm still painting, hiding, and mess cooking. The watch bill has not been posted yet so I don't know if I'll be home or not this weekend. If I get off this weekend, I'll have to stay aboard Thanksgiving. I have no choice one way or the other. I'll know for sure later this afternoon.

I've decided that when I get to be an upper job that I, too, will have a personal servant. I can see it now, breakfast in bed, jumping ship every night, soft quiet music with more time to write to you. Only eleven more months and I'll be a second job. They have it pretty soft. They act as foremen for the 1st jobs and see that the work gets done by the youngies.

September 30, 1954   Some gal wrote to Mr. Callahan (1st job) telling him he was a dirty rat and to stop hazing her boy friend. He first thought it was you. He wanted to check your handwriting against the letter he received. Its a good thing your name is Lou and not Nancy. I would have had it! He somehow learned her name was Nancy and started a manhunt to find the youngie. No luck!

Haven't had a chance to study my Rules of the Road. I've got the 8 to 12 messenger watch tomorrow and I'll miss all my classes anyway. The last time I stood that watch I was at parade rest for the entire time. Later the back of my legs were killing me.

I was on deck after you left Sunday. The fog was so thick you couldn't see the cars in the parking lot. Strange place! Later you could see the railroad bridge with its red lights blinking on and off. It was cold, damp and foggy, as usual. The orange channel markers dot the shore and blink once in a while. Every so often you can see the lights of a ship creep up the canal, pass, and fade away into the night. It's beautiful in its own way but darn lonesome. The quiet of the night is broken only by the ship's blowers.

The duty youngies said the weekend was great. They didn't have to get up until 6:30.

I'm hiding and writing this in the locker room. It's hot, crowded, and miserable as ever. I won't go topside. Every so often I can hear the cry "young man" and I wonder what poor son-of-a-gun has been jobbed. As long as it's not me I don't care. If I don't belt one of these 1st jobs it's gonna be a miracle. I used to be rather happy-go-lucky, but lately I seem to be getting more bitter everyday.

Messdeck coffee is not available until 6:30 AM. I'm required to provide it at reveille for the first jobs in Berry's corner. I'm not the only one that has been assigned this *function*! I don't have a percolator! I do have cold water, a steam supply pipe, stolen coffee grounds, and an old athletic supporter that I found in the trash. The solution to the problem is obvious! Steam the cup of water. When it gets really hot just dip the old jock with the grounds in the cup until it turns dark brown! *They love it*! Other youngies have their own solutions and add different ingredients. As an upper job, I'll never order food or drink from a youngie!

October 4, 1954   All cadets are now wearing undress blues. There's something about them that makes you feel like a sailor. I wonder if it's worth it? The darn things are made of wool. All we do is scratch, wiggle, and squirm. Can't get comfortable in them. Sooner, or many washes later, they'll lose the itch and get soft and warm. I hope!

October 5, 1954   The "Board" is going to investigate the hazing down here tomorrow. I doubt that they'll get what they are after! They made a big speech and left. Big deal!

The 1st jobs are hunting all over for a youngie named Wilson. He has not been seen since the supper formation. I guess he jumped ship never more to return? I wonder who will be next.

The hazing is back (never left)...**"86"**...and the band plays on!

October 6, 1954   Got your letter today. I didn't get to read it until 4 PM. It's against rules and regs to smoke, sleep, eat, or read letters while on watch. It's kinda like putting ice cream in front of a kid and not letting him eat it.

I'm supposed to be studying. In the next room the drums are playing a snappy street beat while some clown is playing "Now is the hour." They really are getting better every day. Maybe someday they will all play the same thing at the same time!

Don't understand why there are only demerits, no merits, just demerits!

This place is a circus. The first jobs are the barkers and the youngies are clowns. I spend half my time trying not to smile. Smiling will get a guy in trouble. As you might have guessed, the hazing continues. I must admit that without it this place is dead.

And the band plays on... and on! The throb of the bass drum is about to drive me mad.

October 16, 1954   We won't leave for the Boston shipyard until Tuesday. If I'm lucky I might get off Wednesday. I smiled in class (study period) last night, it might cost me a weekend? Don't be surprised if I don't get home. It seems like I've been aboard for a month and it's only Tuesday.

October 18, 1954   We were supposed to have three tests today but actually had four. We have two, maybe three, tomorrow. I got little or no sleep last night. Really tired. A few guys are staying in sick bay resting, studying and missing the tests. They will make them up later. Maybe I'll try it too. We got another shot today. My arm is really sore. Some of the guys really are sick from the shot. I'm just not that lucky.

November 9, 1954   As I write this we are somewhere in Massachusetts Bay. The ship has a strange and uneven roll. I'm going one way and this table the other. We left Boston about 2:30, late as usual. Spent the morning turning-to and painting. They took so long getting organized I didn't think we were ever going to get underway.

We've been at sea about two hours and sick bay is loaded. Every so often someone else lets go and usually the guys watching join in. The locker room has a sick and sour smell. Hate the thought of going down there.

Letters to Lou…

We stand watch for four hours on and eight hours off with two "dog watches" from 4 to 6 PM and 6 to 8 PM to break the sequence (and to allow for the evening meal). Time is marked every half hour with a bell system. Eight bells start the watch at noon, four, eight, midnight, four, and 8 AM. One ding is added every half hour between the eight bells. Two thirty is 5 bells…it's also 1430 hours. Different huh!

We'll soon be back in Buzzards Bay. Hate the place and the Cape. Somebody suggested that they should untie the bridges and let the whole thing just drift out to sea. Sounds like a great idea to me…and take the fog with it!!!

I've got your picture taped to the inside of my locker door. Brightens my day each time I open it.

November 15, 1954   I got aboard about nine last night. Hung around the locker room until taps. Just playing it a bit cozy.

November 16,1954   Getting colder every day down here. We're all wearing "P" coats and look like a bunch of true swabbies. I woke up this morning and discovered that somebody had jobbed the big buttons off my coat. So I naturally did the same to someone else. After breakfast I tried to sew them on and sewed my pocket up doing so. I finally got things straightened out and passed inspection.

November 17, 1954   I'm constantly getting jobbed and don't have much time to myself. I'm tired and kinda bitter. Not getting much time to study. Marks came out today. I didn't do too bad. Gonna have to better in January. Didn't make the 1-50 list, whereas a bunch of my classmates did and will spend next weekend aboard.

Bob has just returned from Brighton Marine Hospital. He does not look good. I bet he'll wind up in sick bay again before the week is over.

The upper jobs are playing lots of new games lately. As usual us youngies are losing. There are very few youngies without demerits. I'm overdue!!! I've been pretty lucky (cozy). Hope lady luck stays with me.

November 26, 1954   Here I am back aboard. Only took two and a half hours to get back. Not too bad. Walked the last mile with my seabag real slow. I didn't want to go aboard too early.

November 29,1954   I'm writing this during the evening study period. Study…what a joke! Lee Cueroni (1st Job) is sitting in the corner of the room across from Ted Brown who is sitting in the middle of the room with a burning match between his teeth. Lee is shooting it out with a water pistol. Not a bad shot, but you know he misses on purpose. As fast as they go out Ted lights up another to keep the game going. Ted is losing, natch, but that's expected as a youngie. Ted is soaking wet and mad as hell. He also makes two of Cueroni, but still he sits there furious but quiet.

Spent the day messcooking. Ate around one and washed trays until two. We don't eat using dishes. We use metal trays that have sections for different types of mush. Spent the remainder of the day peeling spuds. Three of us peeled 200 pounds in two hours. We cut most of them into squares. It's faster that way. What a mess we had on our hands.

I've also got a great case of dish-pan hands. The first time they've been clean in weeks.

November 30, 1954   The Q-list (Quarantine) has snared a bunch of guys. So far ten guys made that list. That's one third of my class. Two of them had big dates this weekend that they can just forget. I've been lucky with Q-list. Still can't get off the 1-50 list for two weeks. I'll have to be back aboard at 6 PM on Sunday.

Study period. Cueroni is telling Brown of his many adventures with the opposite sex. He sure can tell a great story. He has the class in an uproar. Ted will never stop laughing. Cueroni is also on the 1-50 list. He's been on so long he's called the toastmaster.

Greer is up for ten demerits. He was sick at home and failed to bring a doctor's note back with him.

We drew duty days for the upcoming holidays. I thought I might draw Christmas or New Years but I was lucky and drew the 29th, Wednesday. Only one duty day with six hours on and six hours off. Not bad, huh!

…won't be home this weekend!

Dad gave me a ride to the expressway. I no sooner got out of the car and guess who picked me up? He gave me a ride all the way to the Bay but we had a flat tire right in front of the Knotty Pine. So naturally we went in for a few. When we came out the tire was as good as new. In fact it was new! If you haven't guessed, it was Cueroni. He directed me to say hi from him! So...Hi, from him!

December 6, 1954   Snowing hard, really cold, and the wind cuts like a knife. The third class spent the afternoon sweeping snow off the main deck. Cold, windy, miserable day! Total snow about 4 inches.

December 7. 1954   Things are running full speed ahead. The officers are laying it on thick and the upper jobs are raising hell all night. I was up until 11:30 last night making toast for Mr. Arnold. I jobbed a few for myself. Not bad!

I hope to be off the 1-50 list tomorrow. If I don't get off I won't be home this weekend.

Berry put me on report last night for talking during studies. If, or when, I go to Captain's mast is worth 10 demerits and the loss of a weekend. I'm beginning to think I won't get home until Christmas. Keep your fingers crossed, it might be close. Joe Lark is going to mast with me. The Captain won't take excuses, so he'll award us 10 demerits and tell us to step back. Our chances of beating this shove are pretty slim. Oh well!

December 8, 1954   The 1-50 list came out today. My name is still on it! Cdr. Connors (the "BUM") was supposed to give our class a make-up exam Monday but he didn't show up. We will probably take it tomorrow. Even if I pass I can't get off until two weeks from today! That means I'll be aboard for the 1-50 weekend. I still have to be back at 6(rather than 10PM) Sunday and won't get home until the 23rd.

I'm off the Physics list cuz I passed the last test. Never expected the "Bum" to pull what he did. I'm tired, bitter, and disgusted with the whole mess!

I rated a long weekend. Now I won't even get home. If Berry paps me, I won't be home until the 24th. I'm beginning to wonder if I'm gonna get home for Christmas.

I guess my Dad's company Christmas party, the 20th, is out. Don't see how I'll ever make it. He'll be very disappointed. Me too! That's the trouble with this place, you just can't make plans. Damn it!

After supper last night a lot of guys got sick. There must have been something in the food or water. All night long there was at least one guy in the forward head throwing. Thirty-three guys turned in sick this morning. Sick bay is loaded. The remainder are sleeping in their racks in the compartments.

I feel kinda lousy, but I think I'm gonna live. I don't want to turn in and miss my classes. I've got Connors tomorrow. Can't afford to miss any of his classes.

December 10, 1954   Lots of guys sick! Maybe the food was OK? Some kinda bug going thru the crew. Yes, I joined the other guys last night. Really sick! We all have the same thing.

December 15, 1954   We went to town today to give blood and to get away from the place. They wouldn't take it because we were all sick recently. The Red Cross gave us coffee and sandwiches anyway! Nice people! We stopped by again later before going back for a couple more sandwiches. Really, nice people!!!

Berry had me painting decks again today. Really weird guy! Going soft I think! Lots of other guys agree with me.

December 16, 1954   The 1st jobs are up to their old tricks. Lots of youngies are bitter about it. Lots of talk about rebelling. It would never work now. It might work after the cruise but not now. Lots of talk but not much will happen. They may play games but they'll never win. I bet when they become upper jobs they'll be meaner than anyone down here now.

Berry is still holding my report slip. I don't know if or when he'll turn it in.

Letters to Lou…

Finally got my MMA sweater today. Its white and blue with the MMA seal over the left side. It buttons up the front with pockets on both sides. Yes, it's yours while I'm on cruise. We are not allowed wear it down here. Think you might squeeze into a size 42 long?

December 17, 1954   Commander ? (Not Named) just came in tearing! Somebody jobbed the wheels off his car. It's sitting on blocks in the parking lot. We probably won't get to sleep until they are returned.

December 21, 1954   We were taken out of study period to shovel snow again today. There's about six inches on the ground.

Still free of demerits and the upper jobs are aware of it. I'm gonna have to be really cozy or a ten shove will cost me a day's liberty during the Christmas leave period.

January 3, 1955   We are doing a lot of work on the ship lately getting it ready for the cruise. The upcoming cruise is gonna be one of the greatest adventures of my life. Can't wait!

January 4, 1955   Bob Stickney's mother passed away today. He left the ship as soon as he got the news. Not sure if he will return?

We received the official cruise itinerary today. Copy enclosed. Looks like we are going visit some pretty interesting places.

I think half of the U. S. Fleet went through the canal headed south this afternoon. It took more than an hour for them to pass one by one. Very impressive.

Can you fix Bob Young up with Kay for the dance? If so let me know by Friday, OK?

The next three days are set aside for exams prior to the cruise. We'll all be doing lots of cramming. Hope the upper jobs are also busy and lay off us.

Rumor has it that we may take the ship back to Boston for repairs before we go on cruise. I hope so! It won't make me unhappy.

January 13, 1955   I'm in the Navy now! Signed the papers today. I'm in for eight years, two of them on active duty. This will keep me free of the draft and out of the Army. I also need the money, about $16 a month. It should pay for half of my second year's tuition, all of the final year's tuition, plus my ring and year book. I can't really work or make much when I get off, so I signed up.   I also got an ID Card which will get me into the Navy Fargo Building and cheap beer...about $3.50 a case.

January 16, 1955   I got a ride into South Boston with friends Sunday night and waited until the last minute before going aboard.

Third Class Year

Letters to Lou…

    Our mail address for the cruise   …Midshipman _____
                                             U.S.T.S. Charleston
                                           c/o Fleet Post Office
                                           New York, N.Y.

    We were told that the mail would be waiting at the "mail buoy" for us to pick up prior to entering each port. Many young men have stood "mail buoy" watches expecting the reward of a letter from home. All were disappointed! No "YELLOW BUOYS" were sighted. Actually, the ship's mail is forwarded from New York to a post office ashore based on our itinerary.

Departing Buzzards Bay

"Youngie Cruise"

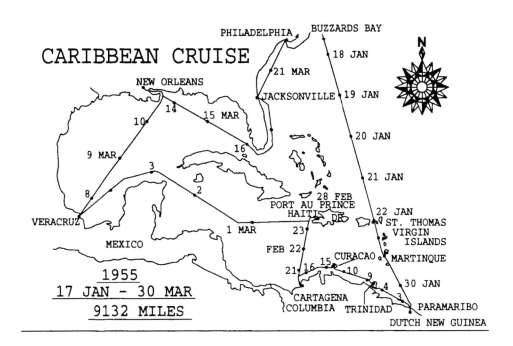

CARIBBEAN CRUISE

1955
17 JAN – 30 MAR
9132 MILES

January 17, 1955 10 AM Underway headed south for St. Thomas, Virgin Islands.

January 18, 1955 Rough seas off the Virginia coast. Lots of guys sick!

Upper job Perkaski gave me a foot long kielbasa to hide for him. I hid it in the barrel of the old 5 inch gun back aft. During the storm off Virginia, as we headed south, wouldn't you know the kielbasa slid out of the barrel and went over the side. Perkaski told me one night to get his kielbasa as he was hungry. I knew the kielbasa was somewhere off the Virginia coast but I told him some other upper jobs, under the cover of darkness, made me give it to them (didn't see their faces and didn't know their names) and they did something with it. Boy, was he ticked-off, and he automatically thought it was the deckies. I was really sweating the outcome.

[Hank Billings]

January 19, 1955 We have been at sea three days and I'm doing fine. Tired but not sick. We haven't seen the sun, another ship, or land since we left Buzzards Bay. We are bucking winds of hurricane force. The ship's bow and the main deck get covered with water when we hit these huge waves. A lot of guys have been sick but seem to have adjusted now.

The sea is really beautiful, especially the Gulf Stream. I'll try to capture it with my camera.

A wave just crashed through an open port and swept Dick Boles clear across the deck. He was mad as a wet hen; all we did was sit and laugh.

Earlier today we were ordered to secure a foam can on the main deck that was rolling around in the waterway. If we had half a brain we should have just kicked it overboard. Another 3rd job, Dick Boles, and I pulled it across the deck to the bulkhead. As we were fighting it a large wave broke over the side, knocked us down, washed us across the main deck into the lowest lifeline on the opposite side water way. We held on for what seemed like hours while the sea water rushed over us. Finally we got to our feet and made a dash for safety. We both came very close to being swept overboard. Very, very lucky! Later after thinking it over we both had the shakes. It took a while to settle down. ***Note: 1992 Class Reunion. Talked to Dick about this. Through the years he and I have had reoccurring thoughts and nightmares over this incident.

"Youngie Cruise"

Letters to Lou...

January 20, 1955 Bob Strautman has been in sickbay for two days. Almost broke his leg during the storm.

The sea is still a little rough. When we get to St. Thomas I think I'll take a long nap on a "solid" white beach. They say when you go ashore you can get "land sick"! You get so used to the ship's motion that when things don't move you can get sick. What a thing to look forward to, Strange huh? The sun finally came out today. Hurray!

We are about 200 miles east of the Florida coast and still headed south. Didn't get much sleep again last night. Fought all night just to stay in my rack. It took about twenty minutes to find my shoes in the mix this morning.

Saw a lot of flying fish today. One of them landed on the main deck. They are kinda bright silver with wings like a butterfly. They don't really fly, they come out of the water and just glide over the waves.

January 21, 1955 We set the clocks ahead tonight. Got a crew cut today, hope it grows back before the cruise ends.

The officers are wearing "Bermuda Shorts". Temperature about 80 degrees.

I'm a messcook again, spending most of my day below decks, washing trays and things in the scullery. Sweat like I've never sweat before.

"The Bum" said that he had never spent a worse night at sea. He said that he has rode out hurricanes before but they don't compare to the last storm. I should explain... Commander Conners has been called "The Bum" for years due to his personal appearance and the shoddy condition of his uniforms.

January 22, 1955 Tied up at St. Thomas, Virgin Islands. Beautiful island with large clean white beaches and clear blue water. I took a few pictures as we entered the harbor. I hope they come out OK! I'm still a rookie with this camera. This is a really nice place to spend my 19th birthday.

January 23, 1955 I went ashore yesterday and was amazed at some of the houses and the way some of the people live. They seem to be dirty and miserable making a living on tourists and taxi cabs. They are U.S. citizens living on a U.S. island.

While we were eating, some negro kids were watching us through the open port holes hoping for a hand out. Later I had to take the garbage ashore. These poor kids fished through the barrels and removed every piece of meat in them. Really sad!

Before going ashore I didn't know what I wanted most a "gin mill' or a "dairy bar". I settled for ice cream! I guess I'm slipping, huh!

Some of my classmates came back under the weather and they are now sorry for it. The Pink Bubble had them up at 5 AM for scrub down until 8 AM. They had breakfast and went back to work until now (2:30 PM). They'll probably loose liberty in a couple of ports and may get 10-20 demerits? It pays to stay dry and thirsty!

It's about 85 degrees now and I am hot and sweating! The heat and humidity is wicked, especially in our khaki job suits. I hope to do a little swimming tomorrow. We can rent a convertible for about $7.50 a day. We intend to tour the island and see everything.

January 25, 1955 As I write this the sun is hot and bright above us. The sea around us is calm and a beautiful blue-green. We're all wearing "T" shirts and some guys are even barefoot. While at sea we can wear almost anything we want. Kinda nice! We left St. Thomas at 9AM this morning.

Yesterday we rented a Willys convertible and drove all over the island.
I took some group pictures with us in the car. I'd set the camera on something, point it correctly, set the timer, push the button and run like mad to jump into the picture. I made it most of the time. Lots of fun!

The hotels are beautiful and expensive. It's $16 a day for the cheapest room without meals. Meals start at $7.50 and go to unbelievable prices. I don't think we can afford to honeymoon here!

18

"Youngie Cruise"

…fantail movie.

THE
MAUBY
WOMAN

K

BARBADOS

POSTAL CARD 1/31/57

January 26, 1955   We have been in Martinique for about six hours. We are tied up alongside a concrete pier with a few French ships around us. The dock is loaded with negroes at work. It seems like the women do more than the men. We've been watching them load cement on a "32" Ford truck. Women were carrying 50 pound bags of cement on their heads. They use their hands only to keep the bags from shifting. I've never seen anything like it!

January 29, 1955   Travel is one way to make a guy appreciate the land and his home. When I finally settle down New England is gonna be my home.

January 30, 1955   Enroute to Paramaribo, Surinam. Paramaribo is only a few degrees from the equator and its gonna be even hotter than here. As a deckie I'm on deck and working in the sun most of the day. It's hot on deck but murder in the engine room. I would hate to be a snipe! The temperatures range from 105 to 140. They have little or no fresh air. The blowers help but it's still hot air. The place stinks something wicked from human sweat.

February 2, 1955   We were the quests of Alcor Co. today. We toured their bauxite mines in a bus. Later we had dinner and all we could drink. We drove for miles through the jungle. I took a few pictures of the natives and their huts. I hope they come out OK!   Hot...boy is it hot!

The movie on the fantail tonight is "The Sea Around Us". Not a bad flick!

We learned today that President Eisenhower stopped all allowances to maritime academies. The state will have to pay for the whole business. The rumor is that this is the last cruise for the Charleston. The state can't afford to pay for everything. The future of the school does not sound very good!

Visits made to Martinque, Paramaribo, Dutch New Guinea, and the Island of Trinidad. Nice stops, enjoyed by all, and all had a ball.

February 9, 1955   We are underway, and clear of Trinidad, headed for Williamstead, Curacao. Most of these islands look the same. All the harbors and docks are located in small bays and inlets. Usually there is an old fort at the entrance.

I'm in sick bay and feeling much better. Food poisoning? The ship's doctor wants to keep me off my feet and under observation. Boy, have I got it soft. Never had it so good. Upper jobs Berry, Collis, and Hannon just came in to visit and gave me a few words to remember (which I promptly forgot) and left me a few pair of shoes to shine. Oh well! Bob is also in here keeping me company. Maybe he'll help with the shoes?

Here comes the messcook with dinner. Wow, what a mess! Don't even know what they call it. Really bad! Another mystery from Moe the Philippine cook.

Finally got around to it and wrote to Duane Drohan. He was left behind with a hernia. Assume he is recovering at home now.

Going ashore has become routine. Usually head for town and walk a lot. Always have a few beers before we go too far. A local pimp, a guy that shows and knows all about the town, takes us where we want to go. He gets a cut on anything we do or buy. Most of the bars are the same on the waterfront.

19

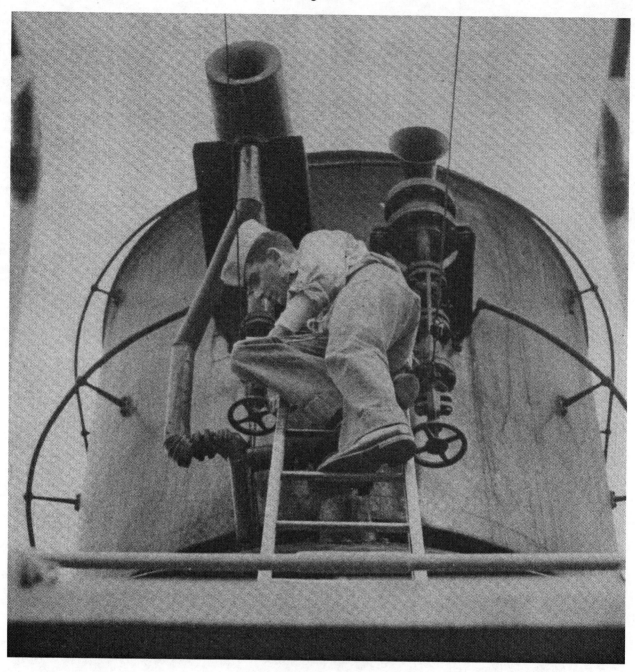

Ed Ascolillo working on the ship's whistle

…no satellite phones or E-mail.

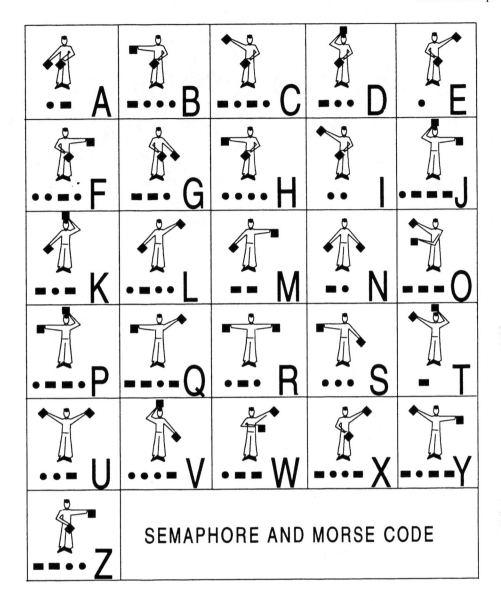

We practice signaling whenever we get a chance. It's one part of the U.S. Coast Guard's Mate's Exam.

I've had no problems with the upper jobs since we left. They seem to aim for the guys that come back to the ship under the weather. It pays to stay sober. Otherwise a guy might get a few hours sleep and be up at 4:30 AM to scrub down on the main deck. Not much fun with a big head. The first jobs will drag their posterior for a few days. The unfortunate youngie or second job will be sorry they overdid it ashore.

Drinking is a first class privilege. We can have a few drinks as long as our eyes are clear and we can walk without a stagger.

They just piped movie call. The pictures are old and pathetic. The youngies don't go. If they go they end up being butt machines and running errands for the upper jobs. Normally they'll find a place to hide and sleep or write letters home. With only 328 feet of campus and half of it officers' country its kinda hard to do but it's done.

We have a following sea which makes us seem to be standing still. Actually we are making 12 knots which is not bad for this old ship. I'm told the new destroyers can make about 35 knots.

Letters to Lou…

February 10, 1955   Valentine's Day. A maximum of only ten words are allowed in a "SEA LETTER". I've spent a good deal of time trying to figure out what to say. It is not inexpensive and I want to get it right.

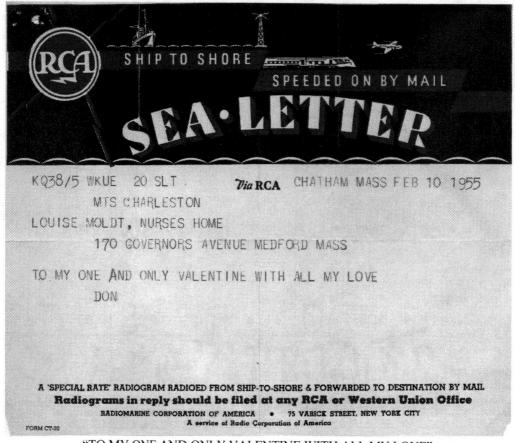

"TO MY ONE AND ONLY VALENTINE WITH ALL MY LOVE"

February 11, 1955   We are tied up here at Willemstad, Curacro. It's a nice clean Dutch port. I'll take a few more pictures and then send the film to New York. They'll send it to you after processing. You should have the first set of slides by now.

February 12, 1955   John Arnold (1/D) was badly injured in a diving accident. He dove off a tower into shallow water. A few hours later he died in the hospital. A special mass was held on the fantail this morning. Several days later his body was flown home.

February 19, 1955   Cartagena, Columbia. The liberty party is starting to return. Some are about half in the bag. The first jobs are active now, checking these guys out. As the youngies return they are ordered to walk along a seam on the quarter deck ten times without stepping off. Its really more difficult than it seems. If you step off they put your name on the early call list for the morning, 4:30 AM, early scrub-down. It's really kinda funny watching these guys trying to concentrate and walk the line.

        Went ashore, and toured the town, we really had a ball. We had a steak dinner in a small cafe; also had beer, ice cream, and coffee all for $1.80. Not bad huh!

        While in a small shop with "The Pink Bubble" and others he somehow pushed his hand through a glass show case. The woman threw a fit. He claimed it was already broken. I don't know what happened next or if he paid up. I just left laughing.

        The beer down here is usually warm, flat, and not very good. We drink it anyway. We had some pineapple and papaya this morning, not bad, but kinda sweet.

"Youngie Cruise"

…bum boats.

Less than forty days remain to the end of this nightmare and Boston. As an upper job the cruise is great. For a youngie it can be hell. However when we get ashore it can be lots of fun. Even when ashore we do not enter any bar where the upper jobs are drinking. When dismissed from the liberty formation they usually get the taxi cabs. The underclass's walk. They also get to go to all the big times and parties. We might get some of the left-overs like very long bus rides thru banana plantations. Lets face it, if you've seen one banana you've seen them all!

Really hot today. The temperature in the laundry is at least 110 degrees. On the messdeck its 96; a terrible time to be a messcook. When underway, sometimes we'll sleep on deck. The deck is hard but it's nice and cool.

It looks like my liberty section will get two days ashore in the final four ports(Vera Cruz, New Orleans, Jacksonville, and Philadelphia). Only one half of the crew goes ashore at a time.

It's sometimes frustrating but fun to talk to the natives. We talk to them like little kids using English, Spanish, and lots of hand signs. The one thing that is always understood is money.

In some ports, bum boats will come along side. The kids will dive for coins. Interesting to watch. Some of these kids can go deep and stay under for a long time.

Underway, normal scrubdowns are at 0530. This is something hated by all youngies. We scrub the decks every morning with stiff brushes on a broom stick (ki-yi) and hose with salt water. A second job operates the hose and some times sprinkles sand on any bad spots. We are lined up and run up and down scrubbing until breakfast. The teak wood decks are clean, almost white, but we scrub anyway. Meanwhile, below decks the upper jobs are sleeping in to 0630.

The homes here are beautiful. Some are close to the ocean with great beaches. Warm weather, nice clear skies with lots of stars; it would be a great place to live. Living near the ocean, maybe on the west coast, should be one of our goals. Never ever want to live in a desert climate that's hot and dry!

Collis (1/D) told us that getting a job as a pilot in the Panama Canal is not difficult once you have your masters license. It takes about six years to get the license. The first six months as a rookie the pay is only about $6,000. Once you get the pilot's papers the pay goes up to $18,000 to $24,000 per year. Hard to even imagine making that kind of money. He also said that they get two months vacation a year.

I'm told that tug boat captains make $6,000 in Boston harbor. Not bad and they are home every night. Maybe someday, when and if, I graduate, and after two years in the Navy I'll look into these type jobs?

I normally don't drink coffee but the coffee here is terrific.

Cartagena was loaded with "fish" (pescado grande). A term used to describe a guy with lots of money that is willing to buy drinks for people like us. When funds are low you hope to run into people like this on the beach.

23

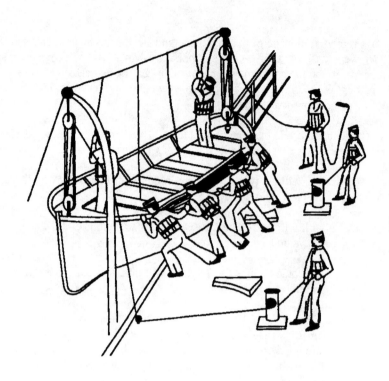

Launching a Whaleboat

Starboard Side Whaleboat

"Youngie Cruise"

M.T.S. CHARLESTON
Enroute from Cartagena, Columbia
To Port au Prince, Haiti.
Wednesday 23 February 1955

PLAN OF DAY FOR THURSDAY 24, FEBRUARY 1955 (Typical)

0800 - Section 4 on watch.   Prepare for entering port. It is expected to enter port about 0900.
Sections 1 & 2 maintenance after securing in port.

1230 STARBOARD WATCH LIBERTY. Section 4 maintenance.

The Captain held Mast at 1300 Wednesday 23 Feb. 1955 and awarded the following punishments:

DATE OF OFFENSE	OFFENSE	REPORTING OFFICER	DEMERITS
2/20 AYLMER, JF 3D	Smoking out of hrs.	LT HIRST	10
2/18 BERRY,PF 1D	Smoking out of hrs.	MAA SANFORD	10
2/23 CHRISTIE,AJ 3E	Having another Midn's gear.	LT HIRST	10
2/23 CHRISTIE,AJ 3E	Gear adrift	LTJG TONELLO	3
2/20 DUCHARME,AE 1E	Gear adrift	LT HIRST	3
2/21 DUFFLEY, JJ 3E	Late hammocks	LT HIRST	6
2/19 FERRERA, JJ 3E	Disobedience of orders	LT BOULDER	6
2/21 FLYNN, EL 2E	Loitering in an unauthorized place.	LT HIRST	6
2/20 GREER, RJ 3D	Missing formation	LT WIKANDER	6
2/22 HEMMALIN,JP 2D	Disregard of orders	CDR WOODLAND	10
2/18 KENDRIGAN,PM 3E	Gear adrift	LT HIRST	3
2/18 LACAIRE, DJ 3D	Absent from formation	LT PAGE	3
2/18 LACAIRE, DJ 3D	Having another Midn's gear.	LT HIRST	6
2/21 LACAIRE, DJ 3D	Late hammocks	LT HIRST	6
2/18 LACH, JF 3D	Gear adrift	LT HIRST	3
2/17 LEWIS, CW 3E	Unshaven, unshined shoes, general appearance dirty.	LT BOULTER	6
2/17 LEWIS, CW 3E	Having another Midn's gear.	LT BOULTER	10
2/18 LEWIS, CW 3E	Gear adrift	LT HIRST	6
2/22 LEWIS, CW 3E	Dirty clothes unmid-shipman like appearance	LT PAGE	6
2/20 MARSTON, PG 1E	Gear adrift	LT HIRST	3
2/16 MIRABELLO,ED3E	Having another Midn's gear.	LTJG TONELLO	10
2/16 MIRABELLO,ED3E	Out of uniform	LTJG TONELLO	3
2/17 MIRABELLO,ED3E	Missing formation	LTJG TONELLO	6
2/18 MONAHAN, CF 3D	Dirty Linen	LT BOULTER	6
2/22 MULQUEENY,JB2D	Disregard of orders	CDR WOODLAND	10
2/23 PUTIGNANO,DJ3E	Purloining another Midn's gear	LT WIKANDER	10
2/12 REID, WJ Jr 3E	Loaning another Midn his blanket	CAPT THOMPSON	10
2/20 SHEELY,DV 1D	Disregard of orders	CDR WOODLAND	10

[Jim McCluskey]

Letters to Lou...

February 23, 1955 Off the coast of Haiti. It was my turn to have lunch with the Admiral and Captain. I smoked a few of the Captain's cigarettes and was treated like a king for more than an hour, even remembered how to use a knife and fork (as opposed to the usual two big spoons). Before I went in, the 1st jobs gave me a bunch of questions to ask about the cruise, etc. I was expected to get the answers and confirm that we would be back in Boston on the 30th of March.

Scuttlebutt has it that we might make our next cruise in September. The government has cut off funds to MMA. Might have to go to King's Point or Maine Maritime next year. It's not clear that the state will come up with money to keep MMA operating. It's also rumored that the Navy is going to take the ship back. Really don't know what they'll do with it. Only one gun aft and it's really slow. Rumors are always going around. Most of which have no foundation.

March 3, 1955 We are crossing the Gulf of Mexico enroute to Vera Cruz. We'll be five days at sea and four days in port. We are painting the entire ship again prior to entering port. This is the second time since we came aboard in August. Gray, everything is gray, ugh!

The Captain has several strange names... "Square Jack" and "Stupid"... I don't know why! His son, who works as a maintenance man back in Buzzards Bay, is called "Stupid Junior". The Captain has an impressive record and is a great seaman. He is well liked by all. He's stern and hard but still seems like a regular guy. I think he's great.

March 5, 1955 Your picture is still on the inside of my locker door. Hanging in there with fresh masking tape.

Some body jobbed my pen. The one that runs out of ink about every page and a half. I hope it frustrates the thief as much as it frustrated me!!!

March 7, 1955 Vera Cruz Mexico   Nice city. I've enjoyed this port more than the others. Best yet! Spent the day walking around, eating Mexican food, drinking milk shakes, and listening to the music of Glenn Miller all afternoon. He is popular down here. It costs two cents(20 centimos) to play the juke box. A peso is worth about eight cents.

We are going to have a dance aboard tomorrow night. The whole town has been invited. They expect about 400 people. Don't know where they are gonna put them? We really don't have that much deck space. I'm sure they will squeeze them aboard somehow!

Jim Lynch and Pete Readel want us to join them at the Totem Pole the first Saturday after our return. Sounds like a good idea to me. Lets join them!

Joe Lark spent the night in the local jail. He was accused of not paying for sandals in his possession! He is now known as "Zapato Joe".

The mail finally caught up with us. Three bags full. Mail call lasted about forty minutes. As you would suspect, us youngies get ours last. Received your nine blue envelopes. Really made my day!

…I was on the helm.

A few of the guys are talking about leaving once we get back. Not everybody is cut out for this type of life. Good luck to them.

As I write this Nat King Cole is singing "The Sea and the Sand" in the background.

March 13, 1955   We had the big dance the night before we left Vera Cruz. Instead of hiring an orchestra they had something like a circus band. We must be polite so the Admiral allowed the Mexican Naval Band to play for us. I really didn't mind dancing to march music but when they added the South American Swing to it, that was the limit. Quote "*You will* dance with these young ladies, *won't you* young man?" There were lots of girls aboard but they all came with their mothers! I asked a gal to dance. Her mother said it would be OK, but would I show them around the ship first? I should have taken off then, but being a good guy I took them on a fifteen minute tour. The mother spoke English and her daughter remained silent. After answering a million questions we finally got to dance. We were dancing for about 15 seconds when the music stopped and the band took a break. When the band returned I was dispatched to dance with another senorita. It just so happens that her mother also wanted a tour of the ship. I bowed out by explaining that I was a messcook and was needed in the galley.

I gave it up and hit the rack about ten thirty. They got all the youngies up at one to turn-to and clean up. I had the morning 4-8 watch which left me with very little rest for the remainder of the day.

Frank Flaherty and Fred Furgerson spent the night in a Mexican jail. They refused to pay a taxi driver. The driver just drove them to the local jailhouse and dropped them off. They later went to mast for being AOL and for un-midshipman like conduct. Frank received 100 demerits and Fred 75. They will only get three hours ashore for the remaining stops of this cruise. Frank could be our four striper but with his 127 demerits it's unlikely.

The trip from Mexico to here was great. Nice calm sea. The temperature has dropped and it seems kinda cool. I stood watch as messenger. A lot happened while on the bridge. Berry was sick (too much to drink at the dance), so I was on the helm for more than an hour. The ship wants to go according to the sea state. It's a little difficult to keep it on course. After a little practice I could keep within four degrees of the course. Steering the ship is a 1st and 2nd class function. I went about 18 degrees off course when I first took over. "The Bum", the Officer of the Deck, almost went out of his mind. The Captain walked around like he knew it all the time when it was happening. He really is a cool character. Everybody else got all excited. Oh well, I tried! Did my best, just need more practice.

We picked up a pilot at the mouth of the Mississippi. Then we spent the night going up stream. The Captain spent the night on the bridge. The pilot was in command giving course and speed changes to the people on watch. He really did a great job with and without the fog. We anchored about six miles south of the city at 0530. Later the ship passed customs and tied up around 1030. Very interesting night. The river is muddy with lots of drift wood and things.

New Orleans. Lots of ships tied up from many different countries. No bridges across so you have to take a ferry from one side to the other. Showboats and others use stern wheel paddles on the river.

Bob Stickney was "picked up" by a gal in a drug store while on liberty and promptly fell in love. Note: While at MMA he continued with this long distance romance. Bob and Jane were married in 1959.

We have fresh milk aboard today for the first time in two months. We are restricted to one cup per meal by Sid. I won't complain, one cup is better than no cups!

This town is loaded with bars and night clubs. We checked out a few and had a good time. It cost us $1.40 for a beer in one place. The show was not bad but the prices were wicked.

I was surprised to see the discrimination down here. There are signs on the street cars that say "This section is for whites only." We're not used to this and it made us "Yankees" feel very uncomfortable.

March 16, 1955   Enroute to Jacksonville, Florida from New Orleans. I learned a lot on the last series of watches. Collis and Lt. Page were shooting stars on the 4-8 this morning. I was allowed to watch. I didn't understand much about what they were doing but it was worth my time.

"Youngie Cruise"

Letters to Lou…

I received a letter from my mother while in port. My new brother(?#5?) is due in July. Started me thinking about what it might be like to be at sea and not be home when your son or daughter is born. Even worse would be to still be at sea for months after. Note: My second daughter Leslie was born, November 1960 in Norfolk, VA while I was on cruise in the Mediterranean. I got home *four months later*. I submitted my *"first"* resignation papers upon arrival. I was finally released from active duty in March of 1963 and hired by the Smithsonian soon afterwards. While in training I learned that Dick Greer was also working for the same organization in Peru. I tried to get stationed with Dick but they sent me and my family to Iran instead.

Looking ahead I won't have liberty upon arrival in Boston. According to the duty sheet I'll get off the following day. Damn it!!! I'll also be aboard for Easter.

March 19, 1955   Jacksonville. Florida. Twenty-one miles up the St. Johns River. We arrived early. Before we anchored out overnight, we steamed around while the Captain did a little fishing off the stern. He never catches anything but it's a good way to kill time.

Saw all kinds of fish enroute. Saw a shark this morning and yesterday a bunch of porpoises were jumping around in our bow waves. Two sea turtles were spotted along with hundreds of flying fish. Interesting trip.

Several upper jobs caught a "Sea Bat" (with brooms) and had him in a large cardboard box on the main deck. The box had a bunch of small air holes in the sides with a peep-hole on top. They were feeding it lettuce when several youngies stepped on the main deck from the midship hatch. "Hey youngie, have you ever seen a sea bat?" "No, sir!" "Come on over here and take a look!" "Just bend over and look in the hole." Just about the time the youngie was bent over and trying to see inside the box he was whacked in the butt with both brooms. Great fun for the upper jobs! The surprised youngie was then told to shove off! The upper jobs then waited for the next victim to surface from the midship hatch.

The day before yesterday we cruised right into a large group of subs and destroyers off the tip of Florida playing war games. Later we steamed by a huge carrier with more destroyers.

We'll get full use of the "Y" and its pool tomorrow. The Propeller Club has a dance scheduled for the other watch section tonight.

"The Bum" has the duty today. As usual he pulls all kinds of inspections and drills. To make liberty when he has the deck you have to be perfect or you won't go ashore.

We are tied up next to the "Sea Cloud", the world's largest privately owned sailing vessel. It's as long as the Charleston and painted a beautiful white. The four masts are twice the height of ours. Washington, DC is its home port. Must be worth millions.

March 30, 1955   Boston, Mass.   Home at last! It was a <u>very long</u> night <u>as we anchored out</u> in Boston Harbor <u>waiting for</u> <u>the sun to rise.</u>

April 5, 1955   Tom drove me to Route 2 Sunday. No trouble, hitch-hiking, getting rides from there. As usual I hauled my seabag with all my laundry, no problem!

Ted Brown is going to come home with me this weekend. Do you think you could fix him up with Leslie? Frank Flaherty and Jim McCluskey said they, too, will make the dance on the 30th. Do you think you could fix them up also?

April 10, 1955   Happy Easter! All kinds of first job girls aboard this afternoon. They used the chart rooms as a dance hall while the radio plays full blast.

We also had guests from Hyannis aboard for lunch. Twenty brats called sea scouts! Us youngies, of course, *volunteered* to show them around. I didn't want to take a nap anyway!

Classes start again tomorrow. In addition to our regular classes, we'll get to see the "Victory at Sea" films as part of our Naval History class.

"Youngie Cruise"

...wants to be a snipe. Imagine!

The first class is back to playing games again. Berry's corner was busy last night. He was AOL and expects 40 demerits at the next Captain's mast. He's a three time loser for AOL. Being a little bitter he took it out on the youngie snipes(engineers).

April 12, 1955 Buzzards Bay, Massachusetts Remember Arzy? He was short, dark, and friendly kid. We went to his girl's house after the ring dance. He left yesterday. It's rumored that Boothman is next. He returned today and spoke to both the Admiral and Cdr. Rounds. Other youngies are also thinking of leaving. Only 60 of the original 75 youngies remain aboard.

Classes are getting tough. We get very little time to study. About a third of the class is on the 1-50 list.

April 20, 1955 Came aboard at 1205. Had hamburger for lunch. Berry, "The Pink Bubble", had a special job waiting for my return. He really is a "great" guy! Bogger Brown and I spent the afternoon cleaning the bilges of the port lifeboat. Ted and I had a great time splashing around making mud-pies in two inches of mixed water, lube oil, mud, and crap off the bottom. Didn't get much studying done for the Spanish exam tomorrow. When I think about it, nobody should be made to conjugate verbs that early in the morning!

April 21, 1955 Here we are in another study period (what a joke)! Berry is playing handball with Cueroni, our class monitors, in the front of the room. They each have a cheering section. When one scores on the other their cheering section acts accordingly. What a madhouse!!!

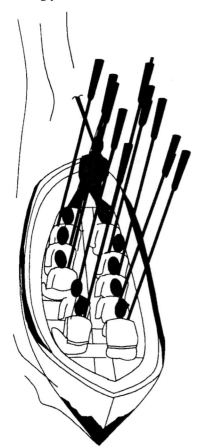

We had a great seamanship lesson today. Practical seamanship in whale boats (a long heavy wooden boat designed for 10 rowers). There were 11 in the boat, 6 youngies and 4 second jobs. After we cleared the ship the second jobs stopped rowing and just went along for the ride. Rowing one of these tubs is not as easy as it looks. Some of these guys have never rowed a boat before and were in for a surprise. It was a laugh a minute when we first took over. Taylor's oar slipped out and he fell into the bilge with two inches of water in it. As he tried to recover he hit Greer in the neck almost knocking him overboard, he then whipped the oar in the other direction belting the man at stroke oar knocking his hat over the side. The second jobs went out of their minds laughing while we just rowed and tried to get back in stride. Bob Taylor and Jim Lynch spent the rest of the afternoon aft of the wardroom with a handful of steel wool.

April 22, 1955 We lost another guy today. "Basher Barry" left this morning. It seems like we are losing a man a week. Before "Basher" left he told Berry, "The Pink Bubble", what he thought of him and dragged his posterior something wicked.

My watch section also lost a guy. He's not gone completely. *Worse than that*, he has gone from bad to worst, the "deckie" wants to become a *"snipe"*. Imagine!!!

April 23, 1955 Learned that Monahan also left yesterday. Plans to go to Cornell. Only twenty five of the original deckies remain.

April 24, 1955 A new youngie, Riley, will join us soon. He is joining us from the Coast Guard Academy. Boy what a let down!

April 26, 1955 Talked to Lt. Smith today. Seems like a regular guy. He spent two years on a destroyer before being sent to MMA. He's the head of the Naval Science Department. He said he is going to make a career of the Navy and expects to retire at 41, with an income of more than $200 a month. Not bad huh!

I've also heard that there will be a dance aboard the ship this summer. It will be a combination beach party in the afternoon with the dance on the fantail that evening. We'll eat on the messdecks. It looks like you might get to go below decks after all.

"Youngie Cruise"

Letters to Lou…

May 2, 1955   When I came aboard last night Dick, Ted, and Frank were all in the locker room. I guess Dick and Frank spent the night in the Medford Brig. Frank got in a fight with some guy over a parking space. The guy came flying out of his car and clipped him over his left eye (what a smack). Frank had him on the deck when the cops showed up. Dick just watched but was hauled in anyway.

May 3, 1955   Marks were posted today. I averaged a 3.044 hope to get at least a 3.2 next term. We have been doing a lot of rowing lately, getting ready for the whale boat races in Boston on Maritime Day the 19th of May.

The "PIER", the snack shack, re-opened today. Good for us! When the food is lousy we can get a hamburger or something at the north end of the parking lot.

The following text in "_Italic_"are "excerpts" from letters sent by Bob Stickney to Miss Jane Smith, his future wife, in New Orleans, Louisiana.

May 9, 1955 I was happy to hear from you again. I thought that the kid had forgotten all about big Bob Stick…
I am waiting for a physics exam to start and decided to write to my favorite southern friend. James [Piner] jumped ship last night with another middie, and they got caught on the way back. It is a shame; that is worth 100 demerits plus a drunk charge and an out of uniform charge. You can guess how they feel this morning.
I lost your letter and I have to use my memory, so please forgive me. My Spanish is not the best, by any means. As a matter of fact I just about get by. The rest of my marks are not so bad. The class standings were printed last week, and the old kid came out 13th, which pleased him the most……

May 10, 1955   Joe Tache was working in the scullery with us and just left? He packed his gear, saw the Admiral about leaving, and left the ship at 12:30. The Admiral gave him 24 hours to think it over and talk to his parents.

May 11, 1955   A "youngie" Jack Alymer (3/D), "a bogger", went before the Captain today for two reports: sleeping in his car and jumping ship. He got 10 demerits for sleeping in his car and he will go before the board later for the jumping ship shove. As a youngie, Collis got 100 for the same charge.

If he gets 100 out of it he won't get off the ship for 2 1/2 months or 10 weekends plus his normal duty weekends. Ted Brown after being placed on the 1-50 List for Naval Science hit the Jack-Pot and went double or nothing...he is now also on for Spanish. Restricted to the ship.

Ted was supposed to go to a prom Saturday night. The only way he can get off is to have a death in the family. His uncle in New York is scheduled to die next Thursday. He plans to submit a special request that morning and leave that night.

May 24, 1955   Another long day has ended. Another week of mess cooking. This place and that dirty old man are gonna drive me bananas. I'm still working in the scullery. It's a small room filled with steam and hotter than Haiti. The deck usually has from one to four inches of water on it. At sea, when the ship is in motion it's just great for washing your legs from the knees down!

Went out with Cueroni today and dug quahogs. We plan to steam and eat them after check muster tonight.

May 25, 1955   Another Captain's mast was held today. As usual Task was on report. He only got 30 this time which brings his total to 314 demerits. He got the 30 for missing 1-50 studies for the third time. Don't think he'll be around much longer.
May 31, 1955

Dave Freeman might throw a party Friday night. Lets go, OK!

Frank is in the Quincy Hospital. Three car accident. It took them 15 minutes to get him out of the car.

June 1, 1955   About 80% of the midshipmen gave blood to the Red Cross today. Nice stall! It gets us off the ship for a few hours.

June 7, 1955 "The Bum" talked about next year's cruise to Europe in class today. It sounds like a great trip. He described some of the ports and the different types of mooring systems we are going to use. He's not such a bad guy, just don't cross him.

June 8, 1955 The Board of Commissioners came down today. Lots of new rules and regs changes. From now on anyone caught jumping ship will be due for automatic dismissal. As a first job you risk everything if you go ashore at night. Also anyone caught in a parked car on the school grounds is subject to 10 demerits (a weekend aboard).

Friday afternoons will now be spent marching from 1:30 to 3:30 (with rifles). This will be in addition to marching every morning for twenty minutes.

Peckarski, 1st class snipe, was thrown out today with only seven weeks to graduation. He was on probation for marks and jumping ship last March. He was in tears talking with his classmates in the after head before he left. The draft board is right on his heels. He may not be a civilian for long!

June 15, 1955 A new rule from the Board. Any midshipman on the 1-50 list more than 90 days will be placed on the probation list and restricted to the ship until his case comes before the board. They continue to cut down on liberty time. The solution to many problems down here is to allow the guys more *real time to study* and cut out all this other stuff.

June 16, 1955 Your friend, Lee Cueroni, put eight youngies on report for disregarding the Officer of the Watch (they gave him the long finger). They all got 10 and the next weekend aboard. Taylor, Lynch, and Manning were in the group. Don't think you know the rest of them. Dick Greer also went before the mast for being up after taps and drinking in the I.C. Room. He's not charged with drinking, but if he puts up an argument, they'll bring up the real facts and let him have it with both barrels (meanwhile they'll also hold it over him). He'll no doubt take the 10-15 demerits and step back.

Still sweating Trig. but I came up with the correct answers today. Harrington must have had a heart attack!

June 24, 1955 .My dear Miss Smith, the Commissioners of the Mass. Maritime Academy have everything to say about what I do. They tell me what time I get up in the morning, what clothes I will wear during certain times of the day, what food I will eat, what I shall study, when I can smoke, when I can go to bed, when and for how long I will go home, what clothes I will wear while I am home, where I may and may not go while I am home, and what time I shall go back to the good old ship. I told you that if I am able at all to get down there [New Orleans], I will do so. I am trying to get enough money together now so that I can come. I have, as far as I know, ten days off. Two-three of these days I will be bumming down. I hope to spend at least two and possibly three days with you and spend the remainder of the leave getting back to take the final exams of the year. Of course, if the Commissioners check up, I won't be able to come, or if I don't get enough money together I won't be able to make the trip.....

I have the duty this weekend, so I will have some time to do some badly needed studying. The weather is starting to get better all the time, and we do a little sailing on week-ends. Too bad you aren't up here; there is going to be a big clambake and beach party on the 19th, and everyone expects to have a ball.

June 28, 1955 Bob Taylor and I spent the afternoon putting floor boards in the punt (small rectangular boat). Bob is unhappy about getting caught writing a false doctor's note by the Commissioners. They could not locate the doctor. He is now on probation.

Our seamanship classes are getting more interesting. The last few days were spent rebuilding the Captain's gig and splicing wire rope. We are doing more and more real seaman like work lately.

The snipes were out sailing this week so we didn't get any sail time. We'll get three years in the boats. The snipes get about eight months.

Bob Taylor and Jim Lynch were supposed to be painting the waterline in the punt this afternoon. They started clowning around with the one oar astern of the ship. Before they knew it they were caught in the out-going tide headed south. The O.D. called away the whale boat crew. By the time we got the boat in the water they were at least a half mile away. They were very relieved when we finally caught up with them, took them aboard, and tied the punt astern. We turned around and started rowing back to the ship. Between the current and the square-ended punt we couldn't make any progress.

Letters to Lou…

The ship signaled "pull harder"... we did, with no change...decided to give it up and changed course for a beach about 3(?) miles south of the ship. Once ashore we built a big fire and waited for the tide to change. We signaled the ship that we were OK and were waiting for a tide change. Spent most of the night, cold and miserable, on the beach. Rowed back to the ship before dawn. "The Bum" called us lots of things I won't repeat, but mostly *worthless*. Taylor and Lynch got 10 and lost another weekend for skylarking.

July 4, 1955 My brother Kenneth was born today. The rumor around the ship is that he is our son...not my brother. Of course everyone believes we have been married for a long time. Wish it was true! Joe Davidson (1/E) will drive me straight to the hospital Friday. I'll pay for the gas. Hope to make it in time for the visitor's hour. (Note: I was Ken's best man at his wonderful wedding years later.)

July 6, 1955 Jim McCluskey, Joe Walsh, and I are going before the mast tomorrow. Late for formation! We were late because the boson mate of the watch claimed the trays were not washed correctly. We washed them again which made us late. Probably get 6, maybe 10, demerits depending on what the boson mate and O.O.D. report.

The Board returned today. "Mickey" Spillane also left today. He was given the choice of returning with the next class or resigning. Being normal, he quit and probably never will return. Nobody would ever want to go thru another youngie year!

July 7, 1955 I am still trying to figure some way of getting down to see you in August, but I must confess that I honestly cannot see how I will be able to do so. .. The mid-term marks came out yesterday, and with them came the Commissioners who have given two more of the boys their walking papers. Those guys are really making a shake-up down here. They are now considering taking all of our week-ends, with the exception of one a month, away from us. In the academy's new dictionary the word "Commissioner" is spelled " B - - - - - -", and it ends with a "D"!

I have four more weeks, and then we start to take the final exams. Boy, have I a lot of work to catch up on. I was home for the weekend, but I didn't do too much celebrating. I went to the movies by myself, which is something I rarely do and saw the "Sea Chase". It was very good. I also read the book "The Good Shepherd" by C. S. Forester, and I suggest that you read it. It is a story of a Bible-quoting commander, the rank, someday, I hope to hold, But I really doubt that I will quote the Good Book.

I have won a scholarship for next year's tuition, which has taken a lot off my mind. ...I should be studying for a naval science exam in the morning, but I cannot keep my mind on naval strategy and tactics in this weather.

July 11, 1955 Everyone is hitting the books getting ready for finals. The 1st jobs are really starting to sweat. They'll take the Coast Guard exams in two weeks. Just learned that their exams have been moved ahead one week! They are really sweating now! They don't bother with us now. All they do is eat, study, review old tests, and sleep. Its our chance to get even! Its really gonna be fun!

July 16, 1955 The new youngies will be aboard in just 15 days! Hooray! Two kids from Medford are on the list, Brady and Sullivan, I don't know them. Do you?

The second jobs are standing first class watches now. We continue with the same duties.

"Wickie" had the deck Friday and Saturday. He's a little bit simple and will believe almost anything he is told. The first class talked him into having a party aboard. It was thrown in the wardroom and officer's country. Midshipmen are never allowed in these spaces. They had a ball! The second jobs jumped ship. The youngies were set up as watch standers including an "86" watch in the parking lot.

July 19, 1955 Jim Lynch read the clipping you sent before the class. He's the class clown and did a great job with it. Lots of laughs!

July 22, 1955 have a copy of "The Caine Mutiny" though I have not read it yet. I expect to do so very shortly. If I can get enough money together, I am going to start my own library consisting of famous sea stories and stories of the sea and its related fields. As you have noticed in "The Sea Chase", the sea is a big pool of dreams that in a second's notice will turn into a nightmare.

"Youngie Cruise"

...or I'll lose another weekend.

There is something about the sea and the people that (feel) for it that you cannot put into words. People will give their lives for the sea, will work like a dog in the worst weather and be glad that they did. Perhaps one thing that people cannot understand about sailors is that there (are) no roots to their life, but yet there is something bigger and better, which I am unable to explain. Jane, I have seen men who have loafed for months because they could not get a ship. Yet there were plenty of jobs on shore; they just won't work ashore. Yet every time they are on a ship they swear on the high heavens that they won't go back to sea. But they always do. The men that follow the sea are the biggest cutthroats and thieves, bums, etc., that you can find. However, under a captain you cannot find a more loyal group. The sea is for men with no room for the squeamish....... [Note: First and last pages of this letter are missing, so this philosophizing just trails off....]

July 26, 1955 Finals. Still sweating Trig and Harrington. Gotta keep my average above **3.0** or I'll lose another weekend.

We had a Communications exam yesterday. English Literature this morning with Trig this afternoon. Physics and Naval Science tomorrow. Thursday Spanish, Algebra, and English Composition. It all ends Friday with U.S.History, Seamanship and...liberty. See ya Friday night

The Propeller Club of the United States
PORT OF MASSACHUSETTS MARITIME ACADEMY
BUZZARDS BAY   MASS

[Jane Stickney]

MISCELLANEOUS RULES AND ORDERS

All Standing Lights in compartments (located on bulkheads near doors about two feet above the deck) are to be turned on and left on from 2000 to reveille.

Lights of all types to be turned on and off by using light switch. DO NOT UNSCREW BULBS OR REMOVE GLASS GLOBE.

Clothes are not to be hung up to dry below decks.

Matches of the "strike anywhere" type are not to be allowed on shipboard.

Avoid spilling oil on deck. Take proper precautions to avoid overflow and smearing of paintwork with sounding rods.

Waste oil, paint, soapy water, or other similar matter which will smear the hull is not to be thrown over the side.

Garbage will be disposed of at sea through the slop chute.

Garbage will be disposed of in port by local arrangement.

Smoking is prohibited throughout the ship when fueling.

"Baker" is to be hoisted while fueling.

Do not line the side to stare at boats or visitors coming alongside.

All bunks of the 00-04, 08-12, and 12-16 watches are to be made up by 0800. Those of the 04-08 watch by 0830.

Midshipmen will not occupy bunks between reveille and 1600.

Smoking is prohibited in bunks at all times.

The maximum number of Radios allowed in each of the Midshipmen's Berthing Compartments and messhall is (2) for each space.

Radios requiring antennae are to be plugged into the Broadcast Antennae outlets which are available in each living compartment. No other Antennae are to be strung about.

Music hours are the same as the smoking hours. Hours are posted.

Volume control of radios to be kept below a level which will not cause disturbance to others.

[Jim McCluskey]

"Youngie Cruise"

Massachusetts Maritime Academy
19 August 1954

MEMORANDUM FOR ALL MIDSHIPMEN:

Because of lack of clerical help it is not possible to make out complete financial statements for all those desiring them. Each student should keep track of his own expenditures and keep his own books. Mr. Anteen furnishes you with a receipt for all books, clothing and supplies. Other annual expenditures which are deductible upon the commencement of the academic year are as follows:

Service fee (tuition)	$150.00
Social fee	$ 15.00
Athletic fee	$ 15.00
Insurance	$ 20.00
Total	$200.00

Since books, uniforms and supplies average about $100.00 a year this makes the total annual cost $300.00. The $200.00 annual subsidy received by those drawing Federal subsidy, therefore, fails to be enough to cover this annual cost by about $100.00. It is necessary for the individual to make up this $100.00. Since practically all of the $300.00 is spent at the beginning of the year it is necessary that those drawing Federal subsidy pay the $100.00 plus $50.00 additional outlay for books at commencement of second class year. Others will be required to deposit $300.00 at the commencement of both 2nd and 1st class years. Those who have bought more clothing than the average will be required to pay that much more.

As for the $400.00 deposit which you made when you entered the Academy the annual charges, and about $100.00 paid for the initial outfit, (for which you have receipts) consumed nearly all of it.

Your receipts plus the above information will give you all the information that you will need with regard to your expenditures. You may check your receipts with those in possession of Mr. Anteen, when he is available.

There is about a two month delay in the receipt of the $16.66 (average) monthly subsidy for those receiving it and therefore none of this subsidy will be available as cash for the first classmen until after the cruise.

s/
J.D. WILSON,
Rear Admiral, USN(RET),
Superintendent.

Note: The $16.66 was paid to those in the U.S. Naval Reserve Program.

[Jim McCluskey]

Massachusetts Maritime Academy

26 July 1955

WEEK END LEAVE

The following instructions concerning week end leave replaces previous regulations and instructions pertaining thereto:

Third classmen will be granted only one week end leave every four weeks.

Second classmen will be granted week end leaves every other week end. Additional week end leave on non-duty section week ends will be granted second classmen who:

1. Have not received more than 15 demerits during the preceding month nor more than 50 demerits during the preceding four months.

2. Have an average mark of more than 3.0 during the preceding term with no mark less than 2.7.

3. Are recommended by their faculty advisors and instructors.

4. Are not on the 1-50 list.

First classmen will continue to be granted three week end leaves out of four.

All midshipmen will continue to be placed in sections with the principal week end leave to be granted immediately following the week end during which the section has the duty. For the third classmen this would be the only week end leave. This would stagger the week end leaves and there would be approximately the same number aboard each week end.

/s/
J.D. WILSON
Rear Admiral, USN(Ret),
Superintendent

Copy to:
Board of Commissioners
All officers (1 each)
All midshipmen (1 each)
OOD Folder
OOW
Bulletin Board

[Jim McCluskey]

    This was posted today. Nothing heard about this until today! The next youngie class is really gonna have it rough. I bet a lot of them drop out sooner and faster than the previous classes. **Just one weekend off a month is insane!** I wonder if they have been told about this policy change?

FIRST JOBS
(Bad Guys)

MUSTER SHEET

Section	DECK(1D)	CHECK OUT	CHECK IN		Section	ENGINEER(1E)	CHECK OUT	CHECK IN
___4	ARNOLD, JD				___4	CLAXTON,PH JR		
___3	BERRY,PF				___4	COLLINS,CF		
___1	CALLAHAN, DF Jr				___3	CONWAY, RF		
___3	COLLIS, RA				___1	DAVIDSON,AJ		
___1	CUERONI, LA				___1	D'ENTREMONT, RL		
___2	FOSTER, AL				___2	DUCHARME AE		
___2	HALLIGAN, JP				___2	FITZPATRICK,BE		
___2	HANNON,JA				___3	FLYNN, DJ		
___3	KEEFE, MH				___3	FLYNN, WJ		
___3	KOCHANOWICZ,JF				___2	FORD, R		
___1	KROCHALIS, EJP				___2	GALANIS, PL		
___1	LE BLANC, JB				___4	GREEN, DL		
___1	MC CARTHY, DJ				___1	GRIFFITH, RE		
___3	RILEY, FK Jr				___3	HAMMOND, ER Jr		
___2	RUSSELL, JC				___2	KORPELA, WA		
___1	SCANNELL, GF				___1	MARSTON, PG		
___2	SCHUFFELS, JF				___3	McLAUGHLIN, DW		
___1	SHEEHY,DV				___4	MOORE, AS		
___4	SIROIS, AC				___4	NICKELL, RE		
___4	STERLING,CI 3rd				___2	OJALA		
___4	WEINFIELD, RM				___4	PANORA, JW		
					___2	PEKARSKI, BJ		
					___3	PYBAS, CE Jr		
					___4	QUALTER, FJ		
					___1	RAWSON, RM Jr		
					___4	SMITH, DE		
					___1	SMITH, RN		
					___2	THOMPSON,WH		
					___1	VILES, PJ		
					___2	WALLACE, RM		
					___			
					___			

MIDSHIPMEN ARE CAUTIONED REGARDING THEIR CONDUCT AND PROPER WEARING OF UNIFORM.

Sec 1 liberty commences _____ expires _____

Sec 3 liberty commences _____ expires _____

Sec 2 liberty commences _____ expires _____

Sec 4 liberty commences _____ expires _____

Midshipmen on 1-50 list return by _____

D - DUTY

R – RESTRICTED   R.T. ROUNDS, CDR. USNR

CLASS OF 1955   EXECUTIVE OFFICER

[Jim McCluskey]

SECOND JOBS

MUSTER SHEET

Section	DECK(2D)	CHECK OUT	CHECK IN		Section	ENGINEER(2E)	CHECK OUT	CHECK IN
___2	CANNIFF, WR				___1	ALDRICH,AG Jr		
___1	CASHMAN, RW				___3	BEE, RD		
___1	CLEVELAND,RN				___1	BERRY,RV		
___3	COYNE, T				___1	BLAZEWICZ,JVF		
___1	D'ANGELO, AV				___1	BRENNOCK, RF		
___2	DONAHUE, JR				___2	BURGESS, FS		
___2	GREER, RE				___2	CHURCH, RL		
___2	HALPIN, EL				___3	CORSARNO, VE		
___3	HEMMALIN,JP				___3	COUGHLIN,EF		
___3	HOWAT, JC				___2	CULLINANE, GEA		
___1	MAC DONALD, RW				___2	DUGGAN, TJ		
___1	MAHONEY, J				___4	EDNEY, JW Jr		
___1	MATTESON, KL				___1	FITZGERALD, JF		
___3	MC ADAMS,CF				___3	FLYNN, EL		
___2	MOWER, PR				___2	GREEN, RW		
___1	MULQUEENY, JB				___1	HAMWEY, RM		
___2	QUIRK, JR				___3	HANSON, AE		
___1	STANDLEY, PR				___4	JOHNSON, DR		
___4	VOGEL, JJ				___4	JOHNSON, JP		
					___2	JORDAN, DC		
					___4	KELLEY, RH		
					___2	LYNCH, PL		
					___3	MACINTYRE, RG Jr		
					___4	MALKASIAN, E		
					___1	MANSFIELD, JL		
					___4	MC LAUGHLIN, TM		
					___1	O'CONNOR, RG		
					___2	PARENT, TR		
					___1	PIOTTI, WT JR		
					___2	RYAN, MT Jr		
					___1	SHYNE, KT		
					___2	SOULE, SL		
					___3	STEWART, GW		
					___4	THORPE, AM		
					___2	TRAPP, CFM		
					___4	TRAVERS, JE		
					___3	VESEY, WP		
					___1	WARD, DI		

MIDSHIPMEN ARE CAUTIONED REGARDING THEIR CONDUCT AND PROPER WEARING OF UNIFORM.

Sec 1 liberty commences _____ expires _____

Sec 3 liberty commences _____ expires _____

Sec 2 liberty commences _____ expires _____

Sec 4 liberty commences _____ expires _____

Midshipmen on 1-50 list return by _____

D - DUTY

R – RESTRICTED

R.T. ROUNDS, CDR. USNR

CLASS OF 1956

EXECUTIVE OFFICER

[Jim McCluskey]

| **MUSTER SHEET** | | | | "YOUNGIES - Good Guys " | | |

MUSTER SHEET "YOUNGIES - Good Guys "

Third Class 1954

Section	DECK(3D)	CHECK OUT	CHECK IN	Section	ENGINEER	CHECK OUT	CHECK IN
_+_1	*ASCOLILLO, ED*			_+_1	*ANDERSON, RN*		‖
___2	**AYLMER, JR**			***1	ARZOUMAIJIAN, PH		
_+_4	*BROADBENT, CW*			***1	BARRY, JJ Jr		
___1	**BROWN, RD**			___1	**BILLINGS, HC**		
_+_4	*CIALDEA, CP J*			___3	**BOLES, RJ**		
___2	DROHAN, DE			___1	BUTHMAN, RA		
_+_1	*GREER, RJ*			___1	**BUTLER, TF Jr**		
___3	**HOGAN, DF**			___1	**CHRISTIE, AJ**		
___4	KEENAN, JD Jr			_+_1	*DUFFLEY, NJ*		
_+_1	*LaCLAIR, D*			___1	ELLIS, HA Jr		
_+_2	*LACH, JR*			_+_4	*FEE, JR*		
___1	LYNCH, JJ 3rd			_+_2	*FERGUSON, FM*		
___2	**MAHONEY, FE**			_+_2	*FLAHERTY, JR Jr*	*** PAT***	
___1	MANNING, RL			___2	**FREEMAN, DV**		
___1	**McCLUSKEY, JM**			_+_2	*GILLEN, JR*		
___4	**McCLUSKEY, JL**			_+_2	*GRAHAM, F*		
***2	McDONALD, JW			___1	**GRANT, KR**		
___3	MEGONIGLE, CE			___2	**KENDRIGAN, PM**		
___4	MEYER, LD			___2	KENNEDY, LM		
***3	MONAHAN, CF 3rd			___2	**KOOPMAN, DH**		
***4	PINER, JWG			***2	LEWIS, CW		
___1	**READEL, PF**			___4	LOPAUS, RC		
___2	**REILLY, RK** (BLACK)			___3	**McCARTHY, JJ**		
___3	ROFFEY, RC			___3	McGRATH, JJ		
_+_4	*STICKNEY, RL* ***JANE***			_+_3	*McKENNA, JE*		
_+_4	**STRAUTMAN, RE**		1/18/98	___3	MIRABELLO, ED		
___3	SWEET, JK Jr			___3	O'CONNELL, JR		
***4	TACHE, JA			___4	**PUTIGNANO, DJ**		
_+_1	*TAYLOR, RK*			___3	**REID, WJ Jr**		
___3	VERDERICO, MB			___4	**RUMNEY, RE**		
___2	**WEAVER, RG**			___4	**SCARLATA, AC**		
***3	WILSON, RE			___3	SOUTHWORTH, FC Jr		
___	RILEY, RE (RED)			***3	SPILLANE, EF		
				___4	**SULLIVAN, EF**		
				___3	TASK, HL		
				___3	WALSH, JF		
				___4	**YOUNG, RA**		
				___4	**YOUNG, WG**		
				***4	ZIMINSKY, PV		
				___2	FERRERA. K		

NOTES: **BOLD names made MUSTER at the 40th REUNION**

*** = Did not Graduate

Italics = Deceased

MIDSHIPMEN ARE CAUTIONED REGARDING THEIR CONDUCT AND PROPER WEARING OF UNIFORM.

Sec 1 liberty commences _____ expires _____

Sec 3 liberty commences _____ expires _____

Sec 2 liberty commences _____ expires _____

Sec 4 liberty commences _____ expires _____

Midshipmen on 1-50 list return by _____

D - DUTY

R – RESTRICTED

R.T. ROUNDS, CDR. USNR

CLASS OF 1957

EXECUTIVE OFFICER

July 1998

[Jim McCluskey]

CLASS OF 1958

Information taken from the "BULLETIN" August 1958

Incoming "Youngie Class" August 1955

Bachelor's Degree
Nautical Science

Arsenault, Roger D.
Boyson, Arthur
Bradley, John
Callahan, John P.
Collis,Charles
Dalton, John W.
Dill, Edgar A.
Donnellian,Robert I.
Dowd, John E
Fisher, Kenneth
Flynn, Richard A.
Knight, Robert L.
Manning, Russell
Mason, Ronald F.
McCormick, Gerald J
O'Neil, James M..
Perrotti, Manual V.
Petit, Nicholas A.
Polletta, Michael P
Schofield, Albert R. Jr.
Sinclair, Donald L.
Stetson, John B.

Bachelor's Degree
Marine and Electrical
Engineering

Atkinson,William R.
Ayers, Raymond D.
Bradley, Joseph F.
Butler, Lawrence W.
Cash, Daniel H.
Chorlton, Charles D.
Crowninshield, Bowdin B.
Crowninshield, George W.
Cull, George E.
Fields, Charles L.
Foss, Donald M.
Frimodig, Robert L.
Goodwin, Robert
Hanson, Alan E.
Harrington, Paul D.
Keane, Chester F.
McCluskey, Joseph L.
McDonough, William J.
Meyer, Karl L.
Morison, Arthur M.
O'Connell, Robert J.
Reid, William J.
Ruest, Paul M.
Salley, Ronald G
Savery, Winsor T.
Shannon, David J.
Shepherd, Wilbur S.
Stickney, Robert L. '57D & '58E
Sullivan, Daniel
Washburn, Francis B.
York, Bruce A.

Note: Only Graduates Listed Above

[John Dalton]

One Gun Chun

Fingernail inspection by "Hop"

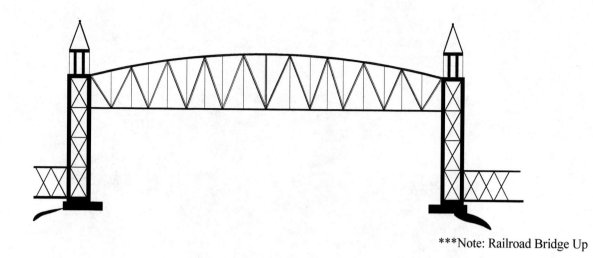

***Note: Railroad Bridge Up

SECOND CLASS YEAR

PART 2 - YEAR 2

August 9, 1955   Since the new youngies (tools) have come aboard I don't have to do the dirty work anymore...kinda nice! In fact I've started to read Mr. Roberts in my spare time.

We are now securing things for a hurricane that's coming up the coast. If it hits we hope to be better prepared than last year.

August 10, 1955   New books were issued today. Mostly professional subjects. No more Physics, Trig, or English Comp. Next term no more Spanish.

Hope things are going OK at Boston Floating! Changing hospitals and your routine takes time to adjust. Good luck!

....I am back at the academy now and will be here for quite a while, until they get the weekend liberty straightened out. I am waiting to draw books and start classes, and I feel pretty good now because we start taking navigation and radio aids [?], plus other professional subjects. I should clean up on those subjects. At least, I will try to....

August 12,1955   I passed Spanish but flunked Algebra. I live in fear of "Hop". I just freeze in his class. Most of my grades are pretty good, especially the professional ones which are the most important, the others are gonna drive me bananas.

Do you remember "Horny" Wilson, a classmate. He quit! Couldn't raise $150 due to sickness in his family. Our class was about to chip in to help him but he is needed at home. Really too bad, huh!

August 15, 1955   Storm warnings. The youngies are due for a hurricane tonight. "Wickie" has the deck. All hell is about to break out from the first jobs that don't jump ship. A few youngies went for a swim up the "Mississippi", a salt water trough in the starboard head. Not as bad as last year. They were allowed to change skivvies before turning in. No running around on the main deck afterwards either. The first class went light on them due to the new youngie leave policy (one weekend off per month). People are concerned that they will start quitting faster than ever.

August 16, 1955   I went out in a whale boat today. Its the first time I've gone out and not done the rowing, just went along for the ride.

August 18, 1955   Ted and I have pulled all kinds of deals this week. We were picked to teach the youngies how to row and to act as coxswains. Cdr. Connors, "The Bum", assigned us a boat and a crew. Let's hope we can continue to stay on the right side of him.

August 18, 1955...I was sorry to hear you mention the uniform that I wear. I do not think I could get over it if it was the uniform that holds your interest and not the person who wears it. [Note: I must have innocently commented on how handsome he looked in his uniform! JS]

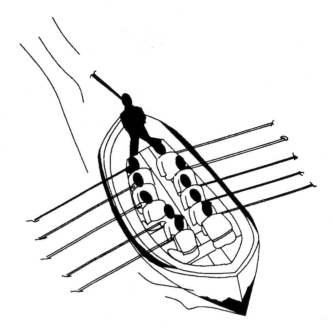

We have started on the new liberty plan; therefore I will be here for the week-end...Jane, it is a shame to see over one hundred middies walking around below decks with nothing to do. They have never had that many men on board ship on a weekend before, and therefore the cooks did not have enough food to feed them. Sunday dinner they had a pork chop, potatoes, bread, jam and a half-cup of sour milk. For supper they had beans, bread, jam and coffee. For Monday morning we had boiled eggs and powdered milk. There is now a big stink about the food, so perhaps we will get out on weekends from now on. I surely hope so.

Jane, I have done more work and studying since I became a second classman than I did last year. We have more professional classes, such as navigation, rules of the nautical road, seamanship, communications, Naval Science, Naval Ordnance and Gunnery, English Lit, Spanish, Naval History, Maritime History, Physics, and Economic Geography. Every night since we started this term I have been getting up at 4 AM to study, but it does get tiresome....

Please write SOON. It is so good to hear from the OUTSIDE WORLD and especially from someone like yourself.

August 22, 1955   Remember the "Pier" (the snack shack)? The state is going to take it and the southern end of Taylor's Point(in Oct.) to build a Naval Science Building and dormitories before the winter sets in. Great news, huh! I'll believe it when I see it!

We've had nine youngies quit in the last two weeks mostly because of the liberty policy. Eight new ones are gonna replace them this week. I never thought this place would ever have alternates standing by.

August 23, 1955   The Commissioners are here again. I wonder what new rules and regs will be issued today? The "Anteen Raiders" may learn their fate today?

A youngie, O'Niel, fell down the fireroom ladder last night and lost the feeling in and use of his legs. He was rushed to Brighton Marine Hospital last night.

Bob Strautman just discovered a ship named the USS Hogan. It was built around 1910 as a destroyer and converted to a fast mine sweeper in 1940. The average life of a naval ship is about twenty years. It must be a really beauty at this point. It was also known as "Hogan's Goat".

Just returned from the make-up exam. All of us on the 1-50 list flunked again! Harrington claims we are not studying! Actually he's not doing much teaching...rarely showed up for class! He, of course, threw another fit! He really gets excited! Some day he's gonna have a heart attack and drop dead! We're all gonna take another make-up exam in a few weeks. God only knows what he'll give us or do then.

Ted and I continue to pull deals. We watched "The Cruise of the Farragutt" and a few other films this afternoon. We'll go out in boats again tomorrow if it doesn't rain.

August 24, 1955   As I write this a few boys in the corner are glued to their seats while a certain party describes his date last Saturday night. It really was just an ordinary date for an ordinary guy but this guy hasn't had a date or been out with a girl in *four and a half years*. He has written about twenty poems and at least ten letters to her. The poor guy has had it!

Letters to Lou…

Everybody strings him along, keeps him all excited, and they drag his posterior something wicked! This guy won't be going ashore for a while and he's afraid she is gonna forget him. He really is in bad shape!

August 27,1955   The Commissioners are here again (Friday). Called the 1st jobs together, laid down the law again, **"NO MORE HAZING"** !!! Do you understand? Also **"NO MORE JUMPING SHIP"!!!** etc. Oh well... we'll see! Also only first class cadet officers and the O.O.D. are now allowed to put a youngie on report. Last year any 1st job could put any youngie on report at any time. Maybe that accounts for our class average of 30 demerits per youngie.

Remember Megonigle? He's from Kentucky (crazy kid) and wanted to go to Annapolis but has a physical problem. He got engaged over the telephone last night. His father bought the ring, gave it to the girl, she opened the box when he called. He, of course, is all excited and is going home this Friday. He is gonna fly both ways and spend sixteen hours at home...we think we have it rough!

Ted just came in. He is trying to figure out the time of sunset. The flag comes down then. As bosonmate of the watch it's his job to know the time. Chances are that the sun will set with or without him!

The duty section now gets four hours of liberty on the weekend. Just enough time to have a beer and get back. Greer, Ascolillo and Brown brought back a quart of beer for me. Great guys, huh!

I've got to run around a little bit next weekend. I've got to buy some drum sticks and a replacement drum head. We had a party in the band locker last night and more than one thing was damaged!

August 30, 1955   Dick Greer and Jim Lynch are on the spot again. The Pentagon, Navy Dept., sent a letter to the Admiral demanding $60 from Jim and $5 from Dick. They rented bikes in Paramaribo, Surinam and left them on the dock. The guy that rented them wants money for one bike(not found) and for a light on the other one. Dick and Jim refuse to pay; they don't have the money anyway! I'm not sure what's gonna happen?

We had the Admiral during study period today and did we tell him what was on our minds. He was shocked and seemed to be at a loss for words. He picked the wrong class to talk to when he picked us. He was constantly shelled with questions, opinions, and wild statements. We are gonna have another bout with him next month.

One of the guys asked the "Good Admiral" if the "YOU ASS HO" (USO) was sponsoring a dance or something or other at one of the Ports of Call on the next cruise.

[Peter Readel]

We met with the Captain two weeks ago and he, too, was amazed at what we had to say. We'll probably lose because of we said but at least they know what's on our minds.

August 31, 1955   We will leave on our Mediterranean cruise March 5th next year. They are afraid the ship won't make it across in the winter. It sure makes me feel good to know that! Another bit of cruise news is that we won't hit North Africa because of the revolution and uprising in Algeria. Where we go nobody knows! Usually the ship stops at three ports on that coast.

I got a letter from my Dad today with a $10 inside. Five of it has to go toward that damn drum head. All I know is that I better have a drum head under my arm when I return.

September 3,1955   I haven't heard from you for over a week, Jane. .... You, Jane, got me in a pail of hot water yesterday. I was rushing to mail call in hopes of hearing from you, and on the way I tripped over one of the kids. He swore, and I swore back at him and left it at that. Then after I found there was no letter from you, I walked back and was plenty mad. The kid was still in the same place, and this time I told him to get out of the way. He said to make him, and I did. Result, I am on report for fighting and, if the Captain gives me what the books say, I will not have any liberty for quite a while. Solution, you should write more often and I will not be mad all the time and get into trouble...

We will have to spend the winter in Cape Cod this year. The cruise has been postponed until the 5 March in hopes of better weather in the Med. That may prove to be a good thing, and then again it may not. If we get a ten-day Xmas leave, as I hope that we will, I am going to do my best to get down to see you. On the other hand, the cruise may be cut down to ten weeks, and it will cut out a lot of ports. As it stands now, we are going to leave in mid-term and have only eight weeks to the finals when we get back. And that is bad.

[Note: I sent him my photograph. JS] Jim [Piner] sleeps below me, and he stops and says "good night" to you each and every night...

How far is New Orleans from Houston, Texas? We will be in that port on our next cruise. Congratulations are in order for Midshipman Richard Weaver, a close friend of mine who has just received his first degree in the Masonic order, an organization that I someday hope to be a member of. It is also the group that a friend of mine is trying to navigate a loan of four hundred dollars from for expense money. That is some sentence structure. But, as you know, English is not one of my better subjects.

September 7, 1955   All are present and accounted for ...for the "Sunday Evening Supper Club". We'll hit the books later for the math make-up tomorrow morning.

We continue to practice for the ring dance next Saturday. The second class always provides the honor guard. Usually six guys with rifles and a leader. We practiced the march on and later the "Queen Ann's Salute". This salute starts from a standing position, the rifles are tossed in the air with rotation, caught and finished with one arm across the chest and one knee on the floor. Kinda tricky but impressive.

In four weeks we'll take this ship to the Boston shipyard. I'll get two weeks liberty, nights anyway, and weekends home. I have only one duty weekend during the overhaul.

September 9, 1955   A party is scheduled at Graham's house after the ring dance. Ted is gonna drive us in his girl friend's car... a convertible I think? Sounds like fun, huh?

I have four hours liberty tomorrow afternoon. A few of us will probably hit a dairy bar in town. I'm dying for an ice cream!

September 12, 1955   had a feeling that you were home yesterday and called your house, but your father said he did not know when to expect you. Who or whom do you know in Memphis? It is twice now that I have called and your [father] has kept asking if the call was from that city. I don't think that he likes to believe that I live north of the Mason & Dixon Line....

Just for the record, I was 19 years old [when we met] and was 20 the day after Washington's birthday. I have 21 months left at the Mass. Maritime, and then, as you decide, (as I hope that you will be my wife) I will go to work as a third officer for $750 a month or be an Ensign in the Navy for $300 a month...

I came out much better than I expected on the fighting deal. After about an hour of fast double-talk to the captain, I finally talked him down to six demerits, which is not a restriction.

We leave for drydock in Boston on the 3rd of August and will stay there about four weeks. That will give me a chance to get some work in because we get off the ship every night.

September 13, 1955   Twelve of us took another math make-up test today. I know I got 10 of the 11 problems right! <u>BUT...</u> Ted Brown and Herbie Ellis were caught exchanging answers when Harrington entered the room. He threw <u>another fit</u> (getting kinda used to them now). He gave us a lecture about the honor system and a million other things before he left.

Harrington has not spoken to any of us since the test and we don't dare go near him. He may make <u>ALL</u> of us take another exam again!!! Damn!!! The way it's going I'll never get off the 1-50 list, to be posted tomorrow, or finish with him.

The following day. Good news! I'll be off the 1-50 list in two weeks. Harrington is taking us off because he needs us on the drill team and for the half time show! We need to practice marching ...never mind studying algebra.

Letters to Lou…

Remember "Cocchi", also know as Ferrera, from Waltham? They found him face down on the oil covered deck plates down below. A steam line parted in the fireroom and burned his back and left arm pretty bad. Gonna be in sick bay for a while!

Nine more days and we'll take the ship for repairs to Boston and dry-dock. Can't wait! Only the duty section stays aboard at night and weekends.

We are still taking the boats out every afternoon. Ted and I pitted our crews against each other. My crew won by about fifteen yards. We sure have pulled a good deal. Neither of us have done an afternoon's work for the last six weeks. It sure beats chipping paint and other things!

Last night we voted for people to represent the class to select the type and style of our class rings. Four guys were selected. Southworth, Jim McCarthy, Greer, and me.

September 17, 1955   Ring Dance. Had a great time! Things went well for the drill squad.

I had the duty the night of the ring dance, but I was thinking of you all the time, Miss Smith. We did not have classes today because of the threat of the storm. We were tying up the ship and beaching all of the small craft. The visibility of the area is down to zero, and the barometer is falling one-tenth per hour, so it looks like we are in for a ride.

Jane, if there is one thing that you learn in this business, it is to make a decision and stick to that decision until you have positive proof that it is wrong. We are trained to make such decisions on short notice and with a limited amount of facts on hand. In the case of a girl who lives in New Orleans, I applied these principles on such things as a short meeting, a few letters, and telephone calls. I think that I have made the right decision on my part and hope that you are able to do the same.

I am sorry to hear that you quit your job in the library [at Tulane]. I wanted you to look up river transportation in Brazil for me, if you had the time to do so.

September 21, 1955   I was discovered writing this letter and the following want to say hello.
Hello from …Ted, Keenjab, Pink Riley, Black Rielly, Pinejob, Dick Greer, Gluk, Jim and Joe McCluskey and the remainder of the class.

September 22, 1955   We had a rally in town last night for the football team. Jim Lynch was the MC and did a tremendous job. The first game is against New Haven State Teachers College (never heard of them).

September 24, 1955   Nine more days to dry dock and every night home. Can't wait!
While the ship is in Boston we are expected to go to the Sperry School to get our "Gyro Ticket" in Brooklyn, New York. The ticket means a lot if your looking for a job and it's required to go from third to second mate. The school is free but I have pay for room and board. I don't know where I'll get the money but I plan to go.

Saturday night on my duty weekend. I'm bored and restless. The TV on the messdeck is going full blast. I haven't been more than thirty feet (fore or aft) all day. As I write this and look around I see guys sacked out, reading, and in general disgusted with life. A radio is playing softly in what we call the gorge but nobody is listening. The rain is beating on the main deck above me.

Every once in a while the damn squawk box makes an announcement. " Now hear this…….." "Now hear this, there will be a movie in the building at 2000 tonight. The name of the movie is… " A Bride By Mistake" (I bet it's just great)." The last movie was "Every Girl Should Marry". I wonder who picks these flicks? We'll probably go just to pass a few remarks and see a little of the outside world. As the movie progresses the crowd usually thins out until the only one in the room is the projector operator(poor soul) and a couple of youngies jobbed to clean up and square away the chairs.

I just realized I'm a MO-DEL (not model) midshipman! I'm dressed in a pair of grubby and salty dungarees and a "T" shirt with a pack of Luckies rolled up in the left sleeve. On my feet are a pair of old black socks; one is inside out and showing many strands of gray thread. My hair was combed last Thursday and I need a shave. Yup, I'm just a real MO-DEL MIDDIE!!! I've decided not to go to the movies tonight. I'm too lazy to change into khaki's and run over to the building in the rain.

THE BOSTON SUNDAY GLOBE--OCTOBER 2, 1955

Atomic Energy Sailors

Massachusetts Marine Academy Cadets Take Instructions in Nuclear Reactors for Propulsion of Ships

By EARL BANNER

BUZZARDS BAY -- The cadets of the Massachusetts Maritime Academy Schoolship Charleston will begin receiving instruction in the operation of nuclear reactors for the propulsion of ships early next year.

Congress has yet to take action on the President's proposal for the construction of an atomic ship. The question is still in committee, but the commissioners of the Massachusetts Maritime Academy, anticipating the fact that progress can't be held in check by even Congress, have taken this action with the blessings of the Atomic Energy Committee.

Which is all by way of illustrating that the Bay State's college for sailors has come a long way since the days of the old Schoolship Nantucket when cadets were still being instructed in the intricacies of sail and coal-fired boilers when the merchant navies of the world were already committed to the use of oil fired steam turbines.

The Charleston, a trim former Navy gunboat, is moored to the State Pier here at the entrance of Cape Cod Canal nine months of the year. Then, March through May, it carries the college (for it could rate this title since graduates receive a B. S. degree - earned in three instead of the usual four years, too) to far distant ports of the world.

Superintendent of the academy is Rear Adm. Julian D. Wilson, United States Navy (retired). The executive officer is Capt. John W. Thompson, United States Maritime Service, former navigating officer of the old Nantucket and commanding officer of the Charleston.

Adm. Wilson was absent in the Great Lakes area last week investigating the opportunities for graduates of the academy in that region.

★   ★   ★

Capt. Thompson told me: "The opening of the seaway is going to boom shipping in the Great Lakes. Great Lakes shipping interests sent their representatives East last year. They're looking for more well trained college degree men to man their ships. We think that an increasingly large percentage of our graduates will wind up in 'lake' shipping in the years ahead. The trend started last year when four of our graduates took jobs out there."

★   ★   ★

Every year the academy receives from three to five times as many applicants as it can handle. Accommodations on the ship are taxed to capacity now with some 200 cadets in three classes (the "young men", as they are referred to by the officers) and the staff of 21 officers, instructors and staff members.

Most of the applicants fail in the strict physical examination. The remainder are weeded out in the scholastic examinations. The result is that those comparative few managing to survive are the literal "cream of the crop".

★   ★   ★

They have to be for the routine they adopt for the three years after admission would discourage all but the best qualified. The ship is run Navy style with strict discipline and an easy road to dismissal for non-conformists through easily-earned demerits.

★   ★   ★

There are no long vacations throughout the three-year grind.

★   ★   ★

"And no college graduate has a better opportunity to build up a nest-egg any faster, either," Capt. Thompson stresses. "What other college can promise its graduates that they will be able to land a $600 per month job right after graduation?"

★   ★   ★

It isn't all that grand though. The cadets have a football team this Fall scheduled to play New Haven State Teachers, New Britain Sate Teachers, Worcester Polytech and the Maine Maritime Academy at Castine. (Perhaps it won't happen this year, but the day may come when the maritime schools will sail their ships to their respective away from home games. That's the scuttlebutt on the Charleston right now, anyhow.)

Letters to Lou…

In season, they will have basketball and baseball teams, too. Thanks to the Spring cruise, the baseball team plays many of its games in foreign ports. Right now, the cadets are looking forward to their next South American cruise and hoping, among other things, to avenge the 6 to 5 defeat they suffered from their Venezuelan counterparts the last time they were down that way.

Better athletic facilities and shore side classrooms are scheduled in the academy's future expansion program. The last session of the General Assembly appropriated money for the purchase of land near the State Pier to enable this program to get underway.

THE FORMER NAVY GUNBOAT "Charleston" currently serves the Massachusetts Maritime Academy as campus and schoolship. The vessel has serious shortcomings as a training ground for merchant mariners since it offers no facilities whatever for training in cargo handling. The Academy Commissioners are hopeful now that a former hospital ship may be obtained to overcome this defect in the school's facilities.

October 17, 1955   Here we are in Brooklyn, N.Y. I haven't seen much of the town but we are going out tonight. Due to weather conditions we had a lot of trouble getting here. We were lucky and caught the last plane to New York. A lot of the roads in western Mass have been washed out and closed to cars and buses. Flying was the only way to get here. It sure is a nice way to travel!

Riley and three other guys still haven't showed up? (Monday PM.)

October 18, 1955   The second day of class and two days in Flatbush is over. The "Y" is almost under the Manhattan Bridge which make it kinda hard to sleep. The traffic here is wicked! Cars rule the day and at night it's one mass of cabs and trucks. We went up to Times Square last night, saw a show, and finally went down to the village. Some sections of the city are tremendous while the village etc. are terrible (just like a foreign land). We usually eat at the "Y" or at the Automat across the street from the Sperry School. Everything seems to be more expensive here. I've got to be careful and stretch my money for the next two weeks. Many meals of peanut butter and long loafs of bread.

October 20, 1955   Tomorrow classes are over at noon. Black Rielly and I are gonna tour the United Nations and the Empire State buildings. Most of the guys are visiting family friends or have dates this weekend.

My cousin Ken and I went to a Broadway show Saturday night. "Will Success Spoil Rock Hunter?" We hoped to see "Damn Yankees" but it was sold out. We had supper at Mayflower Donuts and then went across the street to the Astor Hotel for cocktails. Later we drove to his place in Philadelphia and spent the next day visiting friends in New Jersey. He dropped me off on the N.J. Turnpike. I used my thumb, and my job suit, to get back to Brooklyn. It really was a great weekend!!!

October 31, 1955   Here it is Halloween without anyone playing trick-or-treat. The youngies are very much in the spirit of the day ducking for apples on the messdeck. A nice party. The upper jobs really enjoyed it.

November 1, 1955   Started to read "The Decline and Fall of the Roman Empire." It's required reading for all military schools (MMA-military? that's a laugh)! The Admiral, our great naval leader, recommends it. Rumor has it that after we read it he wants us to explain it to him in three letter words! No kidding! He's not too dense, just a little slow! It usually takes him 20 minutes to answer a simple question. He spends 18 minutes thinking about it and takes about 2 minutes to answer!

I left my black cap cover at home. I hope I remember to bring it back next weekend. We change covers on the 7th. I want to look like a bus driver along with all the other guys!

November 3, 1955   Finally off the 1-50 list. Finally passed the math test. Hooray!!!

November 4, 1955   Lewis is back after three weeks vacation. He was released and called back with 100 demerits. He was caught with thirteen different midshipmen's gear in his locker(Purloined is the termed used). Thirteen must be a new record! He won't get home for months. He does hope to get off for Christmas.

...the raiders.

November 7, 1955   Two 1st jobs were caught jumping ship last night. A sure 100 and...out?

A few guys just ran Laclair's mattress up on the port yardarm. Looks pretty good up there with his towel, blanket, sheets, etc. It will probably take him a long time to find it or before it will be reported. Maybe he'll sleep in the shaft alley tonight?

Great duty weekend. Made a beer run and had a party on the point a few hundred yards from the ship.

The second class snipes rented the Inn here on Taylor's Point while I was in New York. It was supposed to be a dance etc., but the etc. took over! Most of the second jobs aboard jumped ship and came back smashed. The 1st jobs will really be on our necks when they find out and get back. Our class is in enough trouble without this happening. Just one more thing to hold against us.

Today at 1330 eleven of my classmates and two upper classmen received a gift from the Board of Commissioners of 100 demerits apiece, which means they are entitled to stay aboard the ship until the first of the year. One of the kids, a very dear friend of mine who received 100 today, got caught jumping ship on the weekend and is expected to get another 100 on Friday. If that comes, I can only say that we will miss him around here. The others are also going up for jumping ship but they have had a clean record up until now.

November 8, 1955   The "Anteen Raiders", all thirteen of them, joined the "Century Club", 100 demerits. Our class now has more members of a single class in the club than any time since World War II. Another record! In my class eight snipes and three deckies will be aboard for a while. Chuck Broadbent (a raider) is also waiting on board action after getting caught jumping ship last Saturday night.

Jim Quirk and Cleveland, 1st jobs, and Broadbent were sent home pending board action.

Our class now has a total of **3,518** demerits, last night's posted total. An average of **53.3** per man. Just think we still have 21 months until graduation. Task is leading the pack with **502**, seven guys have more than 200, fourteen have more than 100. Seven guys have **"NONE"!!! Lucky and cozy!**

The first class is on us all the time, just like being a youngie again! These first jobs won't get any cooperation from this class. Classmates have done things like quit the band, the football rallies, and other clubs. Our class has received about 1100 to 1400 demerits from them and they still drag our posteriors.

Their Maine Rally was a flop! They want school spirit but they'll not get it from this class.

BULKHEAD SLATED FOR CONSTRUCTION AT FINGER WHARF

Admiral Wilson Notes Possible Target Date For New Buildings

BUZZARDS BAY, Nov. 10 -- Construction of an extensive bulkhead along the State finger pier at Massachusetts Maritime Academy here was announced today by Rear-Admiral Julian D. Wilson, superintendent of the academy. A possible Spring target date was seen.

Construction of proposed new school buildings could be started as early as July 1, the commanding officer noted, pending legislative approval of plans and specifications.

Meets With Approval

The proposed expansion program for the Maritime Academy has already met with approval of the State commissioner, the admiral reported.

Letters to Lou…

Plans call for the construction of a dormitory and mess hall, an expansive drill hall with additional office and classroom space, an athletic field house, boathouse and an engineering laboratory and garage.

Admiral Wilson said money has already been appropriated for the acquisition of more land enabling the academy to clear a drill field which would also be used as an athletic diamond and gridiron.

The proposed bulkhead to be constructed along the pier where the training ship customarily ties up will give the school more footage of land on which to build.

Water will be pumped out of the area and fill-dirt moved in. Size of the bulkhead pier will depend on its cost, said Admiral Wilson. He added that negotiations with the Boston engineering firm of Charles T. Main, Associates are now underway for its construction, tentatively to begin April 1.

Admiral Wilson said money has been appropriated for construction of the new bulkhead.

$12,000 Set Aside

Another $12,000 has also been set aside for drawing of plans and specifications for the new buildings. The admiral stated he did not contemplate any great increase in the school's enrollment following approval and completion of the new buildings. The academy's enrollment at present is 184.

Meanwhile, in other news from the academy, Admiral Wilson announced today that the Maritime school's Winter cruise will be delayed until March 5.

The USTC Charleston was scheduled to get underway early in January for the Mediterranean Sea.

It was explained that cold weather in that area during the early months of the year would hamper shipboard training instructions. The ship is scheduled to call at Spanish, French and Italian ports during its training cruise.

November 11, 1955   I have the mid watch now and am about half way through it. I have to make a set of rounds every half hour, take bearings, which never change unless we have winds of hurricane force, and take the ship's drafts - which haven't changed for the past ten years - every hour. In the meantime, I do what I can to stay awake.

I learned a very good lesson in practical engineering this afternoon. I was told by the officer of the deck to pump the bilge under the wardroom because it was nearly full. This tank is divided into three parts and has three valves in the suction pump. Being very smart, I said if it will pump water one part at a time in 20 minutes, I could pump all three parts in ten minutes. I opened the valves and started to pump. After about five minutes I took a sounding and found to my surprise that I had flooded the tank and water was coming in at a rate of about 200 gallons a minute instead of going out. I don't dare write what the officer called me, but it was good for a laugh with the midshipmen because I was very close to flooding the wardroom.

The reason for the revolt that I was telling you about is that last week a couple of third year men jumped ship and got caught in the act. At the same time a couple of my classmates were making a lot of noise on the mess deck. Well, the upper class blame our class for waking up the O.O.D. with a lot of noise, and , therefore, causing their classmates to get checked out.

That in itself wasn't bad, but the dirty part was they caught a classmate of mine drinking on board two weeks before this happened and have put him on report and had him bounced. That started the progress of revolt, and I don't think it has stopped yet.

Sad news, I just completed the 2:30 rounds, and the engineers have broken a steam line. No one is hurt.

More sad news. Mass. Maritime lost in football today. Maine Maritime - 20; Mass. Maritime - 6.

I am having as much trouble with navigation as you are with physics. We use the Merchant Marine officers' Textbook and the Navy Textbook, and there is a difference like night and day. Bowditch is the Merchant Marine book, and I believe it is written in Greek. And Dutton's , the one the Navy uses, is so simple that it is ridiculous for it doesn't cover a third of what we have to learn. I guess that I will never be another Prince Henry.

As you can see by the newspaper clipping [Cape Cod Std. Times, 11/10/55, "Bulkhead Slated for Construction at Finger Wharf"] we are getting some new buildings, also a new pier. It is a good thing if it happens. Also we are going to get a new hospital ship this coming summer, and the good old Charleston will be given a watery grave by the Navy.

…lost to Maine.

November 14, 1955   We lost to Maine Maritime 20-6 last Saturday. They really have a nice campus unlike ours. On the way back the team bus was in a bad accident. Nobody was hurt but it scared the hell out of all of them. The night before the game a few guys were in a car accident while going to visit Enoch Malkasion (1/E), an injured football player.

[Peter Readel and Tony Scarlata]

Bob Strautman returned Friday and was told about getting 100 demerits. He figures he'll get home three days after Christmas.

The ring salesman came down today. There is not enough time to get our rings for Christmas and some of the guys want to design a new ring for our class.

I'm writing this while standing Bob's watch. He's not feeling well again!
Its just another typical day on the bogs. So help me I'll never come down this way again as long as I live(after graduation of course). Why people come down here in the first place is beyond me?

Navigation is getting tougher. Communications with Morse Code (dots and dashes) is another beauty! After two hours of the flashing light in a dark room you acquire a stutter, a blank mind, and find yourself in a mild state of shock.

November 17, 1955   The weather has gone from bad to worse. This place is gonna be bad again in the winter. I'm not looking forward to standing on the dock tomorrow morning at 6:10 for 15 minutes with the wind blowing like it is.

The class is still divided over the ring style etc. The deckies want one type and the snipes want another. Oh well! I'm really more concerned about my grades which are slowly rising in the professional classes.

November 18, 1955   Chuck Broadbent is back and restricted. He must have a horse shoe in his back pocket.

November 19, 1955   The new academy does sound fine, and it looks good on paper, but this is election year in the state and if they ever start on it, it will be a small wonder. As for a new ship, I will, along with my shipmates, be sorry to see the Charleston go. However, it was condemned by the Navy about four years ago, and they have an epitaph all ready to engrave on her commission plaque.

November 28, 1955   Lewis was caught drinking aboard today. On report for "inattention to duty". Here we go again!!!

November 29, 1955   As I write this everyone is raising hell in the first jobs' study room next door. "Victory At Sea" is playing. It's great music but kinda hard to study with it blasting away!

November 30, 1955 {Postmark]   I had Thanksgiving Day dinner on the state, and it was very good except that I could not keep it down very long. I was struck with a very bad case of the grip and am just getting to feel better again. That is one reason why I haven't written to you before this.

Another is that I was reading a very good book in all my spare time, The Sea Around Us. The last reason and perhaps the weakest of the three is that I had an awful lot of studying to do. Midterm marks came out last week, and I was given a 3.3 average, but I don't think that I will have it at the end of the term. As you know, the final exams are coming in just three short weeks.

[In early December Bob went through the windshield of a friend's car in which he was riding as a passenger. The car was involved in a collision on the icy Harvard Bridge. I received a four-line note from one of Bob's brothers suggesting I write to him at Brighton Marine Hospital. I phoned the hospital immediately, and we were able to talk for about five minutes, during which I learned that his forehead and mouth were badly cut, requiring much reconstructive surgery. Also, he had lost many teeth. J.S.]

December 1, 1955   Please excuse the pencil; I don't have anything else to use. Jim McCluskey hasn't returned my pen. If and when he does, it will be because he ran out of ink. He'll never return it with ink, never does!

A typical ship's office notice

MASSACHUSETTS MARITIME ACADEMY   NOV. 28 thru Dec 9, 1955   /RJC

LOST ARTICLES
MIDN R.K. REILLY - 1 peacoat
MIDN MULQUEEN Y - 1 undress blue hat
MIDN FOSS   - 1 peacoat
MIDN L.W. BUTLER - 1 dress khaki blouse - 1 pair dungarees

ACTION TAKEN BY B OF C
KELLY, E. F. AWOL since 2247 Aug. 27, 1955. EXPELLED as of 27 August
previously reported as dropped.

LEWIS, C.W. Nov. 16, 1955, found in possession of a bottle of whiskey while
on watch, LTJG TONELLO reporting officer; disciplinary discharge with right
of appeal within 7 days; detached from Academy Friday 2 December 1955.

FREEMAN, D.V. Jul.27, 1955, Entering storeroom which had been broken into,
B of C reporting officers; 100 demerits plus probation. It is requested that
following records be changed: Demerits Report for period ending 8 August

1955 - ADD 100 to columns 2 and 3. Summer term marks for period ending
29 July 1955 - change conduct mark to read 0.0

BRADLEY, John III Oct. 5, 1955, AOL 1 hour, LT HIRST reporting officer;
15 demerits but to be worked off so as not to interfere with the December
overnight leave.

CHRISTIE, A.J. Oct. 17, 1955, AOL 17 minutes, CDR CONNORS reporting officer;
To have only one overnight leave between Thanksgiving and Christmas.

FEE, J.R. Oct. 14, 1955, AOL 13 minutes, LT PAGE reporting officer; to have
only one overnight leave between Thanksgiving and Christmas.

McCLUSKY,J.L. Oct. 18, 1955, AOL 12 hours, CDR ROUNDS reporting officer;
to have only one overnight leave between Thanksgiving and Christmas.

McCORMICK, G.J. Oct. 13, 1955, AOL 45 minutes, LT HIRST reporting officer;
15 demerits but to work off so as not to interfere with December overnight
leave.

MEYER, L.B. Oct. 17, 1955, AOL 15 hours 20 minutes, CDR WOODLAND reporting
officer; to have only one overnight leave between Thanksgiving and Christmas.

PETIT, N.A. Oct. 10, 1955, 20 minutes, LT WIKANDER reporting officer;
15 demerits but to be worked off so as not to interfere with the December
overnight leave.

REID, W.J. Jr. Oct. 6, 1955 AOL 45 minutes, LT HIRST reporting officer;
15 demerits but to be worked off so as not to interfere with the December
overnight leave.

RUMNEY, R.E. Oct. 6, 1955, AOL 45 minutes, LT HIRST reporting officer;
to have only one overnight leave between Thanksgiving and Christmas.

WENTWORTH, C.W. AWOL since 1450 Nov. 28, 1955, CDR ROUNDS reporting officer; disciplinary discharge with right to appeal within 7 days.

HOME AWAITING ACTION OF B of C			AWAITING TRIAL
MC DONALD, J.W.	7/29	Resignation	LEWIS, C.W. 2E
HARNEY, F.J.	8/16	Resignation	
WENTWORTH, C.W.	11/28	Appeal	RESTRICTION LIFTED PENDING
LEWIS, C.W.	12/2	Appeal	DECISION of B of C
WILLSON, R.S.	8/10	Enlisted	USCGO'CONNELL, R.J.(AWOL case)
			FOSS, D.M.(SAH case)

MIDSHIPMEN ABSENTEES		RETURNED MIDSHIPMEN (ABSENTEES)
STICKNEY, RL 2D,	PHSH since 4 DEC	WARD,DI, SpecLv 1 to 4 Dec.
FLAHERTY, JF Jr.	2E SAH(AOL) since	BLAZEWICZ, JVF, PHSH 28 Nov to 6 Dec
	2200 4 Dec	COLLIS, CD, ONOP 6 to 7 Dec
		SINCLAIR, DL Jr, Bangor Hosp 12 to 14
		Nov. PHSH 14 Nov to 1 Dec.

Letters to Lou

CAPTAIN'S MAST DATE OF OFFENSE	OFFENSE	REPORTING OFFICER	DEMERITS
23 Nov PINER, JWG, 2D	Out of uniform	LT YARD	6
23 Nov PINER, JWG, 2D	Threatening a cadet officer	LT YARD	15

NOTE:

16 Dec End of December marking period (SUBMIT FAILURES TO SHIP'S OFFICE)
23 Dec End of fall term (SUBMIT EXAM MARK AND TERM MARK TO SHIP'S OFFICE)

[Jim McCluskey]

December 5, 1955   Bad weekend! Harrington came through the messdeck after lunch. He thought I was hazing the youngie messcooks. This time he grabbed me, picked me up off my feet, and jammed me between the Coke machines. He did not hit me, Thank God! I've never been so frightened in my life! I thought he was gonna kill me! I spent the next few hours scrubbing (Ki-yi-ing) the main deck waiting for the report slip and a future 100 demerits. He later found that I was not hazing anyone and he came up and apologized.

December 8, 1955   The only thing that I am worrying about is final exams which start the 19th of this month. I hope to be out of here by that time, I hope.

At the academy the marks start at 2.5, which is 67%, and go up to 4.0, which is 100%.

December 13, 1955   1115 PM. Check muster ...second class, ONLY! Somebody was seen coming back over the stern. The first class blamed us, the second class. We spent a few hours at parade rest on the main deck. The O.D. needed his sleep more than we did...he gave up without putting anyone on report... and sent us below. Victory again!!! Crazy, huh!!!

I have to go see the Admiral tomorrow. He has to approve the ring contract and grant us permission to use the classrooms for fittings.

Letters to Lou...

December 15, 1955   I will go back to the ship Sunday and start taking exams on Monday, but I can feel it in my bones that it is going to be a worthless fight as far as navigation and Spanish are concerned. I was supposed to hand in a 5,000 word paper on the Mediterranean on Monday, but I have not had a chance to even begin it.

I was thinking today that if I should keep this scar, it will be a mark of distinction for me. Did you ever see a picture of the great German naval leaders; they all have scars on their cheeks - so why should I be different from them? Besides, if I ever run out of tales to tell people, I can always explain how I got the scar as I was trying to free a lifeboat on a sinking ship or something equally as good. If I wanted to get real good, I could tell the girl that I was trying to impress that I got cut up while I was defending her honor...

December 18, 1955   We are sleeping in an unheated compartment. The 1st jobs don't want their pathetic excuse for a Christmas Tree to dry out too fast. All steam lines were closed to the messdeck.

Please excuse the pencil again! Jim has borrowed my pen again. I filled it up for him before he left!

December 23, 1955   I am sorry that I have not written to you sooner, but I have been so tied up with finals that I haven't had time to think straight.

I took the last exam and the last make-up test this morning, so that is out of the way. I seemed to do all right in the academic subjects, but if a person loses two weeks in the professional subjects, he is at the end - and that is just where I am. I know that I passed the navigation and the ordnance and gunnery final, but I am not so sure about the rest of them. Well, that is enough of the feel sorry for yourself hour.

Admiral Byrd has nothing on us, Jane, for it has been below zero all week, and the ship is frozen in solid. Today the sun came out and warmed it up a bit, and all afternoon you could hear the ice cracking and hitting the ship. This is no weather for old St. Nick, unless he has anti-freeze for the reindeer. It is surprisingly quiet around here now that all the middies have left the ship for Xmas leave. I have the duty today and tomorrow and then will be off until the second of January.

I am making a proposed cruise itinerary, so if you would like to write to the kid you can send it to the port that we will call at on the dates given. It is going to be a long haul across to the port of Galveston, and I hope that you will have some news for me when I get there.

December 31, 1955...I am glad to hear that you had a good Christmas and were kind enough to spread good cheer to the foreign seamen. [Note: An adult adviser for our church youth group had arranged for a dozen or so of us young women to have dinner with the officers, followed by dancing, on a Dutch merchant ship docked in N.O. for the holidays. It had been a very enjoyable evening both for the officers and for us. JS] When we were in Dutch Guiana a band came down and started to play American songs for us. It makes you feel good inside. That hymn "Nearer Our God to Thee" is believed to have been played on the Titanic while she was sinking. However, that book which you were kind enough to send me states that they played ragtime. My dear Miss Smith, what if I may ask were you doing in the staterooms? No decent captain ever lets young women go below decks. Kidding, of course!

Admiral Julian Wilson gave me a very good break by not restricting me, which he had the right to do, for not reporting to the ship before going to the hospital. It sounds weird, I know, but according to the rules and regulations, he should have restricted me. As for the liberty, I had the 24th and took Megonigle's duty on the 23rd so he might spend his whole leave at home. Megonigle lives in Kentucky and cannot get home on weekends.

January 5, 1956   All the first jobs are in Newport, R.I. for Fire Fighting and Damage Control School. We'll have a ball today and tomorrow. The afternoon calls for sacks with a jam session scheduled tonight during evening studies. Broadbent is very good on the piano.

A new TV was installed on the mess deck. Yeah! We really can't complain, as late as May 1954 forty percent of the population did not own one! NOTE: 1957 more than 90 percent of homes had a TV set.

…Hop is leaving.

Yesterday a destroyer came up the canal and hit everything but the Charleston. As it came up it hit a buoy, went up on the rocks, backed off onto a sand bar and took two hours to get off. The Coast Guard is still looking for the buoy. I wonder how long it will take for the Navy to find a desk job for the Captain?

We ordered rings today. They will be delivered February 23rd. We won't be allowed to wear them on campus until we're first jobs.

January 9, 1956   Several members of the class are now sporting small gold ear rings, off campus. This is an old nautical tradition. Sailors would wear them to insure that the gold would be exchanged for a proper funeral service away from home.

January 11, 1956   Jane, when Jim [Piner] and I were at the Roosevelt [Hotel in New Orleans, briefly during the l955 cruise], the ballroom had on both sides and for the entire length of the hall, tables just overflowing with glasses of scotch and rye. [Note: I think he's mistaken about the rye! It's almost never served down here. JS]   It made a very pleasant sight to a couple of hungry, thirsty, and broke seamen like Jim and myself.

I have a date for the ring dance with a most intelligent and most beautiful girl from New Orleans. I am afraid, however, that if these scars don't hurry and heal , it will be like beauty and the beast.

Not a chance to be self-conscious about the scars around here. Another kid and myself, who were in   the same type of accidents, have picked up the name of "Scarface".

If I take a P.G. in engineering, I will be down in New Orleans for sure on that year's cruise. It will be 1958, however.

Have to do some sights for stars now, honey, so good luck on the exams and be a good kid.

January 16, 1956   I think, honey, that money is one of my biggest problems. In fact, I don't know where I will get the money for the P.G. in engineering (post graduate course).

January 17, 1956   Great news!!! Harrington is leaving next fall. He is going to teach math at Salem State Teachers College. He has recommended to the Commissioners that the Academy drop formal football until proper facilities are available.

We have about six inches of snow on the main deck from last night's storm. The snow must be cleared before classes will be held.

Harrington was supposed to give us another make-up exam tonight but he never showed up. This nightmare will never end!

January 18, 1956   Most of us are back on the 1-50 list again...its now called the Maritime Math Circle. The nightmare continues!

Ziminsky from Arlington left us today. The Academy learned he was married during the Christmas leave period. The Commissioners learned before we did - very unusual. Somebody blew the whistle on him!

MASSACHUSETTS MARITIME ACADEMY   MORNING CLASS SCHEDULE   JDW/RGC
SECOND TERM   SUMMER 1956   (1/3/56 to 7/27/56)
                     2ND CLASS (57)

DAY	PER	RM	DECK		RM	ENG	
	1	6	Trig	LH	5	ShipCo	LW
	2	6	Span	FY	5	Calculus	LH
MON	3	6	Sea	WC	5	Diesel	JC
	4	6	NavSci		5	MarHist	
	5	6	MarHist		5	SteamAux	JC
	1	Lab	MarHist		5	AnalGeom	LH
	2	6	Span	FY	5	NavSci	
TUES	3	6	Nav	RR	Dr	MarHist	
	4	6	Study*		5	Calculus	
	5	6	ShipEcon PH		5	Span	FY
	1	Lab. Study			5	AnalGeom.	LH
	2	Lab	First Aid AT		5	ElecEng	WH
WEDS	3	Dr	Span		5	SteamEng	JM
	4	6	Trig	LH	5	Study*	
	5	6	ShipEcon PH		5	NavSci.	
	1	6	Study		5	Span	FY
	2	6	MarHist		5	AnalGeom	LH
THUR	3	6	Nav	RR	5	ShipCo	LW
	4	6	Sea	WC	Dr	EngLit	AC
	5	6	NavSci		5	ElecEng	WH
	1	Lab	Study		5	Diesel	JC
	2	Lab	EngLit		5	Span	FY
FRI	3	Lab	FirstAid AT		5	Boilers	AL
	4	6	NavSci		5	MarHist	
	5	6	ShipEconPH		5	NavSci	

*Captain Thompson will conduct a class in the Merchant Marine Service and the Superintendent will conduct a class in Naval Customs etc., in accordance with the following schedule:

	1st week	2nd week	3rd week	4th week
4th Period	A MMS	2D MMS	A NavCus	2D NavCus
Tuesday		1E NavCus		1E MMC
4th Period	1D MMS	B MMS	1D NavCus	B NavCus
Wednesday	2E NavCus		2E MMS	

CLASS: FIRST MONTH   SECOND MONTH   THIRD MONTH   FORTH MONTH

Mon:Tues:Wed:Thur:Mon:Tues:Wed:Thur:Mon:Tues:Wed:Thur:Mon:Tues:Wed:Thur:

2DECK   M   M Comm Nav M   M Comm Nav S   S   S   M   S   S   S   M
2ENG P-E M P-E M   P-E M   P-E M   P-E M P-E M   P-E M   P-E M

Notes: S - Seamanship M - Maintenance P-E - Practical Engineering

Except during the fourth month when all third classmen will be assigned to deck divisions(because of cold weather in February making outdoor seamanship impracticable) the third class group will shift divisions monthly. Third class Group A will be assigned to Deck divisions the first month, to Engineering divisions the second month, etc.

Third class Group B will be assigned to Engineering divisions the first month; to the Deck divisions the second month etc.

Shifts will be made in the middle of the shipyard overhaul and in the middle of the cruise.

Half of one group of the third class is assigned to maintenance daily. This group will carry stores and other miscellaneous tasks when required. Others should not be withdrawn for this purpose if possible to avoid doing so.

APPROVED: J.D. WILSON, Rear Admiral,USN(Ret)
                                        Superintendent.

Copy to: Board of Commissioners(6), Instructors(1 each),Naval Science(1 each)
Midshipmen(1 each)

[Jim McCluskey]

1-50 LIST   MASSACHUSETTS MARITIME ACADEMY   /RGC

(ISSUE 1-1956)   17 January 1956

1. The 1-50 list will be published monthly after marks are received. List remains in effect until superseded. Additions and deletions will not be made until following list is published (next marks to be received are JANUARY FAILURES after 27 January.

2. Following are on 1-50 list as the result of failing FALL TERM 1955 MARKS:

BRENNOCK, RF 1E Thermo	2.3		AYLMER, JF,	2D Rules of Road 2.2	
DUGGAN, TJ 1E Boilers	2.3		BROADBENT, CW 2D Alg		2.4
MALKASIAN, E 1E Boilers	2.3		BROADBENT, CW 2D Sea		2.4
MALKASIAN, E 1E ShipCo	2.3		BROWN, RD 2D Alg		2.4
BILLINGS, HC 2E Nav Sci	2.4		HOGAN, DF 2D Alg		2.4
BUTLER, TF Jr 2E Nav Sci	2.3		LACAIRE, DJ 2D Alg		2.4
CHRISTIE, AJ 2E Lit	2.4		LYNCH, JJ III 2D Alg		2.4
MAHONEY, FE 2E Nav Sci	2.4		LYNCH, JJ III 2D Nav		2.2
MC CLUSKEY, JL 2E Alg	2.4		LYNCH, JJ III 2D Comm		2.3
MC CLUSKEY, JL 2E Steam	2.4		MANNING, RL 2D Nav		2.4
MC CLUSKEY, JL 2E Nav Sci	2.2		MANNING, RL 2D Nav Sci		2.2
MIRABELLO, EJ 2E Nav Sci	2.4		PENNANPEDE, PP 2D Sea 2.2		
REID, WJ 2E Alg	2.4		PENNANPEDE, PP 2D R of Road		2.4
REID, WJ 2E Elec	2.4		PENNANPEDE, PP 2D Nav Sci		2.4
REID, WJ 2E Nav Sci	2.4		PINER, JWG 2D Lit		2.0
SPILLANE, EF 2E Boilers 2.3			PINER, JWG 2D Nav		2.2
SPILLANE, EF 2E Nav Sci	2.4		PINER, JWG 2D Nav Sci 2.4		
TASK, HL 2E Nav Sci	2.4		ROFFEY, RC Jr 2D Rules of Road		2.3
WALSH, JE 2E Nav Sci	2.3		SWEET, JK Jr 2D Alg		2.4
			SWEET, JK Jr 2D Span		2.4

GROUP "A"			GROUP "B"	
ANDREWS	Alg 2.4		CALLAHAN	Sea 2.1
BOYSON	Comp 2.4		CAPELOTTI	Alg 2.4
BRADLEY	Alg 2.3		COLLIS	Alg 2.4
BUTLER	Alg 2.4		DONNELLAN	Alg 2.4 & Nav Sci 2.3
DALTON	Alg 2.4		FIELDS	Draw INC
DOWD	Alg 2.3		FLYNN	Alg 2.3 & NavSci 2.4
KEANE	Alg 2.3		HARRINGTON	Draw INC
KENNY	DRAW INC MarEng 2.2		ONEIL	Alg 2.4
MARTENSON	Alg 2.3		POLETTA	Alg 2.4
MC DONOUGH	Phy 2.3		SCHOFIELD	Alg 2.4
SAVERY	Alg 2.4		SHANNON	Lit 2.4
SMITH	Alg 2.4 MarEng 2.1		SINCLAIR	Alg 2.4
STETSON	Sea 2.3		St. PIERRE	Alg 2.4
SULLIVAN	Alg 2.4			
YORK	Alg 2.4			

REEXAMINATIONS 1/4/56 THERMO 3.0 FALL 1955
KELLEY, 1E change 2.0 to 2.5
MALKASIAN, 1E change 2.0 to 2.5. REEXAMINATIONS 1/6/56 STEAM ENG 3.0
O'CONNOR, 1E change 2.4 to 2.5 FALL 1955
VESEY, 1E change 2.3 to 2.5   TASK, 2E change 2.4 to 2.5
                          YOUNG, RA 2E change 2.3 to 2.5

REEXAMINATIONS 1/4/56 STEAM ENG 3.0
FALL 1955   11/23/55 MATTESON, 1D
DUGGAN, 1E change 2.4 to 2.5   Spanish 2.2 summer 55 - 3.4 change 2.2 to 2.5
REEXAMINATIONS 1/6/56 STEAM ENG 3.0
FALL 1955   11/23/55 PUTIGNANO, 2E, reexamined
BUTLER, 2E change 2.1 to 2.5   Spanish 2.2 fall 54 & Spanish 1.6
FERGUSON, 2E change 2.0 to 2.4   summer 55 - mark 2.5 change marks
GRAHAM, 2E change 2.3 to 2.5
KENNEDY, 2E change 2.3 to 2.5
KOOPMAN, 2E change 2.4 to 2.5   1/4/56 BRENNOCK,1E FAILED reexamination
LOPAUS, 2E change 2.3 to 2.5   Thermo fall 55 - mark 2.0
REID, 2E change 2.1 to 2.5   1/6/56 MC CLUSKEY,JL, 2E FAILED re-exam.
                                   Steam Engines fall 55 - mark 2.0
            J.D. WILSON, Rear Admiral,USN(Ret) Supt.

                                                     [Jim McCluskey]

January 21, 1956   Lat. 41'44" N;   Long. 70', 37"W.   It has been a cold, snowy, and lonely week for I have not heard from my sunshine gal since last Monday. I called [home] Sunday night and asked Betty [sister] to send me the book Admiral of the Ocean Sea, but it has not arrived yet. I was put in charge of field day this week-end, and I was running around like a chicken with my head cut off because one of the toughest officers on board made the inspection. Praise the Lord, I got by; as a matter of fact, he complimented me on the cleanliness of the good ship Charleston.

We had eight inches of snow down here this week and had quite a time playing with it. First we attacked it with shovels and then with water lines with 150 lbs. of pressure. The latter works out much better. That night it went down to zero; in the morning we had a fight with new snow, which was ice an inch thick on the deck. You can't beat this New England weather, honey.

January 23,1956   I started the day by finding that I had picked up a case of athlete's feet over the weekend. Next, I had an argument with the good commander, Mr. Rounds, in Navigation. After dinner we had a boat drill, and some fool didn't take in the slack on the line; thus when I let go of the lines, the block came swinging out. I got out of the way, but the block took my hat as a raincheck and put it into the cold waters of Buzzards Bay. All this was going on while it was snowing so hard that you could hardly see a hand in front of you. Next, I flunked a Spanish test, and then I received your letter, and all is well again.

We had Admiral Wilson in class today and found out that he was the captain of the battleship Maryland at the Battle of Leyte Gulf. It is quite an honor to become a captain of a capital ship, you know. In order to be in Spain for Easter, we have made a change in the cruise itinerary. We will got to Marseilles, France and then to Barcelona, Spain.

Carl Megonigle wants you to fly to New York where we will pick you up and take you to his house in Hartford. We will spend the night at his house with him and Betty. Then, Saturday morning, we will come to Boston and show you a little of New England. [Note: Pipedream, of course! J.S.] Dress at my home and eat at Durgin Park and then proceed to the ring dance. Several others have similar plans. Jane, if we don't marry each other a lot of the boys around here will be very disappointed. Jim [Piner] still insists that you have made a mistake and are writing to the wrong one of the middies that you met

January 23, 1956   This place is in an uproar! The Mass Maritime Academy Lonely Hearts Club is holding a numbers raffle. A few of the guys sent a buck to the "Club" and received a fifteen page booklet. You should see some of the names and pictures. Every name has a number. The "select" members of the "Club" have their own rules and charter. The numbers are all in a hat. When they pick a number they have to write to "it". Some of them are really funny! Dick Greer is writing to Mary Jones in New York who is 86 years old. Nobody wants to trade, so I guess he's stuck with her! Her return letter should be a riot.

January 24, 1956   All members of the Math Circle failed the make-up exam again! What a bunch of beauties, huh! He threw us a curve with new material...oh well!

January 26, 1956   Term marks have been published and the kid has dropped from a 3.4 to a 3.095 average. I shall have to blame this on my stay at Brighton's favorite hotel

...Moby Dick.

The Charleston is a grand ship; and I like her as if she were a person, but she is inadequate for the type of work she is engaged in.

I got the ship so clean that the officers decided that I should be in charge of getting the ship ready for inspection by the Coast Guard. That had me going all week-end while I should have been in my bunk like the rest of my classmates. Next time I will not do such a fine job.

I haven't read Moby Dick, but I have seen a whale.

January 31, 1956   The cruise is getting nearer and nearer and the nearer that it gets, the better I like it. I have to close for now.....Why don't you transfer to a school up here?

January 30, 1956   Took another algebra make-up today....results unknown!

MASSACHUSETTS NEWSPAPER CLIPPING -- JANUARY 30, 1956

... ON PUSHING ACADEMY BUILDING

BUZZARDS BAY, Jan. 30 -- Bourne and Representative Allan F. Jones met with Elwood S. McKenney, executive secretary to Governor Furcolo, in an attempt "to activate plans for construction already approved and allocated for" at the Maritime Academy.

This construction includes dormitories and a bulkhead.

The town is interested to see that projects approved some time ago are carried out, Selectman Philip Sanford said.

Matter "Dormant"

The matter has "lain dormant" long enough and the selectmen are interested in seeing the project advanced, he added.

He pointed out that the Maine and New York Maritime Academies are well ahead of the Buzzards Bay institution in facilities and that it is not fair to the men stationed here.

"We are turning out just as good men as those academies and it is a shame that facilities cannot be added here," Mr. Sanford declared.

Secretary McKenney said he would start work on the request probably some time this week. He said he would first secure a copy of a report from the committee set up under Governor Herter's administration to investigate matters pertaining to the academy, particularly the matter of location.

Some time ago drives were under way to relocate the academy in another community. Salem, Marblehead and New Bedford, among others, were mentioned. The committee's report recommended the academy remain in Buzzards Bay, however.

Steps To Be Taken

Mr. McKenney said he will confer with Representative Jones of the Ways and Means Committee and the budget director to ascertain what funds have been approved and allocated for construction.

Then, after discussion with the Governor, who has been described as "interested" in the academy's advancement, steps will be taken to improve the existing situation, he said.

Mr. Sanford said land has been reserved so the academy might build dormitories but that nothing has been done by the Maritime Commissioners to promote the projects.

He said plans for building a bulkhead and dormitories have been made for some time at the Buzzards Bay school but that nothing can be done until the commissioners in Boston "get busy on it".

February 2, 1956   Good luck with your alcoholics! [Note: I was a sociology student at Newcomb College, and we were doing a project on alcoholism.] Jim was drinking so much when he was at home his mother sent his name in to AA. The funny thing about that is, he isn't even old enough to drink with the law's consent.

We have quite a collection of officers here at the academy. Mr., or should I say Commanders, Woodland and Rounds are of the very best type along with Mr Clark and Mr. Page. However, Commander Connors is the exact opposite of them. The commander , "Bum", as he is known to the middies, has one great pleasure in life, and that is to be mean to middies.

Letters to Lou….

Take the [school] seal [decal] that I am enclosing and put it on your favorite glass. Then as you drink your milk in the morning, you will remember the poor little midshipman at the academy in the cold and swampy town of Bourne. If you remember, then I am sure that you will remember us in your prayers. If you do that, we might be saved from that nasty old man on the mess deck.

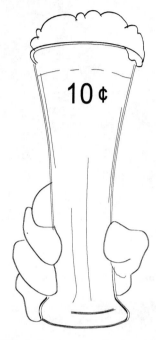

February 5, 1956 Paul Pennapede has not returned? Sick? We went to a dance with him last fall. He joined the class as a second job and is having second thoughts about this place.

I just made it with only a minute to spare last night. We stopped at the "Pine" for pizza and a few "dimies" and lost track of time. I could see my next weekend home being erased from the liberty list.

I forgot to get a birthday card for my mother last weekend. Dick Weaver is gonna save me and pick one up in town today. Nice guy!

February 6, 1956 The dirty old man gave me your letter this afternoon, and I was glad to get it even though it came from such a bad source. To top it off, I have the duty this week and have to stand all of my watches with him..

A sextant is an instrument used for measuring the altitude of celestial bodies. If our friend Columbus had added declination to the answers that he got from his sextant he would have found the correct latitude of the Indies.

I was talking with Mr. __?__ today, and I found out that it is possible to apply for a commission as a full lieutenant in the Navy. Instead of taking a commission as an ensign, I hope to take a P.G. in engineering and after that go to the Great Lakes and get a third officer's license.. At that point, I will have two degrees and three licenses as third officer. With that as a background, I could apply for a commission as a full lieutenant...

The reason I have attended so many schools and not learned a thing is that I usually get bounced out for being a bad boy before I learn anything worthwhile...

We are scheduled for three days liberty in Italy, so Jack Aylmer and myself, as we have of no money to go to Rome, are going to rent bikes and ride around the countryside for three days. We should be able to have some fun that way. I might ride north for forty miles and visit the Italian seaman who was in the hospital with me...

I flunked a navigation test this morning, and that is not good at all.

February 8, 1956 Roffey, Manning, and I were assigned to air bunting today. In other words we flew all the signal flags from the main yard arm. Two of the halyards broke and we had to climb up and replace them. Really cold up there with the wind etc. Not much fun in February.

February 9, 1956 I have had a hard time trying to protect you this week. They have been painting the berthing compartment and the boys can really spread the paint around. I moved you from my overhead to the side of the lockers but after chow I found that you were still in a dangerous position. Therefore, I kept you in the darkness of my locker for two days. The paint is dry now, and again you smile down on my scarred face and keep an eye on me while I try to get some beauty sleep.

I think that my brother is getting married on the morning of the day of the Ring Dance. If that happens, it should be quite a day!

February 11, 1956 Saturday Night I don't quite know what to write with so much excitement down here! We had our regular Friday night class in Judo again last night. Dick Greer broke his little toe, and Joe Lach left with a smashed nose. Other than that it wasn't a bad session. The instructor weighs about 105 lbs., just a little shrimp, but he throws even the biggest guy around like nothing at all. He is teaching us mostly "dock" Judo, like how to disarm a man with a gun, knife, or a club etc.

...a new ship.

Europe is a bad spot with a lot of bad actors on the docks so MMA is trying to prepare us for the worst. It's quite a science and easy to learn once you get used to it, but I don't think I want to play games with a gun or knife.

I spent the afternoon stenciling and re-stenciling my gear. I didn't want to use just black and white so I used a good Irish color, green, for the light colored and white gear and the usual white on the dark gear since I couldn't find any light green.

February 12, 1956   Jim Lynch is next door writing themes for the youngie class. What a character he is! For 50 cents he will write a 500 word theme and guarantee a grade of 3.2 (80%). He has done this also for my class for the past year and a half and really cleaned up! Now he is working for the youngies.

February 13, 1956   The "Bum" said in class today that we may be getting a new ship after the cruise. The ship they have in mind is a Liberty ship which was built during the war. It's huge and for a change it should give us plenty of elbow room. If they decide to take it we will leave sometime this summer (June or July) to go down and get it. We'll sail before the new youngies show up. We'll go down in the Charleston and come back in the new ship leaving the Chun in Texas. There is nothing definite about this whole deal but the "Bum" and Cdr. Murray are going to fly down sometime in the next two weeks to look her over.

I don't know if you met Red Riley's girl, Rose. I don't think so. Well, she has had her big toe removed last week. Some kind of cancer I think! Awful, huh!

[Note: I must have written Bob about some Mardi Gras parades. JS]   The last time I saw a parade, I was coming home and was in uniform. It was the Independence Day parade, and every time that I tried to get to the side of the street a flag would pass by, and I would have to stop and salute. Needless to say, I felt like a complete fool and did not enjoy the spirit of the thing at all.

The letters from Boston and Hyannis are the letters that I give to the cook to mail on his way home. Brighton Marine Hospital is in Brighton. Both are parts of Boston, but the telephone exchange is Newton. Newton, however, is another part of Boston and has the Beacon exchange.

February 15, 1956   There is a lot of talk about us going down to Texas to see a new ship that the Maritime Commission has offered the academy. The ship is in Beaumont, Texas...Do you know where the place is in relation to New Orleans? I hope that we get it, for it is a fairly new victory ship and has far more room than the Char.

February 18, 1956   I have three volumes of the Arabian Nights to read on the cruise, along with Anthony Adverse and the Seven Pillars of Wisdom. I hope that I will be able to plow my way through them. I read the book, Good-bye, Mr. Chips this afternoon and liked it very much. Mr. Chips reminds me of Mr. Wickander an old officer we had at the academy. One night when he had the duty, a phone call for him said that the middies were out in town raising hell, as, of course, they always were when he had the duty. He told the person that it couldn't be any of his boys, for they were all in bed asleep; with that he hung up.

A week of exams and a couple of days leave and we will be off on the cruise. I can hardly wait for the line to be hauled up and the engines to be put astern.

The Latin on the [school] seal means, as far as I can find out, "We demand peace and quiet under liberty." Not very appropriate, I should say. There has not been peace and quiet here at the academy for as long as I can remember.

[Note: In a previous letter Bob said he phoned me because he'd won some money from a slot machine. JS]   The slot machines are also outlawed in Mass. but this one was in a private club. It was the first time in my life that I played one on the level. I was in Curacao and was playing with American pennies when I should have been using Dutch dollars. Fate, however, caught up with me and when I finally did win I got back more pennies than anything else.

The dirty old man, the master at arms, just kicked me off the mess deck, and I will have to finish this letter standing up.

Letters to Lou…

February 21, 1956   The only type of interior decorating that has been done on the Charleston is that of the boys tacking up pictures. Some of these pictures are better to look at than any color scheme would ever be; your picture is one of these.

The trip to Beaumont and the new ship are both out the port by direction of the Board of Commissioners. I don't have to tell you how I and almost everyone else feels about it.

I was talking to Bo Taylor about you and the Ring Dance, and I wish that I had the faith in our meeting that he does. I am afraid that you won't enjoy your trip here to Boston, but Bo thinks just the opposite.   I said, for argument, that I was the world's worst dancer and things like that, but he still wouldn't change his mind. I hope, honey , with all my heart that things will work out the way that I have dreamed they will.

There has been no official word, but so far everyone thinks we are going to France before we go to Spain. Just reverse the dates on the itinerary.

February 23, 1956   [Talks about books he intends to read on the cruise. JS] I also have to stand a watch out of every four and have to turn in a ship's position every day and an azimuth three times a week. You can see that I will keep busy during the cruise, a good way to stay out of trouble.

Navy tests tomorrow, so I will close for now…Wish that I could see you before we leave, but that will have to wait till the Ring Dance.

February 25, 1956   Class rings and mugs arrived today. We are not allowed to wear the rings aboard until we're first classmen. Home and weekends will have to do for now.

February 29, 1956   [Note: A twenty-year-old's social commentary, but not directly related to academy life. JS] Thank you for your fine opinion on the segregation problem. However, dear, the residential segregation is by one's choice. South Boston is all Irish, Jamaica Plain, all Jews. The West End is all Italian, and East Boston is all Spanish. I do believe that there is more segregation in the South but more prejudice in the North.

This might be a great week. Jim has gone home to Florida, and Meyer is in sick bay. That leaves two watches to be stood by three of us.

Just took 39 cans of motion picture films aboard…for the cruise.

March 2, 1956   0400 I have just been awakened for the morning watch on this cold, dark day. The temperature is 8 degrees above, northerly winds 20-25 miles per hour.

I am glad that you liked the mug, honey. It was supposed to come with my ring but the mug is the member of my order that has come, though the ring won't be ready until a week after we sail.

Spring 1956   One event I can remember at the academy is the night I jumped ship and Hop held a check muster. When he came to my name "Scarlata, Scarlata, Scarlata where's Tony?" When there was no response he told everybody to sack in, at least that was the way it was described to me.

[Tony Scarlata]

Lets face it, Hop, the coach, was not about to put his star athlete on report. No way!

[Ben Hogan]

LIBERTY CALL – BOSTON SHIPYARD

SECOND CLASS CRUISE

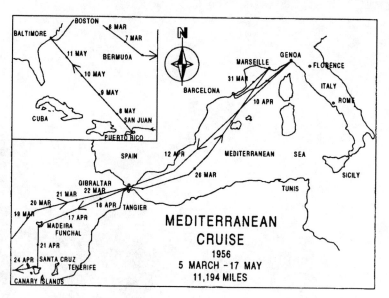

March 5, 1956   Underway. Enroute to the Mediterranean Sea.

A few guys, as usual, were sick on our run to Bermuda. The weather and sea were rather mild compared to our first days out to sea last year. A couple of youngies rode the rail for a few days but they seem to have recovered.

It sure is nice to get a break from classes for the next ten weeks.

The Admiral is not with us. He was in the hospital (don't know why) when we left. He'll join us later.

MASSACHUSETTS MARITIME ACADEMY
M.T.S. CHARLESTON   5 MARCH 1956

The Board of Commissioners have directed that midshipmen be always mindful to conduct themselves in a manner that will reflect credit upon themselves, the Massachusetts Maritime Academy, the Merchant Marine, Naval Reserve and United States Government.

Loss of liberty may or may not entail assignments of demerits.

Any midshipman whose conduct while ashore on the cruise, occasions disciplinary action by the civilian authorities, will be detached from the ship and sent home at his own expense with right of appeal to the Board of Commissioners upon arriving home.

Midshipmen's liberty, while on the cruise, will depend upon his conduct while on the cruise, and not be limited by any liberty restriction existing on March 1st 1956

[Jim McCluskey]

March 8, 195   Hamilton, Bermuda I received your very nice letter today, after we dropped anchor in Hamilton Harbor. Bermuda is a lovely place, but the cost of things is very out of line. The reason that everything is so expensive here is that all things must be imported and the biggest business is the tourist trade. Jack Keenan and I spent four and one-half hours riding around the island of Bermuda today. We saw everything from the city dump in Hamilton to the lighthouse at the end of the island. The city has many multi-colored houses and beautiful gardens. The harbor extends into the heart of the city and it is a beautiful sight to see with its various colors and many sailboats.

We went to the Hamilton Lighthouse, which is 390 ft. above sea level and we could see the whole island.

...use the huge lifeboats.

The Charleston developed a leak in her fuel tank on the way down and we have lost about a thousand gallons of fuel oil. The whole side of the ship is black from the oil slick. Therefore, we will be busy tomorrow.

The trip down made some green faces on the third classmen, but the trip across the pond will really make seamen out of them.

March 9, 1956   I am trying to write to you between the runs I have to make with the liberty launch,. I have been in the wind and sun all day and look like a lobster. I burn badly, but it goes away the very next day, I never get a tan.

Did I ever tell you we have a ship's carpenter whose name is Mr. Chips?

March 9, 1956   Anchored in Bermuda. Jim Lynch was on the radio for three nights prior to leaving Boston. He's a friend of the DJ. They talked about the ship and the cruise between records - WBOS - 1600 10-12PM - "Night Train". Jim would like to be a DJ after graduation and needed some experience before a mike on the air.

Red Riley has been here before with the Coast Guard Academy, sailed with the Eagle. He recommends the "Elbow Beach Club". No doubt we'll check it out tomorrow. Beer is expensive about $1.50 a quart.

To go on liberty here we have to use the huge lifeboats. It sure looks strange to see about a hundred (or so) middies in job suits all crammed into one pot-bellied bath tub.

A second job's life at sea is great. I haven't done a days work since we left. I'm on watch now; my function is to take bearing on several points to see if the ship has moved in the anchorage. I do this every fifteen minutes and write letters or read in between shots. Pretty soft huh?

I don't think we want to honeymoon in Bermuda, OK? Not much to do and the prices are too darn high. The average meal is about $5.00 or better. The guys that went ashore came back hungry. The cheapest thing on the menu was a grilled cheese and that was $.85. Kinda high huh! It would be OK I guess if there was a little more cheese in between. A small bottle of beer runs from $.50 and $2.50, no dimies on this island.   Note: Two years later this is where we spent our honeymoon!

This has to be the cleanest port we've ever hit! There are no slum areas and most of the homes are very nice. No pimps or bum boats.

March 14, 1956   Here we are still in Bermuda. We moved the ship two days ago but only to change our anchorage. We had a little rough weather on the way down that took its toll on the ship. We have discovered a few new leaks in the hull, nothing serious but some things that had to be repaired.

We were supposed to cross the big pond in eleven days but now we'll have to do it in eight to get back on schedule. We should be underway today. Hope we won't be late getting back to Boston.

The rumor was that we were going to return to Boston and take the ship out of the water for repairs. Some of the guys got all excited about it but it was not necessary. There was a four foot gash or crack in one of the fuel tanks and we lost a large amount of fuel (6,000 gallons in 3 days). We now have just enough fuel to get us across the pond. The other leak is small and just a pain in the butt. Every morning and before we turn-in at night we have to go down and bail out the dry stores spaces. The youngies do all the work and we of course do all the heavy looking on. Such a deal, not bad huh!

Letters to Lou...

March 17, 1956   St. Pat's Day with no green beer! Enroute to Gibraltar on holiday routine. Sacks all day is OK and the smoking lamp is always lit. We now have 2,350 miles to go at 14 knots, a slow crawl. Kinda like driving from Boston to San Francisco at 16 MPH for 10 days.

My navigation is getting better. As second jobs we are required to get a fix at noon. Yesterday I was nine miles ENE of our true position. Today I was only 500 yards off. Tomorrow I'll probably find myself in Vermont. Practice, practice, I need lots of practice! Like the guy in New York that asked a cab driver, "How do I to get to Carnegie Hall?" "Practice...practice!"

"Now hear this... The movie tonight is... The Cattle Queen of Montana." Sounds great huh! A real shoot-em-up at least forty guys get wiped out in a little more than an hour.

On deck we have a real salty crew, but a long ways from the King's (well dressed) Navy. No two guys are in the same uniform. In fact some don't have any uniform at all...sun hours! It's just like a nudist colony for one sex, not much variation but designed to get every ray of the sun!

Only 2,000 miles to go to Gibraltar. The closest land is straight down about three miles. Columbus must have been crazy. He was at sea 42 days. The Pilgrims took 64 days in a ship only 120 feet long. We can't complain!

No church services yesterday so a few guys in the "gorge" were reading the Bible aloud and came across the following..."Those that go down to the sea in ships, and do business on the sea, see the wonders of God!" True, very true, the sunrise and sunsets are really beautiful and the sea is really awesome!

NOTES TAKEN FROM THE SHIP'S NEWS LETTER RECEIVED VIA RADIO....

WHEN THE MOVIES ENDED ON DECK LAST EVENING WITH A SOFT BREEZE WAFTING ACROSS THE DECK AND FRIENDLY STARS TWINKLING DOWN UPON A SMOOTH SEA A FAR DIFFERENT SCENE WAS BEING ENACTED IN BOSTON BAY. THE ITALIAN STEAMER ETRUSCO WAS CAUGHT IN A NORTH EAST GALE AND PROBABLY BLIZZARD AS WELL AND WAS SENDING OUT A DISTRESS CALL FOR HELP. THIS SOS RE-BROADCAST SHORTLY AFTER WAS AS FOLLOWS: "SS ETRUSCO POSITION ABOUT HALF MILE FROM SHORE AT PLYMOUTH MASS, VISIBILITY VERY POOR. WE HAVE A RED LIGHT GIVING A FLASH EVERY SEVEN SECONDS BEARING 180 SEA MOUNTAINOUS POSITION VERY DANGEROUS." THE SHIP WAS THEN, OR SHORTLY AFTER, AGROUND. CHATHAM RADIO AND BOSTON COAST GUARD RADIO GOT TO WORK AND THE COAST GUARD CUTTER "COOS BAY" WAS PROMPTLY DISPATCHED AND DUE TO ARRIVE AT THE DISTRESS SCENE AT 11 PM CHARLESTON TIME.

March 19, 1956   LAST NIGHT WAS A ROUGH ONE FOR THE STORMY NORTH ATLANTIC. TO BEGIN WITH, A SHIP SANK OFF THE NORTH WEST SPANISH COAST ABOUT MID-EVENING. CAUSE OF SINKING UNKNOWN HERE BUT BELIEVED SEVERE WEATHER. FIVE SHIPS WERE SPEEDING TO THE RESCUE AND AT LEAST ONE HAD ARRIVED THERE AND WAS STANDING BY UNTIL DAYLIGHT TO PICK UP SURVIVORS. THEN ANOTHER SHIP WAS SPEEDING FOR NORFOLK, 120 MILES FROM CAPE HENRY, WITH A FIRE IN HER HOLD. NEXT, THE DUTCH COASTAL PICKED UP AN SOS BY PHONE FROM A SHIP AGROUND ON THE DUTCH COAST AND FINALLY A SHIP WAS REPORTED AGROUND NEAR CARTAGENA, SPAIN BY GIBRALTAR RADIO.

Going to sea can be a dangerous business!

March 20, 1956   The first day of spring. To those of us studying navigation that means the sun has crossed the equator and its declination is now north. We changed course yesterday and are now headed due east on the 30th parallel straight for Gibraltar. The wind and sea have changed and we are taking the waves broadside which increases our roll. Every now and then, too often perhaps, the bow goes under and everything on the main deck forward is buried in salt water. The stern never goes under but does come up and out of the water. When it does the screws are almost clear, and spinning like they are, at 140 RPM, vibrate the entire ship and send out a huge spray. It actually looks like a cloud, and when looking aft there is a clear trail of fog and mist.

Please excuse this mess but under these conditions I can't write much better. As the old boson says "this ship is going up and down more than a w____'s pants.

The last three days have been rough. Until Monday the crew was happy, rested, and taking the crossing pretty well. Since the weather and sea changed life has been hell. You can't eat right and when you do you hold the tray in one hand and eat with the other. If bread is available you always take an extra slice to put under the tray to keep it from sliding around. Trays will slip off the table and smash against the deck. The cups break, the food or coffee or anything else that's on the tray just spreads out across the deck.

Sometimes the messdeck can really become a mess. I can remember how last year, as a messcook, we spent a lot of our time swearing and cleaning up the damn place especially in heavy seas.

Going into Gibraltar I'm gonna be the quartermaster of the watch which means I'm gonna be pretty busy making entries in the logbook of all kinds of events and things. Sounds like fun!

March 24, 195   Gilbraltar The hole in the fuel tank that I told you about got bigger and bigger until the chief reported the loss of 10,000 gallons of oil. We moved from Hamilton to the north anchorage, and there we stayed for three days. It got to be funny after a while, for not one of the crew or the officers would go down and weld the hole. The captain didn't want to take the responsibility of crossing the pond with the ship in that condition.

After two days at anchor we moved to St. George's, where a welder from shore came out and did the job. We left Bermuda Wednesday night and sailed for five days without any trouble. Then the port engine broke down and we drifted for half a day without any power, three thousand miles from nowhere. Well, anyway, we are now in Gibraltar.

I am sitting in the Captain's gig, of which I am a member of the boat crew. The rock of Gibraltar is certainly some rock. It goes up and up and up. I looked at it through the glasses today and it has more guns in it than it has rocks. The city is built on the base of the rock and goes up; the more money you have the higher up the rock [you] live. Its inhabitants are Spanish and English with a small amount of true Gibraltanians. [sic!] The three of these races make up a population of about 25,000. As I look aft from the gig I can see Africa, Spain, and Gibraltar. Tomorrow, I think that I will go to church and then to Spain.

As I look at Africa, I can see the mountains upon which Hercules held up the world. The top of it is way up in the clouds, and he might still be there, for all I know.

…When you come to the ring dance I will buy you a ward eight. It is a drink of a mixture of things. The basic one is gin, I know, but the rest of them I do not.

[Note: More social commentary. JS] I have not read Mr. Faulkner's letter on de-segregation and would appreciate it very much if you sent it to me.

…The weather has changed a little, and we are back in blues again.

March 25,1956.   Gibraltar   Starboard watch came through again! Local bar, great party, and the Navy Shore Patrol broke up two fights. Lynch and "Red Riley" were taken to the station house. It seems they were talking to some "limey" seaman about the Queen. Who knows what was said but it broke into a hell of a fight. The bar was later declared out of bounds, only to us.

March 26, 1956   Enroute to Marseilles, France. The sea is calm and the ship is riding easy. This is only a two day trip about 600 miles. No time zone changes, we won't lose another hour of sleep.

Cigarettes are only a dollar a carton. Not bad huh! A ten cent pack can get you a taxi ride across any city on this cruise.

We learned in Gibraltar that the best bar in Marseilles is the "Strip-Quiz." I'm sure we'll check it out!

Letters to Lou…

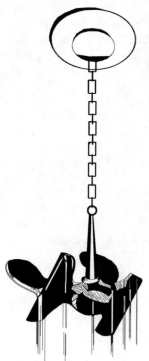

For the last few weeks I've been living almost as well as a first job. The youngies are polite (imagine) and anything I need or might want done is done without questions or complaints. You'd be surprised how their attitudes have changed. Sounds strange huh! I've never had any trouble with them anyway but now it's really something! Of course there is a reason for it! I've been assigned as the permanent keeper of the anchor chain. What an honor huh? At any rate every time we drop the hook I drop it. When it comes up the boson handles the wheel and the deck gang while I supervise the youngies in the chain locker. If a guy gets wise or is just plain arrogant his name is placed on the list. Two guys are chosen and given the privilege of "faking the chain".

The appointed pair are sent into the chain locker which is a dirty wet and small space up forward. There is only one small light in this dark space. As the chain comes in it has to be "faked" and put in place properly so it won't knot and stop the anchor from going out when it is dropped. The chain can come in fast. It's heavy, muddy, wet, and usually smells bad. A real nasty job!

I was down there twice last year and hated every minute of it! If the chain should slip and start to run out you could go out with it. Right up and through the spill pipe, on to the main deck, around the wildcat and into the sea below. It's one hell of a way to die! After recovering the body you'd probably only be recognized or identified by the stencil on your dungarees. Pretty grim huh!

Sheehy was caught in the chain as a youngie and smashed his leg and knee. He still walks with a limp and can't go Navy because of it!

My function while the chain comes in is to watch and see that it is done right. From where I stand, above the youngies in the locker, I can see the guys and I'm right beside the one and only ladder out. Not a bad deal for me! No work, just watch, hold the light, smoke, and keep my eyes and ears open!

I sure would like a great big glass of cold milk. Real milk! Oh well!

March 27, 1956 Enroute to France. We followed the coast of Spain with its snow covered mountains all the way. We are still wearing "blues" on liberty. Kinda cool here! We had a movie on the fantail last night - darn near froze to death. The wind was bitter and cold. It was a good movie though, "Devil's Canyon", another shoot-em-up western.

While on watch the "Bum" always asks the upper jobs what they would do in different situations if they were the watch officer. Then he may do something but never explains why to us.

Our speed was 15.7 knots at times. I don't think we can go any faster. The old Chun was in rare form.

March 28, 1956 Marseilles, France. Tied up, at La Canebiere Street (Can of Beer St), Old Port Dock. There are more small boats tied up then there are cars on the street. Hundreds of small boats of all types. It's a very busy street with lots of restaurants and bars.

Our Spanish teacher recommended we try a very special local dinner called "Bull-ya-Base". He told us it was terrific and don't miss it. A bunch of us went into a place on the waterfront that specializes in "Bull-ya-Base." We had a few beers and waited for our order. It finally showed up. It was a long deep dish with a big fish hanging out on both ends. It had several types of vegetables that we could identify and was covered was a light brown sauce. It did not smell very good! After looking it over and having a couple of guys sample it, we sent it back and ordered spaghetti!

Actually I'll take Spam, or peanut butter and jelly, any day, over that mess.

…the crowd goes mad.

March 30, 1956   Marseilles, France.   Well, honey, here I am in France, with the Charleston tied up stern to at the end of "Can of Beer Street".   The weather over here is not as good as one would expect it to be.   It has been raining all day and quite cold.

I got into trouble with the dirty old man, so I went ashore yesterday and will be restricted tomorrow.   I had a delicious French dinner and drank quite a bit of that good French wine.   I saw what the bouillabaisse looked like, but I didn't have the nerve to try it.

I am standing up and writing this letter against the bulkhead and it gets tiresome after a while.   [It also gets impossible to read. but was better than no letter.JS]

I have not seen so many beautiful women in one place in all my life.   The city is quite large and everything runs about the same price that it does in the states.   I hope the package that I sent reaches you in one piece.

April 1, 1956 Easter Sunday. Arrived, Barcelona, Spain.

April 2, 1956   We went to the "Bull Fight" yesterday. Wow! It was tremendous! I've never seen anything like it! At first it seemed cruel, mean, bloody, and you pitied the poor bull. After seeing a guy thrown in the air and rushed by that 2,000 pound mass of muscle and bone you change your mind fast. The crowd goes mad and boy do I mean <u>mad!</u>   I took some pictures and hope they come out OK.

There is another fight tomorrow and I don't plan on missing it! Never saw anything like it!

PLAZA TOROS MONUMENTAL de BARCELONA

POSTAL CARD 4/2/55

Seat number 21, Sol y Sombra (in the shade), with a cool one!

....……………………………………………………………………………

MTS CHARLESTON
Barcelona, Spain
Prepared 2 April 1956

<u>PLAN OF THE DAY FOR TUESDAY APRIL 3 1956</u>

0800 - Section 4 on watch. Boat Drill
        Sections 1 and 2 maintenance following drill
1245   Starboard watch liberty
        Section 4 maintenance

Letters to Lou…

Each watch section will be given about 48 hours leave while in Genoa to <u>visit Rome</u> or <u>visit Florence</u>. Requests from parents for these over-nights will not be required for those granted leave to visit Rome or Florence.

There will not be sufficient time to grant three days leave to visit Rome and still grant equitable liberty to the remainder of midshipmen.

Port watch will be granted the first 48 hours leave period in Genoa.

[Jim McCluskey]

Still on a "pure tour!" Don't intend to change! A few guys have got "Old Joe". The Navy issues every man a "Pro Kit" before they go ashore. Here the guys just chance it! As the sixth fleet moves so does "Old Joe." Everyone on the ship is checked at least once before we go ashore in the states and Boston.

April 4, 1956 Enroute to Genoa, Italy. This cruise is almost half over. Jim Lynch and I are planning to visit with his brother-in-law in Washington when we tie up in Baltimore. Jim has been to Washington before and knows what to see and do. I'm really looking forward to it.

April 5, 1956 Genoa, Italy. Went ashore this afternoon. We bought a pizza for dinner. It was terrible and cold. Won't do that again!

Genoa reminds me of the time Joe Walsh and I were walking down the street and a paison stopped us and asked if we wanted to exchange American dollars for Italian Lire. We spent about one half hour trying to get the best deal. He wanted ten dollars and two cartons of cigarettes for 100,000 Lire. He kept on pointing the 100,000 bill up to the sun for us to look at the picture to show us it was authentic. We beat him though, we told him we would only give him $10.00 and no cigarettes. Good deal, huh!

Later when we tried to buy something we found out that we had just bought 100,000 Drachmas worth about 30 cents. You can't trust those Italians!

[Tony Scarlata]

April 8, 1956 Genoa, Italy...The Charleston wants a lot of attention, I'm afraid. The engineers are having all sorts of trouble with the port main engine and the condensation pumps which break down about every two days.

… My father writes that he received a card from them [the commissioners] saying we arrived in Gibraltar one day late because of rough seas. Not a word about the ship breaking down.

I spent the past 2-1/2 days living like an Italian. I wanted to go to Rome but I didn't have the money. I went to Florence and several other small towns. It was really very nice. The people were a little hard to get along with until they found out I was an American. They have no love for the British, I'm afraid.

April 9, 1956 Ed Ascolillo, Joe Walsh, and I spent the night on the train going from Genoa to Rome. It was a seven hour trip as second class passengers. We were in small room that holds six people, kinda like you see in the movies. MMA rented about two train lengths for the middies. The wine and brandy flowed like water.
After an hour or so nobody drew a sober breath. It was a great trip...no officers or first jobs.

We didn't want to wear our uniforms to Rome so we changed into what might be called civvies. Black rain coats, white dress shirts, khaki pants, white socks, and black shoes...our civilian uniforms.

We didn't have much money so we traded packs of black market cigarettes for taxi rides, food, beer and other things.

We hit Rome about 7:30 AM had breakfast at the USO and then went to mass at St Peter's. After mass Eddie, Joe and I spent most of the day in and around the church. It really is huge! In fact nine masses were being said in different sections of the church at the same time. Confessions were held in any language. While we were waiting we met a brother from Malden Catholic High School. After having or taking him to dinner, he spent the afternoon explaining the Vatican to us.

…the ship is fine.

This place is a masterpiece! You can't imagine the size or the beauty of St. Peter's. I don't expect to see anything like it again.

We did not get an audience with the Pope but he made an appearance on the balcony of his home. He was a long way up and a long way off but we did see the Pope. He was there about ten minutes. He said a few things in Italian(I guess), then blessed the metals and holy items that people held in the air. Afterwards he said a short prayer and returned to his room. There were thousands of people in the square below him. It was really something to see and I was really impressed!

USO *home away from home*

It certainly was in Rome!

April 14, 1956 Tangiers, Algeria. Mail is really costing me a small fortune but it's worth it, I think? In Spain it cost me a buck to send a three page letter. Oh, when we get back to Boston liberty will run like last year. First day off then five days on duty <u>or</u> first day aboard with the next five off. I don't know now which it will be?

About the "Strip Quiz Bar", we never did find the place. Must be slipping, huh? From what I've been told it's a different type of strip tease. The guys in the crowd help out and some get on the stage. The guys ask questions while some gals dance around. When someone in the audience gets the answer correct a designated article of clothing is removed. This goes on until she is dancing around with nothing but a great big smile. We wouldn't have made out very well anyway...we don't speak French!

Yes... the ship is just fine...it's not about to sink or anything!

NOTES FOR PERSONNEL ON LIBERTY

Prevailing rate of exchange:
>about 400 Moroccan francs to dollar
>about   43 Spanish pesetas to dollar

Pickpockets are numerous and skillful, especially some of the children.

Only registered guides should be trusted. Each of these has a license with photo and number

Only Chico-Taxi or Taxi Minor are reliable taxis and pay only the amount shown on the meter.

Beaches outside the Bay are treacherous.

Entrance to Mosques is strictly forbidden.

Do not approach or speak to Moslem women on streets.

Photographs of <u>individuals</u> should not be taken.

Swiss watches, French perfumes and Spanish leather goods are most popular items to buy.

People are friendly towards Americans and should be treated courteously.

Letters to Lou…

April 14, 1956   Tangier, Morocco   received your letter this morning from the hands of the dirty old man. Your wise suggestion about not antagonizing him was a little late. We had another disagreement this morning.

Yesterday we stopped at Centa(?), Spanish Morocco to refuel the ship. By the time it was done, the engineers had dropped enough oil on deck to keep us, anchor clankers, busy for the next two weeks.

Jane, what makes you ask about bugs? Yes, we have a goodly amount of roaches, but that is the extent of it.   In fact, if we got rid of them, I think the ship would fall apart. Once, as a third classman, I had to find 75 roaches and paint them white, then deposit them in the wardroom pantry. I don't believe that the officers would like that if they found out about it.

Our film on Sunday is "A Farewell to Arms".   It would be an insult to Mr. Hemingway if I even tried to think of a different ending. I do believe, however, that the death of the lady was a tragedy and a shock to any reader.

My throat is so sore that I can hardly talk, but I am still smoking as much as ever, therefore, I think it will stay with me for a while.

April 16, 1956   Arab music is awful! Really weird! I bought a few records to play for the upper jobs later! They'll love it around 6 AM some Sunday morning.

Tangiers was a real cool port (yes the word <u>cool</u> was used in 1956…I've copied it directly from the letter). The people are a real mix. There was a French, Spanish, and English Quarter along with the Arab "Casbah". The Spanish section was the best as far as the people go and the French was not too bad except for the smell. The "Casbah" was a huge section on the outskirts of town. The streets were just small alleys and loaded with people. People of all kinds! This section had its own bars, shops, pimps, crooks (pick-pockets), and red light district. It's just like you've seen in the movies!

The Arabs have their own kind of dress, a lot like you might see in Bible stories. The men wear slippers, no socks, bags on each leg called knickers, long drab robes and a dark red fez to top things off. Some wear turbans but most wear the red fez. I bought one with a long tassel draped over the back. They were a big hit with the cadets. Lots of them returned to the Charleston.

No picture taking is allowed. Five guys lost cameras cut from their straps and more than a dozen lost their wallets. The kids will rush a guy or guys and when one of them gets something he takes off. There's no hope of ever catching him!

The women are something else! They all wear a dark cloth cover from head to about an inch off the ground. Only one eye is visible…"One Eyed Honeys". One of the guys offered two gals 1,500 pesetas to remove their veils. Did they ever get mad! About two seconds later everyone on the street was around us. One guy told us quite frankly in English to "Get the hell out of here!" We did!

A long awaited salesman finally showed up at 8 AM this morning. He has followed us around the Med with lots of stuff and took orders in some of the earlier ports. He came aboard with all his gear and started to set stuff out when he was told to leave. We would not delay sailing at 9 AM. Sorry, no cashmere sweater from this port!

April 19,1956   Funchal, Madeira   Putting our liberty boats in the water was a problem. A large wave will pick the boat up, throw it against the ship and rattle the falls that we use to lift and lower the boat. It's a lot of fun until someone gets hurt or goes over the side.

Joe Fee (2nd class snipe) went in yesterday. He wasn't hurt, just wet and mad.

Megonigle (2/D) went in today. What a splash! He hit flat face down and got the wind knocked out of him. We threw him a life ring but he paid no attention to it. I was in the boat and pulled him out. The O.D. gave me hell later. I guess he'd rather have one go down instead of two. The guy could have drowned. If they had their way they would have just kept bouncing life rings off his head.

…lots of free samples.

All the boys are back from a day in town and the local wine cellars. Nobody comes back really sober and some are really loaded. It really is funny to watch them come aboard and pretend to be sober. The O.D. picks them out when they reach the top of the ladder. They just won't go ashore for a few ports.

Usually the proud young midshipmen of the Charleston are perfect gentlemen. According to rules and regs they don't drink, swear, or cause any disturbances. The boys are always living up to rules and regs by following them to the letter, keeping the tradition of the Charleston pure and wholesome. You can walk the decks of the ship for weeks and never hear a foul word. Just a great bunch of guys to cruise around with! I'll be lucky if I get out of here with my senses, half a brain, and without becoming a complete alcoholic.

The boys are playing a hot game of poker on the next table. Curse and swear, deal and re-deal that's all that seems to go on. They have to play it cozy since gambling is not allowed aboard. They play with two or three decks of cards. One is used to play with and the others are used as chips. Each card has a certain value and the system works rather well.

April 19, 1956   Still anchored out here at Funchal, Madeira. Just completed a special run for the Captain and the "Bum". They really are a pair! They went to a party held by the consul and I guess they had a few. The "Bum" sang all the way back while the Captain just sacked in! How they ever made it to the boat dock I'll never know.

This port is famous for its wine. Lots of free samples and the guys are taking advantage of the opportunity. They don't buy anything...just drink everything!

CRACKED CORN, FEATHERS AND SID

Island of Madeira. Bob Roffey and I went ashore with upper classman Jim Quirk. Met a tour guide who invited us to his home for dinner. Had a great time talking to him, his wife, and daughter. His hobby was raising and racing homing pigeons, something I did in high school and a sport that Jim's brother participated in. Our tour guide host offered to give us two pair of his pigeons in exchange for copies of pigeon magazines to be sent to him we got back to the states.

Jim and I, under the cover of darkness, created a cage for the pigeons in the 0-2 deck life jacket locker and went ashore to met our new friend, the tour guide, the last day we were in Madeira. He gave us some cracked corn for feed and we brought the birds aboard in two overnight bags. The "cage" worked out well and every night after taps, we would bring the pigeons to the forward showers and water and feed them and also let them flap their wings a bit. As Jim was the ship's barber, it worked out well because we would sit in the barber shop with the lights out while the birds were in the shower.

About half way across the Atlantic we were surprised one evening when Sid came through the forward berthing compartment into the forward showers area during his post taps tour. Of course, he saw the birds doing their thing on the deck. Sid said "I've got them now" and he headed quickly aft. As soon as he cleared the berthing compartment, Jim and I grabbed the pigeons and the water and feed bowls and started to go towards the messdeck when we heard several people coming forward. We ducked down into the small stores area and looking up the ladder, saw Sid leading Capt. Woodland and Cdr. Rounds toward the forward showers. Several cadets in the forward part of the berthing compartment heard Sid say - "here they are, we have them now" as he entered the shower area. Of course the birds were gone but in our haste Jim and I were not able to pick up the corn spilled on the deck by the pigeons nor were we able to pick up the feathers shed by the birds. Sid pointed to the corn and feathers as evidence that the birds had been there but he could not explain where they went. Capt. Woodland reportedly said to Sid that the birds were most likely lost and came aboard through one of the open ports in the showers. Sid suggested that while that might be a possibility, they sure didn't bring the corn with them!

The remainder of the cruise was replete with chow line comments to Sid indicating that there was a spotting of an elephant on the maindeck, sighting of alligators in the scullery, etc. Sid never found the pigeons nor did he identify the pigeon keepers. When the Charleston tied up to the pier in Boston, the pigeons left the Charleston in the same manner that they came aboard, in two overnight bags.

[Bob Roffey]

Letters to Lou…

Coo-coo, coo-coo in chorus by the guys in the mess line. "Stop the line, you guys want to eat, cut it out!" "Hey Sid, ya wanta buy a canary that sings rock and roll?" As soon as he turned his back the chorus would start again.

April 22, 1956   Santa Cruz de Tenerife. This is our last port before crossing "the big pond" and ten days at sea. It's gonna be a long time between mail calls!

This is a real nice island - it just seems to rain every five minutes!

Port watch (those guys are all animals) had liberty today. It was Sunday and liberty went as soon as we tied up. They had a dinner and dance at the Embassy. Liberty expired at 1 AM Monday instead of the usual 10 PM.

I wish we had a cargo ship instead of this excuse for a man-o-war. If we only had one boom, a cargo net, a long wire lead, and a strong donkey engine we would have no trouble getting these car loads of drunks aboard. Officers and cadets alike were driving up in the same cars, falling out, and helping each other up the steep gangway. They all had a ball and will pay for it later. They won't be worth a damn at 6 AM. Big heads have trouble getting thru hatches etc.

Some of these parties…Wow! There wasn't one guy that came back entirely sober!

The cabs were loaded with men. To begin with the cars are small(kinda remind me of Mutt & Jeff's car) and painted black and red. They are allowed by law to carry only four passengers but a few coins will alter the law a little. One car had eight guys in it counting the driver.

April 24, 1956   Tuesday.   The first day of the crossing. The sea is calm and living is easy with weather like this. Tempers are cool and everyone is in a good mood.

I went on liberty yesterday. The Spanish Navy arranged a tour, and a dance was held later that night. We <u>had</u> to go…"You <u>will go</u> and you **will have a good <u>time</u>, won't you?"** " Yes sir, I know I'll have a ball Sir…Thank you, Sir."

The tour was another bus ride to the north side of the mountain. The island is about 45 by 15 miles. They drove us over every inch of it! It really is beautiful, rugged, and high with bananas everywhere.

After about an hour of riding everyone was bored with the winding road and the jerky bus. Let's face it…if you've seen one banana you've seen them all! We all knew we could have a better time on our own. We started at 2 PM and at 5 PM we were still headed away from the ship. We were not happy!

A little after five we found ourselves driving down this huge mountain toward the sea ahead. The guide told us we were invited to eat and drink at some French Beach Club. It sounded like another cracker, cheese, and an ounce of wine deal. As we drove up, four buses full of hungry, and disgusted middies were greeted by some beautiful girls on the beach. I don't understand French but what ever they said sounded great! Everybody came to life for the first time since we left the ship.

It was a beautiful resort with a pool, a huge bar, and a Spanish string orchestra playing in the background. Everything was on the house! Watch three deckies, six of us, found a table, gave the waiter a pack of smokes and proceeded to live it up. The waiter treated us right! First he brought a us a case of beer, a tray of chow each, with olives and chips. We started off just fine!

The beer wasn't too good but it was free. It was unusual to have more beer than we could drink! At last count I remember 22 bottles on the deck with another 12 on the table. We were there only an hour and a half but everyone was smashed getting back on the bus.

I wonder who picked up the check for the 140 thirsty and hungry guys? It must have cost a fortune!

Everyone was feeling so good that the bus broke out in song. In fact they didn't stop singing until we were back at the ship.

The buses stopped at another place to refuel. The Hotel set us up again and we were really loaded when we left. We got back to the ship at 9 PM sober again, or at least half sober! We then set out for the dance at the Casino which had another huge bar. Drinks were cheap and it gave us a chance to get rid of our Spanish money. Beer was twelve cents a glass, mixed drinks were cheaper. Coke was the most expensive drink.

It was a great dance, I think! I returned to the ship with arms full of pastry and bread (another chance to part with my Spanish money) and feeling pretty good.

The next morning I woke up with my head in a vice, red eyed, and feeling lousy! A few guys were put on report for not getting up. A few more were up early for 4 AM for scrub down. Somehow they missed me. I thought for sure I would be up for scrub down. Lucked out again!

I had the watch with Vogel (1/D) coming out this morning. We sent the messenger down for some morning after pills but they didn't help much!

Really looking forward to the next ten days at sea...I need to recover!

April 28, 1956   The average person at home is probably watching TV. Here on the Chun a bunch of guys are watching V.D. It's no joke! Some of the guys are really sweating it!

Of course every cruise of the Chun is sure to bring back a few pets. You can find aboard rare and common pets. Usually they are small and easy to hide. Last year they brought home puppies and chameleons. This year we have a few racing pigeons and canaries but this year the most popular pets are "crabs!" You can find them in every compartment deckie or snipe.

They are kinda cute and always good for lots of late night action. A few of the guys spend their spare time picking them out and training them. They are kinda smart you know! Really! They multiply like rabbits and in a short time you can have your own "crab circus" or "colony." No kidding!

To get rid of them is a long hard job, but the smart guys on the Chun have come up with a few quick solutions. One of them involves alcohol, a sand barrel, and getting them drunk so they will kill each other off by stoning each other. The other, better solution, which is more successful but painful, and sometimes fatal, involves a little lighter fluid and an ice pick. I won't go into the details here but I'm told it works great! Really!

I wonder if either of these procedures are outlined in your Merck's Manual?

April 29, 1956   Only a few more days and we will arrive in San Juan. We have been underway for five days - no land - no ships - just water and sun. The water temperature is about 72 degrees, the air temp is about 85 everyday. To make things cool and comfortable we have the northeast trade winds on our starboard quarter. Really nice! We should have the same weather all the way across the ocean.

I'm getting the hang of this navigation stuff. I'm usually within a mile of the navigators position at noon. Not too bad for a rookie! I'm gonna try some star sights this week. We will be required to shoot stars on next year's cruise. It's more complicated but much more accurate and interesting!

Still underway. Movies on deck, on the fantail, nightly. Last night we had what is called a "happy hour". Jim McCarthy sang a few songs and drafted a few youngies to do a few assorted stunts. Lots of laughs and it helps make the time go by faster.

May 5, 1956   San Juan, Puerto Rico. Less than two weeks and we'll be back in Boston and no more letters for awhile. Can't wait! I'm getting kinda tired of bars, bar maids, and our usual liberties ashore. Looking forward to returning to normal!

San Juan is a nice large city but we spent most of our time on the Navy base. Checked out some real American chow and beer at good prices. We made the rounds of the "E", "C", and "O Clubs". Beer was only 15 cents a can or two for 25 cents.

Letters to Lou…

Not bad huh! Mixed drinks varied from 20 to 40 cents each. Because we are in the R.O.T.C.(that's what they thought anyway) they asked us to leave the Enlisted Club and sent us to the Officers Club. Big difference! Really nice! They even had "one arm bandits."

J.J. Lynch was drinking at another table with a few guys and a LCDR..'s wife and 18 year old daughter. Everyone was trying to put the make on the daughter. Nobody was paying much attention to the mother. J.J. being a good sport and hoping to get on the good side of the daughter through her mother started to talk to her telling her she was a doll etc. and later calling her "Mom!" She didn't say anything at the time and seemed to enjoy the attention. Our liberty time ran out and we returned to the ship.

Once aboard we spent fifteen minutes, twelve of us, at attention on the maindeck getting our posteriors chewed up and down by both the Captain and the X.O.(CRD. Rounds). They were fit to be tied! It seems that the mother talked to her husband and he called the ship and reported the event to the O.O.D., the X.O., the Captain. I guess the only one he didn't talk to were the cooks! We've had it!!! Every dirty detail aboard has been coming our way! J.J. has been packing grease valves in the hot steering engine room for hours. We have been turning-to on the maindeck with scrub down after scrub down. The teak wood deck has never been so "virgin isle." Its kinda funny now, in fact it's a riot, but when we were on the maindeck it was no joke! The whole thing will be talked and laughed about for years to come.

I rated liberty again today. However our visits to the town and the base were not appreciated. The Navy and our X.O., being very kind and considerate, have arranged a bus tour of the island for us. I don't know what we would have without this fine all day bus ride. I bet they won't run out of gas until after 10 PM. We can't get out of the tour so touring we will go! Plenty of chances to take more pictures of more bananas!

Two days prior to our arrival at San Juan we had the usual "short-arm-inspection." All 180 of us were piped on deck for a check muster. The guys on watch were checked later. The next pipe ordered us to strip to nothing but our socks and shoes and remain at parade rest with our clothes in hand. The doctor and the pharmacist mate were up on the bow waiting for the crew. A dozen guys at a time were taken forward for inspection. Doc Boyle checked everything but the roots of our teeth. An hour or so later he had his list! A few guys had "Old Joe" and another bunch had "critters"…a star was awarded to those that had both! If you just had pets you were allowed ashore. The other guys would stay aboard until they passed a smear test. This would include Boston! It pays to keep the tour pure!

May 12, 1956 Baltimore, MD. Jane, the reason that I am now restricted to the ship is that the language that I used with the dirty old man was not the king's English. In fact you might say that I was "just a little obscene."

We made the Gulf Stream up from San Juan, and what a difference in the weather it made. The sea temperature went from 80' F down to 53'F in less than one-half hour. On the way up here, while I was at the helm, we ran into a graduate from the academy who had a kid brother aboard. The ship was steering very nicely, as a matter of fact, so good that I wasn't watching the gyro at all. Mr. Page came into the pilothouse and told me to watch my steering because there was a ship on our quarter. I turned and looked out the slot in the wheelhouse and almost had heart failure. The ship, which was a tanker, looked like it was sitting on our fantail. The next thing I knew the tanker was alongside, with a distance of about fifty feet between ships, and the two brothers were talking to each other. It is certainly a small world when two people can meet under these conditions.

There is a lot of talk about the Navy cutting out its program here at the academy and at the other maritime academies. Jane, how can the Navy be so stupid as to cut its maritime academy programs? The reason, I understand, is because of the (?)Lyndies(?) case at King's Point. The men that the Navy gets out of these academies are some of the finest officers that the Navy has.. They know more about ship handling and about navigation than the graduates from Annapolis. Sure, they do not have the academic background, but that is to be expected in a professional school. The Navy gives us about $16 a month, while at the same time they pay the jokers at Harvard, Yale, and Tufts, who know about the Navy and ships as much as my kid brother does, $76 a month. Jane, it makes me sick to think of what the Navy is throwing away when they make line officers out of these ROTC grads.

…Home at last.

When they go into the Navy they know nothing about it. They have only two years to serve and they get out. The Navy says they are not in long enough to warrant special training, which they aren't. Therefore, they fumble around here and there for two years and come out of the Navy knowing as little as they did when they went into it. If they took these ROTC grads and made them staff officers only I could see the usefulness, but until then I cannot.

I guess that is about all you care to hear about that. It probably is too much. I only wish, however, that I could get to see Admiral Burke, who's CNO of the Navy, for I talk a much better argument than I am able to write.

We had milk and ice cream for the first time since the cruise began today. The supply officer was very good about it. The ship tied up at eleven o'clock and he had it down in time for lunch.

Did I tell you that our friend Mr. Taylor got engaged before we left? I have never met his girl but from what Bob tells me, she sounds very nice.

I had a dream on the way up here that you were waiting on the dock when we came into Baltimore. Needless to say, I was very disappointed to be woken [sic] up for the watch. I am definitely worried about the Ring Dance affair...I lie in my bunk nights and think about that very much......What will you think of my face. It was bad before, but it is worse now - scars, false teeth, and things like that..

What will you think of my friends, my family, the shambles that I live in. I have few clothes and less money. All these things enter my mind, but the best solution I can think of is just to let you see me as I really am.

May 17, 1956 Arrived Boston, Mass. Home at last! Liberty call!

May 1956

Shortly after returning from the cruise to the Med., another cadet and myself had the opportunity to date two lovely ladies who were euphemistically known as "bone-in-the-nose" and "that's all brother". We showed the girls all that Onset Beach had to offer that night. During the course of the evening ____ and I each drank six quarts of Budweiser. The girls drove us back to the ship so we could show them the fezzes that ____ and I had bought in Tangiers. The girls waited at the car at the end of the finger pier. At some point, while staggering across the mess deck, we determined that the girls would **REALLY** appreciate our fezzes if that was **ALL** we were wearing. We each stripped down to nothing more than a fez and a T-shirt. As we staggered back down the finger pier, the girls ran back to the car, locked the doors and rolled the windows up. Undaunted, we continued our romantic pursuit and pleaded with the girls to let us back in the car. For reasons that are still not quite clear to us, the girls declined to let us in the car until we put our pants back on. I believe that the rest of the evening was a glorious success.   [Dick Boles]

May 28, 1956 This has been a very pleasing day for me. The dirty old man is not here, and I received five wonderful letters [Note: Letters written to cruise that finally caught up. JS] from you untouched by his hands.

I had planned to go into the hospital for additional plastic surgery] the 6th of June but the executive officer will not let me off. Therefore, I will try to get it done in the August leave period.

I have had several interviews with different people and got another scholarship for this year with little or no trouble.

Bob Taylor is one of the best friends that I have here at the academy. He sleeps below me, and we have many conversations lasting long into the night. He is the one who keeps telling me not to worry about the impression I will make on you when you come up here.

Letters to Lou…

The school had to take part in the Bourne Parade yesterday. I was stuck with the color guard and felt a little foolish stuck way out in front of everyone else, but it lasted for only a little over an hour. It started to rain as soon as we got to the cemetery and all of us got slightly drenched. Great fun.

May 31, 1956 Jane, in talking with some of the guys, when I came back from leave I found that their parents had to pay duty on the things that were sent to them. I had completely forgotten about duty or I would have sent you that package when I got home. Please tell me if you had to pay duty on it and, if you did, how much, so that I will be able to reimburse you.

I am glad to hear that you are still coming to Beantown. I can hardly wait for you to get here. However, I don't want you to work so hard; you are supposed to be on vacation. [Note: To make the deal work, I had assured my parents that I would pay my plane fare myself. Accommodations would be with Bob's family. But I only made 75 cents or $1.00 per hour, at most, on my campus jobs. So, I did have to work hard! JS]

June 4, 1956 Buzzards Bay. Back again on the "One Gun Chun!" As usual it's cold, damp, and kinda foggy. I wonder when my cold will return? Maybe tomorrow! Can't wait!

June 7, 1956 I received three letters today, all of which brought me exceedingly good news. The first and most important was yours… The second was from Capt. Williams at Brighton Marine Hospital telling [me] to report on the 29 July, 1956. I don't believe that the executive officer will turn this down. The third was a letter for my scholarship, and all that it needed was my signature.

Speaking of the dirty old man, he just chased me off the mess deck and I am forced to finish this letter sitting on a trunk in the dimly lit pea-coat locker.

Jane, I would have preferred to march in Boston or some other big city rather than in Bourne. The reason is that the boys really look good on parade and it would be good advertising for the school.

Speaking of ads, I will have to get busy, for I am working on advertising for The Muster. I don't think I am appreciated, though. I tore up all of the old contracts and made an order for $400.00 with the printer for new ones. Mr. Clark asked me why, and I told him I did not like the type of paper they were printed on. He had a small fit, but when he sees the new contracts I think that he will get over it.

June 11, 1956 I'm writing this from my rack prior to taps and lights out. I'll put it under my mattress pad and drop it in the mail box first thing in the morning. Greer hasn't sacked in yet so the rack next to mine is empty. Meyer just swung in above me. He usually falls asleep fast. Red Rils is next to crawl in after he gets his gear hung up, below me. Ascolillo is getting ready to crawl in beside him. Dowd, a 3rd job, is the only one missing. He sleeps below everyone just above the deck and a bunch of old shoes. No doubt he is turning-to somewhere, being a youngie must be tough!

In a far corner the radio plays some 1920's music. No R and B or Rock and roll! The first jobs are the rulers of the radio and kinda square!

June 12, 1956 Not much new here! Studies are starting to catch up with us. Cdr. Rounds, "Tricky Dickie", doesn't help much! He goes through something, Navigation, like a shot and expects it to be as easy as falling off a log. What a guy!

June 13, 1956 Some of the boys down here are sitting on pins and needles. It seems the ship's doctor, "et-et Boyle", wrote a letter to the Bd. of Commissioners with a list of the boys that got you know what on cruise. Some figure the maximum punishment will be 100 demerits and probation. Ten weekends aboard; it will probably be August before they get home.

June 20, 1956 Glad to hear that you finished that d____ typing. I didn't think it would take so long. I thought you said it would only take about half an hour? Well anyway---<u>Thanks a million!</u>

Next week, the 27th (Weds), the premier of the movie "Moby Dick" will be in New Bedford. Because it's a sea picture and is based on New Bedford whalers they figure they should have some maritime personnel. So old MMA will leave on buses at 1:15 and march down main street in dress uniforms. Tremendous, huh! All the boys are really excited and dying to leave!

…worth a million.

Maybe the show will burn down between now and then. Stranger things have happened you know, and some of us have liberty this weekend.

There has been a lot of talk about the Ring Dance in the last few weeks. Its my duty weekend, Sept. 15th, so I'll only get 24 hours off. I've gotta get some dress whites soon. Another 14 - 16 dollars for the uniform and 10 - 15 for shoes! I'm up to my ears in bills and there doesn't seem to be any end to it! Just gotta work weekends! I'll talk to Pete Rubico ('43-'44) about driving again for Medford Blue Cab. He got me in this place and he'll help me now, I hope!

June 21, 1956   Captain Tom Burke ('39) was down last night. He has placed most of the first class with good jobs and great pay. All they have to do is pass the Coast Guard exams.

John Halligan (one of our upper jobs) was also aboard. He is sailing 3rd for U.S. Lines..."American Manufacturer"...on 38 day runs to Europe. His pay is an unbelievable $1000 -$1250 per month or about $800 a month after taxes! Not bad, huh! My Navy Ensign's base pay will be about $220 per month.

June 21, 1956   What a day we've had today. Two classes and five study periods. Most of the officers are on their Navy cruises (Reserve Units), sick, or on vacation. The ones that are aboard are prepping the 1st jobs for the Coast Guard Mates Exam.

This time next year I'll be in their shoes studying, sweating, praying, and hoping for luck in that exam. You have to get 90% in the first two days and 80% in the minor subjects later in the week.

It's a pretty tough test and 27 guys from King's Point failed a few weeks ago. That's a pretty high percentage. Maine Maritime has taken theirs and everyone passed. Let's hope that MMA has the same good fortune.

What a battle we had with the first class last night! It seems that they have been treating us like youngies all year and all of a sudden (two weeks ago) they gave us second class privileges. They want us to do them a favor now so they are giving us the ship with lifeboats included! It's a long story and I won't go into it! Dick Weaver had his tape recorder on in the back of the row (unknown) to the first jobs and for half an hour there is nothing but fighting, arguing, and a few other choice phrases. That tape is worth a million dollars, maybe someday you'll get to hear it!

June 23, 1956   The Ring Dance is going to be held at the Sheraton Plaza on the 15th September. I do hope that you will come up. The invitations have not [gone] out yet, but I will see that you get one as soon as they do.

War is hell, and it is rough all over. I came across some extra money today and so I went into Boston to see if I could buy a suit. There was not one store that had a jacket large enough for little stick.

June 24, 1956   Well I'm writing this from my rack again! Above me only six inches away is your picture. Actually there are three pictures in a cardboard frame taped to the underside of Meter's rack. Two of you and one of Kenny. Of course, everyone figures we are married and Kenny is the first of a rumored ten! Wow! What do you think about that?

June 25, 1956   Wednesday we have a nice long parade to keep us entertained. New Bedford what a place to march! If this keeps up we'll lose all our holiday liberty and march instead! Rumor has it we will march again on the 4th.

Last Saturday morning Chuck and I took the drums apart and painted them blue. We finished painting today and put them back together. They really look nice. The large sections are blue and the rims are yellow. Just to "job it up a bit" we put a yellow fouled anchor on the left side.

I guess I'm stuck with a drum, like it or not! Don't know which is worse to carry a rifle or a drum for five miles! Lots of laughs with the boys in the band. At least we get a chance to look around a little and take in the sights!

Tomorrow will be the real test. Old MMA makes its second public appearance of the year--all jobbed up!!!

Jim Lynch is still running around in his fur lined vest. He looks and acts like Art Carney on the Gleason Show. He is rarely seen without the vest.

Letters to Lou…

June 25, 1956 Saturday 8 PM Check muster. All hands present and accounted for waiting for darkness. Harrington's Uncle Joe and some other guys tied up alongside this afternoon. Looks a lot like Hop. Around 6PM none of them were feeling any pain. The Cadets figured it would be a good night to jump. We waited for the first class to leave. Brown, Taylor, Roffey, Broadbent, and I planned to leave about 10:30. At 10:15 only two first classmen remained aboard (of ten) and maybe a dozen of 30 of the second class. Learned later that 26 guys were ashore before we decided to leave. We planned to leave two at a time swimming ashore pushing a bucket ahead of us with our clothes. No problem...it's worked before! Broadbent was on his way with Anderson (he was in another gang). Roffey, Taylor, and I were next. Only having a couple of buckets restricted our departure. Ted was running all around the ship looking for us. I guess he thought we left without him. He ran up the main deck and started across the gangway with no hat, a "T" shirt, and white bucks. He was on the end of the gangway when who should step out of the Captain's passageway but Harrington. We were 200 feet forward of them when we heard the scream. We all assumed he was sacked in with his buddies in the wardroom (that was our last report form the messenger of the watch). We ran aft to check and ran right into Hop, Ted, the 1st class O.O.D., and the messenger. Some of the guys in the parking lot also heard the scream .... **"Brown, where are you going?".** At that point there were 10 guys in the water or close to it. Task almost didn't make it When we got him aboard he just laid there soaked, exhausted, unable to move. When he heard the scream he ran from the end of the building (parking lot) taking off all his clothes enroute, losing them, his watch, ring, and one shoe before he hit the water and swam to the bow more dead than alive. "Where have you been, Task?" "Just taking a shower, Sir!" "You and a bunch of other guys, right?" "Yes Sir, but I was in the **forward head!**" Hop pulled check muster and found 26 midshipmen missing. I don't think he has put anyone on report yet! But who knows what he's gonna do! Ted is really shaken...**probably never pass Algebra.**

Never again!!! I'll **never** try that again. Much too close for comfort. Once again I lucked out! Maybe I still have a chance of passing trig; Harrington didn't catch me doing anything wrong, right?

June 28, 1956 I have received word today that I have permission to enter the hospital during the August leave period. I will be in the hospital from 29 July to 5 August. I hope that you still have the address of the hospital.

We had to march in New Bedford yesterday for the world premiere of Moby Dick. It was a long parade but we took first place and brought home the cup, which makes everyone feel better.

July 5, 1956 Well here I am back "home" in the bogs at the Massachusetts Merry Time Academy. What a place this is! Rain, fog and really damp! It seems like it's always that way down here! If it keeps up I'll never lose this cold!

Coming back I was supposed to meet Strautman, Weaver, Greer, Young, and Roffey in Needam at 7 PM. They left for a beer somewhere and I was kinda out of it for a while until I found Young. We stayed to watch the fireworks. A tremendous display, how was the one in Medford? We also stayed to watch the "Miss Needham" contest. They all paraded around in gowns, no bathing suits. Don't know who won as we left early!

July 5, 1956   [Minority opinion dept.!] I saw Elvis Presley on TV the other night, if I ever saw a disgusting act, that was it. Pardon the expression, but he was the most fagish looking person I have ever seen.

July 8, 1956   Sunday. Our annual leave starts 27 July and ends Monday the 5th of August. Ted (Boonya) wants us to come down to the Cape for a beach party. Let's do it, OK! I'll have the duty for a couple of days but I'm really looking forward to a break!

July 9, 1956   Another day with cold, rain and fog. Anyone that would live down here all year must be a little mental!

The youngies shut off the first class today! Remember we did the same thing last year? They refuse to be hazed and will do nothing but their regular(legal) routine duties.

Learned today that Ziminsky, married last Christmas, is about to have twins.

We've missed three or four of "Spook's" (Strautman) parties either because I had the duty or you were working and had to be in early. I guess he's planning a blast and I don't want to miss this one! It should be a large crowd since most of us will be on leave. Just a warm up for the Ring Dance!

Talking about the Ring Dance I ordered my dress whites today, $18 and I still have to get shoes! I think I'll get a pair of white bucks and paint the red edge around the side. Not much sense buying regulation shoes and maybe never wearing them again!

Kenny, a youngie with only a few weeks to go, left yesterday! Guess he was just fed up! He returned today to stick around until finals are over and get credit for a full college year. "College", ha-ha!!!

July 10, 1956   No change in the weather! Still foggy! Didn't have a beer this weekend except for Saturday. Have you seen the new "Imperial Quart" that Narragansett is putting out now! Really huge for the regular price!

Only 35 more days and you'll be an RN and out! Wow, it sure sounds great and Congratulations!!!   In three weeks I'll be a first classman and get 3 out of 4, or 7 of 8 weekends home! Sounds great huh!

I think the "new" youngies are coming on the 31st?

The upper jobs figure on getting their orders to report about the 5th of September. They won't get a chance to ship out on their mates license! One of the NavSci instructors was telling us that carriers are pretty good duty! They left every Monday with orders to B.B.F. (be back Friday). He had every weekend off for two years. Not bad huh!

I think I'll put in for sea-going tugs. Saw one going through the canal today pulling a barge. There's seldom more than a few officers aboard with about twenty white caps. Small, fast, strong and good experience, if I like it, for a civilian job. They are paid well and are home most nights!

July 12, 1956   Good news for a change! The Navy is gonna pickup the check for next year's tuition, social fund, my ring, and a few other expenses. The grand total amounts to $300. Not too bad huh! Last year they paid half and this year they pay it all. That plus driving for Blue Cab should get me through the year very nicely. It's also good news for the folks back home and their pocket book.

July 12, 1956   In one more week we have final exams and as of yet I have done little in the way of studying for them. I suppose I will have to get on the ball but so far I have followed the usual procedure for flunking, that is, "I have plenty of time, I'll do it tomorrow."

The first of the week was very foggy, and a fishing vessel ran aground about 100 yards off the dear old Char. If the fog is at all heavy, it is hard to see the other side of the canal, which is only 1000 yards away. About a month ago a Navy destroyer ran up on the rocks across from the school.

We had to go out into the bay yesterday for some small boat practice. There was no officer along so we drifted down into Buttermilk Bay and tied our boat up there. Some went ashore and bought some beer. That was very good as it was unbearably hot. I sat and drank beer and read Jules Verne's Around the World in Eighty Days, a very good book. However, we worked all the beer off on the way back for the wind and current were both against us.

July 16, 1956   More good news. We had the Admiral for class today and he said that our first class liberty weekends will start for us Friday! Yea! Should be home about 7:30.

July 17, 1956   Lots of rumors. No stripes passed out yet. A couple of guys broke into the Admiral's cabin last night to check the list that needs to be confirmed by the Board. They didn't find or learn much.

We have a big race Thursday. Ted, Greer, Red Rils, and Megonigle are in the boat and I was picked as coxswain. Four boats are in the race. A first class deck and engine crew are entered with a boat from the second and third class. I've got a great job, one nice long fast boat "ride" with no pulling just barking! We've got a good boat, a good crew, and we should be right up and in there for the money!

Letters to Lou…

July 23, 1956   Finals today and tomorrow. One test right after another!

The compartments are all upside down. Bunks are all rearranged, gear is scattered throughout the ship and it's all just one big mess. The officers are all complaining about one thing or another and there is no pleasing them.

While making my rounds last Saturday night I discovered a line of guys in the after berthing compartment after taps and lights out. "What's going on!" "There's a gang bang in the port isle!" I can't believe this place! To top it off a guy that had the next watch was allowed to job (to go to the head of) the line.

I'll be glad when the "new" youngies show up to square this place away!

July 24, 1956   Harrington didn't show up for class today? The exam has been postponed until Thursday. We'll just sweat it out a little longer.

A new class of youngies will be aboard next Wednesday!

I studied until 10:30 last night, watched "Victory At Sea" on TV, and went back to cramming until 12:30. Meg and I split the mid-watch so I was up at two to 4:15. What a night! I got up at 6:30 and started in again. With all the time I've put in lately my marks are pathetic, passing, but pathetic!

I'm now a Cadet Officer, one stripe, amazing, really amazing! I'd gladly swap the stripe for a passing grade in Algebra. Let's hope Harrington shows up Thursday so I can get this madness over with!

July 24, 1956   We just had a lecture on drinking and were told that all the drinking places in the Bourne area will be closed to us.

The exams were coming along fine until this afternoon. I believe that I flunked the navigation exam this afternoon. However, my marks will pass me for the year. I have never made such silly mistakes in all my life....I have an English Lit test tomorrow, for which I have prepared nothing. Spanish is also going to be a good one for me. I haven't done a thing.

July 25, 1956 11:10 PM Thursday.   The Andrea Doria and the Stockholm collided 50 miles southeast of Nantucket. The Andrea Doria was lost with 46 passengers. The Stockholm limped back to New York at 8 knots having lost 5 crew members. This collision resulted in the greatest rescue at sea in history.

This collision and the ensuing sinking of the Andrea Doria was one of the major news stories of 1956. It competed with the Suez Canal crisis, the re-election of President Dwight D. Eisenhower, the Hungarian Freedom Fighters and a host of other headlines of the day.

The incident, of course, touched the lives of those that lived and died in it, as well as their families and friends. Regulations were changed and travel on the high seas became safer. The Golden Age of the great ocean liners was drawing to a close as air travel became the preferred means of travel to and from Europe.

August 2, 1956 I am dying of boredom here at the hospital... The doctor is going to take the stitches out tomorrow and I hope to get out shortly afterward...Great leave this has been!...There are several people from the Andrea Doria here at Brighton.

"Typical Snipes"
J. Flaherty, F. Ferguson, D. Freeman

CLASS OF 1959

Incoming "Youngie Class" - *Our new tools!- August - 1956

NAVIGATORS

Bastille, Robert J.
Bresnahan, Maurice J. Jr.
Capelotti, Michael E
Dauksevich, Chester L
Collins, James F.
Dauksevich, Chester L.
Donnell, William C
Dunphy, John J.
Edson, J.M.
Flanagan, Joseph T
Fuller, J. M. *
Gaides, Charles A.
Johnson, Francis X. III
Lee, Robert E.
Litchfield, Rodger A.
Loftus, John M
Mackinnon, David O.
Mann, Timothy J.
Martenson, David C
Melvin, John A. *
Metcalfe, Allen G
Nolan, James S.
Rodes, Theodore Jr.
Ryder, D.A.
Saponaro, Joseph A
Sarnie, Robert W.
St. Pierre, Henry J.
Webb, Warren R.
Westgate, George A.
Whelahan, Andrew M.
Wilson, Albert B.
Woodside, Robert D

ENGINEERS

Arnett, Rexford R. Jr.
Atwood, Barry M. *
Baker, Earl F.
Casey, Richard J. Joseph
Chaisson, W. P.*
Colomb, William A.
Cutter, R.H. *
Ellis, David W.
Fitzgerald, Malcom E
Flynn, Edward L. Jr
Hautanen, R. W.
Lavender, Raymond G. Jr.
Litchfield,RobertW.(Blk)
Joyce, Charles M
Kadlac, Donald E
MacAulay, John M
MacGregor, Douglas R.
MacGregor, John Edson
Monson, Arthur C. Jr
Moriarty, John A
Mulkerm, Coleman J
Pike, Lee J.
Rehfield, Austin W
Shay, E. T.
Sweet, Charles Jr.
Tierney, Paul S.
Troungo, Gordon R. *

[J. Dunphy and A. Wilson]

Note:Actual graduates listed above.
  * Deceased 4/98

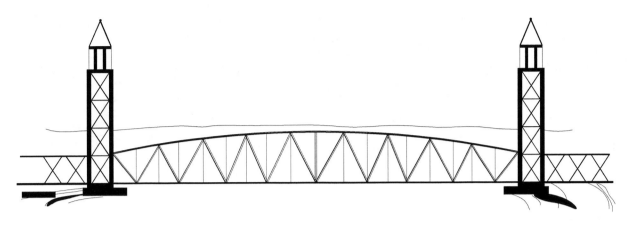

FIRST CLASS YEAR

PART 3 - YEAR 3

August 3, 1956   The new youngie class arrived! Hurray!

August 8, 1956   I missed writing yesterday and I'm sorry! We've been kinda busy with classes like they are and with this new class of young tools! Lots of laughs! I won't tell you about them or what has happened aboard the Chun until I get home since it would take pages and pages. I will say one thing, it's real nice to be on top of the pile and not on the bottom.

We had first aid again today and discussed the usual subject (you know what). Tony also told us a little about different pregnancy tests. I still don't understand how the rabbit gets pregnant! Is that really what happens!

The officers are giving us plenty of work to do hoping that we'll relax on the third class a little. We get the work done but the hazing doesn't even slow down.

I'm writing this from my salvaged stuffed living room chair. Never did I ever think that the "Pink Bubble's" corner would become "Hogan's Haven of Heavenly Bliss!" As I write this, four young men, seeing your picture over my bunk, "just happened" to ask me if they might write and introduce themselves by means of the mail. Naturally it's O.K. with me if they would like to drop you a line, I mean who am I to stop them? A Medford kid, Dunphy, might write tonight!

I've never studied or crammed as much for finals as I have for the last week or so. The hazing has been kinda rough so the officers figure if they lay on the studies the hazing will ease off. Actually it gets worse since the first class is on edge all the time and have little or no patience.

After such a poor showing by the last first class up at the mate's exams I guess the officers ain't gonna let it happen again. I turned in about 1 AM and got about five hours sleep which is not too bad compared to some of my classmates.

Some youngie was seen last Saturday night at the V.F.W. Drive-In in his job suit. A certain first job brought it to our attention Sunday night. He'll never do that again! Poor kid!

August 12, 1956

I got back to the academy on Monday and was issued books. Classes started that afternoon. From the look of things it is going to be a pleasant year. We have gotten into the meat of things at last. In addition to the old standby of navigation, we have rules of the road, rules of steamboat inspection, admiralty law, ship's construction, cargo storage and handling, meteorology, damage control and engineering administration.

Jim Piner has left the academy for good. I think that he is going into the Army.

The following is a copy of an extremely eloquent description of a young man's trials and tribulations. It has been placed here with permission of one of **"our youngies"**.

"Once There Was A Youngie"

A Tale of Life on the Good Ship Charleston
by RADM M.J. Bresnahan

Forty years ago on a beautiful August day, I was one of about one hundred aspiring midshipmen traveling to the Massachusetts Maritime Academy to form the class of 1959. We had much in common. We were bright-eyed, eager, highly motivated, and almost none of us had any notion of what was about to transpire. As we converged on Buzzards Bay, we had no idea that we were passing into another dimension. Our first week at the academy was about to be indelibly etched into our memories.

Landing at Taylor's Point in Buzzards Bay was in itself a shock. Despite its natural beauty, it was a barren place. Not a tree or a bush was present. There were a few worn and weathered summer cottages surrounded by sand, but very little grass or other vegetation. For one standing in the midst of today's Academy, it would be hard to fully understand the feeling of isolation. The classroom building, gym, library, dining facility, parade grounds, and playing fields were yet to come. The major highways leading to Cape Cod had not yet been built, and the wind-swept peninsula that was Taylor's Point had never really recovered from the great hurricane of 1939. It was a lonesome site.

A single building stood at the end of the pier on the edge of the canal. At right angles to the building was an old, wooden finger pier that looked as though it should have fallen into the sea years before. Tied up to that pier was the *Charleston*, my new home.

The *Charleston,* was built during the 1920's Naval Arms Treaty era. It was designed to look like a cruiser from the air, but it was in fact the size of a small destroyer. The Navy had classified it as a patrol gunboat, and it was a sleek ship with good lines. For all of that, it was still over twenty years old and had long since seen its best days.

My first step onto the *Charleston's* quarterdeck was akin to being shot. "Stand at attention....Drop that bag....Who let you in here, you worthless tool?.... What's your name?.... No, it isn't.... Your name is young man.... Your name is young, worthless, stupid, wedge.... Do you understand?" "Yes sir!" "I can't hear you." "Yes sir!" "Do we have hazing here at the Maritime Academy?" "No sir!" "Don't ever forget that."

My classmates were starting to form up around and next to me. The din and roar were rising. We were doing pushups, standing on our heads, and trying to sing as directed.

"We will now go below and draw dungarees so we can get to work... You midshipman, stand fast." That order was directed to a young man who had just minutes before been thinking of himself as a "freshman." He stood out from the rest of us because of the way he was dressed. We had been advised to report in "light clothing." Heedless of this instruction, this chap was dressed in a sport jacket, gabardine slacks, and a white shirt and tie. An obvious target. I will never forget the look on his face as the upperclassman relieved him of his golf clubs and walked up and off the ship to the edge of the pier. As he dropped the clubs into the water he yelled back, "You won't be needing these." That "freshman" was gone by week's end.

The rest of that day was spent "drawing gear"- uniforms, books, towels, mattress, pillow, and a knife to hang around your neck. "Stencil it all. Everything that you own must have your name on it." All of that was to be done and then stowed quickly. I was receiving that firm guidance from an upperclassman who was circling like a shark, screaming at the top of his lungs. It was my general orientation. I was a "youngie." A simple tool, and the lowest of the low. When anyone shouted "young man" or "wedge," I would stop, drop everything, come to attention and answer, "Here sir!" "I can't hear you." "Here sir!" "That's better, stupid."

I was a youngie. My mission in life was to be subservient to the upperclassmen. All else - education, training and nautical enlightenment - would flow from that

Did I understand? "Yes sir "I can't hear you." With turned up volume: "Yes sir!" "No you don't understand anything you simple tool." When I once again answered "Yes sir!" I really meant it. I didn't have the vaguest idea as to why I was here being subjected to such indignities, but I had no time to ponder this question.

All that had been stenciled so far was to be stowed. Nothing was impossible. A good midshipman could roll and stop twenty cubic feet of clothing and stow it in a locker that was a little bigger than a medicine cabinet. He could do it very quickly. It was possible to carry his mattress, books, clothing, all at once, across the pier, up the gangplank and down through the midship's hatch.

Don't be distracted by the gauntlet of roaring upperclassmen, who were not past giving you a gentle nudge as you bent to pick up something you'd dropped. If self-confidence flagged, some time spent standing on your head surrounded by hostile people screaming at you brought a rush of blood to your brain and with it a new resolve.

The class of 1959 did all of that and more during our first six hours aboard *Charleston* before we were introduced to our bunks - our home inside our home. After some very basic instruction, we made them up "nose to toes."

Those bunks were stacked four high from deck to overhead without much space in between. The sage advice offered at 135 decibels was to "make up your minds as to whether you want to sleep on your back or your belly before you get in because there isn't enough room to roll over.

We were slow to learn the knack of making a bunk around a three-inch-thick mattress laid on a sagging piece of canvas that was lashed to a metal pipe frame. I think I was wasting time trying to figure out what was sanitary about sleeping nose to toes. Mine was not to reason why but just to hurry or I'd be late for cleaning stations.

In an instant, everyone was running for cleaning stations. "Now hear this.... Turn to.... Sweepers man your brooms.... Clean sweep down fore and aft.... Wipe down all ladders.... Carry all trash to the pier.... Go to your cleaning stations." Loudspeakers all round me thundered. "That's the 1MC, stupid." The voice of God. What is a cleaning station, and where is mine? A typical stupid question from a worthless youngie. It was answered by a now familiar "upper job" who seemed to be angered by my mere existence.

I found myself part of a group being herded down into the boiler room via what seemed to be a very steep and slippery ladder. In the midst of heat, humidity, and noise, we were offered some very basic instruction on the cleaning of deck plates. As new as I was, I had the feeling that we were better off than some of my classmates who were going into the bilges under the steaming boiler, armed with bundles of rags.

Cleaning deck plates was simple. Down on your hands and knees with a wire brush, a rag, and a number 10 tin can half filled with diesel oil. Scrub and wipe. Scrub and wipe. It was hard to understand why we were doing that because they were not dirty. "Never mind, you worthless tool, scrub and wipe." It was Marine Engineering 101!

None of us proved to be adept at this our first lesson. Because in this culture there was a strong sense that repetition was the mother of all learning, we worked right through what was then called the evening meal. It didn't matter. I wasn't hungry. The heat, noise, verbal abuse, popping up and standing at attention, providing upper jobs with cigarettes and lights, seemed to have dulled such mundane things as appetite. It was the kind of chaos you have to live through first hand to ever fully appreciate.

Our spirits were starting to sag as we made our way up the ladder and passed through the mess decks. People were cleaning up, securing tables to the overhead. The scullery was steaming and banging away. Not a morsel or scrap of food was in evidence. No light lunch left out for the tardy on this ship.

"Get the lead out.... You're already late for evening studies.... Everyone off the ship.... Get over to your assigned classrooms." More running without any idea of where we were going.

Huddled in the building, stenciling books under the tutelage of a fresh crop of upper jobs, we were a sorry lot. Physical and verbal punishments were the orders of the evening, and there was more than enough to go around. No one could escape attention. There was no anonymity in this maelstrom.

"ONCE THERE WAS A YOUNGIE"

We had our first introduction to "nose to the wall." It was a new level of torment. "Put your nose on the wall, hands behind your back, extend your feet as far back from the wall as possible." It was almost funny for the first 30 seconds because the position was so ridiculous. Then the pain set in and all the humor ended.

In the midst of all that, a cry went up that echoed through the building: "86!" We had been schooled on that and in fact, some of us had already been posted as 86 watches. That was a simple but very efficient sentry system set up to warn everyone that an officer was near. It was the basic building block of the Midshipman Mutual Protection Program. There was much yet to be learned and appreciated about that. Whatever complex relationships existed between classes, and despite the rules of conduct that governed them, there was never any doubt that we all shared a common enemy. It was a Byzantine code that had yet to be fleshed out for us, but as new as we were, we understood the basic premise.

The building fell silent as the officer of the day approached the front entrance. It was our first glimpse of an officer. And not just any officer. It was the "Bum," Commander Bill Connors a weathered, salty character who spoke in low throaty growls. We could tell from the reactions of the upper jobs that this was not a man to be trifled with.

As the "Bum" wandered through the building, casting looks of disdain in all directions, we youngies reveled in this brief break from torture. I was sitting at my desk fighting back tears from the intense pain that was shooting through my face from my "nose to the wall" stint.

Never let them see you cry or sweat. It would be an invitation to turn up the pressure. Macho stoicism was an equally bad approach, looked upon by upper jobs as a challenge.

When Commander Connors had finished his all-too-short inspection and headed back to the ship, pandemonium broke out. "Back on your head.... Nose to the wall." "Here sir!.... Yes sir!... No sir!" The clock seemed to have stopped. This was the land of the thousand minute hour. Nine o'clock finally arrived.... 2100. What the hell did that mean? They even tell time differently here.

We were shortly back on the ship for formation on the main deck for check muster. It took about twenty minutes of "Here sirs: to get through the long roll call, before moving on to cleaning stations.

Cleaning stations had not yet been permanently assigned, and we were pushed hither and yon. I was much relieved to find that I was not heading back to the boiler room. I found myself, along with three of my classmates, sweeping down the main deck in the dark. Our upper job mentor was heaping abuse on us for our obvious lack of talent in such matters. His language was beyond the pale. After just one day, it was clear that this was only the norm.

I had grown up in the inner city and was no stranger to rough talk. However, cursing and swearing here on the school ship had been raised - or lowered, depending on your point of view - to new levels of inventiveness and imagination. It was common practice to take a two-syllable word, break it in the middle, and insert a curse for color and emphasis. In one day we had learned not to take offense. It was just the vernacular.

We all knew the next scheduled event was taps. "Now hear this, taps, lights out, silence about the decks and spaces. The smoking lamp is out in all berthing spaces." "This is as hard as it gets." That was of course, before I learned about hurricanes.

"Not so fast, young man." Many of us were handed pairs of shoes by upperclassmen with these orders: "I'll have these back in the morning with a gleaming spit shine." Those shoes looked as if the owners had walked across the country with them. But how could we do such a thing? It was bedtime. The lights were out and our shoe polishing kits were stowed away in our lockers. Rapid instruction solved all of those problems. Just below our berthing compartment was the locker space. Youngies could huddle down there in their skivvies and spit shine shoes in the beams of their flashlights. Posting an 86 watch was necessary, because if we were found up after taps it meant going to Captain's Mast and thus demerits. If we were found shining upperclassman's shoes and somehow implicated their owners in our stupidity, the unthinkable would happen. But what was the unthinkable? Never mind, it was also unspeakable. We already knew about the demerits. They were instruments of terror. We had one weekend off a month and ten to be to stack up those demerits. They were to fall on us from the heavens like a driving rain.

Down in between the lockers, while spit-shining shoes, we youngies were talking in whispers, forming the "classmate and shipmate bonds" that arose from the need for mutual protection and shared pain.

"How long does this go on?" Is it some kind of indoctrination and when will it end? A few of my classmates knew because of brothers that had preceded them at the Academy. The answer was sobering. "It lasts all year long. After the cruise it slacks up a bit, but you stay a youngie all year." After that was settled, we lapsed into silence, each lost in their own but common thoughts.

Three hundred and sixty-four days to go. It was beyond the scope of our imaginations.

About midnight, we crept through the ship and deposited the shoes under the bunks of the upperclassmen. Stealth and silence were critical. If we had awakened anyone, who knew what would follow. It was the earliest development of the school ship skill called "cozy." That was staying out of the way, bending with the system, and flowing through it with the lowest possible profile. As you passed through classes, the nuances changed. It was a complex skill. There was no higher praise from peers than to be labeled cozy.

Once the shoes had been silently deposited, we headed forward to our bunks. Sliding into that tiny space was another skill that had to be learned by trial and error. How do I get in without stepping on or waking everyone around me? No one was a natural. I opted for the "on the back position," and at about my third try, I had wedged myself into place.

The berthing compartment was small and had about one hundred midshipmen packed in as tightly as cord wood. It was August and very hot. I was dirty and reeking of diesel oil. My still sore and throbbing nose was just a few inches below the canvas bottom of the bunk above me. The sound of blowers, the snoring, and other noises from a hundred exhausted midshipmen filled the compartment. I could hear the continuously running water from the heads that were located about ten feet forward of my bunk. As I lay there sweating on top of my standard-issue woolen blanket, I thought, "I'll never be able to sleep here." Primal survival skills must have kicked in because I was unconscious in a matter of seconds. My last thoughts of a hurricane was started by a group of upper classmen returning from a run on the beach during the mid-watch. They entered the compartment, turned the fire hoses on full blast, and tried to blow us youngies out of our bunks Next we were roused from the sleep of the dead at first light by the 1MC, "Reveille, reveille, up all hands, heave out and trice up reveille. No one stirred. There was not a sign of life. Then, up from amidships came the sound of a gravely old man's voice. "Get outa da bunk, grab your socks, wake wakey, rise and shine." The man behind the voice appeared in the compartment. He was dressed in dirty rumpled khakis and he was smoking a pipe that was blowing sparks and ashes into the air like the stack of a coal burner. His poorly fitted false teeth were whistling and rattling, but his voice was strong. The same litany. "Get up or you'll be going up to see the old man."

SID

There was such a burst of activity and confusion that I had no time to dwell on how much I would grow to hate that routine, or the Master at Arms who was at its root, Sid Sanford, the devil reincarnated. If officers were the enemy, they were at least in the distance. Sid was always with us.

Climbing out of my bunk, stepping on those below me while the guy above was falling into me was a mad scramble. All the dungarees and shoes looked the same and sorting them out was awful.

The crescendo of yelling and howling was starting to pick up, directing us to "check muster on the pier."

"ONCE THERE WAS A YOUNGIE"

The "Bum" watched over us as we once again responded to the roll call. He had a way of looking at us as though we were something distasteful that he had just discovered on the bottom of his shoe. Clearly, he was a man of unpleasant disposition. It was much later, December in fact, when he was presiding over another check muster on the pier that he started to work to his full potential.

It was just breaking first light, and the wind was howling as it usually does at Buzzards Bay. I don't remember what the temperature was, except to say that it was painfully cold. Commander Connors decided that the time was right to check the stencils on our skivvies. Wearing another midshipman's gear was a serious offense and violators of that regulation were forever being sought out. We dropped our dungaree trousers to our ankles and stood there in ranks as the "Bum" trooped the line. A long stare at the skivvies' stencil was followed by piercing glare into the face of the wearer. It took a long time, but it was another building block for our new characters.

At the close of my second morning check muster we broke for cleaning stations. Without being told, I headed for the focsle and started to sweep. The upperclassmen had already begun to eat, so we youngies were alone. A quick sweep, stow gear, and go below to shower and shave. A simple enough thing, you might think. That was not so on the patrol gunboat *Charleston*.

It took a couple of weeks to figure out that a youngie could shave and shower in the morning only if he got up at least an hour before reveille. It was simple. Go to the quarter deck the night before and put in an early call. Your classmate on watch would come down and shake you out at 0500.

On our first visit to the forward head, my classmates and I were pretty confused and stood around watching the routine, trying to get the hang of things. The head and its devices were not of this century, There were no sinks. One took an enamel basin from a stack and filled it with cold water from a single tap. You then carried it to an open pipe whose end you placed in the water and slowly cracked a valve. Auxiliary steam bubbled in and heated the water. Then you got in line, waiting to put your basin into a metal frame that sat in front of a mirror. There were six positions for one hundred midshipmen. The word crowding took on a new meaning. While you were in line, any upperclassman would cut in just to get in front of you. It was called "jobbing the line." By the time you reached the mirror your water was cold. However, getting out of line to reheat it meant that you would lose your place. There were lots of ways to identify youngies, but the surest way was the cuts on their faces from cold shaves.

The showers were equally challenging. They had a single tap that emitted cold water from the nozzle. Once you had the water flowing, you manipulated a second valve to cut steam into the system to get the right temperature. That sounds simple enough but there was a hitch.

The water pump was of the old reciprocating type and the flow was uneven. It frequently paused in midstroke and the water stopped for a second or so. Just long enough to get a straight shot of steam out of the shower nozzle. No long and leisurely showers on this ship.

The new hands, the youngies, all left the heads that morning with bleeding faces and burnt skin, feeling neither clean nor refreshed. Our skills and timing needed to be developed to prevent such things from happening, but they lay in the future for us.

As we moved aft toward the mess decks, the morning meal was uppermost in our minds. We had been at the Academy for over twenty hours and hadn't had a single bite to eat. We queued up in the chow line that snaked its way through the berthing compartments onto the mess deck. Progress was slow because the upperclassmen kept "jobbing the line." It was a period of anxiety because feeding stopped, not when everyone had eaten, but purely by the clock. If you were stuck at the rear of the line when the morning meal was over, you didn't eat.

The other challenge associated with eating was the presence of upperclassman who had finished their meal, then simply demanded yours, sending you back to the rear of the line to get another for yourself. That worked only if Sid didn't notice. If he remembered that you had passed through previously, he sent you packing. Despite that, it was a good feeling when you drew up to the steam line. You picked up a steel compartmented tray, still very hot and greasy from the scullery, and plopped an equally hot bowl on it to carry a small packet of breakfast cereal.

Then you moved on to the bacon that had been cooked at 0430 and had the consistency of shingles. The fried eggs were stacked in a steam tray that had 8 inches of grease at its bottom. This was not brunch at the Ritz.

At the end of the line stood Sid who dispensed warm milk from an old enamel bucket that was hanging from the overhead by a piece of nine thread. One cup each. That was the absolute limit. The still warm cup into which it was poured made it all the more appetizing. Sid was growling and his pipe was aglow with the attendant ashes drifting into the milk bucket. "Move along... Move along... Keep the line moving." As though we had slowed down for the purpose of prolonging this delightful experience. Sid and his Filipino cohorts working the steam line were a surly lot who held all the midshipmen in very low esteem. They let us know of their bad opinion in no uncertain terms.

It was a poor meal but not by any measure the worst that I would experience over the next three years. That special memory was reserved for a dinner served during my last cruise, consisting of a single boiled potato and a can of sardines, all slapped down on my tray by the ever insolent and hostile MO.

Innocent of those things yet to come, I found a place at a mess deck table, asked permission to be seated, and started to eat. Only the day before, I would have turned up my nose at such fare, but hunger is a good sauce. I cleaned my tray.

We did have lots of coffee available in the mess decks. I was sent to get two cups for the upperclassmen at the table. When I returned, I waited my turn for a small can of condensed milk. These cans were set out on all the tables since fresh milk was far too precious to be used in coffee. As the upperclassman sitting across from me was adding condensed milk to his coffee, something came out of the can too quickly to be identified, and dropped into his cup. It only took a second to float to the top of the coffee. A roach! I wasn't stunned, I'd seen bugs before, but I will never forget the scene that followed. It will stay with me forever.

The upperclassman took a spoon, lifted the roach out of his coffee, snapped it onto the deck, and started to drink. I must have turned green because he said, "You'll get used to those things." In fact though, I never did. I hadn't had the time to get the ship into focus enough to realize that it was overrun with roaches. Trying to stay ahead of them was a three-year-long battle. We never even won a skirmish. They were everywhere. Because the ship's food was so poor and there was so little of it, personal snacks were secreted in every nook and cranny, It was formula for disaster and the roaches ruled.

The rest of the week went by slowly, but I was learning very fast. I learned how to splice line, clean boiler burner tips, chip paint, wipe bilge's, spit-shine shoes, steel wool tile decks, march in ranks, peel potatoes, stand an efficient 86 watch, roll and stop my clothes, stand on my head and sing, and support the full weight of my body on my nose and forehead. Most of all, I was convinced that I was a worthless tool.

In just a few short days I was made to believe that I was a simple wedge, part of a whole class filled with creatures of no value and only the tiniest speck of potential for any future growth. I was being molded and I didn't even know it. How could I? I was averaging four hours of sleep a night, my body was filthy, and I was starving. By the time the week was over, I knew my classmates who were in my watch section better than I ever knew my own brother. It was total immersion in madness, without a minute of your own, or a second to think. The process wasn't hard to swallow because it was being shoved down our throats. Digesting it all was another matter.

When Friday afternoon arrived, we were mustered on the pier dressed in our new khakis, less collar devices. No one thought we should be identified as midshipmen because we were so sorry looking. Our civilian clothing was packed in our bags. "Return them to your homes. Midshipmen do not have civilian clothes. Neither will they have a horse, a wife, or a mustache. Remember that!" "Yes sir!" "I can't hear you." "Yes sir!" "That's better." We were released to go on liberty with strict instructions to return to the ship not later than 2200 on Sunday evening. That was the official part.

Every youngie left with food orders from upperclassmen. "I'll have four tuna fish sandwiches... Bring me back three bologna and cheese and one ham on rye... Bring me back some instant coffee, three cans of deviled ham, and a loaf of bread... Got it?" "Yes sir!" "Good, because you are my food servant."

I trudged up the road and over the old wooden bridge that led to Buzzards Bay with my classmates. All but a few of us were hitchhiking home. It was a common method of travel for young people in those days.

"ONCE THERE WAS A YOUNGIE"

There were few cars. In fact, having one was rather a disadvantage. It meant that you ended up providing transportation service to the upperclassmen.

We shared an almost giddy feeling at our release. We were back in the real world after what seemed to be a very long time. I can't remember exactly what I did that weekend upon arriving home. I probably slept and ate in great measure. Neither can I recollect what was going through my mind. I think I had some image of the Massachusetts Maritime Academy being a local version of Annapolis. I had expected to be parading around in a gleaming white uniform with bands playing in the background, all in a pristine and orderly environment.

After only one week had passed there were no such illusions remaining. I had come to a hard place where the levels of discomfort, deprivation, and pain were very high. What I do remember very clearly was the arrival of Sunday afternoon. It was like the approach of an execution. I was getting ready to go back. The act of "going back" was probably the most significant act of self-discipline that had occurred in my young life. Although I surely didn't realize it at the time, it was one of those truly seminal events that shape one's future, that are passed through without recognition of their importance. At the time, I simply did not want to return to bedlam. But I did.

Because hitchhiking was uncertain in terms of time, I left home early and arrived at Buzzards Bay in the dusk of a beautiful summer evening. Uncertain steps took me back over the bridge and down the small country road toward the ship. We called it "leaving the world."

As I proceeded up the wooden finger pier, I could see first classmen lounging about the quarter deck. Vultures awaiting the arrival of prey. When I stepped onto the main deck I was promptly braced up and told to report on my weekend. "What did you bring back, young man?" The tuna fish sandwiches that were neatly wrapped in wax paper and tucked into a small brown bag were snatched out of my hand. I had a problem. The upperclassman who took the sandwiches was not the one who had ordered them. To protest on the basis of that sort of logic was out of the question. Stand by for heavy rolls.

I managed to avoid conflict until the word was passed for check muster. We fell into ranks on the main deck and the roll was called. There were lots of silences as my class's muster was called. The faint of heart had started to drop. A significant number had simply walked off during the first week. Many had reversed course on their first day.

One look at the *Charleston's* accommodations with the backdrop of first classmen attentions had been enough for some. Almost one hundred young men had started with my class. At the end of thirty days, nearly half were gone.

Of the 55 that remained to start our first cruise, 50 graduated three years later. The system found the weak early.

During that check muster, I also learned that the whole first class was back aboard. Good grief, we had been dealing with only the leave period duty section and restricted men. What would life be like now that we would be receiving the full attention of the entire class?

The question was quickly answered for me. The upperclassman who had made me his food slave showed up looking for his tuna sandwiches. My feeble excuses were rejected out of hand and only seemed to infuriate my food master. "Down below and into your dungarees, you stupid oaf. I'm going to give a lesson in following orders."

In ten minutes I was down on the deck plates with an armful of rags. "Into the bilge's, young man." That was the first time I'd been given such an order, but it was not to be the last.

Cleaning bilge's under a steaming boiler is a task that has to be experienced to be understood. It's cramped, very hot, and requires kneeling or lying down in the oily water sloshing around on the bottoms. Hot condensate drips down and falls onto the bilge cleaner with regularity. It was not hot enough to scald, but it did hurt. It was the death of a thousand cuts.

At about midnight the midshipman on watch ordered me out of the bilges. I think the upperclassman that put me in there had forgotten me. "Get out of here and turn in. Don't get caught up after taps by the OD or your ass will be in a bag. Got it?" "Yes Sir!"

After my silent passage through a sleeping ship I was standing next to my bunk. Passing back and forth very quietly were my classmates who had been jobbed for a wide variety of tasks. After taps, a shadowy world of youngies was moving about the ship doing the upperclassmen's bidding.

I was trying to figure out what to do with my dungarees. They were soaked with oil and other effluvia. They were beyond rescue by the strongest of detergents. Roll them up and put them on a locker top. I'd developed a youngie essential - a bilge outfit. They were to get some heavy use in the months ahead.

After I had deposited my dungarees in a safe place, I was making my way to the head with a towel and soap. I was filthy. As I entered the berthing compartment, I heard a loud whisper: "86! The OD is coming." I made a mad dash and dived into my bunk, stepping on a number of people in the process. No one showed up. It was s false alarm. It must have been about 0100 by then, and I drifted off to sleep clutching my soap and towel, covered with fuel oil. Welcome home young man.

My last thoughts of that day centered on the words of my upper class mentor. "Did you have a good liberty?" "Yes Sir!" "Good, because it will be a long time before you go down that road again." That prediction came to pass.

Tolstoy said, "Man is the animal that can get used to anything.: He was right. Of course, he neglected to mention that it wasn't easy. Neither was life on the school ship but it could be endured.

The next three years were made up of a thousand stories, but none of them have remained with me as vividly as my first week's adventures.

Life did get better. I learned a lot of things. How to survive by being cozy and getting better at "playing the game." The upperclassmen lost some of their interest in the hazing that was not allowed at the Maritime Academy after the cruise.

They were busy preparing for their license examinations and graduation. Perhaps they also thought that they had completed the job of building our characters.

We youngies, my classmates, had been woven tightly into a mutual protection society by ten months of shared adversity. There was probably a sense of confidence built up among us because we had endured. We had the ability to live, study, go to sea, and do all of the other things demanded from midshipmen, while under great pressure and stress. Soon we would be swaggering second classmen. That took a lot of heat off the daily routine.

All we had to be alert for now were the officers and Sid. That and dealing with the environment wasn't an easy task. But it was relatively less aggravation than the day-to-day, minute-to-minute attention of an upper class with whom we had lived cheek to jowl.

Tolstoy had it right. Some years later, when I was a young Naval Officer, I was berthed back aft in a destroyer in what was called the "Ensign's Locker." Three Ensigns shared the stateroom, and my bunkmates were appalled by the spartan conditions. One was from the Naval Academy and the other came from Amherst College. I was amused by their complaints. To me, life in the Navy seemed like a bed of roses. But then again, I was from the *Charleston*, and had been annealed in a very tough crucible.

I am unsure of why I started to write this story. It is a tale of life in a world long since past, and it has no bearing or relation to today's Academy. Progress and enlightenment took hold many years ago, and the school has operated in a sane and reasonable fashion for a long time. Certainly it is strict and stern in comparison to other state colleges. The nature of the professions for which its cadets are educated, demand such training. But it is definitely operating in the vanguard of the present times.

In the days of which I write, the Academy was run by men who were graduates from classes of the 1920s. They had served their time as midshipmen and cadets on the sailing ship *Nantucket*. In turn, they had gone to sea in an era when American merchant seamen were treated like bond slaves. The lot of those men had remained relatively unchanged for a hundred years.

"ONCE THERE WAS A YOUNGIE"

When those officers returned to the Academy as instructors, with licenses that read "Master of Steam and Sail," they recreated for us the world that they knew. As I look back on it all, I realize that we were locked in a time warp. The Class of 1959 was being prepared for life in the previous century. That wasn't all bad. Because when we did graduate, we were ready for much harder existence than we encountered. Unlike us, the rest of the world had moved on and become a kinder more gentle place.

Since I have returned to the Academy myself, I am frequently tempted to tell at least a short version of this tale to cadets. I can't imagine why, except to perhaps let them know that their own lot in life is not so bad, I try to resist doing that because I remember how I felt when I heard such things from graduates of the *Nantucket*. Generally, when you are in pain yourself, the knowledge that someone else was once in greater agony provides you with little relief. And so, in the end, the only real reason to tell this story is that old sailors are prone to do so. It is the warp and woof of the profession.

The End
[RADM M. J. Bresnahan]

August 14, 1956   There is gonna be a little band concert on the fantail tonight. It's always a lot of fun and puts a little life in the daily routine.

The youngies are working on the brass binnacle for the ring dance. You'd be surprised how it shines with a little elbow power and young strength.

August 14, 1956   I just received your letters from the hands of the dirty old man. He and I have started the year off fine. He has me before the mast this week.

The courses are "horribly difficult", I have flunked three out of four of the tests that we have had this past week. We are getting more work now than we ever had before. It seems I have less and less time to read and write to you.

August 15, 1956   Ship's store opened yesterday so I picked up a pair of shoes for Dad and "T" shirts for Paul. I've been waiting for "Honest Al", otherwise known as "Arm Pit AL", to open for weeks.

I'm gonna sign off now and take a break from my professional sea-going subjects and read "Away All Boats!"

A few youngies have decided to write to you! Imagine that! Enclosed you'll find a few words from several third jobs. How they ever got out of high school I'll never know! Read them and please have a little pity, "English Classes" start tonight on the "mid"! Note: A total of fourteen letters were written in the following months, mostly on the "midwatch."

Dear Louise,

I am very sorry for this poor excuse called handwriting. I'm obliging with Mr. Hogan's request for an envelope and a stamp. I was compelled to address this envelope, please excuse for I am <u>mucho</u> sorry for this mess.

Signed
Midsn. Earl N. Baker, 3rd class

August 21, 1956   Back on the 1-50 list again. Failed Trig again! Also was notified today that I goofed Friday on my Spanish. Damn, I'll get through it somehow but what a pain. I have no interest in either subject! Gotta do it; they're required for the degree, the degree is required for a Navy commission, and graduation is required to take the mate's exam.

August 22, 1956   My luck has been running terrible for the last few weeks and continued this morning. It seems I had the <u>4 to 8</u> this morning. While making an entry in the logbook I made a mistake in grammar, mis-used a comma, etc. I'll go to Captain's Mast Friday and probably get 10 demerits and another weekend aboard. If it's Labor Day I will at least get Monday off, I hope! Captain Woodland stated   "No excuses!"   "Get it right!"

...and more letters from Bob.

My entry was as follows:

0745 - Received on board one box (1) of pipe fittings and four (4) boxes of small stores from the Boston Navy Yard and Nepco Co.

It should have been written as follows:

0745 - Received on board one box (1) of pipe fittings from the Boston Navy Yard and four (4) boxes of small stores from Nepco Co.

The "Bird" spotted the errors right off the bat!   Oh Well!

August 23, 1956   I have just finished typing the special request for liberty commencing at 1600 the 13th September and expiring at 0800 the 17th September in order to be with you as much as possible. Pray, as I will, that it comes through... I wrote a letter to your father finally, as you know. I hope it makes him feel better about your coming up here.

Commander Conners

Great news, I came into 4th place for the summer term. However, if the new subjects do not get any easier I will be the anchor man for sure.

August 25,1956   I am glad that your father liked the letter. It took me a good two hours to write that out, after the third try. I didn't want the innocence and virtue part to be so obvious, however I thought your father would like the idea of it.

The "dirty old man" is Cdr. Connors and it is with him that all my trouble stems from. When I say that he will have me before the mast, it means that he will have me do all the dirty work as if I were an ordinary seaman. In the sailing ships' days, to ship before the mast was to ship as a seaman, while to ship after the mast was to ship as an officer or cadet. ..If I said he would have me before the mast, it would mean to bring me to the Captain's Mast for disciplinary action. This he quite frequently does.

I found out today that the boys have ordered 60 quarts of liquor for the party after the Ring Dance. I hope that they have included some scotch in that order. [The word "order" was written over in this letter, as if he wrote it incorrectly. JS] I can spell "order", and I have been put on report at least three times for disobedience to them.

The weather has been alternately hot and cold for the past five or six days. As a result, I have a good cold. I coughed last night and it started my nose bleeding it didn't stop for two hours. If this keeps up I will be dead before you get here.

The articles on Elvis have been very interesting indeed. I believe the man is a complete fool.

Note: 1956 Elvis Presley had his first No 1 hit, Heartbreak Hotel.

September 10, 1956   Pictures were taken today. The first six were in cadet one stripe boards, the next six could be in Navy or "Merchie" uniforms. I'd rather be seen in a "Merchie" costume than as a lowly "Enswine", in 90 day wonder dress.

I'm back again - no news! Nobody seems to know when the "Boys" will get around to coming down and hear our case. The longer they put it off the worse it's gonna be for us. Maybe they won't come down this week and I'll still have my stripe for the Ring Dance?

THE NIGHT BEFORE WEDNESDAY (or Reilly's Rabble-rousers)

Twas the night before Wednesday,
And all through the ship,
Not a light was aglow,
Nor a movement of <u>lip;</u>

All of the youngies were sleeping,
Each tucked in his bed,
While visions of turn-to,
Dance through his head;

The night watch was set,
By the gangway with care,
The rounds were in progress,
"The Bird" in his lair;

Twas easy to see,
That if all went to plan,
A full night of slumber,
Was offered each man;

Just a little past ten,
There was a disturbance,
<u>And to those who awoke,</u> *
It caused a pertubance;

It seemed that up forward,
Where slept Mr. Meyer,
Some dark colored Mick,
Was holding a chair;

…feathers everywhere!

Now it happened by chance,
And mostly by luck,
In a round about way,
There came a loud "Cluck";

A rustling of feathers,
A flutter of wings,
A voice that demanded,
"Who is it that sings?"

A look of amazement,
A cry of alarm,
As through their shocked minds,
Ran the twenty-third Psalm;

The rest was procedure,
The ax had descended,
The reign of the "Choir",
Had suddenly ended;

A lesson was learned,
By the expense of a few,
If a Mica wants a song,
Its a good time to screw:

"86"

Written by Hank Sweet   Cadet Lt., 1st Division   * Censored(?) and "slightly" revised in 1956

Note: Reilly got away...free...with a bunch of other guys...

As the hatch opened..."Is that Woody?"..."Yes Hogan it is I!" "I'll see you in my stateroom in ten minutes in dress uniform!" "You're on report!" "Yes SIR!" Just singing a few songs and now I'm up for a 100 demerits. Damn!

How well I remember...It seems to me it was "What do you do with a Drunken Sailor", sung in the 'round', starting on the "Port Aisle" that did us in!!! For once in their lives the "young men" were making sufficient noise that the "86" was too soft...and too late. Never did I expect to come out of that with 10 for "up after taps." Who said that politics didn't play a part in what happened to cadets? Wasn't the "Black Rils" wearing 'stripes' at that time??? I know the only thing I ever got was Cadet CPO during the cruise and they wouldn't let me sew on the CPO Badge on my uniform. Geez, there were tail feathers all over the Mess Deck that night!!!!

[Pete Readel]

Many weeks later my "trial" was held in the Admiral's quarters on the main deck aft of the quarter deck. I remember standing at parade rest outside the door to officer's quarters on the starboard side for a very long period of time. The Board reviewed the charge, "hazing the third class by singing after taps." Captain Woodland described the incident in detail while I waited on the main deck. Finally I was called in and allowed to plead my case. I stated that I was sorry, and that I had indeed had the young men singing after taps. I then explained how I felt that they were downhearted and depressed and needed a boost to their morale. I thought a few popular songs might brighten the end of a long day. They asked a few questions, grunted in unison, and dismissed me. I wasn't before the board more than five minutes before returning to my assigned waiting station.

While I awaited my fate my classmates two levels above on the 02 deck were giving me the "thumbs up and OK" hand signals. While the case was discussed two decks below they had their ears to several electrical conduits, listening. These conduits acted just like a voice tube. I pretty much knew the verdict before I heard it from the Board. I was given a warning and the case was dismissed! I was even allowed to keep my cadet ensign stripe.

[Ben Hogan]

Letters to Lou...

YOUR TAXES PRESERVE SEA TRADITION

Boston Traveler Features - Sept. 12, 1956 (Unable to scan or copy the 4 old photos accompanying this article)

THE SEA'S A HARD TEACHER, but the sturdy cadets of the Massachusetts Maritime Academy master her rules and whims in their tough three-year training course. No small part of their training is life aboard the training ship Charleston (left) either moored in her berth at Buzzards Bay or on her long annual cruise. Other vessels small and large, also provide part of the training in practical seamanship which supplements intensive classroom work. For example, Cadet A.S. Gaton (center) of Wellesley Hills takes a turn at the wheel of a sub chaser.

Aboard the Charleston or in the barracks ashore (right), study, discipline, and self-discipline are the rule of life for these future masters of the seven seas. Rigid schedule enables them to win college degrees in three years.

Mr. and Mrs. Massachusetts Taxpayer are chipping in to keep the states gallant seafaring tradition.

The money goes to train some 200 cadets at the Massachusetts Maritime Academy at Buzzards Bay.

The cadets live in a salty, shipboard atmosphere on the training ship Charleston.

Sea-going military discipline turns them into sharp capable officers for the nations warships and merchant vessels.

Others become airline navigators, Panama Canal Pilots, or executives in waterfront jobs ashore.

But the modern age of science also puts some of these sailormen in jobs far from the sea.

Such land-locked posts include engineering jobs for refrigerator companies, power plants, and other industrial firms.

But, whatever their future job, all cadets go through rigorous training that crams a four-year college course into three.

The spice of foreign travel evens the tough routine.

Each cadet goes on three three-month foreign cruises during his training. Two are to the Caribbean, one to the Mediterranean area.

Each cadet eventually graduates with an armful of official papers. A bachelor of science degree, a merchant marine officer's license and a Naval Reserve commission as ensign.

The variety of papers indicate the number of government agencies that play a role in the Academy's operation.

The Academy is partially subsidized by the federal government and is administered by the Maritime Administration. It is run by the Massachusetts Department of Education.

Massachusetts pays the lion's share of the Academy's expenses. The 1957 budget appropriation sets aside $355,000 for the school.

Uncle Sam pays the state $25,000 a year to help defray these expenses. The federal government also pays for major repairs to the training ship Charleston.

In addition, most students are enrolled in the Naval Reserve. The federal government pays the state a ration allowance of about $200 a year for each reservist.

Each student also pays tuition.

…bachelor of science degree.

First year men pay $400 when they enter the Academy. That goes for books, a $150 tuition fee and some clothing and equipment. In addition they pay about $200 for a dress uniform, making a first year cost of $600.

Second and third year students pay $300 each year. Half of that is for renewals on books and equipment.

Newly enrolled cadets become part of a tradition that goes back to 1893.

Most of the some 4,000 graduates since then have become top sea dogs.

The sea is never far from the students. They live on board the Charleston moored to the state pier.

A new class of about 75 students enters each Aug. 1. Ninety per cent go on to graduate.

Many are following a family tradition by attending the academy. One was the son of Capt. John W. Thompson of West Yarmouth, academy executive officer.

His son, Richard, graduated in 1947 and has since been around the world on the Navy cruiser Worcester.

The academy's commandant is Rear Admiral Julian D. Wilson, a veteran of the regular Navy. He runs a taut and happy ship.

The 20-piece academy band plays martial music every morning at 8. But it is not "wake-up" music; the cadets get up at 6 to clean their quarters, stand inspection, and eat breakfast.

The cadets then go ashore for instruction in a large classroom building on the state pier. They study in two classes, both leading to a bachelor of science degree.

One class-future deck officers-studies seamanship and navigation. The other studies marine and electrical engineering   The grind of studies keeps students busy during their three years. They even attend classes while making the yearly cruises.

Third year men (seniors) get three weekends off each month. First and second cadets get one and two free weekends respectively each month.

This rugged schedule is necessary to complete four years of college training in three. It also familiarizes cadets with the working routine of shipboard life.

Cadets stand watches. The corps undergoes infantry drill every Friday afternoon as the student band plays.

It isn't all a grind though.

The cadets football team plays such colleges as New Haven State Teachers, New Britain State Teachers and Worcester Polytech. The big game each year is with the Maine Maritime Academy.

There are no married men among cadets. Applicants must be single and remain so while enrolled.

Graduates of the Academy have served in every war since the Spanish-American War.

One was Capt. Emery Rice of the class of '97. He commanded the transport Mongolia that sank the first German submarine in World War I.

Academy men get the top in peacetime, too. Capt. F.J. Devlin, class of '20, is general manager of the United States Line and Capt. Phillip Fanning is vice president of Jarks Corp. of new York, a stevedoring firm.

Letters to Lou...

Fall 1956   One of the items required on lifeboats is a signal pistol with a lanyard attached. Twelve parachute signal cartridges were to be kept in a portable watertight metal case; cartridges to be: 20,000 candle power, height 150 feet and burn 30 seconds. Ref: American Seaman's Manual.

On a nice calm rare sunny day we were treated to a demonstration of practical seamanship. We were actually going to fire a Very Pistol under the supervision of Commander Conners. The class was assembled astern of the Charleston on the corner of the concrete pier. We were shown how to load the pistol, extend your arm, how to test the wind and pull the trigger. A cadet was selected to put the flare in the air. He followed instructions and fired a round out and over the canal. A cheer went up as the parachute opened and started to descend. Then the wind shifted! It reversed direction and started to drift back towards us. It went over us and landed on the hood of a car in the parking lot. The "Bum's" car!!! We all ran to inspect the damage and to get the thing off his hood. The flare pealed the paint back and left an elongated bare spot about fifteen inches forward of the driver's side windshield. More than a few choice verbal curses were directed at the cadet responsible. The pistol in my hand felt like it weighed a ton. The question was "will I ever get see the sun rise again?" I told him I was sorry but I don't think he heard me. My classmates vanished! I was in shock and repeated that I was sorry! After all I did follow his instructions!

He stopped steaming when I told him I could fix it, my father was in the auto repair business. I drove the car home Friday night. Early Saturday morning we worked on it and re-painted the hood. I returned it to the parking lot Sunday night as good as new

[Ben Hogan]

RING DANCE

September 15, 1956   The biggest social event in the three years as a Midshipman's life at the Academy is his own Ring Dance. The ceremony symbolizes being wedded to the sea, with the placing of his ring in the water from the seven seas of the world by his escort of the evening. It is old in the tradition of the Academy; it has a meaning of deep significance to all those that take part. The ceremony is impressive with the second classmen providing a color guard.

J .Ferrera, F. Graham, J. Gillen, L. Kennedy
and Lovely Ladies

MASSACHUSETTS
MARITIME ACADEMY
Class of 1957
Main Ballroom
Sheraton Plaza Hotel
Boston, Mass
CLASS OFFICERS
PresidentRichard Greer
Vice President   John F. Flaherty
Secretary   Richard Weaver
Treasurer   Forbes Graham
DANCE COMMITTEE
Chairman
Lincoln M. Kennedy
Committee Peter Readel Robert Strautman
Robert K. Rielly Forbes Graham James McCarthy

From: Class of "57'
To: Invited guests
Via: Company of Midshipmen
Subject: Ring Dance
1. The following is hereby announced.   Respectfully Submitted
2000 Commence Dance   Class of "57"
2100 Commence Ring Ceremony
PATRONS:
2215 Commence Intermission   Mr .and Mrs. Richard Gillan, Mr. Chester Lopaus
2245 Commence Dancing   Mr. and Mrs. Ernest Strautman, Mr. and Mrs. Joseph L. Kenny,
2400 Taps   Mr. and Mrs. Daniel Sullivan.

RING DANCE HONOR GUARD

Jane Smith - Bob Stickney

...one hell of a party.

September 17, 1956 Monday after the Ring Dance. I've got a study period now and it's my first chance to drop a line. After talking to a few of the guys please <u>excuse</u> and let me <u>apologize</u> for anything that might have been said or done Saturday night!

About that wild time, first I got home O.K., parked the car out front and fell asleep with a blanket in the chair in the living room. I remember when I got in the hands of the clock were straight up and down. Around seven-thirty I woke up and just happened to look out the window. A gray form was leaning over my engine and tapping something with a wrench. At first I thought somebody was striping my engine for parts so I bound out of the chair and made for the door. At the door I took a second look and saw it was my father working on it so I went back to my emergency bed.

I finally got up about eight-thirty and got my gear together. Around 9:10 Roffey showed up with a big head after dragging his father out of bed. We had a cup of coffee and talked to my folks a while and left at 9:30. They said they had a good time and left long before we did. Made it down here in one hour and forty minutes never going over 60 mph. Nobody was on the road and it was easy driving considering my head and lack of sleep. Roffey slept most of the way!

When we got back, Manning was still not aboard. Joe Fee was three minutes over leave and put on report. On his way down he saw a bad accident about thirty miles from here. As he went by he saw a guy with his head split open so he stopped. After looking in the car he found   Russ Manning in the back seat suffering from a bad back and shock. The cops took both Russ and the driver to the hospital. Russ still hasn't called in or shown up? I guess he was hitch-hiking and riding in the back seat.

Bob Sarnie belted his car before ever getting to the dance. St. Pierre was driving down Washington Street in Salem doing about 50 mph and hit a parked car which in turn hit another car for a total loss of two cars and about $1900. He came back all stitched up and was sent to sick bay. The state cops took him to court this morning. Nobody was hurt as he was all alone after dropping his girl off.

After the ball had ended two cadets were booked at the local station house, two wound up in Boston City Hospital. It would take me hours to write about what happened, I'll tell you about it later, but it all took place about five minutes after we left.

Damage to the rooms have been estimated from $250 to $500. The Admiral will probably get one tremendous combination letter, bill, and require a letter of explanation. We'll have to pitch in and pay the bill!

The hotel employees found some guy under the bed in a blue suit and some gal in the closet in a gown. She was fine except for a big head and not knowing quite who she was or who she was with!

Remember the bell hop and the house detective outside the room who spoke about calling the cops? Well the house detective had just been thrown out (I didn't see it) and really took a beating.

Do you remember Mahoney dancing on the TV with the lamp shade on his head? I heard about it later (I missed that, too).

How much of this did you see or remember? Maybe we should compare notes? All I remember are vague shots of different things and Hank running into the door (splitting it up the middle) after we were caught watering a potted palm in the passageway.

After all that was done and what happened, I hope you had a good time and are not too offended! I should have taken you home a lot sooner than I did! I know it's too late now but next time we'll leave a lot earlier! That was a once in a lifetime--- <u>and once is enough!!!</u>

PS: One of the cops that broke up the party told Jim McCluskey, after looking the place over, that he wished he was off duty <u>cuz it looked like</u> one <u>hell of a party!</u>

Letters to Lou…

September 18, 1956   I think that everyone in the academy, from the officers down to the cooks, have spoken to me about the girl that I escorted to the Ring Dance. You certainly have made a hit up here, especially with the Stickney family. Even my grouchy old father said that you were a very nice young lady.

September 19, 1956   Oh, that white gown of yours might come in handy say in August next year! Can't you kinda have it fixed up somehow(add a few more hoops and a little lace here and there) and convert it to a wedding dress? I kinda like that gown and hate to see it go to waste in a closet somewhere. See what you can do huh! A white gown, a few flowers, and a white "job" suit might be just the thing for the great day! What do you think huh?

Congratulations on your graduation. The world can always use another great nurse. Debated about jumping ship to get you a card, but didn't dare, I'm in enough trouble now. Sorry, really sorry! Also really sorry about missing your graduation...again I don't dare jump ship. I couldn't get to and from Medford without missing formation or check muster.

September 20, 1956   The Board of Commissioners have not arrived as of yet. They have postponed the final bout until next week. I am getting awful tired of waiting for them.

I got proofs from the pictures that were taken at the dance and have a beautiful shot of your back. I also have the proofs from my graduation pictures and as soon as I have them made up I will send you one, if you would care to have it.

September 21, 1956   I had my first class with the dirty old man this week, today, and after class he stopped to tell me that he did come down to see Mr. Page on Sunday [Note: Refers to the Sunday of the Ring Dance. JS] and that Mr. Page told him that he would not give me permission to stay with you, but he would not put me on report if I did not come back. It's a great time to find that out.

As the commissioners have not yet come, I am still free to go home this weekend...

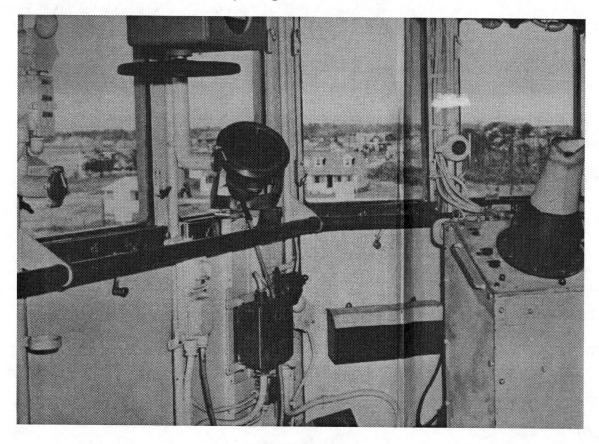

PILOT HOUSE

September 23, 1956   Here it is Sunday night the start of mid-term week. Next Monday we'll take the ship to Boston for dry-dock and repairs. It's gonna be great to get <u>off every</u> <u>night</u> <u>for a month</u>...let's hope! Between my duty week (3rd week in Oct) and maybe five to ten days restricted for that singing deal in the compartment, my time in Boston will probably be taken up pretty nicely. Ten days in East Boston is better than three months in Buzzards Bay!

Thursday we'll know for sure! The "B Of C" has a lot on their minds besides our case. One second job is up for cheating on a youngie final exam. Putignano is up for marks and his eighth offense for unauthorized absence from class - 6 X 8 or 48 demerits. Four second jobs are to see them about changing from deckies to snipes. Twenty of my classmates are up for failing <u>three or more subjects</u> last term with one more week to pass the make-up exams. Manning is gonna be a second job "again" after failing the second try to pass the navigation make-up. Harrington has a fight with them about football this year - will there or will there not be a football team next year?

They are also faced with the problem of the cruise route January 10th and repairs to the Chun whether she'll make it or not? In other words they'll have a full day down here.

No doubt my next title will be "Cadet Ensign Retired" or Midshipman Hogan member of the "Century Club."

September 24, 1956   ...Another shot of us at the Ring Dance has come down and this time more than your back is visible. I shall have it made up and send it to you if you would like it.

Starting Monday, my friend, my address shall be U.S.T.S. Charleston, Bethlehem Ship Yard, East Boston, Mass. That will be for a week. Then it will be somewhere else in Boston, just where I am not sure.

I have to see the commissioners tomorrow and will send you the results as soon as I have them.

September 26, 1956   This has been a trying week for me here at the academy. The Board of Commissioners came down yesterday and tried every case except for mine. I was in a very nervous state all day waiting for them to call me before them, but it never happened.

This does not mean that we are through with this thing, but it does mean, at least I hope it means, that our case had very little significance to the jolly captains from Boston. I think we should find out what is going to happen to us before the week is out.

September 27, 1956   [Note: Bob is trying to figure a way to come to New Orleans over the Christmas holidays. JS] Thank you for your concern about my ride down there at Xmas but if I go in uniform the railroad will charge me $67.50 for a round trip. Thirty hours in a seat will be hard, but it will be worth it if I can see you once again.

Rumor, we might go to Mobile or even back to New Orleans this year. However, Houston is still in the air.

Still no word from the jolly captains, perhaps they have neglected us.

October 2, 1956   Honey, the dear old Charleston has been up on the blocks for less than a day and already she looks like a piece of Swiss cheese. I was checking the hull with the "dirty old man" today and he went to test a spot with his little hammer. As he lifted the hammer away from the hull, a stream of dark black oil followed it out and hit him right in the face. I laughed so hard I nearly fell out of the bucket. Needless to say that my laughing did not please him at all , but I couldn't help it. Honest.

Met a rebel chief at dry-dock this morning, and he was very arrogant!

October 4, 1956   I don't know what the Commissioners are going to do about us, but from the looks of things, they have forgotten about us.

The poor old Charleston is really getting a working over here at the yard. We have found some holes in the side that are so big that I am going to have them measured for venetian blinds and use them for portholes. Seriously, though, the ship is in tough shape.

Letters to Lou…

I should use this extra time to get a little ahead in my studies; however, as of now I have done nothing but eat lots of Italian sandwiches.

I am glad that the dolphin is not able to smell. If he could he would leave my ring. I have been working in the bottom of the peak tanks, and I smell like Hogan's goat.

[Note: Nostalgia and inclusion. JS] You should go on Queen for a Day and tell them you want enough money to commute to Boston. I can go on the Heartline show and do the same.

October 6, 1956 The Charleston is still in the dry-dock and will be for the next week or so. Therefore, there are no phone connections. *[Note: Bob was trying to figure a way to phone me on my birthday, Oct. 13th, but he had the duty that day, and there were no phones he could use near the ship. He decided to try to phone me on Oct. 10th instead. JS]*

Speaking about the Char., there are over 28 holes in the hull which are going to be fixed at a cost to the state of $25,000.

October 6, 1956 Good News! It's very doubtful that we will make the cruise in the Charleston this year! The Chun has not passed the Coast Guard inspection yet and unless the Coast Guard changes its mind it won't! The Admiral said today that the commissioners are discussing a P-1 (troop transport ship) that is now on the Hudson River in upstate New York. Judging from what he said if we get it we will leave Buzzards Bay on the Chun in January and go up the Hudson to get it. It would take at least a month (probably two) to exchange gear from ship to ship. That would leave us about a month for a short shake-down cruise to Cuba and around the Gulf and then back to Boston for final adjustments.

Let's hope it works out that way! The Chun is on its last legs and weekends home in Jan. and Feb. wouldn't be hard to take! Just don't get your hopes too high yet, lets wait until they make it official.

October 8, 1956 A couple of young men had a little brawl on the main deck today. One broke his nose (or I should say his classmate broke it for him) while the other kid can't see out of his left eye. They were really going at it for a while there! They won't get liberty for a while. The Captain usually gives ten to fifty demerits at mast for that sort of thing. Fifty will mean more than two months aboard for them.

Next week will be a short one with Monday being a holiday and the Newport Navy Damage Control and Fire Fighting School coming at the end of the week.

October 9, 1956 Moby Dick was playing in Lynn not too long ago; however I was financially embarrassed at the time and was not able to see it.

I wish that you wouldn't pick on my appetite the way that you do. It is what keeps me strong and healthy. Not only that, but I am a small eater compared to some of my family.

October 11, 1956 The Charleston has finally come out of the dry-dock after three fruitless attempts. Each time the yard filled the dock with water so that we could get out, the ship took so much water that the lower level of the engine room was completely under water. Well, the leaks are all fixed now and we are ready for another year's run, as far as the hull is concerned at any rate. There is still a lot of work to be done on the engines and rigging.

[Note: About this time Bob started including LKUF ("little known and uninteresting facts) in his letters, i.e., that dolphins can't smell, etc. The following is one of those. JS]

Did you know that the Vikings visited Buzzards Bay in l007 AD? They were looking for Vinland, but when they got a look at sandy and barren Cape Cod, they turned around and went back to Iceland.

Would you consider living in the Canal Zone? I understand that the Navy has all sorts of facilities down there now - schools, churches, clubs, and things like that. It is a civil service job and pays $15,000 a year.

…no more thumbing allowed.

October 14, 1956 Jane, during the ten day Christmas leave there has to be 22 men a day on the ship. Not only this, but the Admiral has an order to the effect that each man has to have at least one day's duty but not more than three.

October 15, 1956 All sorts of things have been happening around here but as far as I can find out we are still going to leave here for Buzzards Bay on schedule. We will leave Boston on Monday 21 October 1956 and classes will resume back at the Bay on Tuesday 22, October, 1956. October is almost over and then we have only November and December to wait for.

I should like to call you again real soon but I am broke and will not be home to earn money for a few weeks. The reason for that is that Mr. Page believes that I am a rogue, also, and put me on report this morning for shirking duty. Just for laughs Greer, Reilly and myself are going to think up some ridiculous excuse to tell the Captain. It will get us more demerits to be sure, but the poor Captain is so concerned about the condition of this ship that he has not smiled for weeks.

I was not glad to find out yesterday that the Charleston is taking a foot of water an hour in the bilges. This was due to some strain on the keel while the ship was on the dry dock. By the way, some fool pulled one of the many switches here yesterday, and one of the yard's dry docks is now permanently sunk. No lives lost, but a lot of money.

October 20, 1956 Classes will start on Monday, much to my sorrow, but I suppose that it is better now than later. I shall have to do a lot more concentrating on my work in the next eight weeks than I have done in the past eight weeks. I should like to be accepted back in the academy for the engineering course but one has to be in the top of his class to do so.

October 22,1956   Things have changed again! We were given the cruise ports unofficially today. Nothing to write about since most of the ports are terrible! Mostly Navy ports and three stateside ports.

October 23, 1956 We have just finished a class with the Captain and he told us about hundreds of good jobs that are open to graduates of the Massachusetts Maritime Academy. It makes me feel very good.

Mid-term marks have come out and I had better get on the ball and do some work or I will flunk out of this place. I should like to be able to [tell] you when we see each other again that I have come out in the top of my class. It is going to take a lot of work, however. If I can stay in the top third of my class I can be accepted back for engineering without much trouble.

[Note: He is always dreaming up some scheme to get time together. They rarely work, however. JS] Jane, if you are able to take four days of me, and if you and I both write to the Commissioners saying that we are engaged to be married, they should give the Admiral an order to let me off the ship all four days we are in Mobile. That is a long-winded sentence.

The doctor has been worried over the amount of auto accidents that the midshipmen have gotten into. He spoke to the Commissioners about it and very soon, I believe, there will be no thumbing allowed or any cars allowed on the academy grounds.

I have been swindled out of five dollars for the 1956 yearbook. The Admiral has given an order that every midshipman shall buy the 1956 yearbook for the price of five dollars. We hope to make enough money on ads this year to give the book away.

Johnny Fitz told me to give you his best, and he hopes that you still love me, for he says all I talk about is you...Mr. Hunt told me if I don't get off the ship in Mobile and meet it in Florida, I am a fool.

October 26, 1955 I am writing to you from Butler's Cove here at the end of the canal. I have the 8-12 watch of a couple of boats out here tonight. It is damn cold, and I have a fire going. The smoke kept getting into my eyes as I was reading your letter.

I wish that you were here, honey. It is very romantic. The sky is covered with stars and the skyline of the bay is just beautiful.

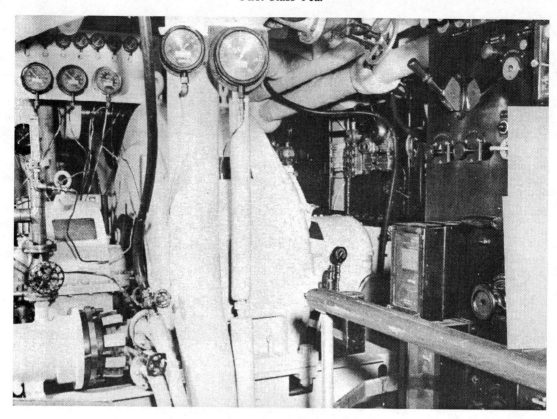

ENGINEERING SPACES

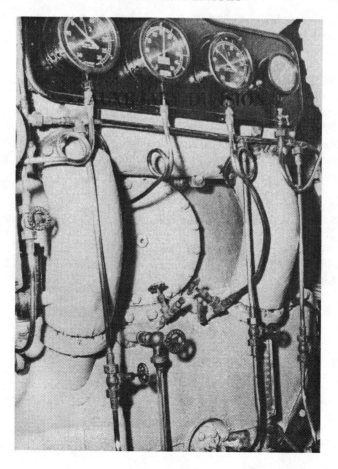

…Schlitz.

There has been a gale wind in this area for a few days. A couple of men were working over the side in a punt today and drifted into the wind and current. Consequently they floated out to sea. A pulling boat was sent after them and could not row back with the boat in tow. They pulled into Butler's Cove and then waited for someone from the ship to pick them up. The men were exhausted from rowing and from the shots that they were given this morning.

I received 48 demerits today and won't be going home until Thanksgiving. Besides the shirking duty, I got into an argument with the dirty old man. That is the main reason that I am out here this evening.

October 28, 1956   I met J.J. and Tony at 4 PM after driving like a madman. I'm just gonna have to leave earlier from now on! Anyway we made it with plenty of time to spare.

October 29, 1956   I am writing this during noon hour so I can jump ship this afternoon and mail the letter from the post office….I shall be restricted to the ship until after Thanksgiving so I would appreciate it if you would send me thousands of letters.

October 30, 1956   Tuesday. I've got a question to ask you! We were talking about taxes etc. in First Aid today when Greer asked if there was a "food tax" on intravenous shots (I hope that's how you spell it). Do you know or can you find out? I'll be expected to know when I get back Sunday night. I know it sounds kinda strange but is it true?

Collis (one of our first jobs) was down last night with a case and a half of my favorite (Schlitz). A good time was had by all involved Boles, Lynch, Collis, Koopman, and Benjie. Finally hit the rack around 2:30! Got up this morning with a mouth that tasted like the "bottom of a bird cage."

November 1, 1956   The weather here has been very foggy but very warm for the past few days. There must be a temperature inversion or a shift of our currents hereabouts.

We are having a great battle to get rid of the roaches here on the Charleston. We may lose a few middies with the spray, but I don't think it will be any more than what the roaches are getting now. We have so many on the ship they are in the bunks and lockers. Every once in a while I have a third classman catch a hundred or so and have them deposited in the Admiral's cabin. Once I had them painted white and put in the dirty old man's room.

November 3, 1956   Well, honey, a lot of things have happened since I started to write this letter to you this afternoon. I have been in a fight ("scrap" would be more proper). I read a 200 page novel by Maugham; had the HELL scared out of me when a 3rd classman damn near broke his back, came close to getting caught jumping ship, plus had a discussion of literature with the head of the English department.

First things first. I went below to get a different pen and had a run-in with Hal Task. It was a foolish thing to do, but he has been getting on my nerves. The outcome is that I shall expect no trouble from him in the future. Next some fool had a third classman stand on his head in a barrel. This barrel was next to a ladder and the kid lost his balance, and down he went. When I got to the bottom of the ladder, I thought that we had another Sergeant McKenan [Note: I hope somebody knows what this refers to. JS] on our hands, but fortunately he was only shaken up. After that I read a book about the Italian Renaissance by Somerset Maugham. A little later Carl and I went out for pizza and got back to the ship just in time to hear second call to check muster. After check I had a talk with Mr. Clark about different books and authors…So, here I am writing a letter at 10:15 that I started to write about 3:00 this afternoon.

I will commence leave on 21 December 1956 and will have to be back to the ship on 3 January 1957. Still planning to come to New Orleans for Christmas.

November 6, 1956   I plan to see the Admiral today for the procedure for getting special liberty in Mobile. I hope that he will give me a direct answer instead of beating around the bush as he usually does.

Letters to Lou...

November 7, 1956   The ship was to be fumigated in dry dock but there were so many holes found in the hull that all the money was spent for them. Congratulations on killing your first roach; I didn't have that pleasure until I became a cadet here at the academy. Admiral Wilson told us that we might get a new ship this year. If we do, it will curtail the cruise.

I am going to have a hard time getting all four days off in Mobile. If you do not have direct relatives in the port you are allowed only overnight liberty for the days that your watch section is scheduled to get off. If this happens, I would get two days and nights off, but they would be separated. Of course I could jump ship on the alternate nights, but that would have to be after two.

November 7, 1956   I came across something on a chart today that struck me as kinda interesting. It seems that a certain second mate on a U.S. Lines ship threw a bottle over the side while in the Caribbean in 1953. Nine months later it was picked up 2,500 miles away from where it was dropped.

Sometimes they will drift for years. One was at sea for six years after being dropped off the west coast of South America and recovered in Australia. How would you like a little <u>delayed</u> mail (postcards, etc.)? Imagine getting a letter months or years old. Next cruise I'm gonna try it!

More "new" rumors about a new ship on the Hudson. We'll see, maybe?

November 8, 1956   Good news! The roaches have retreated to the dock and selected corners of the Charleston, a great victory for the master-at-arms. The ship is now alive with rumors of a new ship. The Captain and the Admiral have taken a week off and that is the reason for most of them. Some think that they have gone to Washington to see the Maritime Commission. Others believe that they have gone to New York to look at the ship. I have not formed any ideas as of yet.

We had a big quiz in ship's construction this week and everyone flunked. After we talked, we found Capt. Woodland had tested us on three chapters which were assigned for the first of December, not the first of November. He erased the marks, something I didn't think he would do.

November 9, 1956   There is no excuse that I could give for the fighting at the dance. I think it was in very poor taste and did little for the appearance of the school. However, a lot of friction is brought about here at school because of two reasons. The first and perhaps the most pronounced of the two is that the middies are packed in the ship like a bunch of animals. Each man has one locker (which is two by one and one-half) and his bunk, and that is all he does have. The other reason is that the system of indoctrination here at the academy is so much of a strain both physically and mentally that the anguish is too much for a person to hold in. That is one of the biggest reasons for getting a newer and larger ship.

While we are on the subject of things here at school and its lack of the proper facilities I shall give you an example that happened here this morning. A couple of first classmen thought that they needed some recreation and started to build a booby trap for the master-at-arms. Well, they rigged up a bucket full of water which, when pulled from a string in the far corner of the ship, would tip and hit the master at arms at the time he usually comes to check the decks. The master at arms got hit with a deluge of water from the overhead. At the time it was good for laughs and everyone felt better for it. Now, however, word of it got to the Captain and everyone must stay aboard next weekend until the culprit comes forward.

Oh, another youngie has decided to drop you a line. Really nice of him, huh!

November 11,1956 - Sunday (11:10) P.M
Massachusetts Maritime Academy
U.S.T.S. Charleston
Buzzards Bay, Massachusetts

Dear Louise,

Before I start, I realize that you have never met me and certainly know nothing about me, however the nights are long on the decks of the Charleston and I am at a loss to know what to do with my next hour of watch.

…get Sid.

First I will introduce myself as Dave Ellis, third class at the Academy. I am now standing Messenger watch on the main deck amidships with Mr. Hogan. Mr. Hogan (Ben) is now engrossed in what must be a good book called "The Adventurer", by Mika Waltari (author of the Egyptian) and pays little or no attention to me.

Of course coffee and toast are my first functions of the watch, (since Mr. Hogan doesn't have to make it, he enjoys it to the utmost), and I hope I don't stain this stationary with the juice of oranges (orange juice being another favorite of Mr. Hogan's watch menu).

With 20 minutes remaining before my relief comes on deck for the "mid", I shall continue to write. It seems only fair that I should mention Mr. Hogan's concern over Lt. Harrington's wife ("Hop" being his favorite instructor here at the Academy). Poor Mrs. Harrington has "Hop" in a state of mild confusion (this Mr. Hogan enjoys also - confusion I mean). Being a very nervous, excitable, and unpredictable character adds to the humor of the whole affair. The reason for this dilemma is that "Mrs. Hop" is driving him slowly insane because she is 21 days overdue. She now has six girls, and God help the midshipmen at the Academy, if its not a **"boy"**. Mr. Hogan being thrilled and delighted hopes for **"twin girls"** (Ha-ha !!!) Let's hope for my sake she has a boy within the week since I still have him for class.

I am distressed at the fact that I receive only one weekend liberty a month at home and I am about to loose it on account of Mr. Hogan's classmates. A certain incident occurred last Friday morning and a 1st classman will not confess to the crime. A state employee, a dirty, grubby, old man, known throughout the ship for having no compassion for the midshipmen at 6 o'clock in the morning, met his well deserved fate. Every morning he comes through the compartments, screaming, yelling, slamming on locker doors, raising hell and rolling the boys from their bunks.

A large tin can (very large) was ingeniously rigged the night before, filled with water, tested and approved by all, for Mr. Sanforth. This can was hung on the overhead with great care between two large air vents, hidden from anyone that might step beneath it. The ingenious part of this rig is that it could be tripped (or triggered) a good distance away by a long cord that was also hidden in the maze of overhead steam lines, and wires.

The following morning at 5:30 a certain few select cadets sneaked out of their racks and filled the can with a mixture of sticky bug-juice and water. Accomplishing this they took their places and waited for the bugle.

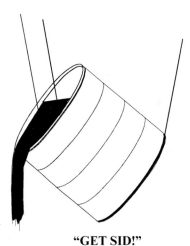

Shortly afterward, the bugle sounded and Mr. Sanforth started to make his usual harassing rounds. After waking everyone back aft with his loud hoarse voice he came forward to get the remaining company of midshipmen (walking his usual route). Slamming one locker door too many he was hit with an avalanche of bug juice and water. The shock of the cold water stunned him, washed his sparse hair over his eyes, re-seated his "square" glasses on the end of his nose, put out the tobacco in the bowl of his pipe and soaked his shoulders and arms with a sticky mess (a direct hit).

Everyone enjoyed this thorough shower, until Sid reported it to Capt. Woodland who in turn reported it to Crd. Rounds. Needless to say there were no bitter faces on the dock at the 0615 formation that morning.

"GET SID!"

All the 1st class cadet officers were mustered on the main deck for a little speech by Capt. Woodland and told to find out who was responsible for this **"accident"???** and to turn the name into ship's office by 0800 that morning.

Confession is not needed for everyone knows who did it, except the officers back aft and poor Sid, and certainly the cadet officers will not turn in their own classmates. Consequently the whole company is restricted next weekend (including Mr. Hogan...Ha-ha!). Only the next five days will tell. Let's hope I get home. I haven't seen my family for six weeks and would love a home cooked meal.

It is raining and the watch is over. I am now seated in Mr. Hogan's corner of the compartment. I must make a confession before I go any further. As you might have guessed already I am just the secretary of the letter and not the author (Mr. Hogan has broken his right arm). But it has been fun anyway and we have killed another long watch. Hope to meet you at the dance on the 1st of December.

Letters to Lou…

I remain,
David H. Ellis 3/d

Questions: 1.) Who, in the class of "57", pulled the cord?
Ans. Jack Aylmer "took the rap." 50 demerits and he spent several months restricted to the ship. Bresnahan assisted with the rigging.
2.) Did Harrington have a boy or girl?
Ans. A Boy! We were upper jobs when Harrington had the baby boy. I remember he was named Paul Tolan Harrington after the end that caught the winning Touchdown when Hops alma-mater, Holy Cross (I think), beat Boston College. Someone, and I know it was a football player, asked Hop what he would have named him if the end's name had been "Brother Erastis Jones." I also think everyone who laughed did "laps" after Hop got his blood pressure down to 980 over 300.
3.) Did Ellis graduate with his class?
Ans. Yes, David Ellis graduated with his class. He's retired from Arizona Power and now has his own consulting business in Phoenix.

[Pete Readel]

November 16, 1956 I received your letter today upon my return from Fire Fighting School at Newport Naval Station.

This deal about the water-throwing has had me upset for the past few days and it came to a head about an hour ago. The first classmen had a massive meeting in the Navigation Room to find the culprit and have him confess to the crime so that the others may go home. Jane, I wish that you could have been there tonight. It was a real example of human nature. I have never in my life seen so many people in one room who, from all outwardly [sic] aspects seem to be sincere, turn into the cowardly, backstabbing animals that I saw this evening. People who were supposed to be friendly with another person, for the cost of a few days liberty, throw a person to the dogs. The thing which is really incongruent about it is that these same people are training for a profession which will keep them from home for months on end. Our friend Goat is now on report for breach of discipline and good, upstanding classmates are home on liberty.

This is my last restriction, honey. I will be home for the holidays. During the leave I intend to go into Boston and see the Commissioners about leave in Mobile. I surely hope it works out as good as I have planned.

This fire fighting is quite a thing, my friend. I never thought that I would willingly crawl into a boiler room ablaze with a hot gasoline fire, but I have done it several times in the past few days. We were taught how to use all the different types of gas masks and breathing apparatus. We were led into structures that were ablaze with gas, oil, and wood fires, and we extinguished them with little trouble.

November 20, 1956 "War and Peace" is playing in town, but after the last shake-up around here, I don't feel like taking a chance jumping ship to see it.

…About the new ship, the Captain has looked over the plans and likes them very much. He and the Admiral are going down to New York to look at the ship. If they like what they see, we may get it right away or wait until next year. I personally would like to get it this year.

There were 67 first classmen brought to mast today. The proposition of safety in numbers worked out fine for the Captain gave us only a warning. We had been put on report for missing the supper formation last night.

The pictures are here, but I have no money, so I will bring you one at Christmas if you like.

November 21, 1956 Goat got 50 demerits for dumping water on the master at arms. I think that it is a stiff punishment for a practical joke. He will have to stay until Christmas to make up the restrictions and also loses part of the Christmas leave.

The dock strike has affected the traffic in the Cape Cod Canal. There hasn't been a merchant ship through for two days. I don't understand what they are striking for. I think, however, that they are killing the goose that is laying the golden eggs.

…another scholarship.

The last letter was mailed by Carl Megonigle and was supposed to be mailed in Hartford. Evidently he forgot and mailed it in his home town where they collect mail about once a week.

November 23, 1956   Good news! I have a string of tickets for the train from Boston to New Orleans. I leave Boston at 11:00 AM on the 22nd December and arrive in New Orleans at 8:30 PM on the 23 December, 1956.

I saw the Commissioners in Boston today. They didn't promise me anything but they did say that they would look into the matter with great concern.

The reason that I was mad about the water deal was that though Goat did do the dirty deed, he did not do it alone. But the others would not own up to it.

I now have in my possession 118 letters from Jane F. Smith. [Note: Bob continued to save my letters throughout our correspondence, but, after his father's death, when the family moved from Lowell St. Court, one of his sisters threw all of my letters away. She had so much to deal with, I can't fault her.....but Bob was sickened when he found out. It would be fun to have the other half of this correspondence! I had 110 letters from him at this time, so I was eight ahead of him...,]

November 26, 1956   I have to watch myself around here from now on. Last night I came back, and the first thing I did was to get into an argument with the "dirty old man". Consequently I am on the restricted list again. However, I will get home this weekend but not again until the leave period, unless I do some fast talking.

[Re: Liberty in Mobile, Alabama] Jane, I think that it would help our situation if your brother or father wrote to the Board of Commissioners, but the thing is that I have told them nothing of my trip to New Orleans at Christmas and I have referred to you as my fiancée. Rather than have them lie, I will try it on my own.

November 27, 1956   Great news posted by ship's office. The class now has **6001** demerits. A new record. Deckies total 1997 or 78 per man average. Snipes 4004 or 91 per man average. Task still leads with 657 followed by Put with 407. Four guys are still cherry (please excuse the expression) with no demerits! An almost impossible task!

November 28, 1956   The cruise is only weeks away. The best part of it is that it will give us a chance to practice navigation and rules of the road for the mate's exam next July.

The uniform for the dance Saturday is dress blues with my knitted "Beer Mug" socks. You really did a great job! I had a few lads, one for each sock, wash and hang them up to dry last night on the "mid." They really did a good job!

November 29, 1956   The USS __?__ is here loading supplies for the Texas Tour and the academy dock is just covered with cases of beer. Very tempting, I must say.

I have just discovered that I have made arrangements to go to a frat party with Bob [Alukonis, a friend from home] on Saturday and that it will be at the same house, same place and exactly one year from the date of our accident.

Last night we were listening to "Moscow Molly" on "Radio Moscow". We have a short-wave radio and started to fool around with it and that is what we came up with. A man gave a spiel about the judicial setup of the Communist government. A woman talked about the Hungarian Revolt and blamed it all on the ___Illegible__. We are going to send her a letter and ask if she will play more records and do less talking.

December 1, 1956   I found out...last night that I will not be able to take the train [to New Orleans] that I told you that I would. It seems that the railroad sold me a ticket for a train on which they have no more room.

I went to see the Admiral this week and talked about returning to school next year for engineering. He told me that he would be very glad to recommend me to the Board of Commissioners. I don't know what I will use for money but I was talking with people today and there is a possibility that I will be able to get another scholarship.

Letters to Lou…

December 3, 1956   "Boonya" found a huge cockroach in his soup and complained to both Sid and Arm-pit Al. Anteen told him to "take it with a grain of salt" and get a refill. Ted is really ticked off!

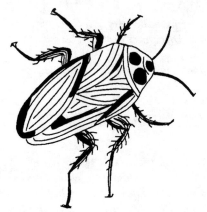

These guys can find some real winners to take to the dances. One of them thought "grape nuts" was a venereal disease.

December 5, 1956   In class this morning we went over the stability problem of the "Andrea Doria"; it was very interesting. The Captain explained how she had a very low metacentric height and thus a high center of gravity. After the trip across, the ship was light from fuel consumption and thus even a higher center of gravity was introduced. As the ship was struck, water was taken in and forced the center of gravity past the metercenter, and the ship capsized. Captain Woodland believes that the Captain of the "Andrea Doria" should and could have controlled this. I am inclined to believe this.

December 8, 1956   Well, honey, a week of classes and a week of exams and then a week of bliss before I start the cruise. I had a regular field day Friday fighting with the Captain and the Admiral. They had sent back my request for leave in Mobile with a statement on it to the effect that I would get overnight liberty and the days that I rated liberty, and that was all. I went to the Admiral and told him I was not pleased with the results and that I had been to the Commissioners. When he found that I had gone over his head he wasn't pleased but told me to send in the request again and that he would see that it got to the Board. Therefore I still have a chance of getting it granted.

December 11,1956   Strange weekend! First I made it back Sunday night with no trouble at all. It seems a few of my classmates were not so lucky. Boonya, Broadbent, Aylmer, were 6 hours and 10 minutes over leave. Roffey and some second jobs were even later getting back since they were delayed by an accident on 128 in Woburn. Dan Sullivan got hit on Rt. 138 and Bruce Andrews got it in Dedham on 128. Both cars are now down at my father's shop for repairs. All told there were 22 cadets A.O.L. and restricted to the ship awaiting action of the board.

"Old Man Flaherty" was in another accident Friday night. He's now in Brighton Marine with head injuries and ten more stitches on his forehead.

Well I took a shower today...surprise! The problem was how to keep my bad finger dry? One of my classmates came up with a solution. I tried it and it worked, everything is just fine now!

December 13,1956   Captain Woodland (the bird) has the deck today. The same guy that caught us with the youngies singing up forward a few months ago. He really is a character, a little weird, "Be Honorable", but good for a few laughs now and then.

I lose my stripe next week. New stripes will be picked back aft by the brass for the cruise. Starting next leave period I'll be "Cadet Ensign Retired" or one of many classifications of S.A.(M.M.)O.C.-U.S.N.R. In English its Seaman Apprentice (Merchant Marine) Officer Candidate - United States Naval Reserve. What a mouthful huh?

A youngie, Mr. Horgan, made a comment about the first class snipes ...Quote... "The dog can have toast but I can't." A stray dog gets more food than a young midshipman! That used to bother me too! I can remember as a youngie, while in my rack, how the first jobs would throw chow overboard before they would offer us any! No change!

...peacoat locker.

It's damp, foggy, and cold down here again. Colder than a witch's nose!

December 13, 1956 We had a wonderful time this afternoon at the diner. It seems that someone at the diner said we had a lot of roaches on the ship. The woman told us she had never had the pleasure of seeing one, and it started from there. I wish that you could have seen her face tonight when we went back there and sat a jar of roaches on the table. After that we made little chariots of matchbooks, paper, string, and buttons. We got two of the largest roaches and tied them to the chariots. At first they wouldn't move, but a shot from a cigarette lighter made it quite a race.

I shall be glad when we leave on the cruise. I have been restricted so much this year I don't know what I will use for money. Usually I work weekends and save out of that for the cruise, but now I shall have to discover another means of getting some dough.

By the way, I am no longer the advertising manager of The Muster. It seems that a large concern sent in money for an ad in this year's book and I sent them back a receipt for the balance of last year's account. This made them very angry and they wrote to the Admiral. The rest of it I will not have to put down.

I am now lying down on the bridge with honest intentions of studying for a naval science exam tomorrow. It is after taps, and the ship is very quiet....Carl has just come up to the bridge in his shorts. He has had a pint of wine and is full of hell. He has been walking around on deck in his shorts and doesn't feel a thing. The wind velocity is up to 25 knots and the temperature is about 35 or so. Carl has been complaining to me about the Navy using too many abbreviations in their textbooks. Now he is telling me not to write letters because I will get into trouble and numerous social problems. He has thought of jumping off the bridge because the water looks very interesting. He's gone now to find all the engineers and have a fight with them.

December 16, 1956 Carl is here again but much more sober than he was last time. He doesn't remember anything of what he did last Thursday night.

Exams start tomorrow and I still don't know a thing about the subjects at hand. If I get by these at all it will be by the grace of God. I cannot think of anyone who has read so much and retained as little as I have. For the past sixteen weeks we have been studying rules of steamboat inspection and rules of the road in the seamanship class. Now the "dirty old man" tells us that we are going to be tested on seamanship. I can tell you that pleased a lot of people.

[DESPITE HAVING NO RESERVED SEAT FOR THE TRAIN, BOB USES HIS TICKET TO BOARD THE TRAIN AND, BY SHUTTLING BETWEEN THE CLUB CAR AND THE REST ROOM, HE MAKES IT TO NEW ORLEANS. JS]

December 31, 1956 Bye bye to my '36', sloped backed, Plymouth. My insurance ran out. It's up for sale. I can't afford the gas anyway at twelve cents a gallon.

Winter 1956 Duty weekend. Saturday night, Captain Woodland had the deck. Dick Greer had the after dinner watch. Dick made a comment that the messcooks did a sloppy job of cleaning up after dinner and requested permission to call them away and "to do it right." He was granted permission and commended by Captain Woodland for being concerned and conscientious.

About an hour later, four young men crossed the quarterdeck with two 35 gallon metal trash barrels, with lids, headed for the garbage battery in the parking lot. Upon arrival they dumped the trash, and nearly filled both barrels with Narragansett Imperial Quarts of beer. They marched smartly back aboard, past Captain Woodland, and disappeared into the galley hatch. All beer orders were filled for the thirsty midshipmen aboard.

After check muster and reporting the decks secure the party started in the peacoat locker and in other small dark spaces on the ship. An "86" watch was set on Captain's Woodland stateroom door after he turned in.

In the peacoat locker the contest was about to begin. A large sea chest was used as a table. "Youngies" were assigned various tasks as timers and pourers of the beer. At least six upper jobs were about to attempt to drink a jigger of beer per minute for one hour. About half way into the contest a couple guys got sick and vomited into a bucket that was provided. The dedicated "youngies" and contestants continued to toss-em-down on schedule. The winner, yes he did it, was awarded the prize of another Imperial Quart!

Letters to Lou…

The beer flowed freely in all classes. The watch standers were the only ones sober that evening. Around midnight a drunk "youngie", with a name appropriate for a Pope, was turned loose wrapped from head to foot in toilet paper. As he ran through the berthing compartments, waking those scheduled for the next watch, he yelled "Hey look at me, I'm King Shit!" "I'm King Shit!" A few of his classmates caught up with him and managed to secure him naked in his rack.

The next morning while on watch I remember talking to Captain Woodland about the large number of beer bottles that had washed up on the beach from the tourist's Saturday night parties.

The truth is, the cadets failed to fill the empty bottles with water before throwing them overboard! If they ever dredge the slip alongside the finger pier they probably suck up more glass than mud!

January 1, 1957   The wind is up around 20 knots; the barometer reads 29.82 inches, the sky is covered about 3/10 with cumulus clouds at around 4000 ft. Temperature is 18 degrees above zero and the drafts are 12'01" and 15'01" fore and aft respectively. That is the weather picture here today.

January 2, 1957   I see in the papers the U.S. Government has passed an act which makes Merchant Marine officers exempt from the draft.

The more I think about coming back here for another year the more I realize it is a good thing for me to do. If I come ashore after a few years of experience as an officer in the Merchant service and have two degrees, even if they are from here, I should have a pretty good chance of landing a fairly good job.

The weather here is keeping to a constant cold; right now the temperature is about 5 degrees above zero. The water has frozen in a water supply from shore, and we are drawing from the peak tanks. We leave here on the seventh, my friend, and two days after that we should hit warm water and travel the gulf stream along the coast.

I broke out my sextant and am getting it ready for the cruise. I have a lot of navigation to do this year; a star sight and a meridian altitude, plus a meridian sight to turn in each day.

January 3, 1957   We are getting ready for the big plunge into the deep blue, Jane. This means that we have taken aboard 21 tons of Grade "B" meat and numerous other supplies. The best thing to go into the freezer was the chicken. It looks like we will have a steady diet of that for a week or so.

The weather is still holding to a constant cold, but a slight rise to 15 above zero this morning. The ground is still covered with ice and snow and people are falling all around the place.

January 6, 1957   It is snowing here now, Jane. It is reported that we shall have a blizzard tonight but I hope it is untrue. I have to meet a kid in Boston at five in the morning. He and his mother are going to give me a ride back to the ship. The Charleston shall get underway about noontime.

Tomorrow we sail to warmer waters. The sooner we leave the sooner we get back! Thanks for the truck load of chow! It must have set you back a bit! I put it all in my locker down below. While I was doing it a few of the guys spotted the jar of red cherries! That's the end! They'll never let me live it down!

A month ago Larry Meyer got a surprise in the mail. He has been engaged to a gal in PA. for about six months. The gals in her class had a shower for her and from what I heard they gave her the world with a handle on it. They didn't want Larry to feel slighted or left-out so they sent him a box of "chocolate cherries." Strange custom! He'll not live that down either!

WHO ME?

Frank Flaherty   Dick Boles   Joe McCluskey

MESSDECK BLACK & WHITE TV WATCHERS

First Class Cruise

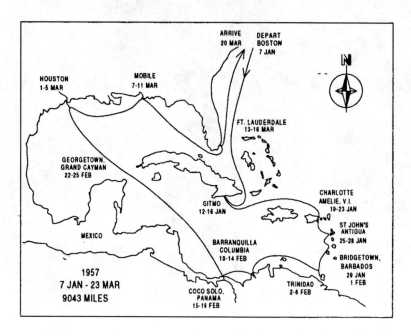

January 7, 1957   Underway. The Christmas leave came and went and then all of a sudden it was January 7, and the Chun was backing out of the slip to turn its nose south once again, for the final school ship cruise. It was snowing and rather cold, but undaunted we were on our way to the warm Caribbean.

January 7, 1957   [Re phone call]   A funny thing happened with that phone call...You and I know that we talked well over the three minute time limit but when I asked the operator how much I owed for overtime, she said, "Nothing." I know that we had talked overtime, so I asked her if she hadn't made a mistake and she told me again that there was no overtime charge. I believe that the operator must know me and didn't charge me for it or that she had listened in on our conversation and felt sorry for us. At any rate, I was glad to save the money.

The weather is still bad, the snow is still coming down fast and the roads are terrible.

I will be glad when the ship leaves today so I can get some sleep. I have been sitting up all night so I can wake my father at four to take me to Boston to meet the kid who is going to give me a ride back. I can never hear an alarm clock, so I figured the safest way was to stay up.

January 8, 1957   It is now the second night since we left Buzzards Bay and I think a lot of people wish that we were still there. We hadn't been out of the place for more than two hours, and we started to ship green seas over the bow. Last night we ran into a small gale and I think all the ties with shore are gone now. It really is a shame to see how people suffer with sea sickness. One kid kept rolling around the deck and screaming that he wanted to die. However, I think that is going to extremes.

Four bells have struck, my friend, the end of the first day's watch. We are now off the coast of North Carolina and will be hitting Cape Hatteras at midnight. We are in the Gulf Stream now and the weather has moderated quite a bit. The ship is now down to a lazy roll.

Oh, I almost forgot to tell you the departure of the Charleston was on TV last night. They had a couple of cameramen down at the dock from WBZ-TV and what a phony thing that was. The train from Buzzards Bay to Boston left at one, and the fellows had to be on it. The Charleston was not scheduled to leave until two, so we had to fake everything for the men and it was terrible...or at least I thought so.

…I was bemused.

January 8,1957   The "One Gun Chun" is headed south. Kinda nice to be at sea again. Really enjoy it. Why I choose to sleep up forward with a bunch of youngies I'll never know. This compartment has a terrible odor. Most of these young men were sick last night. Some of them made it to the forward head and some of them didn't. The barrel and four or five buckets all have their share. Really kinda funny...one kid would get sick and the three or four watching him would join in. The Medford youngies, Dunphy and Sarnie were both sick, pale, and hoping to die. Another kid, Bresnahan, stands much taller than the rest. He's a nice kid with eyes that look like two burnt holes in a blanket

The following is a letter (written 30 years later) by Captain Maurice Bresnahan ('59') to the Academy President Jack Aylmer ('57'), one of his first class tormentors. It is self-explanatory and extremely well done.

Dear Sir:

I was bemused by your description of the USTS Charleston appearing in the first edition of the MMA magazine. Although it was accurate enough it left an awful lot unsaid.

The short blurb just didn't convey the thoughts of the years I lived in her that have always lingered fresh in my memory. The recollections of sleeping in four high bunks in the forward compartment that was hot in the summer and cold in the winter all nicely ventilated by aromas from the abutting head remain vivid to this day. The CHUN'S gentle roll in addition to being very relaxing also produced a chilled water cooling system to the interior of the ship. Every time she was in a seaway that put the badly deteriorated and un-doggable port holes, that ran the length of the ship below the main deck under water, a 60 PSI jet of salt water sprayed through the gaskets. The standing water in the compartment richly mixed with the effluvia produced by a seasick crew carried a hundred or so shoes with it all moving in consonance with the gentle roll of the CHUN. The smell of wet wool and soaked leather superimposed over those emanating from the forward head, crowded under such conditions by middies praying for an hour under an oak tree, created a unique and unforgettable ambiance.

Aside from the shoes, gear adrift wasn't a major problem as the rest of our meager possessions were rolled and stopped and stored away in lockers approximately the size of a household medicine cabinet. The rest, our "hanging gear" was stuffed into the Pea Coat locker. That was a deep and dark place that posed as a torture chamber or a site of total sovereignty depending what class you were in.

Equally memorable were the mess decks and especially on the first night of a cruise. That January departure from Boston directly into the North Atlantic's clutches always involved a few inevitabilities; i.e., the mess cooks struggling down the midship's ladder from the galley with a steam tray could be counted on to fall and spill the contents on the deck. And just as surely those contents would be spaghetti and meat balls. Even the brave lads who elected to eat on that night would be soon driven out by the ensuing mayhem and rantings of the venerable "Sid" standing at his post behind a swaying milk bucket secured to the overhead by a piece of nine thread

Maurice J Bresnahan Jr. RADM, USN (RET.) President

Letters to Lou

The stout hearts whose iron stomachs stood by them were through sheer necessity consigned to the scullery or huddled on the main deck amidships with the life boat crew of the watch. They envied the gang on watch in the fire and engine rooms all warm and dry, unaware of the treat that lay ahead for them when they reached the tropics. Those were the days before heat stress had entered our lexicon. Always fair and objective in the assignment of such benefits, everyone soon gained a full share of bilge cleaning, cleaning burners and scrubbing deck plates with wire brushes and diesel oil under the gentle tropical sun. An especially savored treat was that forty-five minutes of sleep one could snatch between the end of the mid watch and being rousted out to line up and scrub the teak main deck with sea water and sand. That was the real battle ground that separated the deckies from the snipes. After the hours of back breaking work required to make the teak decks gleam it was another inevitability of life that an engineer on a break would pop out of the hole and leave a track of grease and fuel oil as a testimonial of his distain for the ki-yi crew. Attitudes soon stiffened under those circumstances.

Those memories are all intermingled with flashes of standing in line outside of Al Anteen's storeroom seeking health and comfort items fully convinced that he was cheating us out of the major share of our federal subsidy, of collecting pet roaches, the ever present "turn-tos" and the daily struggle to avoid the wrath and evil eye of Tricky Dickey and his faithful companion Sid, that master of dispensing weekend destroying demerits. We carried four movies on each cruise and we all faithfully showed up on the fantail for each and every showing. After a while when the sound went out, and it did frequently, we would all chant the dialog in unison. It didn't take much to amuse us in those days.

Our medical needs were catered to by the highly esteemed Dr. Boyle whose major disinfecting agent was the scotch breath that he concisely expelled. On one memorable evening the Dr. was called to tend to a ship's cook who had returned drunk, fallen into the motor whale boat and split open his head with a fearsome gash. Doc Boyle took a strain and stitched the cook's forehead up so tight that only a few centimeters separated his hair line from his eyebrows. We mercilessly nicknamed him Wolfman. Who, of those of us who lived through them, will ever forget Dr. Boyle's short arm inspections?

Our strength was sustained on the CHUN by what could best be described as a frugal repast. Most of that fare was a monotonous litany of greasy eggs, SOS, Jell-o, fruit cocktail and the ever present withered hot dog. Probably the nadir was the meal in which those at the end of the chow line were presented with a can of sardines and one boiled potato, smacked down on a greasy tray.

For all that, she was a wonderful ship. Our officer instructors seemed at the time to be philistines bent on inflicting pain but in reality as I look back they were for the most part pretty tough and savvy Mariners from the old school. They were characters but they really knew their business and during my almost three decades in the Navy I've reached back toward their teachings on countless occasions. Unenlightened by modern management practices they operated on the "levels of misery leadership theory." Simply stated that was, i.e., "If you think things are bad now, just fail to do what I tell you and I will show you how miserable things can really be."

For all of that - the Charleston and the tests and trials she presented for her crew were unique. She was a crucible in which a lot of good sailors were forged.

[Capt. M. J. Bresnahan, USN]

January 9, 1957 The ship is riding easy now. Wonderful for relaxing and sacks. It's just like a great big gray rocking chair. We are still afloat! Looks like we are gonna make it after all.

The youngies got a good taste of scrub down this morning. They started around five and scrubbed the main deck until after seven. I still remember how great it was to be a young man with nothing to do but work and play games!

January 10, 1957 The sun was out today with little or no clouds to hide it so I tried a little navigation. I made an error in time so that when I worked out the sight I found we were sailing through northern Georgia. Not too good huh? I found the error later and took another sight, crossed it with the first and discovered I was only two miles from Captain Woodland's position. That's much better!

We had a boat drill this morning and the snipes pulled another beauty! The boat had water in it so they had pulled the plug in the bottom to drain it but never put it back! Lt. Page got a tremendous shower when we put it in the water. He was soaked from head to foot! Of course we broke out laughing and the S.O.G. took an hours liberty from us.

The movie on the fantail tonight is "The French Line" with Jane Russell. This is the movie that was once "Banned in Boston." We had the un-cut version and enjoyed it very much!

January 11, 1957   The trip has been quite uniform. The first few days were cold and rough, but now we are in the Caribbean, and the seas are like glass and the weather hot as a furnace.

One of the seamen has gotten very sick and it was at first thought necessary to make for a port and drop him off. However, he has got a little better and we will take him to a hospital in Cuba tomorrow. I think I shall have to take him in since I have the 8-12 watch in the morning.

I have made one achievement, however. I am restricted for the first liberty. I have a very salty pair of work pants which I enjoy wearing. The officers do not approve my wearing these pants. I had been told about three times to get rid of them but I have had them for so long, I hate to part with them. I wore them one night on the midwatch thinking no one would see me but the Captain happened by and saw me.

The Southern Cross is very close and very beautiful tonight. The whole sky is lit up with millions of stars in sundry constellations.

Red Riley has brought his tape recorder with him and one of the tapes is our song, which you listened to at the Napoleon House. [Note: I am as sentimental as the next person, but I have no idea what this song was! JS]

Marks have come out but not the class standings. I have fairly good marks in my classroom instructions but, for conduct, I have a 0.0 and for aptitude I have a 2.6 which will, I imagine, cut down my class standing considerably.

Last night there was a movie on the fantail; it was "The French Line". I know now why it was banned in Boston. The acting and plot were all terrible.

January 12, 195   Guantanamo, Cuba Here I am in Cuba and no word from my friend in New Orleans. I am lying on my mattress on the main deck and sweating up a storm. My God, it is hot here in the daytime, but at night it gets real cool.

The harbor here at Guantanamo is really very pretty but all the Navy ships spoil the effect. There are a number of tin cans and tankers at anchor around us, plus one large cruiser and an uncountable number of small craft.

This place is a resting place for Navy men and there are uncountable clubs, bars, lounges of all sorts and other forms of entertainment around, but nothing for a young midshipman who is in love with a very pretty young lady, to do. If I were able to get off the ship today I think I would have rented a sailboat and spent the day that way.

Last night I was running the liberty boats and when I went in for the _____ [Undecipherable!], what a sight I found on the dock. There were about 300 sailors coming back from liberty and all in whites , or at least they were supposed to be whites. Half of them were lying on the dock dead drunk with their friends sitting on or standing by them trying to keep them quiet. A couple of them were fighting in a "cesspool" and what a sight they were.

The next port will be as beautiful, but as dead, as this one. The only thing different is that anything you buy in the Virgin Islands costs about five times as much as it should.

January 13, 1957 Guantanamo Bay, Cuba (Gitmo). The Navy Base rules and regs are so tough that it's not worth going ashore. We got liberty only from 1 to 6 PM while here! They have a Post Office out here but they don't sell stamps. Since they deal with just Navy mail they just stamp it and send it on. Of course we are not in the Navy so they won't stamp our mail and they can't sell what they don't have so this letter will be posted in our next port of call. Mail has arrived but won't go out! This base is for the birds!

The "word" is now "Official" - I don't have to go in the Navy! But I must go to sea to be draft deferred. I hope they don't change their minds again! I've got a three page letter from the NavSci Office in Buzzards Bay when we left. I'll send it home if I can find it!

Letters to Lou…

Maritime Academy
Graduates Can Get
Draft Deferred Jobs

WASHINGTON, Dec. 22 (AP)   Graduates of the Merchant Marine Academy henceforth may become Navy Reserve officers on active duty or take draft-deferred jobs in the merchant service. The Maritime Administration, announcing this today, said an agreement reached by the Defense and Commerce Departments and Selective Service will apply to the State Maritime Academies of Maine, Massachusetts, New York, and California as well as the Federal Academy at King's Point, N.Y.

re: Newspaper Clipping

January 14, 1957   We are still at anchor here at Gitmo. The North Hampton, a guided missile cruiser, is anchored on our starboard side. This ship is the flag ship of the fleet. It left this morning with about twenty destroyers, two tankers, five or six destroyer escorts, and several other smaller ships and returned today at 5 PM. Eight hours at sea and they are tired! Just a big cruising party! A big bunch of kids spending a little time in uniform! Looks like a good deal to me!

It was explained to several "youngies" that the radar on the bridge was not working and needed a special electronic tube for repair. They were given a typed requisition and sent to the Navy Supply Depot for a 5NS7 Fallopian tube. "Don't come back without one!" This is an old stunt that the supply staff recognized immediately and directed the young man to another source. He spent most of the day going from one place to another trying to locate this special tube.

January 15, 1957 - Charlotte, Amalie, V.I.   I found the letter the Navy sent today. Quote, "The Navy does not, under any circumstances, desire to be obligated to consider the Merchant Marine Academies as a basic source of Naval Reserve Officers, nor be obligated to call graduates of these "institutions" to active duty. To assume any other position would violate our concept that the Maritime Academies are for the purpose of supporting a strong Merchant Marine. The Navy conceives of the schools as primarily required for the manning of our Merchant Marine." All I hope is that they don't change their mind or that a war does not break out! Keep your fingers crossed!

January 15, 1957 - Guantanamo, Cuba

Today I went sailing around Guantanamo Harbor and had a very enjoyable time.

My friend the battalion commander, Jack Keenan, got himself into a lot of trouble today when he took the Captain and the Executive Officer in the gig and went around the wrong side of a buoy. ["He is a condemned man" or "This is a conduct ___ " ... [Note: You all don't realize how horrible Bob's handwriting could be. It was a strain to try to figure out what he wrote at the time; forty-one years intervening hasn't helped. Some letters are very clear, but when he was in a hurry, writing standing up or whatever, it's really a puzzle. I'm going to take the first option in this guess..... JS] "He is a condemned man" in the rules of small boat handling or any boat handling for that matter.

...The hot weather here has given the roaches on board the good old Charleston almost a double size in population.

As for the special liberty in Mobile, Jane, you know that if it was only a matter of my standing extra watches, there would be no problem. As far as I know, the Admiral and the Captain have had no correspondence with the Board of Commissioners since we left Boston. I shall be able to get one overnight liberty, of that I am sure, but any more than that would only be a guess. [Note: My logical, if naive, question was, "Why can't you trade duty with someone else in another port? As long as the ship had the proper number of people on watch, what difference did it make? " As you can see, I'd never make it in the military. JS]

I understand that the day that we left Buzzards Bay there was an incredible amount of snow. I shall have to interrupt this letter to eat some delicious rolls that I have stolen out of the galley. They were hot and burned my tongue. The day we left there was seven inches of snow in Boston and the very next day there was another six. I must say that I am glad to get out of it although the way I feel now I would not be too sure about it. God, honey, it does get hot down here. The temperature was 105 when we left the ship today. It is now 2015, and the temperature is still in the eighties.

January 20, 1957   Charlotte Amalie, V.I.   The impossible has happened, my love.   Here in 1957 a ship has run out of water. We will not have any water for washing until Tuesday or Wednesday.   The drinking water will be turned on for 15 minute periods four times a day.   It seems that while underway we were unable to get the machinery working to make water and now that it is in operation we are not allowed to make drinking water from the harbor.   The island has a very bad drought and has to have water brought in from another island.   It has been raining for about one hour quite hard.   Perhaps it will help them out.   I surely hope that it does.

This morning the engineers got quite a workout.   A check valve broke down, and we were without power for about an hour or so.   It is a good thing that it broke down in port.   We put four running boats in the water but only one is left in working order.   Jane, this is a tired old ship and the Commissioners should let it die.

The rain has stopped, and there are many beautiful rainbows stretching over the harbor.   I should like to find the pot of gold at the end of one of them.   Earlier today there was one rainbow from the top of the mountain to the roof of an old fort at the entrance to the harbor - very impressive.   The harbor has many beautiful boats in it.   Last night I met the Captain of my first ship.   He is now the captain of a very fine yacht here in St. Thomas.   I do believe, however, that he has let drinking get the best of him.

There is an Alcoa ship here loading bauxite bound for some gulf port.   I wish that I could go with them.

The island comes right out of the ocean and has very high mountains surrounding a beautiful natural harbor.   The weather is cool in the mornings and late evenings, but other than that, very hot.   Things come in only two extremes around here - very nice, like the Virgin Island Hotel or very disgusting, like the French Village section of town.   I think everyone and his brother is a cab driver around [here], and they all charge outrageous prices.   Coke [the cola! JS] could cost you three times as much as rum.   Food is very good but not very filling and expensive for what you get.   The beaches are surprisingly clean and have many trees around them.

I have sent to you what I hope you asked for.   [Note: I'd asked him to get me a coral necklace, which I wore until it was stolen, with all my jewelry, from our house in 1983. JS]   As strange as it seems, coral is not very plentiful around here.   As a matter of fact, I had a hard time to find what I wanted.   Bermuda was the place to get that sort of stuff.

Yesterday I went to the beach and then walked around.   I was unable to rent a sailboat or a car.   Monday I have liberty again and I will try to get a car then and drive up in the hills or to the other side of the island.

I shall try to put all I have to say about this place in one letter and thus save some postage - see how cheap I am.   I sent a wire to my good brother and asked him to please make restitution for I am in dire need of the cash.   I wonder if it will have any effect.

The only word that I have received from the Board of Commissioners is that they have received my special request for engineering but they said nothing other than that.   I think that I am getting a big run-around.   Too bad that you don't know some important person who might write a letter to Admiral Wilson.

I am now the navigator of the watch and have very little to do.   The ship is at anchor and the bearings are taken by the quartermaster of the watch.   Yesterday I sewed all new halyards on the port yardarm and will do the starboard yardarm on Monday.   We were flying George on the way in and the line parted.   That is the reason for all the work.

January 22, 1957   Charlotte Amalie, V.I.   Tomorrow we shall hit the briny deep again for a few days.   Then again the unsuspecting populace of some exotic island will be hit by hordes of hell-raising middies.

I watched the last liberty boat return last night and I don't think there was a sober person aboard.   From the number of animals that crawled or were carried out of that boat one might think it was Noah's Ark.   The hot sun and the cheap rum were too much of a strain on the young men, I believe.

ROYAL UNIFORM CORPORATION

MANFACTURERS OF ROCHESTER MADE
UNIFORMS - HEADWEAR - EQUIPMENT
83 MAIN STREET EAST   ROCHESTER 4, N. Y.

Mr. James M. McCluskey
Massachusetts Maritime Academy
Buzzards Bay, Mass.

January 21, 1957

REFER TO FILE NUMBER

Dear Sir:

On the third of this month, we wrote you with reference
to your past due account in the amount of $16.00 cover-
ing white naval officer's uniform.   Etc......

...probably still <u>not paid!</u>

If they do not grant me liberty, in Mobile, Alabama, I shall take it anyway. I don't think they will throw me out for being over-leave at least, I hope not.

This morning I made the mail run and, while waiting for the ten o'clock boat to come, I walked into a section of town called the Spanish Main and there found a coffee shop very much like the one in New Orleans.

January 25,1957   I bought a bottle of good scotch in St. Thomas for two dollars which has made the past few evenings much more enjoyable.

The Charleston is anchored out of St. John's harbor about six miles. It takes twenty-five to thirty minutes to run in with a small boat. The harbor has barely enough water in it to float the small boats. The seas are very choppy and I have been kept occupied all day raising and lowering the running boats.

The engineers really did a fine job on the water, Jane. Last night we finally got the evaporators going for the third time. There was only one discrepancy in their work, however. They hooked up the wrong lines and made salt water for about three hours before they noticed it. So, my friend, we are now drinking very salty water.

January 25, 1957   Barbados   A whale boat race is scheduled against Maine Maritime in Panama February 16th. Jim Piner quit the crew when we turned first class. Joe Walsh replaced him. He was on the original crew but didn't race due to an injury.

The Maine crew must be pretty good. We learned that last summer, in competition, they did a mile in 10 min.-56 secs. and their second class boat was only 6 seconds behind. A lot depends on the type of boat and weight, weather, sea conditions, wind, etc. Our best time in the Bay for a 7/10ths of mile is about 11 min. 27 secs.

We will race against them February 16th in Panama for the first time in 13 years. The "Bum" said we lost to them only once in 1944.

There'll be three races, one mile or more, in a double ended whale boat that weighs a ton or more without the crew (11 guys). A lot of boat to push for an awful long ways. Shear agony for the crew and their bodies!

It seems that Maine has been practicing and planning for this race for along time. We have about 13 days in port to get in shape! Many in the crew have not been in a boat for six months. Oh well, we'll give it hell!!!

I didn't get ashore in Gitmo. It seems I had a spell in sick bay. Yeah, four days on my back with something Doc Boyle called food poisoning. Nothing serious just a little rest and a few pills cleared things up. Lost a little weight (17 lbs.) and got down to an all time low of 138 lbs. As it stands now I'm back up to 148 lbs. and trying to get back in decent shape.

P.S. - Thanks again for the chow, it sure came in handy these last few weeks!

January 26, 1957 Still swinging on the hook about two miles from shore. The wind was up to 32 knots today and no liberty boats were allowed to leave the ship.

January 27, 1957 I shouldn't even write this I'm in an awful bitter mood ("Bitter Ben"). This is my third Charleston cruise. The first few ports always have been mean drunks but I've not seen the likes of the past few and this "hell hole!"

The liberty boat returned with a few "kids" (3rd jobs) that were out of it and badly cut up. I don't know what the story is but it looks like it must have been a bad brawl.

After checking the decks tonight, two fights broke out. Lucky nobody was hurt but it takes a while to stop them when they really get going. Second class this time!

Last night two first classmen went at it. First they almost killed a limey cab driver and then started at each other. Both were fished out of the water after falling off the dock. These two guys have gone through grade school and grown up together yet last night they could have killed each other! Strange!

Morale is very low. Liberty has been cut to 3 1/2 hours. Formations and check musters run all day long. We can't seem to take a breath without permission!

Warm powdered milk ...Ugh!

We've had **"Green Eggs and Ham"** long before **Doctor Seuss**.

We also have **"SPAM",** long loafs of it, great for mid-watch snacks. It's affectionately also known as "horse cock!"

January 28, 1957 John Keenan (our 3 striper) tried to defend and speak for Joe Fee(drunk, etc.) at Captain's Mast today. They both lost! Joe came back last night with the help of a few classmates and a boat. Actually he was sent back by Conners and Hirst who found him in a bar on a table.

The boat came alongside and everyone got out and made it up the ladder except Joe. He was carried up! Couldn't even stand on his feet. It seems that once on deck he stayed on his feet, with the aid of a few second jobs on watch. Capt. Woodland told him that he was on report and to lay below! Well he said he was O.K. and didn't need any help! They released him and he fell flat out cold into Captain Woodland's arms!

He's been referred to the Board of Commissioners. Lach, Graham, Cashman, Shannon, Walsh, Jim McCluskey, Putiginano and now Fee are scheduled to go before the Board. Wonder who will be next?

Mass was held on the mess deck today. Silence is observed during any religious service. Probably seventy percent of the crew is Catholic. While the priest was holding the communion wafer overhead the damn bitch-box pipes up with "Now hear this, <u>DINNER</u> for watches below." We couldn't believe it! Stickney and Taylor were on watch. Taylor made the announcement. Stickney refused! When confronted later all Taylor had to say was "he didn't think God minded!".

Only one day of liberty for me. A dance is being held for us by the American-Barbados Woman's Club. "Great Dance!"- from 1 to 6 PM, for the American (gentlemen) Cadets. In other words, it's a well planned afternoon tea for the animals of the "one gun Chun."

Definition: An animal is (1) an organized being, (2) like an animal, or (3) a Mass Maritime Middie. Noah's Ark (the liberty boat) has a strange collection! From Apes to mice, to flies - bar flies, to just plain run of the mill, honest to God, ANIMALS! They can (4) sleep anywhere and (5) eat off tin trays, also applies! Also pronounced as "An-E-Mals!" The Stoneham Zoo on cruise!

Letters to Lou…

Bill Lacasse, C.P.O., a state employee had his appendix out in Gitmo. He'll meet the ship again in St. Thomas. This is an awful place to get sick but I won't go into that, I'll tell you about it later sometime. It's a long ways from being like Mass General where you are!

I fell asleep in my stuffed salvaged chair in the haven and missed chow! I broke out some stuff from my locker---thanks to you I've lost my hunger pains!

Saturday noon we had ham, Sunday morning we had ham, and again today we had ham again! Sure is a well planned menu! You wouldn't mind so much but the ham is terrible! It has many different colors (yellows) with green veins running across it! Weird! Nobody, and I mean nobody, eats the stuff! Thank God for Spam!

Lots of action tonight! Now hear this, "Fire in the galley! Fire in the galley! Etc.!" Never saw the boys move so fast! Within a matter of minutes I bet there were ten hoses and six CO2 bottles set to go. It was out as fast as it started but the cook was burned. He was treated in sick bay and is now good as new!

I had the O.W. watch on the way in and all we did was "shift" with bells and drive the snipes crazy! In a few months maybe I'll be an O.D. on another ship. I've waited for three years. Gotta pass the Mate's Exam first! Hope I can remember all I've been taught! And you think getting a driver's license is tough! How about a six day, all day, test by the Coast Guard? Everybody really worries about it!

January 29, 1957   We are underway now with the typical jerky rock-and-roll of the Chun. Times are tough! The water we are making, from the sea, is so salty we can't drink it! All we drink is Coke lately! The powered milk is made from the same water…its even worst than ever! It will take a week for the snipes to get the water clear of our fresh water tanks. The strainer(s) in the evaporator and about six other things went wrong for a day. Just long enough to fill the tanks with salt water and ruin what good water we had aboard. Damn!

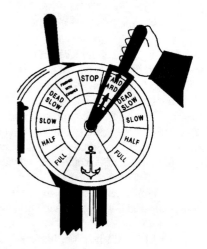

Underway as before in the Caribbean, steering sinuous courses and various speeds, aboard the good ship USTS Charleston. Upper jobs Billings and Graham had just relieved the 0800-1200 watch in the engine room. As was the custom one of our engineer classmates (Frank Flaherty) was functioning as junior watch officer on the bridge learning how to become a deckie. It was SOP to have this individual test the engine order telegraph at precisely at 1200 hours by moving the telegraph handle through all it's positions (ie: Flank to Emerg. Astern). Frank did a wonderful job doing this except he placed the handle on STOP and left it there. Forbes looked at me and I looked at Angus the Watch Engineer and we decided maybe the bridge wanted us to stop, so we closed the throttles, started the main recirculating pumps and waited thinking we were going to hit something or whatever. I think Pete Sullivan was the upper job in charge of the fireroom and he did a good job of getting burners pulled because I don't think we lifted safeties. About this time all the engineering officers arrived in the engine room to see what was happening. We all waited and waited, and then someone got the brilliant idea to call the bridge for info. It just so happened that Frank answered the call and was told to reposition the telegraph to it's normal position, Standard Speed. He did this and the plant was returned to it's normal underway status. All this time the real deckies on the bridge didn't know we had stopped!

Moral to this story…"Mamma, Don't let your Engineers grow up to be Deckies.

[Hank Billings]

Whoever is driving this bus must be off course or something cuz we are really tossing around. Remember the metal trays I showed you? Well they just came crashing down from the top of the Coke machine. What a racket! The messcooks are picking them up to wash again.

Sid, the dirty old man, is tearing mad. A dozen or so of his cups and bowls also hit the deck and smashed into a hundred little pieces. The worst time for a guy to go off course and get the ship broadside to a wave is during meals. One hand is used to hold the tray while the other is used to eat and hold your cup of milk. Lots of laughs! The mess deck is really a mess now.

...dirty old man.

I'm kinda stiff this morning. We worked out again yesterday (after dark) and didn't get caught out of uniform. Only a few more weeks to Panama and the Maine Maritime Academy. You've got to hand it to this crew, they've got a lot of guts! It's a wonder that they don't just quit and say "to hell with it", but that would be the easy way out.

Panama will be a <u>riot</u> and I mean a <u>riot!</u> Both ships have liberty at the same time. Mass has to be back earlier and probably will have to put up with the posterior drag of Maine. We've been told that a lot of money will be bet on the race from the canal pilots from both schools. Big money! Oh well!

January 29, 1957   Bridgetown, Barbados   I am in a very bad way. I have not yet heard from the Commissioners... I have had no word from my good brother [re sending him the money he owed him]. Top it off with a restriction in this port, and you can imagine how I feel.

Sunday a priest came out to the ship and held services for the Catholic midshipmen. I was officer of the watch at the time. Well, the master at arms came up and wanted me to make some ridiculous pipe about mess cooks, and I told him, "No, I won't" and that I thought it was very disrespectful for him to ask it of me. Well, he took me to the "dirty old man", Mr. Connors. Connors, by the way, knows that the only place I care to get off at on the cruise is Mobile, and he has been making threats not to let me off all year. Well, he told me that again Sunday with such a smile on his face that I had all I could to do stop myself from hitting him.

He saw this, so he added that he would make sure I wouldn't get off. With that I lost almost all control and almost did hit him but refrained just in time. However, I told him that it would take a bigger and better man than he to keep me on the ship when we got into the port of Mobile. Well, he put me on report for insolence to and threatening an officer, with the result that I am restricted here. The Captain told me later that I had the right idea but the wrong tactics, which proved nothing for I am still here, restricted. [Note: I heard tales at the reunion of Bob, while on watch, interrupting a Sunday mass with some inconsequential announcement and suspect that this is the story, only he changed some crucial details in retelling it to me. JS]

Yes, there are natural harbors......most of them are that way. The reason I did not write again from St. John's was that after the first day, because of high winds, there were no boats going in at all - thus no mail left the ship. You saw the best of the natural harbors in the U.S. - Marblehead, Mass. which has the deepest and best natural harbor on the continent.

[The fruits of deception. JS] I have just finished a letter to my father asking him to write to the Commissioners and to the Admiral for information. It would help, perhaps, if your folks wrote to the Admiral, but there is a catch to that. In order for the specials to have more punch I have been claiming you as my fiancé, which I doubt your folks like at all. Also, I told them I have not seen you since the Ring Dance because I was not supposed to leave the state at Xmas without the Commissioners' consent, which I did not ask for.

January 31, 1957   Yesterday I got ashore for about four hours though I had to go as a mail orderly. I finished the things I had to do in about ten minutes and then had to wait three hours for another boat back to the ship. I met this very nice and very pretty girl at the consul and she gave me a quick, but very complete, tour of Bridgetown. She has never been off this island, but one could never tell it by looking at her or talking with her. We had coffee together .

As far as Sue [Monrose, my friend who lived in Houston. Later our bridesmaid. JS], it would be very nice to see her again. As far as a date, if she wants to or has the time, there are three friends who would love to have some young lady show them around Houston. There is only one trouble with that for Sue. I don't know, but believe, that by the time the Charleston hits that port there will be little money left in anyone's pocket. You remember how rich I was when I met you...Still, it could be a lot of fun for the people involved. [Note: Get together never materialized, as I recall. JS]

Tomorrow we shall pack up the boat and make for Port of Spain, Trinidad, a very quiet and clean English port. I believe that we shall tie up at the Navy Docks in the place, which will certainly be a relief. It is a pain in the neck to run small boats.

Letters to Lou…

January 31, 1957   Still anchored in Barbados. What a blast we had last night! Remember that "afternoon tea" that I wrote about? It turned out to be a bar-room blast! Left the ship with four American dollars and returned with fifty cents after spending about a buck for stamps. Drinks were cheap. Rum and Coke $.10, Great Dutch beer only $.40 (Barbados money).

The dance was great! They had a Steel Band for music and they are really tremendous! Just amazing what great music they can get from oil barrels and drum sticks.

Lots of animals on the late-late Noah's Ark back to the ship. There were so many men over leave they didn't dare put them on report.

Before the boat showed up to take us back to the ship we all took turns riding around on some guy's bike. Tires, my weakness in life, cost us five dollars. I just rode up the street and the tire developed a tube bubble about the size of my fist. As I stood there looking at it one of my brilliant classmates put a pin to it putting the wheel on its rim. Some big black guy ran to get the harbor police but didn't get too far. He claimed he was gonna talk to our Captain, etc., so we gave him five dollars to take his one wheeled bike and forget it! He did!

I was with a group, Lynch, Ellis, Christie, and Reid, that had to be back on the ship at 9 PM. We got to the dock about 9:20. The penalty is usually one demerit per minute over leave for first jobs. I hired a "bum boat" to take us back figuring that the next boat won't be out until 10 PM. About half way I started to take up a collection to pay for the guy rowing. Nobody had a dime so he turned around and brought us back to the dock. When we arrived there was a whole crowd of guys waiting. All A.O.L!

As the boat pulled up, Herbie got up, fell down and knocked me down and smashed my head on the gunwale. What a lump I had! It's gone down a lot now but what a headache I had. Went to sick bay (spending a lot of time there lately) where they looked it over, washed it clean, painted it, and gave me a couple of A.P.C.s. Dr. Boyle pronounced me sober (no mast for Ben) and the O.D. let it ride. The O.D. had his hands full with the boys on deck. Yeah, - another big brawl, (shades of the ring dance) nobody really hurt - nobody put on report.

A typical water front business card..

Well I've got the next watch as coxswain of the "snake pit", the officer's "Noah's Ark." J.J. Lynch has the party boat. Lots of laughs with a special crew in the boat to maintain order. We were about to establish a Shore Patrol as another watch section. I don't think the officers will go along with it since they feel the S.P.'s will never stay sober!

Enough of our "Escapades in Barbados" a fine port! Trinidad (we've been there before) is our next stop. The boys are looking forward to it. **Animals Away**!

February 4, 1957   Secured in Trinidad at the Navy Base. We went to the "E" club for a good "meal." One large coffee milk shake and a couple of grilled cheese sandwiches. Afterwards we went out to town and off the base. Lou, we have had some real wild times but this liberty takes the cake! Remind me to tell you about it when I get back. It's quite a story and much too long to write now!

We are tied up on the same dock used to film Mr. Roberts.

Our first day here we met Maine again. More plans for the whale boat race were made. Before they came aboard we were in the boat practicing for the race. We did not know they were watching or we would have done a few things differently. It seems they know a lot about us and we know nothing about them. Damn! We'll have four days to practice here in Trinidad. Covered about three miles yesterday.

February 4, 1957   Trinidad   Yesterday I went into Port of Spain and had a wonderful time. I met a fellow from New Orleans who lives in the French Quarter when at home. In the evening I met a nice young Trinidadian girl and we went to a dance at the country club. Her name is Kay and she drives a bright red MG like a mad person. I am glad to be here after a drive with her.

I have the duty this evening but most of the ship is up at the Officer's Club for a dinner dance. Admiral Wilson left an order to the effect that if anyone is seen not fraternizing with the girls he will send them back to the ship. It sounds very encouraging, don't you think?

The Maine Maritime Ship pulled out the day we got in. We shall meet her again at the Canal Zone. I was in the hospital with a kid from there and shall look him up when we get to Panama.

Jane, have you received anything from St. Thomas as of yet? Bo sent something to his girl at the same time that I did and she got it about two weeks ago.

February 5, 1957   Trinidad   Today, my friend, I forfeited my luncheon date with our young Trinidadian to visit one of the seven wonders of the world. I have just returned from the famous asphalt lake here in Trinidad. The people here say it is a wonder of the world but if one was to count the seven new, the seven old, and all the other things people claim to be wonders, you would end up with about fifty.

All in all, Jane, it was very interesting to see, but if one is not careful, he will end up in a bottomless pit of hot, black asphalt. The guide told us of all the prehistoric beings and animals that have come to the top of the lake. As soon as the men dig out some asphalt, which they do to the extent of 1,000,000 tons a year, the hole is filled up in another seventy-two hours. The amount of gas and sulfur fumes is so great that it turns the coins in one's pocket black. It was a surprise to find that the lake will support plant and animal life. Up to the present they have not been able to determine the depth of the lake. In the past 65 years that they have been taking asphalt out of the lake it has sunk only 26 ft. below its original surface. That, I think, is enough for the asphalt lake.

No more news on liberty. I think that I will get two overnights only. I see that we will be in Mobile on a week-end, so you won't miss too much school.

February 5, 1957   We sail tomorrow on a four day run to Baranquilla, Columbia, fifty miles up river from Cartegena where we secured as youngies.

February 6, 1957   Went to a great dance last night. Learned a new (to me) dance called a "Limbo". Got a big charge out of it with the Calypso music and a Steel Band, Man! Lots of fun was had by all!

Letters to Lou...

Today was a bad day for old Ben. Yeah, they finally caught up with me and put me to work. The first time this cruise! I'm navigator for two days and the bridge had to be painted. We finished this morning. Three first jobs, all alone, no youngies to aid us! Painted gray most of the morning.

I'm kinda looking forward to these four days at sea. Gotta have a rest after that last port! Really had a ball! Remind me to tell you about our little bar room brawl some time, you'll never believe it!

When we went to the dance all the girls (all twenty of them for twenty-five guys) had an awful strange attitude towards us! I found out today that the "Maine Lads" tried to queer it on us. As I understand it they told the girls of a few happenings back in St. Thomas (nude swimming, etc.) and how the whole ship was restricted because of a verbal battle with the Police Commissioner?

They expected a bunch of animals and the animals obliged after the happy hour at the bar. Lots of action and laughs but it really was rather quiet and dead compared to some of the "liberties" we've had.

Maybe we can get even in Coco Solo. That's the only port we hit where both ships will be tied up together and both crews get liberty at the same time.

The "Fancy Dan's" from Maine, the perfect gentlemen, had better be careful with the red-eyed and rowdy animals from the decks and bilges of the old Chun! Just ten days and Panama. Can hardly wait!

February 9, 1957 To my right is Riley's tape recorder playing full blast. He has about five tapes and combined with Ascollilo's we have at least ten good tapes aboard. Plenty of top hits, good music, steel bands, and of course one complete tape of nothing but "Victory At Sea".

A few of the first jobs are up here with me on the '0h1' deck just forward of the bridge. Twenty minutes ago this deck was full of 1st job deckies taking stars and running into the chartroom for chronometer times. It's now too dark for stars and those that took them are now doing the mathematics involved to find our position. Whoever sat down and figured out how to put a star or planet on a globe or the charts we use was without a doubt a real "brain"! One look at the tables in our books and the corrections that have to be made for such little things will convince you of it.

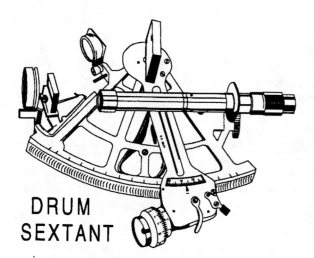

DRUM
SEXTANT

The light I'm using to write this is coming from the charthouse porthole. It's too hot to go below decks. To walk thru the mess decks and up to my haven will start the sweat pouring all over your body. I pity the poor engineers in the engine room. Actually they rate it! They could have been otherwise! The generators are acting up and one "snipe" has to be between them at all times. The temp ranges between 130 to 145 degrees. A living hell! Nobody can take it for more than 10 minutes without relief and fresh air. Oh, I just thank God I'm a deckie getting all this fresh air, sunshine, and a decent tan! I hope that when and if I go in the Navy they never make me a lowly snipe. To be a member of the black-gang in a hot body-odorous engine room would kill me. I can't take the heat, it really gets to me! [Note: Here in Arizona it still does! Happy to have lived in the valley and worked for 28 years on a cool mountain top!]

As I sit here and look out at the stars that shine so bright in a dark sky and feel the ship with its gentle roll in this quartering sea, with it's smell so pure and refreshing, I thank God I'm alive and here! The trade winds behind us are pushing the sea and spotting it with irregular white streaks and spots. Boonya and the boys are singing, accompanied with a guitar, it is very peaceful. The evening turn-to has begun and Cutter (a 3rd job) is sweeping the deck around me while I write this letter. Tough duty huh?

Going to sea as a young man with all its hardships and loneliness has done me a world of good. It has changed me in many ways, taught me many lessons, and broken my heart more times than you'll ever know. I love the sea with its beauty and its storms and violence. If I had to do it all over again I wouldn't hesitate one minute! I know I'll never forget the time I've spent on the good old 'One Gun Chun'.

Hey, think about it, I've got it made! No worries, no cares, no sweat (except in the compartment), three meals a day, (of course it's not the best of chow but it does have some nutritional value-I hope) and plenty of young men (butt-machines) with Winstons. It's kinda heaven and hell at the same time - the hell of it is you're not here...I miss you something terrible!

February 11, 1957   The next port looks like a good one with lots of deals. We received an interesting brief of the place that I sent on to my folks. I cut the top off one page and did not send the following to them:

Barranquilla is Columbia's principal sea port on the Caribbean Coast, and traditional rival of the interior cities of Medellin and Cali for the position of second most important city in the country. Population is 350,000, and we are sure that the good ship U.S.T.S. CHARLESTON will do its bit to help us out with our next census count.-

I guess they've got us pegged!!!

February 11, 1957   Barranquilla   [This letter contains the following "Barranquilla Brief", which I assume, was part of a fact sheet given to the midshipmen, though I can't imagine that it came from the official school administration. Perhaps it did.... JS]

Barranquilla is Colombia's principal seaport on the Caribbean Coast and traditional rival of the interior cities of Medellin and Cali for the position of the second most important city in the country. Population is 350,000, and we are sure that the good ship U.S.T.S. CHARLESTON will do its bit to help us out with our next census count.

I have just sorted four bags of mail totaling over 1,000 letters, and only two [are] for Mdsn. Stickney.

I am enclosing this piece of the Barranquilla Brief, which I thought you would get a [kick] out of. It shows you the difference in moral matters between the U.S. and other countries.

We were given quite a welcome here in Barranquilla. Last night there was a big dinner dance at the country club. Speaking of the club, it was one of the most beautiful places that I have ever been in - a huge patio with beautiful flowers and a big swimming pool. The drinks were free and beautiful girls were plentiful. I was drinking scotch and talking with a very pretty and very nice young lady, who, I found   out afterwards to be only fifteen years old. Today, tomorrow, and the next day there will be tours, cocktail parties and more dances. In fact, we are having a dance on board tomorrow night.

I put down my thoughts of striking the "good commander" and substituted them with sympathy as I actually believe that there is something lacking in the man's makeup.

I don't know what we will do in Mobile, honey, for I don't have a dime and no idea of how much time I shall have off.

Last night as I was getting out of a cab returning to the ship I caught my jacket on the door and put a fine rip in it. I shall spend most of tomorrow looking for a tailor. [sic]

I was looking at some ceramics and saw a couple of pieces with the Newcomb mark on them. Did you ever work on any of the stuff that is made there, if it is still being made there at all? [Note: This is really amazing to me! Newcomb pottery has become rather valuable and quite collectible, and to have found it in Barranquilla in 1957 was really something. Some wealthy Colombian families may have sent their daughters to Newcomb College, is my guess. The pottery he was looking at probably dated from the 1920's and 1930's, the heyday of Newcomb's art nouveau pottery. Enough on that..... JS]

February 13, 1957   It's now ten in the morning, the sun is shining bright, the wind is strong, no boats in the water today, no practice for the race next Saturday, and all I have to say is ...Thank God! I've never been so hung-over in my life! I have better than a head and a half!

First Class Cruise

Letters to Lou…

These Columbian Naval Officers <u>really</u> know how to throw a party! Wow, what a tremendous blast! Only one complaint...no beer! Old Ben became a scotch and soda man. The strange part is that it's the first mixed drink I've ever enjoyed. Also had a little Columbian gin - great stuff!

As I said before, it was a tremendous blast and without a doubt the <u>best port</u> we've <u>ever</u> hit! The people here are going all out for us, from the Governor (we call him Pedro), nice guy, on down. The Captain and Admiral have given us all kinds of special liberty to eat with people, play golf, chess, and for any number of other reasons.

You know how we are supposed to be back aboard at 10 PM. Well last night we were at a hotel party, after the dance, drinking with Captain Thompson (yeah, the guy we stand before at mast) and get this, the time was close to 2 AM! Got back aboard about 3:30 - up again at 6:00 - What a head!!!

Actually I was sober <u>most</u> of the night. When we came back I was as sober, if not more, than the rest of my red-eyed and rowdy buddies. One hell of a great bunch of guys.

The part that I can't get over is that I only spent the total of two dollars all day yesterday. Half of it on smokes and stamps. The bill for our table at the hotel was forty dollars - and the really nice part was somebody else paid it

It's hard to write about a thing like last night since I don't remember too much. All I know is that we couldn't speak much Spanish and had lots of fun trying. Tom Quinlan was called "Messcook" by the girls who don't have the slightest idea of what it means!

Maybe it means something in Spanish cuz everytime they heard it great laughter would break out? I still have no idea what the joke was but they would laugh so we would, being polite young animals.

A few other names used during the night was W.T. Door, Charlie Noble (a pipe in the galley), Scullery Maid, Dry B---s, Young Man, Ape, and I was labeled Butt Can. Here we are in an exclusive hotel using these weird names, and shooting the breeze (a dozen Spanish words) with the cream of Columbian Society. This would have gone over like a lead balloon in the states. This high society has a lot of fun and drink like fish!

The gal I was with was called Melba, I think? I don't have any idea what her last six names were; we wound up calling her "Melba Toast". The cadets, or animals, of M.M.A. really had a ball, and there is <u>another dance aboard tonight</u>.

The Columbian Merchant Marine Cadets from Cartegena will eat aboard with us and then attend the dance. They sure are in for a shock! I just hope they are <u>clever with a spoon!</u> We don't have any knifes or forks on the messdeck, <u>hundreds of spoons</u> but that's all! Maybe they'll serve different kinds of Jell-o to go with the big spoons? Yeah, we've been eating animal style for weeks now off metal trays. As we go thru the chow line we always draw <u>two big spoons,</u> one to eat with and the other we use as a knife. Have you ever spread peanut butter with the backside of a spoon or cut meat with one? Try it sometime! Lots of laughs! Now just imagine a bunch of guys eating at a table going at the food with <u>two spoons</u>! Hollywood could make another Mr. Roberts from things that happen aboard this ship. <u>For instance</u> - all of the big wheels, high society, Admirals and Generals and their wives etc., are invited aboard tonight. The boys, running true to form, went to all the local "houses" and invited the "employees" to the dance! I hope they all wear bright red and frilly things!!! The same thing happened in Vera Cruz when we were youngies!

February 14, 1957 Back at sea. We had our dance on board last night. It was a <u>good</u> dance but the girls were all the same. The local "employees" never showed up! A few of the animals were disappointed to say the least! The girls came in two buses from some local academy - high society weird ones! "Melba Toast" showed up with her father, brother, uncle, aunt, and six other relatives! Down here anyone that dates a girl also dates one of her relatives, and get this - you ask the father <u>before</u> you ask her. Thank God we forward Americans don't have to go through that ordeal! I'll tell you more about this some other time!

It was a good dance if you like "Junior High School Dances". All I could think of was Western Jr. H.S. in Somerville...remember? Actually it was great stuff when we were 13 or 14 but now when you look back it was kinda boring.

As soon as this "Melba" (what a name) came aboard she tells the <u>O.D.</u> she would like to see "Ben Butt Can"!

Commander Connors, the "Bum", damn near died laughing! He didn't have the slightest idea who it was! Then others started asking for "Mr. Messcook", "W.T. Door", "Charlie Noble" etc. right down the line. A first job on watch squealed on us and the "Bum" came below and found us in the "P"-coat locker room sitting around a fifth of C.C. The funny part was he didn't say a word ...he joined us and had a drink! After a toast to "La Tramp" we were herded up the ladder like a bunch of animals to the main deck. The next morning he had all of us first jobs up for scrub down!

Well when we hit the fantail we were greeted by a polite "Buenos Noches"; we all said "Good Evening" (even though it was a lie) and made with so much polite conversation it was ridiculous. Tom started it by telling some "beautiful doll" that she had a nose like a brook, always running, etc., etc., etc., etc... Dead serious he lit into her and she ate it right up - she didn't understand a word of English - and he wouldn't stop! I thought my pants would never dry! Really funny! I remember somebody telling someone what a "beautiful set of teeth" she had and that she was built like a "brick you know what." Just couldn't believe my ears! The part that put me in stitches was that she kept saying "Sí tis true!", "Yes you are correct!", and "Yes I understand!" and all the time she thought he was talking about the ship and the weather! Mucho humor on the "Uno Gun Chun!"

February 14, 1957   Valentine's Day. Before we left Trinidad I put my order in for a Radiogram and flowers to be delivered today. A dozen of red roses with a note. Did you get them? I hope so...nearly cost me an arm and a leg!

February 15, 1957   Postmark, Coco Solo, CZ   In Barranquillla I think there were more dances, parties and very nice people to greet the middies than in any port in which I have gone in the past three years.   The women were almost as good looking as the ones in Barcelona. I did think the Spanish ports the most friendly of all.

We have some Saturday's heroes here, also, my friend. One of them was taking a star sight the other night as I walked by and said to him, "Say, Bob, that sextant is upside down." He looked at me and at the instrument for several minutes and then said, as only he could say it, "Oh, go to Hell."

This is a very interesting place...The homes of the pilots are very nice and the base here is on the edge of a city. The pilots make $15,000 a year and have sixty days off with free transportation to and from the states each year. I do hope that I shall be able to go up and look at the locks and perhaps go through the canal and get my first look at the Pacific Ocean.

February 17, 195   Coco Solo, C.Z.   I have not yet gone ashore here, except for a visit to the Maine Maritime Academy ship which is tied up in back of us.   We had a pulling boat race with them today and won one and lost one. I am told that when we tour the canal tomorrow we shall meet the California Maritime schoolship which is tied up in Balboa.

I was talking with a Captain White who graduated from here in 1940 and is now a pilot at the canal.   He has been here for five years and has a wife and three very nice children. Captain and Mrs. White like it down here very much. The only fault that they find is that a couple of months of the year it gets rather hot. However, you should be used to that...   All that I have to do to get a job here is to have seven years sea experience with one of them as captain. The pay, as I told you, is good, and the government does provide a lot of things for nothing. In addition to that, everything you need can be bought at the Navy PX at a greatly reduced price.

I don't know about the financial condition of the friends whom I intend to have Sue meet, in Houston, but I can tell you that each of them is of the highest esteem in my opinion. It should be a lot of fun for Sue as well as the middies.

[Note: He is suggesting Carl, Red, Bob, Dick, and Jack as possible companions for Sue in Houston, and gives me a brief rundown on their father's occupations as references, which seemed to me very odd at the time I received the letter and more so now.. JS]

February 17, 1957 - Coco Solo, C.Z. Tomorrow we shall leave this place and make our way for a little island called Grand Cayman. This island has a population of about ten thousand with about one hundred of that amount being white. The main export of the island is turtles.

Today I went to see the canal locks at the Gatun Lake section of the canal. At the time I was there, three ships were passing through the locks. One of the ships that was going through had a friend of mine aboard as third officer

Letters to Lou…

> *.I also got a look at the section of the Canal Zone where the pilots live. That was very interesting. They have an area on top of the hill overlooking the Atlantic entrance into the canal. It is a little village in itself, with a fire department, a Navy exchange, a child care center, and a country club with swimming pools, tennis courts, and a golf course. There is also a school for the first eight grades. The pilots live in five room cottage-like houses. I do believe that every deck midshipman in the school now fancies himself as a future canal pilot. There are 170 pilots here at the canal and forty-three of them are graduates of the Massachusetts Maritime Academy.*

> *Well, Jane, soon you shall have a man. [Note: Bob's 21st birthday was Feb. 23, 1957.] I once looked to the day when I would be 21 with awe, but now it holds wonderment for me. Rather, I find it as a step which, once I have taken it, I will be liable for all my actions, taxable, and eligible for such things as the draft, etc.*

February 19, 1957 Enroute to Grand Cayman Island. I owe you a few letters after the last port. Really was very busy with O.W. watches, the race with Maine, and Eddie was down both liberty days to show me around Panama. Nice guy and we had a good time!

We lost the whale boat race in Panama by 13 seconds. It's a shame but the thing that beat us was "City Hall!" We only had one port to practice (on our liberty time) and that was nine days before the race. One h--- of a lot of good it did us with such a long lay off! The second class won - I'll tell you more about this later and we beat them in basketball! Joe Lach made their chess champ look like a complete fool! He won every game (and a few bucks) easily!

February 21, 1957 Another beautiful day at sea! The finest we've ever had! Dead calm!

This morning we had a man over board drill that didn't go too well! The sea was rougher than it is now which explains why the guys in the whale boat couldn't find the buoy. It took them 12 minutes to retrieve the buoy and the life ring. it seemed funny to some guys but it is really pretty serious. I'd hate like hell to be waiting in the water to be rescued and watch the pulling boat going the wrong way! The Captain and the watch officer were not very happy!

This afternoon we had a Captain's Inspection. While he was making his rounds we went through the line for another short arm inspection. Much to Doc (Eh-eh) Boyle's surprise he didn't catch anyone.

I know of a few cases (3) of V.D. and plenty of crotch crickets but the Doc missed them. As soon as the word got around (never more than a few minutes), the unlucky ones prepared for it and weren't caught. It seems a damn shame that sick bay won't treat them without recommending them for dismissal to the B of C.

They feel it would be foolish for them to even enter sick bay so they get treated ashore <u>every</u> port and keep it quiet! Of course between ports they are out in left field.

February 22, 1957 Grand Cayman Island. This place is just beautiful! Clean, quiet, and with out the usual number of tourists etc. Great for relaxing on the beach! The water is clean, light blue, and you can see below for a long ways. Really nice!

Our next port of call is the good old U.S.A. Getting awful close to home now. Time sure drags about this time every cruise.

When I get back I'll have to decide whether "I'm Going Navy" or not in 30 days? In other words, will I take the Navy Commission or not? I'll have to check with the Medford draft board about my status. During the leave period I'm gonna go pay a visit to the Coast Guard and see if they will take me as an officer after going Merchie? It's a long story and I'll explain when I get home. I sure as hell don't want to go in the Army! I'm not about to walk when I can ride!

As I write this, there's a big chess game going on beside me. It's a tremendous game that takes a lot of skill and practice. I'm as big a fan as anyone aboard! Really like the game!

So you've got almost a $100 saved for the wedding, huh! Wow! It sure seems like a lot now but you know and I know it won't last long. Especially towards getting married. Well we've got time I guess, just give me a few months at sea.

…three more weeks and home.

Glad to hear that you got the flowers but you didn't say what kind? I ordered long stem roses, I hope you got them!

So my father got me a '51' Plymouth, O.K., thanks for telling me! He hasn't said a word! What style, color, etc., etc., etc., ??? All you wrote is that it is a real nice car!

February 22, 1957   Georgetown, Grand Cayman   I am glad that you finally did receive the necklace and that it did please you. I have it in my mind to write a nasty letter to that store upon my return. Today I spoke with a mother and daughter here in Grand Cayman and was surprised to find out that they consider themselves lucky if they see their husbands or beaux once in a year. The men on this island have always been seamen, and the women here have resigned themselves to the fact. I have always known that the seaman of Grand Cayman, known as Grand _____ [Note: He has not written "Caymaners" but something that looks like Comanches, which I know is wrong! JS] have been the best seamen in the world, but I had no idea how many have gone to sea. There isn't a man in the town over twenty or under sixty unless he is a cripple or something like that. This place is very quiet, clean and very beautiful. I should like to come here on our honeymoon.

All I can say to you on the religious matter is that I am a Protestant with no particular sect. I usually say "Baptist", for when I'm home that is the church that I go to. I do believe that there is a difference between the Northern and Southern Baptists.

February 23, 1957   Georgetown, Grand Cayman (Bob's 21st Birthday)   I feel crushed. Yesterday was Washington's Birthday and the ship was in full dress. Today is my birthday and they aren't flying even one flag or pennant.

This going to sea is a necessary evil to which I will be bound for a couple of years. At the end of that time, I hope to buy you a beautiful home with lots of flowers and, in time, three or four children. Jane, I might, if I try real hard, be able to buy you $40 shoes

February 25, 1957   Only three "3" more weeks and home. Sounds great huh! Miami is about 500 miles away and its radio station is coming in loud and clear.

It's an awful thing to say but I've worked no more than four hours in the last two months. We're always busy between watches, liberty, navigation, and writing home but no real work is done by the first class. Wonderful life!!! It sure will be hard to go back to work once I leave this famous (?) gray hulk.

Ah yes, this is a fine ship! Lots of laughs, work, heart-breaks, and a constant battle of wits. One hundred and eighty red eyed and rowdy "midshipmen" (excuse the expression but that's what they call us) vs. a small greatly outnumbered group of heartless (grown-up graduate animals), cruel, and bitter officers (also excuse the expression, but that's the name they put to them). Maybe they (or we) should put something else to them? Of course we try but you just can't beat "City Hall."

Sometime I'll tell you more about our fine group of grown-up animals. They really are a smart group that once had a lot of promise. I'm told one man spent ten years on the beach for shooting a seaman during a mutiny, another made a small fortune until he was caught bringing jewels into the country, another studied medicine in three U.S. colleges and Oxford for his master's only to doctor to inmates at "Sing Sing" for ten years and now on the one gun Chun. And still one more tried to start his own union in Panama and left after being shot at and almost killed.

Well I'll end this little discussion of rumors about our officers now! I really don't care for jewels, unions, beaches, and being an Admiral.

February 27, 1957   This is a bad day for the Chun. The weather is the same as yesterday. Rough seas, strong winds, and a small ship makes for plenty of rock and roll. The same group of guys are sick and give a foul smell to the heads and the locker room (one poor guy didn't make it to the head).

It's like one of those days when I was a kid about 12, and stayed in because it was raining. The morning is gone, I'd just hang around the house doing nothing, and I'd ask my father for a quarter to go to the show this afternoon.

February 28, 1957 Last night when the storm started to blow itself out we had one huge wave hit on the bow. It woke us all up, and that takes a lot of doing, it was bigger than usual and hit pretty hard. This morning as the boson made his rounds he found the peak tanks flooded, yesterday they were dry. Yeah, we have a new leak! We pumped the tanks but the water came in as fast as we pumped it out. Nothing to worry about cuz it's supposed to hold water. We just secured the hatch on deck and forgot it. Let's hope we don't get any more!

Liberty tomorrow - lunch and a dance at the Navy base! Hope it's like the blast we had in Barranquilla. Texas is known for doing things big, let's hope they hold true to form. Sunday is the real blast - "A Texas Bar-B-Que" can hardly wait! Square dancing is in order following the chow. Sounds like a real good time, wish you were here! Oh well, only 19 more days and Boston.

LIBERTY IN HOUSTON

175 Midshipmen Arrive Aboard Training Ship

Houston Newspaper(?)- March 1, 1957 Just like it is on land, school was out at 3 PM Friday aboard a pock-marked World War II reconverted gunboat at the foot of 75th St. Instead of howling youngsters, though, there was an exodus of liberty-loving midshipmen. About 175 of these cadets arrived here Friday aboard the Massachusetts Maritime Academy Training Ship Charleston.

The 2,300-TON ship, converted to a training ship after its wartime service in the Pacific, came to Houston after completing more than two-thirds of its 11-week tour of the British West Indies, South America and points in the Caribbean. Their four-day stay in this city is being sponsored by the Houston Port in co-operation with various civic groups and military veterans organizations. Midshipmen aboard the 333-foot-long Charleston, like Duane Drohan and Robert Roffey Jr. train while at sea for later assignments as ship navigators or engineers in either the U.S. Navy or the Merchant Marine Service.

The Massachusetts Maritime Academy, one of four such academies in the country, authorized by the U.S. Congress, is headed by Rear Admiral Julian D. Wilson, (Ret). **FOR ADM WILSON**, Friday was like old home week. Aboard the ship he saw his two brothers and a sister for the first time in 13 years. His brothers, John Hart Wilson and Aubrey Wilson are both from Wichita Falls, while his sister, Mrs. William A. Price, is from Corpus Christi. The captain of the ship, John W. Thompson, has been in command of the Charleston since it was recommissioned as a training unit in 1948."The men aboard this ship," said Capt Thompson, "are trained to handle ships for the U.S. Navy or the Merchant Marine Service, both while at sea and during the remainder of their three years in the service at home."

THE CLASSROOM work is done at the academy in Massachusetts. While on board, midshipmen study engineering and navigation and allied technical subjects as well as naval discipline. Saturday the midshipmen who are not on duty will tour Houston and then take in the Houston Fat Stock Show. Open-house aboard the Charleston will be held between 2 PM and 4 PM Saturday and Sunday. After a series of sightseeing tours and special functions for the cadets and crew members the ship will leave for Mobile Tuesday morning.   Houston, Texas

March 5, 1957 We are about to leave Houston. Saturday we had a great seafood dinner at a place called Pier 21. Afterwards I returned to the ship about 3 PM to watch the Bruins play on TV. I bet there were 50 guys on the messdeck watching. They lost even with our support, 3-2.

I went ashore with two striper snipes later that night. It took us about an hour to find the place but we really enjoyed "Plain and Fancy", a stage show, as guests of the U.S.O.

Sunday we went on another bus ride to a dance at the Houston Yacht Club. Another Junior High affair! A great meal, no drinks, a good time had by all but the dance was terrible! The Red Cross Women were pushing the guys to dance with a bunch of dogs! Also No drinks - No Courage - No Dancing! We returned to the ship at 10:30, an unheard of early hour for the "Kay-Dets" of M.M.A.

If you get a chance and should think of it, look up a book called "My Husband Keeps Telling Me To Go To Hell" by Dorothy Dix. I got a kick out it and maybe you will too! We were in Trinidad more than a month ago - an awful long waiting list - the book was passed from hand to hand - I just got it! Kinda funny! You'll probably find it in the "Fine Arts" section of the Medford Library. One of our intellectual types has it out on loan from the Trinidad Naval Base Library! I think he signed out as "Charlie Noble!"

The Mobile Press - March 7, 1957

U.S. TRAINING SHIP ARRIVES IN MOBILE

The U.S. Training Ship Charleston arrived in Mobile this morning with 175 midshipman who are completing a three-month training cruise to various foreign ports. The vessel, commanded by Capt. John W. Thompson, will be open to the public between 2 and 4 p.m. Thursday, Friday, Saturday and Sunday. She is moored at Berth 2, Pier B South Alabama State Docks. Rene A. Stiegler, Jr. president of the Mobile Propeller Club, said a series of activities have been planned here for the officers and men of the ship, which is operated by the Massachusetts Maritime Academy, under the supervision of the U.S. Maritime Administration. Future officers of the merchant marine and the U.S. Navy are trained at the academy. The Charleston is a former U.S. gunboat and will sail from here at 9 am. Monday for Fort Lauderdale, Fla., and then return to Boston. Rear Admiral J. D. Wilson USN(ret) is superintendent of the school and is aboard for the cruise.

March 10, 1957   Mobile, Alabama. The night I called we were at another junior high dance! Liberty expired at 2300(11 PM) but some of the boys decided to stretch it a little. They are all "PAL'S" now! otherwise known as "Prisoners At Large!" Twenty-two first classmen, restricted until Boston and the B of C's act on their case. Ted Brown was 1 hr-15 mins. late and is really sweating it! I won't go into the reasons for all the "PALs" cuz you'll probably hear more about it from me when I get home.

As it stands now, two 1st class deckies are now members of the 2nd class and six (6) snipes have been dropped out of the class. Pretty serious business!!!

I had liberty Friday but didn't go ashore for a number of reasons. First and foremost the town of Mobile is like Reading (MA)...DEAD!!!

Thursday the 21st the Bruins play their last game at home in the Garden. I'm gonna write home and see if my brother Paul can get us tickets. I'd really like to see a game in person, how about you? We watched the game on TV yesterday. The B's won 4-2 over the Red Wings. Tremendous game with lots of action and mixing it up!

March 11, 1957   Postmarked Ft. Lauderdale, FL   I got to Mobile. We got to see each other, but I think all his talk about "special liberty" turned out to be baloney.   My brother and sister-in-law loaned us their car briefly. We decided to start buying silverware (essential!) for our future home.   It was wonderful to see each other again.

March 13, 1957 - Ft. Lauderdale, FL   Commander Rounds asked me who the very attractive young lady was that I was showing around the ship in Mobile. I told him that you are my fiancé, and he said I was a very lucky guy......Those four days did fly by.

This Ft. Lauderdale is quite a place. It looks like some port in the Caribbean. I have never seen so many small boats in one place in all my life.

March 14, 1957 - Ft. Lauderdale, FL   Captain Woodland sorted the mail and thought I was ashore. Consequently I had no letters at mail call. He was not happy to open the ship's office to get your two letters for me.

Jane, I hope that you don't take up smoking because cigarettes remind you of me. It is not only a bad habit, it is also an expensive one. Red Riley just stuck his head in the porthole and told me to tell you "hello" for him.

I hate the thought of going back to the academy. I have so damn much work to do, it isn't funny. I have completely forgot all that I have learned. I was thumbing through my notes last night and they are all Greek to me.

As for the pants, my love, I can only say that I do not like them. I have always fought with my sisters over them and it looks like I will have the same trouble with you. I think, Jane, I have told you before that to me a girl looks, if not cheap, at least out of place when she is wearing pants. I am not a puritan, far from it, but pants and painted nails do not appeal to me. However, I will admit that I am in the minority, for pants and painted nails are almost universally worn .As far as my becoming a dictator, Jane, I think you have little worry .I shall close this letter...with the hope that we shall never refer to it again.

Letters to Lou…

March 14, 1957 Port Everglades, Florida. I'm in my bunk now, propped up on one elbow with one light after taps. It will cost me 10 demerits if caught, but do I care? With only six demerits in 2 years 8 months I feel like a piker in this class!

Can't wait to get home! Only six more days! I can hardly remember the rain, cold, fog, snow, and summer nights. Especially making rounds through the dark ship with a flashlight then over to the building to check the doors and windows. Just an unpaid night watchman with a weekend (an all important weekend) at stake if I missed just one punch on the round portable time clock.

After I write this I'll have to borrow a stamp and envelope. Been broke this port and last. Spent my last dime on stamps etc. for the most important person on this cruise...you!

The days are getting longer! Next Tuesday will be longer than it should! We'll arrive in Boston Harbor, Tues. around 6:30 PM and lay off Castle Island all night. The only good part of this l o n g night is that we will be able to listen to Artie Ginsburg - "Night Train" - who will no doubt mention M.M.A. and the good old Chun. J.J. Lynch wrote to him from here. I've got a special reason for listening and hope things go right! Why don't you tune in WBOS-1500, I think?

These places are all designed for couples and not for a single guy in uniform. Wish you were here! Wish this school was Co-ed!!! Always have!!! Never happen!!! Just can't wait to get Home!!!

February 20, 1998. Update! Nearly 41 years later. Some things never change!!! The following has been "excerpted" from the Captain's Log on the School Ship's MMA Web Site Page.....Quote....

We will arrive in Cape Cod Bay on Friday evening 20 February slightly ahead of schedule! We will anchor in the Bay and remain there completing required training and prepare to enter port. We will transit the Cape Cod Canal and tie up on the tide, Sunday Morning 22 February 1998 at 0530.

I must confess, the well being of many Cadets is beginning to concern me. some are showing signs of the dreaded but all to common malady, "Channel Fever". The first symptoms usually appear three to five days out from home but may occur earlier if the Sea Term has been particularly long and arduous. The onset typically, is quite sudden and generally includes unexplained loss of appetite, anxiety, and intense insomnia. Those afflicted walk incessantly from deck, to deck, as if searching for Elmo. They are frequently observed to be in a trance like state, staring at the navigation table while babbling incoherently.

A common utterance is, Rwetheryet, Rwetheryet, Rwetheryet. They often become wildly exuberant and describe even the most hated enemies from home in glowing terms. Those in the final stages of the disease have been known to shower three times a day, to pack and unpack everything in sight, and to linger on deck at the exact spot where the brow last sat. It is absolutely pitiful but, what can I do? To my knowledge, the disease has never been successfully treated at sea and the symptoms mysteriously vanish after entering port and before the afflicted can be transported.   TS Patriot State Sea Term 98.

March 15, 1957 Ft. Lauderdale, FL We will leave here on the morning tide and have a quick and troubleless four day run back to Beantown. I really do think that this will be the last trip the honorable Charleston will make for MMA. There is a lot of serious talk about getting a new ship. I certainly hope that it becomes a reality.

March 19, 1957 We are now off the shores of Cape May, making for Buzzards Bay lightship. I surely hope that we find it better than we did last year. Buzzards Bay was fogbound when we hit it and we darn near cut the lightship in half.

To show you how things go around here, Jane, I will give you an idea of today and tomorrow's plan of the day. We will hit the lightship at six in the morning and proceed from there to the Cape Cod Canal. We shall leave the canal at about nine and make for Boston. Upon arrival in Boston, which should be at around four o'clock, we will anchor for the night. Can you imagine anchoring within a mile of the dock and waiting for the next day to go in?

Today the Charleston came upon a pod of whales. I have never seen so many whales in one group. It must be mating season or something. At one o'clock I saw about twelve in one group, and throughout the afternoon another five or six came by separately.

…another Admiral.

Home again. A little early and unexpected, but welcomed just the same. There is a big storm blowing up around here, so the Captain decided to make port while the making was good. It gave the middies a few hours extra liberty, which is a godsend at any time.

I shall go into Boston tomorrow to the office of Naval Personnel to see what kind of a deal I can get. I will go to see my father's employer in the afternoon to see if I can get a job as a cab driver. I have to go back to the ship in the next couple of days to get my gear and my books. I want to get some studying done in the leave period...Good news, I called the laundry and my dress whites are still intact. Now all I need is the money to get them out.

March 20, 1957 Tied up in Boston...home at last! Those that could, left the ship like crazed rats without giving a thought to the "Good Ship Charleston" having completed its last Academy cruise and headed for the scrap yard! Kinda sad huh?

Training Ship Held Unsafe, Kept in Port

Boston Newspaper(?)- March 22, 1957. Acting Gov. Robert F. Murphy yesterday ordered the Massachusetts Maritime Academy's training ship Charleston to be kept at her pier in Boston because the captain considers the vessel unseaworthy after its recent two-month, 10,000-mile cruise. Murphy said he is fearful for the safety of 175 cadets who arrived here Tuesday and are scheduled to sail Saturday for Buzzards Bay.

Captain Thompson of South Yarmouth reported the Charleston developed a leak in its bow cruising last month in the Gulf of Mexico. Murphy said the captain reported the 21-year-old vessel had leakage trouble on earlier trips and "is letting go."

The Coast Guard has revoked the ship's certificate but issued a temporary certificate permitting it to sail to its home harbor. Murphy said the Coast Guard feels the ship can be sailed safely to Buzzards Bay tomorrow.

March 22, 1957 I went to the Coast Guard and filed for a duplicate copy of my seaman's papers, which cost me $1.50. Next I was photographed and fingerprinted at the Lynn Police Station at the cost of $1.00 for my cab license. I am enclosing a notice I found in the paper this morning. ["Training Ship Held Unsafe, Kept in Port"]. I know nothing other than what is in this article, but I will find out the particulars when I go back to the ship tomorrow.

March 26, 1957 Bo Taylor came back to the ship last week-end unengaged. I certainly hope that won't happen to me.

March 29, 1957 I haven't heard about school for the next year yet, but I have seen the condition of things around here, and they are not good. My father is not feeling well at all, and if it gets any worse, I might have to go to work in August whether I want to or not.

April 1, 1957 School started off with a bang. I got back last night and found that four midshipmen had been excommunicated from the academy, two of which were my classmates. I understand that the Board of Commissioners have not yet finished their work and a couple more middies expect to get their walking papers.

We received a class schedule and to my great surprise and pleasure (?), I found that out of the first two days of the week we shall be entertained for six periods by the one and only William John Connors. We have him two periods for rules of the road, two periods for rules of steamboat inspection and two periods for seamanship.

We started to fill out applications for our licenses and commissions today. We will be doing that for weeks by the looks of the application blanks. There are questionnaires for things on not destroying the stamps on cigarette packages to have you contracted V.D. or been addicted to the use of narcotics. The personal history part alone takes thirty-two pages.

There has been a lot of talk about a new ship...In fact a few of the officers are going down to New York tomorrow to look at the stockpile they have up the Hudson. If I know the people around here, they will come back with a four stack, twenty-year-old destroyer but that will be all right because it will be a NAVY ship.

April 3 ,1957 The seventh graduate of the Mass. Maritime Academy has moved up to the rank of Rear Admiral. The latest one was a graduate of the class of '23 and is now an admiral in the Coast Guard.

Letters to Lou....

I was talking with a couple of Coast Guard Officers not too long ago and found out a lot I didn't know about. It seems that if I go to sea for four years in the Merchant Service I can sit for an examination for an inspector in the Coast Guard. If I successfully pass this exam I will be taken in the establishment and put on sea duty for two years. After the tour of duty at sea, I will be sent to a marine inspection office, and there I will stay. It seems like a good deal to me. The pay starts around $7,000 and has all the retirement benefits. It will be like every other office job except that I will wear a uniform.

More applications, Jane. I have been signing my life away for the past two days.

April 4, 1957 It seems that Pete Readel met a girl in Houston with whom he fell in love...or believes that he did. He has called her three times since we got back, and she called him about eight. The name is Brooksie [Note: As best I can make out... JS], and she is coming up here for graduation. Brooksie put a return address on one of her letters as follows: Brooksie F. Readel, Houston, Texas. The MMA sorted the mail and saw the return address, and old Pete was before the Captain in about three seconds flat. It took him about three hours to convince the Captain that he was not married to the girl and that it was only a practical joke.

Mr. Freeman is receiving letters fast and furiously from Colombia.

We are not the only ones in our favorable position.

The officers who had gone down to New York are back, and the prospects of getting a new ship look very good. I don't think, however, that my class will see it.

April 8, 1957 It has been decided that we are to get the ship that is in New York. However, it will not come about for three or four months. The reason the officers like a Navy ship, Jane, is that it attracts more attention when it comes in and out of port.

Our friend Bo had better get back with his girlfriend or find another one or he will get himself killed. He has been doing a lot of drinking, but worse than that, he has been drinking and driving.

I found out about going to work for Babcock and Wilcox. I can be a salesman for them, but first I will have to put 3-4 years in the service department and 1 or 2 years in service at some other branch. When one finally makes salesman, he gets a straight salary of $15,000.

I have to write this quickly, my friend, for I have a class in about ten minutes with the one and only Mr. Connors. I shall have to eat a little humble pie with that character for the next four months, for I want no more trouble

April 11, 1957 I passed the physical for Ensign, United States Navy today, Jane, which makes me very happy. I shall apply for a commission in the inactive reserve. While I was in Boston, I talked with one of the officers there and found out many interesting facts about the Navy Reserve. It seems that if I take a number of correspondence courses and go on active duty for two weeks a year I will be entitled to a pension after twenty years.

For the time involved, it is a very good deal. The courses take, at the most, three hours a week and when I go on active duty I will receive regular pay. I was thinking that if I took the active duty pay and put it in the bank each year it would put at least one child through school.

I have to leave for a few minutes to make evening check muster.

[I wrote about some incident with my physics lab instructor that had not been pleasant. I have no idea, in 1998, what that was about. Bob's reaction follows:....JS] I think that you are learning a very bad habit from me, at least it sounds that way from your experience with the lab instructor. You don't know when to keep your mouth shut. I had a similar experience about the same time with Cdr. Rounds. He had given us some questions on the different quizzes with two different answers. I was selected to tell him about it and when I did he refused to admit that he had made a mistake. That got me very angry with him and I picked the whole test apart - result, a 10 for Mdsn. Stickney and the same week's pay for Cdr. Rounds. Why, Jane, is it so hard for some people to admit a mistake? If I can be right 50% of the time I am happy.

…another license.

April 12, 1957   It is another cold and windy day on Sunny Cape Cod. I don't think that the weather will ever clear up.

My father saw the stack of letters I have in my drawer and told me that I am crazy to keep them and that someday I shall pay alimony on them.

Today I have been looking over the old exams for third officers and if I don't learn a lot more in the next few months I will surely flunk. There are questions on those papers that I could not begin to answer. ….They are so ambiguous that one does not know where to start. I talked with a couple of Coast Guard inspectors recently and they told me the exam this year would be even harder than last. This is because of the football heroes that failed last year.

There are a couple of girls aboard to see the middies. One of them is a very attractive and seemingly nice young girl. I don't know what the hell she is doing around here. But when I go on watch I shall tell them to leave. If there is one thing around here that is bad for a girl's reputation, it is coming aboard this ship - especially at night.

[Bob mentions several of my friends and asks me why I haven't mentioned a male friend, Richard, who was simply that - a friend. Then goes on to do a "Dear Abby" number. JS] …As much as I kid you about "Poor Richard", I am very glad that he is around. We have been thrashing that sort of thing out around [here] for the past week or so. Bo claims that he lost _____ because he told her and encouraged her to go out with other fellows while she was at school..

Carl says he tells Betty that he doesn't even want her to mention another boy's name while he is around. I have been telling them that if two people are in love they will stay in love no mater how much social intercourse they have with either of the sexes.

April 13, 1957   I was thinking today that if I do come back for school next year and do get an engineer's license, I can go to sea for a while and then sit for a stationary engineer's license and work at some large plant. Then I would be home every night. That is what I want. I want to spend as much time with you as I can. Perhaps I should forget about going to sea and get a job as a school teacher or something like that.

Everyone has told me this weekend that I look very sad. And I really feel that way. If only fate would be a little less cruel to us everything would be fine. I shall wind up this tearful note…

April 16, 1957   I filled out data cards for the Navy today. If I go on active duty they will use this card to place me. For the three selections of sea duty I put down DD's, DE's, DMS's out of the Gulf. [Note: I have no guarantee that I've interpreted these letters correctly. JS] For shore duty selections I put the Gulf Naval District. When and if I do go in the Navy I could have a good chance of getting a ship out of New Orleans or Mobile.

Carl Megonigle had to report to the Boston Army Base today for an induction physical for the draft. I hope that they will give him a deferment until graduation.

If there is one kid who is in love with the Navy it is Carl. He plans to go on active duty right after graduation and try to get sub school. If he makes a career out of the Navy, and I think he will, he will be an admiral as sure as the sun will set.

This has been a hectic week around here so far. In two days we have had four tests and are scheduled to have more starting tomorrow morning. The Nautical Astronomy is coming thick and fast and right over my head. The same is true for Ship's Stability and Construction.

I have been thinking of going right to work after graduation instead of attending school for another year. I keep getting rumors of making $700 a month, and I can't get them out of my eyes. It's not only the money that attracts me, my love, but the things that I will be able to do with it.

April 18, 1957   I am thoroughly disgusted with myself today, Jane. Last night I sat up and studied the Navigational Triangle until it came out of my ears and today in class we had a quiz on it. The work was finally done and I thought I had it all right, which I did, until I transferred my answer to the answer book and added 10 degrees for no reason at all. I got it back marked zero and I almost flipped. It took me over an hour and one violent headache to find out where I had made my mistake.

Letters to Lou…

For some unknown reason there will be no liberty for the underclassmen this Easter. I don't know what the hell they are keeping [them] here for but I know it has no logic behind it. I have been telling all the third classmen to send a telegram to the governor but I don't know if they will or not. Something is going to have to be done around this place and it will have to be done fast or the state will find itself with a school full of nervous breakdowns. The underclass has to stay here three weekends out of four for no good reason as it is. When they stop them from going home on Easter it is too much. Perhaps with the new ship things will get better. At least they will have a little more room to live in.

The weather is at last getting a little better around here. At least the sun is out more often than it has been. This, of course, is New England in general, not Buzzards Bay. It is always cold and windy here in the Bay. Last night the Redbud (?) went off our quarter. It stopped there until this morning when a big tanker came by at full speed and washed it off. It came darn near, parting our lines in the process. I don't know or understand what the Navy uses for navigators, but they sure as hell don't know what they are about when they come through this canal.

Last year about this time a destroyer ran aground on the other side, and two years ago a patrol craft sunk at the other end. And still they are too damn conceited to take a pilot. I believe that, after this, the Army Engineers who have control of the place will make it mandatory for Navy ships to take pilots. [Q: Do Navy ships have to take pilots through the canal today? JS]

I was reading in the [Nantucket, Nautical? JS] Mariner today about a collision that was caused by a captain crossing Ambrose Channel on the wrong side in order to wave to his wife. I would like to see his wife. She must be a beauty to cause a million dollar accident.

April 19, 1957 We have been having quite a day today. Since eight this morning we have been having practical problems in damage control. From cutting through steel doors with torches, to flooding compartments, to wire splicing and cable jumping. I have learned a dozen ways to sink the good old Charleston.

There have been a lot of repercussions from the third class not being granted Easter liberty. I just left the quarterdeck and Cdr. Rounds was talking on the phone to one of the Boston papers.

I am enclosing a snapshot. It will give you an idea of what my home on the Charleston looks like. The six bunks in the background belong to myself, Keenan, Riley, Megonigle, _____, and Taylor.

I hope that I will be able to drive a cab this weekend. I surely need to get some work.

April 22, 1957 I have found a new occupation for myself, Jane, but since you just ridicule me for them, I shall not tell you in what direction my pot of gold lies this time.

I have been a good boy of late and have had no arguments with any officers for over a week. I hope that this will keep up until I get out of this place.

April 23, 1957 [The knees, in the snapshot he sent me, belong to Mr. John D. Keenan, and the person in the bunk is Red Riley. JS]

I got caught writing a name under a cartoon of a funny-looking naval officer today. I wrote down R. T. Negative, the nickname for Cdr. R. T. Rounds while he was standing right in back of me. He asked me if I thought it was funny and then told me to destroy it, but what a look.

April 24, l957 There is not much time left for you to be sending mail to me in care of this address - I hope.

I still have not heard a word from the Board of Commissioners as to whether or not they will permit me to return to the academy for another year. I had a call from a couple of people this week to let me know that the FBI had been around looking for detrimental information on the kid.

Riley and myself have just returned from out in town and as we came aboard we picked up Carl Megonigle and carried him with us. As Carl is the officer of the watch, he did not appreciate the humor of it.

I have the duty this weekend again, but only one more time after this and I will be through for the year. If I come back, however, the ball will be rolling again and every time that I will want to do something I will have the duty.

I shall have to get down to some serious studying in the next twelve weeks, Jane. This exam that I am to take for the third mate is part of a permanent record kept by the Coast Guard and the Navy. I do not want to get a low mark in it.

I have to construct a curve of static stability for the good ship Charleston, so I will close for now.

April 24, 1957 I wish that the Board of Commissioners would give me the word one way or the other....If I were in a better financial situation I would go into the Navy after graduation and get my military obligation over with. But at the pay of an Ensign I'm afraid that I cannot make all of my [financial] obligations. Today is one of the days that I envy Joe R____ [?], the mess boy. That character doesn't have a care in the world.

April 25, 1957 I should not waste my time writing to you, Miss Smith, for I should be writing to the steamship companies. (Please do not take this literally.) I was talking with Riley's brother today. Frank, that is his name, graduated from this academy in 1955. He is now the second officer on the SS AFRICAN _____ Frank has been home for a couple of weeks and he came down to see his brother and some of us today. When we were talking with him and asking what will be expected of us after we go aboard ship as third officers someone asked him how much he makes. Listen to this closely now, my friend. He just returned from a seventy (70) day trip and he received pay of two thousand six hundred and ninety-five dollars (2,695). It figures out to be around two hundred and seventy (270) dollars a week.

He drives a 57 Cadillac and wouldn't think of wearing a suit if it costs less than a hundred dollars. On top of that, honey, he loves his work. He said if they cut his pay to a hundred a month he wouldn't change. (He is so taken with the figures, impoverished as he is, poor baby, that in almost every case he's put both the words and the numbers of the dollars....almost like there's a mystical charm about writing it both ways.)

[I was telling Robert, our son, about Bob's work as a "re-po man" with his brother Charlie. This is an example. JS]

Getting back to reality... Each time I have the duty, [I lose out on] something. I won't be able to drive the cab this weekend and on top of that, Charlie called this morning and told me he wanted me to fly to N.Y. on Friday with him and drive back a couple of cars. Another chance to earn twenty or thirty dollars gone to pot.

April 26, 1957 This has been a very fogbound day here in Buzzards Creek. I don't think the visibility has been over 50 ft. at any time today. The forecast is more rain and fog for the weekend which should make it very pleasant.

Carl and I went into town tonight to get a pizza but it took over an hour to get it. By the time we got it we had lost our appetite for pizza. The time, however, was not a complete loss, for the man who made them was very funny. He kept telling us what a bad deal it was to get married - for all you do is work, work, work and no one appreciates it.

April 28, 1957 I hope that you had a grand time at the theater last night. While you were sitting inside watching a show I was standing on a cold and foggy quarterdeck. I have never seen so much fog around here before. All day Friday and Saturday the visibility was below zero. The fog lifted this morning, however, and the canal is making up for the business it lost in the past two days.

I have done little or no studying this weekend...I think that I shall change my middle name from Lawrence to Procrastination.

April 29, 1957 This week...in addition to the studies, I have to stand deck watches. I have little time, Jane, honestly. I am lucky if I average five hours of sleep a day. There is a lot of work for us to do in the next 12 weeks and the situation will get worse before it gets better.

April 30, 1957 Well two long drawn out days are over. Tomorrow will tell the story. A double period of Conners and one of Rounds ought to take its toll! Playing "you bet your weekend" again! Learning through "fear" sure raises hell with a guy's nerves. As you know we live down here for several reasons all based on liberty and freedom. Weekends, leave periods, and finally graduation always seem so far in the future. Don't think I'll ever make it!

Letters to Lou...

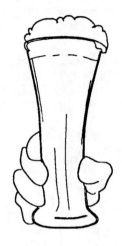

April ? 1957   It was late on a Friday evening. Flarabag and I had been drinking beer since about 5:30 PM in the Brookline Grill. As we were on our way home, we were still wearing our midshipmen uniforms. After about 142 beers, Flarabag suggested that we have another one for the road. Unable to speak, I nodded my head in agreement. The conversation and events went something like this:

Flarabag:	We'll have two more beers!
Bartender:	No! You're both drunk. Go home.
Flarabag:	No, we're not. Give us two beers.
Bartender:	Go Home, Franny, you're drunk!
Flarabag:	If you don't give us another round,
	I'll drive my car through the front door
Bartender:	Franny, the two of you are so drunk you can't stand. Go home!

With this, Frank staggered out the door. I continued to sit on the bar stool staring into space, my eyes glazed over. Shortly thereafter, Frank drove his car through the front door in all his glory. In the ensuing melee, I managed to escape spending the night in jail. Frank, however, was a guest of Brookline's finest. It had been another typical week-end liberty.   [Dick Boles]

May 1957   One week some of the officers disappeared down to New York, and then nothing was heard. and then all of a sudden we had a new ship, the USS Doyen (PA 1), a former troop transport. It spent several weeks at the Bay and was off again for yard work   ['57 Yearbook]

May 1, 1957   Today I saw a strange but beautiful sight, Jane. It was a dirty and rusty old fishing boat that was coming through the canal. However, her steadying sail was painted with a very beautiful picture of the Virgin Mary and the Christ child. The scene was on a rocky seashore. Very impressive.

I...would like to become an admiral. However, [my] habit of telling people what I think would be detrimental to my career as a Naval Officer. If I were to go into the regular Navy I would most likely stay an Ensign for the entire time. The promotion system in the Navy is set up for yes men rather than a man with initiative and ambition. Not only that, but there are too many requirements regarding social life, both public and private, which I do not agree with.

Tell your mother not to worry, for the normal area of operation for the Sixth Fleet is in the Near East and Med. If I do follow them it will be in a merchant ship, I hope.

Tomorrow we again have two tests. It is getting to be a habit but with the mate's exam only ten weeks away I feel it is a good thing. Jane, if I flunk that exam, I think that I shall just go away and never come back. We were given some sample copies of them today and it looks like nothing that we have been preparing for.

May 2, 1957   I am glad that you gave up writing rather than giving up TV. It makes me feel so wanted.

While I was on watch tonight an Army training ship came up alongside the State Pier. I think that they made the worst landing that I have ever witnessed. It is some sort of ship for training Army men for tugboats.

I was informed today that if I wanted to sign a contract for a year and one-half with the Farrell Lines I could make a bundle of money. If I want to make $10,000 a year I can take command of a river feeder on the Congo. It is a job where they give you a ship, a .45 pistol, a black crew and you move cargo from the mouth of the river down to Capetown.   The only trouble with that job is that you have to stay over there for a minimum of one and one-half years. However, it is a very good way to get in with the company.

Keenan has his finger stuck in a hole in one of the desk drawers and Riley is pulling him around the room by the desk.

May 6, 1957 I made some money this weekend and if I do as well next weekend I should be able to pay for my ring.

...a new ship.

I neglected to tell you that I saw the comet last Thursday night. It will not be visible again for 90 years.

May 7, 1957   [Note: Bob is going to take a family friend's sixteen-year-old daughter to her senior prom. JS]   Riley told me today that he has a lot of experience with teenage girls and will give me the proper instructions in rock and roll before Friday. The closer this thing comes the more I believe that I made a wrong decision.

May 10, 1957   I was reading your last letter and one of the kids said, "Stick, is that from the girl down South? She has pretty legs. I watched her climb up one of the ladders on the ship."

The forest fires around here are really putting this state in an uproar. In addition to that, a couple of jet pilots were killed in plane crashes in the past two days.

We had a very interesting morning yesterday, Jane. We were given instructions in the use of ships' and life boat distress signals. The pyrotechnics really are very pretty hanging from their little parachutes.

May 13, 1957   Miss Smith, the mates or license exams are what I have been coming to this academy for. If we fail to pass the mates exams we cannot be commissioned as third officers in the Merchant Marine and thus are not qualified to graduate. And if we don't graduate we cannot get a commission in the Navy. Hence, Jane, our claim to fame is our marks on the mates exam.

These exams are made up in Washington especially for us and consist of a series of exams. The number of exams are usually 18 to 20 but there have been years when there are as many as 25 different parts. Each part is on a different and complete subject, with from 20-25 questions. The exams start on a Monday at 0800 and if we finish before noontime on Saturday we will be doing well.

[It had been a rainy weekend; he'd driven his cab over 300 miles. JS] Soon I will be able to pay off the balance on my ring.... Still no word from the Board of Commissioners as to whether or not I will be able to return to the academy for another year.

May 17, 1957   You would laugh if you saw me now, Jane. I had half of the hair on my neck burned off today. We were doing some practical work with fire and damage control. I had the job of cutting an access hole through a deck with the torch. I lost my helmet in the scramble, and a blowtorch caught me square in the nape of the neck.

A crew of 12 midshipmen and two officers have gone down to New York to pick up the academy's new training ship. I would have liked to make the trip myself but since I have to drive my cab this weekend I thought better of it. I understand the ship is in dry-dock in Hoboken right now getting her bottom sandblasted and painted and will be towed to the academy over the weekend. The ship will stay at the school for about two weeks where inspections and job orders will be made. From here she will move to Boston to have her work done and will be ready for service in the early part of August. Although my class will not have the benefit of the new ship, I am very glad that the school consented to get her. It is a step in the right direction, and that is what this school has been really in need of for the past ten years.

There is also a lot of talk about Mr. __?__ carrying out his threat to make this the best-equipped maritime academy in the world. It is already the best academy. All we need is the physical plant. Of course, I will settle for less but it does seem as if something is being done.

I still have had no word from the Board.... I think I shall forget about it entirely and commence my life at sea, if I am ever fortunate enough to graduate from this place. There were six more of my classmates released from MMA on this date. I think we shall be lucky if our class numbers fifty at the graduation exercises. I have much studying to do but no taste for it.

May 20, 1957   The new ship has arrived and it is tied up to the starboard side of the state pier. It still has no power or lights but [that] condition shall be remedied in a few days. It is covered with an oily protective coating which leaves a terrible red stain on everything that gets in contact with it. On the Charleston our problem has always been not enough room. I think it shall be a reversal on the "Doyen".   Keenan, Riley, Meg and myself took a ten dollar tour of the ship today and all were amazed to find out how much room is available on that ship. [Note: This is interesting for me to read because I remember later letters describing how the ship has been re-compartmented disproportionately to suit the officers, etc. and the middies get what's left - not all that much more space than they had on the Charleston. JS]

Letters to Lou…

There is even a snack and soda bar as large as the one in Walgreen's [the drugstore in N.O. where we met] aboard it. There are tailor shops, barber shops, a cobbler shop, machine shops, carpenter shops, etc. - all of which are bigger than the living spaces aboard this ship. The laundry on it looks like an industrial laundry.

The "Doyen" shall stay here for a couple of weeks for various inspections and job orders to be written out and then she will be towed to Boston to be put into commission as the Bay State Mariner.

There is talk of the construction of a new pier and classroom buildings being started in July but I will believe that when I see the work actually being done. Nevertheless, I want to see the school improved so much that I am delicate prey for all such rumors.

May 21, 1957 Things are happening on the "Doyen." Today a crew went aboard to try and start the diesel operations to get some lights on it; I doubt if they will have it running before a day or so. The seamen have been aboard with cutting torches getting rid of the Navy gingerbread such as gun tubs, speed lights, etc. I believe that the hatches will be opened tomorrow to get some fresh air down in the holds as there is a lot of work to be done down there. The Admiral has stated that it shall be given a coat of gray but the middies and some of the officers are trying to overrule him and get it painted white. I, myself, would much rather see it painted the latter color. I believe that the law requires it in any case.

There is a rumor of graduation being moved up or back. I have heard both of the versions, and I believe neither of them. Nor do I believe that it would be a smart move. I have a lot of work to do in the next eight weeks...

May 22, 1957 All sorts of ideas for the new ship, Jane. Everything from what rooms will be for whom to where the ship will leave on its first cruise. I have heard the Admiral and the Captain are dissatisfied with their small rooms. That means that there will be a lot of cutting up done in the wardroom area.

I was talking with the Naval Science yeoman today and if the ship does not get on the ball quick there will be no commissions at graduation. It seems that all the work has been completed except for the recommendations from the Admiral, which are holding up the whole deal from going to Washington. After they are sent to Washington, it still takes three months to be cleared, and since there [are] only ten weeks until we are through here, it looks very doubtful. However, it is typical of the way things are done around here.

May 23, 1957 I did a very honest day's work aboard the "Doyen" today,, It was very dirty and very hard but I did learn quite a bit. So , one cancels out the other. I tore down all of the radio and transmitter equipment, cleaned it, and moved it from radio two to radio central. The ship is looking better each day. However, it will be a few months before it will be in any condition to live on.

I have the duty this weekend...and I have ideas of getting all sorts of work done. I have several notebooks I have to get into presentable order and pass in, and a couple of papers to write, in addition to studying for another exam. So you see...that I have an enormous amount of work to get done.

May 24, 1957 I've just found out that we are to have an inspection today and my dress uniform is in the cleaners. I shall have to do some fast talking to get out of this. Today is the first good day that we have had on the Cape for a couple of weeks. It is one of those days that brings many people to the grounds of M.M.A. In fact, this morning we were honoring a couple of lovers on the dock.

I have a class in electronics in a few minutes. If we have another of those ping movies I shall get nothing out of it. Each time I see one of those movies, I get more involved in outwitting the "ping" than in watching what the movie has to put over.

We have just got the word that the "Doyen" will not be painted gray. The colors used will be a dark gray hull, white superstructure and buff stacks. This may not be the best combination of colors, however, it is much better than plain gray.

May 25, 1957 (Arrived with 3 cents postage due...) Today has been a fine day on Cape Cod. The barometer is still rising which indicates a good day for tomorrow. It is nice to have a few good days here on the Bay once in a while.

The new ship is the "D-O-Y-E-N" (PAI) a shallow draft transport. L.O.A. 418'; M.B. 65'; M.D. 18'02"; S.H.P. 6,000; D.W.T. 6,580. It has six battle stars from the major island battles.

May 28, 1957   Capt. Burke was down again last evening, Jane, with the word that the U.S. Line will put us on the payroll the day we graduate. I still don't know which line I shall go to work for. The general manager of U.S. is a graduate of the academy, which is a point worthy of consideration. However, Moore Mac is building three large new liners and is scouting for young officers to train for those ships.

I want very much to see the Far East, Northern Europe and Australia - all of which come under lines of the U.S. Farrell is a very good line but it has only the runs to and from Africa. Moore Mac is in Northern Europe and South America. A.P.L. covers the globe but it is a West Coast outfit.

I think that I shall decide to work for U.S., but I am not sure. If I want to come ashore and go to school it would be good to have worked for U.S., the reason being that it is a big line and has a lot of ships in a lot of ports. If I were a student, I could stand night mate watches for them which pays about $40 a night.

May 29, 1957   Today has been another fine day on the Cape. We are to march tomorrow, and for that reason it will rain like hell. It usually does. After the exercises tomorrow we shall go on liberty for the weekend. We have to report in the Science Museum on Friday for a lecture on Atomic Power. After that we have to report to the Coast Guard to write out some more applications, etc. It shall be a long weekend...and I hope to hear from you.

If I get through these exams the first time, honey, I am going to get very drunk for at least a week. I believe that I have worried almost as much about the exams as I do [about] you.

June 2, 1957   Only twenty more days and home again. Seems like I was on cruise again. Not much to write about really. When my orders come I'll know where I'm headed and when so we can at least make some wedding plans. Here we are going together for three years and not married. I wonder if they will ever change the rules down here? Doubt it!!!

Only eight more weeks and I'll have seen the last of the "One Gun Chun."

June 3, 1957   I have spent about sixty dollars this weekend paying off my ring and other small debts. The more I pay out, the more I find I owe. I shall be in good financial condition by graduation, except for the money I want to pay back to the Grand Consistory Office.   [Note: The Masons had given Bob a scholarship, I never had the impression it was an actual "student loan". But he did pay it all back because he felt very strongly that they could then use that money to help another student.]

I did drop into Captain Hurley's Office over the weekend, Jane.   Mr. Hurley is one of those cold-hearted ...commissioners. However, he told me that he would try to have a definite answer for me in about two weeks as to whether or not I can come back to school

June 5, 1957   I think you spoke too soon about my being a model midshipman. ..Today I got put on report again. It seems as though the dirty old man and myself have come to blows again. I was in a heated argument with him this morning and unintentionally told him to go to hell. I believe that this is the fourth offense for insolence. [Note: How can you "unintentionally" tell someone to go to hell??? JS]

I passed the qualification tests today in communications. It makes me feel a little better. I received a paper from the F.C.C. stating that [I was] examined and found qualified to be a communications officer. It is not much, I agree, but if it ever comes to when I would be matched with another officer it would be an added article in my favor.

The mates exam has me scared stiff...I want to pass it the first week so that I can go to New York in the two weeks between exams and graduation.   The reason for this is that I want to attend the Sperry Loran and Radar Schools.

Midterm marks came out yesterday, honey, and we lost another first classman, along with two second classmen and one third classman. I did much better than I had expected. I had one 2.7, two 3.0's, three 3.4's, and the rest were 3.8's. That should look good to the Board of Commissioners when and if they look at my marks

Letters to Lou...

Tomorrow is the 13th anniversary of the invasion of Normandy. [Note: On June 6, 1982 Bob began a tour for military history buffs, landing on Normandy and following the troops' path to Belgium. JS]

June 6, 1957   Worked on the new ship today. They won't have her in shape for months. If it wasn't so close to graduation I think they would cancel classes and really put some time into it. It's a great ship, too bad it didn't come sooner.

I've got 12 of my 24 extra duty hours worked off. I've got plenty of time to get the next 12. Never was restricted before and it seems kinda strange to spend a weekend aboard with no watches to stand. Nothing to do but sleep, eat, study, and maybe sneak a beer or two on Saturday nights. Two and a half more weeks aboard. Seems like a such a long time. The part that really hurts will come later. My conduct mark will be 0.16, usually I get a 4.0. The old average will sure take a drop and so will my class standing. <u>Note</u>: I've given a lot of thought to the above. There is no charge mentioned in the letters I've reviewed, and I do not remember what I did or got caught doing to be awarded 24 demerits? (2/1998).

I wish I could say we've had some weather good enough to get a little sun. It's always cloudy or damp down here! When the sun does break through it is followed by a strong wind. Maybe I'll be able to get some "benefits" this weekend and lose this cold?

June 7, 1957   I was making fun of you for getting shot with Salk vaccine only a short while ago. I got stuck with the same needle today. Not only that, but I have to get two more shots tomorrow and another on Monday. I don't know what they are...

Today is the day that the Board of Commissioners are supposed to meet. I hope that they have discussed my case. If I don't get any word in the next week I think I shall call Mr. Hurley and tell him what he can do with his promises.

It is really a shame the way that they are cutting up the "Doyen". I honestly think that everyone and his brother will get a room aboard it except for the midshipmen.

I had to fill out more applications today. This time it was for a commission in the Maritime Service.   This, however, may pay me 200 dollars back pay. I hope that it does. It would be nice to get that much money around graduation.

No mast today, Jane, but I still have tomorrow to lose my weekend. If there isn't a mast tomorrow, I shall be safe for the weekend.

June 10, 1957   If you so desire, you can get me a pen for graduation.

I was talking with a graduate yesterday who has just got called into the Navy. He graduated in 1955 and was, until about two weeks ago, employed as the second senior officer on the S.S. America - a job that I would like to have very much. It pays about 900 a month and every two weeks you are in New York for four days.

I still have no word from the Board. I think that rather than get myself worked up over this I will just forget about the whole thing.

I think that I shall go to work for the U.S. Lines. I had thought of going with Farrell, but I understand that U.S. will take Farrell over within the next year anyway.

June 11, 1957   Nothing new has happened around here today, except that I have had a to-do with the Admiral. It was over my getting the word from the Board as to whether or not I shall return. Once again I have had a promise from them but no action.

A lot of talk of the academy moving out of here has been spread around but I doubt if it will ever come about. Today, however, was a grand day for the middies. It seems that the middies have always complained about their accounts being short and the admiral has always told them it must be a mistake. Today the State Audit Board found the school books short a considerable amount of money.

I shall have to leave this note for a short while...I have to turn my sextant in to the head of the Navigation Dept. It is Capt. Woodland, and he takes about three hours to check them over. I don't know why, either. The darn things aren't worth a dime.

…the Great White Dove.

Studies are starting to slack off now but the marking is getting harder. We have started to do review work now. It is surprising how much one can forget in such a short time. I have not been to mast yet for Mr. __?__ but the captain is out this week, and it looks like I shall go unpunished for another week.

June 12, 1957 This is a very gray and gloomy day on Cape Cod. The sun hasn't been around since yesterday sometime. The cape is crowded with people waiting for the Mayflower. That is a shame the way that it is being commercialized. I think that the Mayflower will stay in the Cape for two days and then go to New York. Once it gets to New York it will go to a specially built dock and people will be fined a dollar a head to look at it.

Capt. Burke was down again last evening and gave us some particulars on the different companies. I still don't know which one I want to go to work for. MooerMac has some choice runs and in addition to that you are allowed to take your wife with you on one trip a year. Would you like to take a 45 day trip to Northern Europe, my love? U.S. is the biggest company of all and treats the M.M.A. boys fine. They have three good runs, one to the Far East, one to Australia, and one to Europe. Farrell has the West, South and East African runs. Not only that, but it pays the best and offers more of a challenge to a young officer. The only problem is that they will can a mate for the slightest error....

June 12, 1957 Hitting the books pretty good lately, getting ready for the Mate's Exam. So much to remember! In Navigation there is a saying we use to remember the steps used to determine compass errors. It is in the form of a table that goes like this...Compass Deviation |Magnetic |Variation |True...Rounds told us to use the saying "Can Dead Men Vote Twice?", but to impress us further he reversed it to read "True Virgins Make Dull Companions!"

In Rules of the Road we have another little jingle along the same lines designed to aid in describing lights that ships are required to carry....Name |Visibility |Height |Arc| Location |Color. to "No Virgin Has A Small Child!" Of course these little jingles are old and have been passed down for years. Strange what will be remembered and what will pass by the board!

No word on Navy orders...things are pretty quiet down here.

June 1957 I learned today that Boles was about to graduate without demerits. I put him on report (and I'm glad) for being out of uniform (6 demerits). No way was "The Great White Dove of Purity" gonna leave cherry! Especially wearing a <u>fez!</u>

June 14, 1957 Yesterday I was instructed by Captain Woodland to show a reporter around the academy and the ships. If he prints all that I told him about this place and how it operates Mass. Maritime will skyrocket to fame.

June 17, 1957 I am writing as many letters now as I can for in a week or so my letters will come to a grinding stop....The reason, as you well know, is the mate's exam.

I think that Dick Greer is also thinking of returning for the extra year.

If I do come back to school next year I will have to get a car. The reason is that I will be an officer and since I can't bum in an officer's uniform or in civilian clothes I will have to get my own transportation.

There was a representative from MooreMac here at school today. He answered all the questions I had about the company. When the time comes for me to go to sea, I shall go to work for them.

Father still thinks that we do not have a full sea bag and even more so when I told him I would spend any back pay to see you.

June 18, 1957 Cdr. Rounds told us the other day that there had been a certain amount of speculation as to whether or not we would [take] the mates exams early. The Admiral, however, has said that will not be.

I am still waiting for the word from the Board to come in...

June 21, 1957 (Sent to "Sun-Ray Cottages", Gulf Breeze, Florida) I went to mast today, my friend, but I did a lot of fast talking and the Captain was in a good humor. So, he gave me a long talk and let it go at that. However, if looks could kill, I believe Mr. C. would be up for murder. I honestly believe that; that man has no use for me.

Letters to Lou....

I received a letter today from Maine Maritime and it stated that they did very poorly on their mates exams up there in the woods. I shall take that as fair warning...

A graduate of the Academy who I knew very well died a hero today, if being a hero is any compensation for dying. A steam line parted on the ship he was on, and he entered the compartment to shut it off and got burnt to a crisp. The poor kid. He [was] only 22 and just got married three weeks ago.

I had a good time today...All the engineers were in class so I had to take some Coast Guard Inspector through the "Doyen". It was a lot of fun, for I had been down there only three times myself. While we were in the No. 1 fireroom the lights went out so we stood still and chatted in the dark for four or five minutes.

June 24, 1957   We have the reports from Maine on the results of the mates exams and they were disastrous.

I still have not received word on paper from the Commissioners

June 27, 1957   I don't think I have accomplished a damn thing this week. With standing watches and a beach party the other night I have lost track of studying.....This is the most important part of my time here and I can't get into the spirit of sitting down and doing some real work. ...This is the time of year when the Cape is really jumping, which does not add to the chances for study. I'll bet there has been a beach party every night this week.

The "Mayflower" will come through the canal tonight on its way to New York. A lot of people will be down to see it but I have no desire to do so.

Finals at school come on the 14th and the mates exams on the 20th. ..It leaves me very little time.

I have the 8-12 tonight...the last watch as officer of the watch for MMA. It seems now that it was just yesterday that I reported aboard as a third classman. See how life has passed me by...

July 3, 1957   Captain Woodland told us what to expect on his final exam. If what he told us is true I won't even try to study for it. [It] would be a fruitless effort. Honest, Jane, we compared Woodland's exam with that for a master and it made the master's look like it was intended for a novice.

After the Fourth weekend we come back to take three exams for the dirty old man. Can you imagine sitting in a classroom for six hours waiting for that joker. I'll die if I pass from his looks at me.

Admiral Wilson told us today that the back pay from the Navy won't be in for about four or five months.

Not much else to report...except that the Charleston is dying a slow death. You would not recognize it now if you saw it. The lifeboats and deck machinery have been taken off and moved onto the "Doyen".

The second class are acting as first class and the third class has followed suit. It amounts to...a lot of loud talk and threats but nothing to be taken seriously.

July 10, 1957   I feel much better now ...three exams from Mr. Connors are out of the way. Each I passed with considerable success, I believe. We have seven more exams next week and then the mates exams the following week. Since I can't get down to see you, my love, I shall try to get to New York for two weeks' school. After that there is graduation and then my problems start all over again with another year at MMA.

I have so many things to crowd into the next few weeks that I have a constant pain in the head.

Riley's brother, Frank, is back from Africa and he tells me that Farrell is the only company to work for. He is home now for a month and then he goes back as first officer on the African _____ which is not a bad position to be in at the age of 24. He not only loves his work, but with the first officer's job he will make about $15-18,000 a year.

First Class Cruise

July 11,, 1957   Today I finished my last official class at the Massachusetts Maritime Academy. Next week we have the finals and then the mate's exams. I sure will feel better when a week from Thursday next comes along.

I wish that I didn't have to work [driving the cab] this week but I don't feel that they would like it if I failed to show up.

Jim Hannan showed up here today with his new Jaguar. He graduated from here two years ago and now is a pilot in the Baltimore Association. Not bad for a kid of 23. He makes about $35,000 a year. What happened to him is very rare indeed but it shows what can come if one is on the ball.

I didn't tell you about the American [Packer ??] because I feel sorry for the Master. He will hang for that to be sure. Not only that, but I bet there were l0,000 people down here to see the Captain who couldn't run his ship right. If he was out there saving life, etc., there would be no notice of it at all.

I received a few more shots today. I'm beginning to feel like a pin cushion. I have a list of the shots I've got since we have been here and it's almost as long as my arm.

July 13, 1959   I took a couple of women in my cab today who were just that. When a girl starts to go downhill, they really hit the bottom. I am beginning to lose faith in the opposite sex.

July 19, 1957   Evidently I passed all of the finals for I was able to leave yesterday...From the courses with Mr. C., I received a 3.6, 3.7, and 3.8, respectively. He even wished me good luck at the gangway.

In the final for Electronics, Mr. Lynch, a classmate of mine, was stuck for an answer to the question, "Explain electron theory and give a detailed account of the electron's passage through a conductor." Mr. Lynch, who is a real character, replied, "Electrons flow from South to North, around the world in eighty days." The instructor was so fazed by the answer that he gave him full credit for the answer.

After, and if, I pass the mate's exams I am going to sit for a license as a radiotelephone operator. It is not an essential thing to have but once again, if I have more than the next fellow I will be that much better off. The exam is relatively eas and it takes only a few hours to complete.

The weather has been hot and sticky for the past few days, which is not conducive to study at all. From the looks of the examination room ...it is not going to be pleasant to take exams in.

July 24, 1957   I wish that I could have some way of finding out [how] I am doing on these mate's exams. We will not get the word until the examination is over.   I feel sure that I have flunked at least two parts of it so far. The only consolation I have is that everyone else seems (or claims) that they are doing equally as poor. It is crazy, Jane, but everything we were told to know letter perfect, we have not been asked. And what we were told would not be asked of us has been asked in full force.

The weather has cooled down considerably in the last few hours. I hope that it stays that way for the next few days. It gets unbearably hot in that exam room

Well, my friend, the mate's exams are over. .I finally got a definite confirmation to my request to return to school for another year - this time on paper.

August 10, 1957   Well, tomorrow is the big day. I have all my things in order and hope that it will be a nice day. I think that there will be more Stickneys at graduation than anyone else.

August 11, 1957   The Class of 1957 was the last class to graduate from the good ship... USTS Charleston.

MASSACHUSETTS
MARITIME ACADEMY

115th
Commencement Exercises
RECREATION HALL
United States Naval Center
E and Fargo Streets
South Boston, Massachusetts

August 11, 1957

2:00 P.M.

BOARD OF COMMISSIONERS

AUTHUR C. SULLIVAN, *Chairman*

CAPT. CHARLES H. HURLEY

S. P. JASON

CAPT. JOHN R. PETERSON

WILLIAM W. PETERS

Musical Selections by Navy Band of First Naval District

Presiding Officer   Capt. Charles Hurley
Class of 1915, MMA, Member, Board of Commissioners,
      Massachusetts Maritime Academy

Invocation   Capt. Roy C. Bishop
       District Chaplin, First Naval District

Greetings of the Commonwealth   Dr. John J. Desmond, Jr.
Commissioner, Massachusetts Department of Education

Greetings of the Navy   Capt. Robbins Allen, USN
            First Naval District

Greetings of the Coast Guard   Capt. R.J. Borroney, USCG
          First Coast Guard District

Administering of Oath of Office for Licensor
          CDR. A.G. Mobers, USCG
Officer in Charge, Marine Inspection, Coast Guard

Presentation of Bibles   Rev. Robert Wood Coe, D.D.
      Executive Secretary, Massachusetts Bible Society

Presentation of Degrees Rt. Rev. Msgr. Cornelius T.M. Sherlock
      Chairman, Massachusetts Board of Education

     Musical Selections by Navy Band

     Presentations of Awards to Prize Winners

Address to Graduates   Hon. Thomas E. Stakem, Jr.
      Member, Federal Maritime Board

Benediction   Rev. Robert Wood Coe, D.D.
      Executive Secretary, Massachusetts Bible Society

Star Spangled Banner   Navy Band, First Naval District

MASSACHUSETTS MARITIME ACADEMY
Buzzards Bay, Massachusetts

REAR ADMIRAL J. D. WILSON, USN (Ret.) Superintendent

CAPT. J.W. THOMPSON, USMS - Executive Officer and Commanding Officer

Heads of Departments

CDR. R.T. ROUNDS, USNR - Navigation and Seamanship
CDR. J.M. MURRAY, USNR - Marine and Electrical Engineering
LCDR. T.C. GALLAGHER, USN - Naval Science

Instructors

CDR. R.T. Rounds, USNR - Navigation and Meteorology
CDR. J.M. MURRAY, USNR - Steam Engines, Thermodynamics, Atomic Power
CAPT. L.A. WOODLAND, USNR - Ship Construction, Communications
CDR. W.J. CONNERS, USNR - Seamanship
CDR. W.A. HEMMERLY, USNR - Diesel, Steam Auxiliaries, Electronics, Refrigeration
LCDR. J.R. CROSBY, USNR - Diesel, Steam Auxiliaries
LCDR. A.G. CLARK, USCGR - English, English Literature
LCDR. T.C. GALLAGHER, USN - Naval Science
LCDR. L.F. HARRINGTON, USNR - Mathematics
LT. P.G. HIRST, USMS - Maritime Law, Stowage and Cargo
LT. L.T. PAGE, USMS - Seamanship
LT. R.R. POITRAS, USN - Naval Science
LT. C.E. JAILLET, MMA - Spanish Language
LT. C.L. LIVSEY, USNR - Steam Boilers, Properties of Materials Rules and Regulations
LT. M. TONELLO, USNR - Machine Shop, Welding
LT. T.W. MINNOCK, MMA - Economics, History, Mechanical Drawing
LTJG. D.W. GERETY, USNR - Naval Science
MR. G. CAVANAUGH - Physics and Chemistry
LT. A. ANTEEN, USMS - Maritime Academy Steward
DR. J.T. BOYLE, LT. MMA - Medical Officer

Former Graduates Awarded Degrees...

SEAMANSHIP AND NAVIGATION

ARSENEAULT, ARTHUR J. JR	Charleston, South Carolina
JAKEMAN, WILLIAM C.	Watertown, Massachusetts
STEELE, LAWRENCE W.	Rochester, New York

MARINE AND ELECTRICAL ENGINEERING

BARNES, GEORGE W.	Westbury, New York
BEATTY, JAMES F	Great Neck, New York
CULVER, JOHN A	Rockville, Maryland
DONOHUE, DAVID A.	Worcester, Massachusetts
FRISCH, ALFRED J.	Springfield, Massachusetts
MILO, JOHN	Canton, Massachusetts

AWARDS

Prize awarded by the late Mr. Irwin Wood: Wood Memorial Prize (The income on $5,000), given to the graduate having attained the highest standing in seamanship and navigation. Mr. Wood made this award available through his will because in great part he attributed his success in life to his early training at sea. Presented by Mr. Arthur C. Sullivan, Chairman, Board of Commissioners, Massachusetts Maritime Academy, to

LAWRENCE B. MEYER

Prize awarded by the Boston Marine Society to the graduate excelling in those qualities making for the best shipmaster, including aptitude, prompt and cheerful obedience of his superior officers, devotion to duty, integrity, force of character and ability to attain and maintain leadership. Presented by Alva D. Parcell, to

CARL E. MEGONIGLE

Prize awarded by United States Lines Company to the graduate who is outstanding in leadership. Presented by Captain R. Stevens, to

DAVID V. FREEMAN

Prize awarded by Society of the War of 1812, to the engineer graduate for excellence in studies, good conduct and the possession of those qualities of leadership and a willingness to assume responsibility which have characterized the Navy and Merchant Marine of the United States. Presented by CDR. Ross Currier USNR, to

DAVID V. FREEMAN

Prize awarded by the Massachusetts State Society, United States Daughters of 1812, to the graduate in the engineering division standing highest in engineering and electricity. Presented by Miss Josephine G. Richardson, President, to

PETER M. KENDRIGAN

Prize awarded by the Propeller Club of United States, Port of Boston, to the seamanship graduate and the engineering graduate whose scholastic class standing during the last year shows the most marked improvement over the previous two years standing. Presented by CDR. A. G. Moberg, USCG, to

DAVID J. LACAIRE - DECK
HERBERT A. ELLIS - ENGINEER

Prize awarded by the Maritime Association, Boston Chamber of Commerce. Presented by Mr. John J Halloran, Manager of the Association, to

For general excellence in seamanship and navigation

CARL E. MEGONIGLE - SEAMANSHIP CLASS
For general excellence in marine and electrical engineering

JOHN J. FERRERA - ENGINEERING CLASS

Prize Awarded by Columbian Rope Company to the deck graduate showing greatest proficiency in Nautical Science subjects - seamanship, navigation, communications, ship construction, rules of the road and marine law. Presented by Mr. Reynold Spriggs, Advertising Manager, to

ROBERT EDWARD RILEY

Prize awarded by the Military Order of the World Wars, to the seamanship graduate and the engineering graduate standing highest in Naval Science. Presented by Colonel William M. Tow USA (ret.) Past Commander, to

DAVID V. FREEMAN - ENGINEER CLASS
ROBERT K. REILLY - SEAMANSHIP CLASS

Prize awarded by Society American Military Engineers to the graduate standing highest in engineering. Presented by Brigadier General Alden K. Sibley, USA, to

JOHN J. FERRERA

Prizes to the coxswains of the winning and losing crews, and presentation of Plaque to the Academy, awarded by Port of Boston Marine Square Club. Presented by Captain William W. Storey, USCG, Class of 1917, MMA, President of the Club, to

COXSWAIN OF WINNING CREW - DONALD F. HOGAN
COXSWAIN OF LOSING CREW - DEXTER H. KOOPMAN

Prize awarded by RETREADS, World Wars I and II, Hut No. I of Massachusetts to the graduate standing highest in Spanish. Presented by Past Commander Ross H. Currier, Hut No. I to

DAVID V. FREEMAN

Prize awarded by the late Captain Joseph John Sawaska, Class of 1928, MMA, to the graduate making the highest mark in navigation. Presented by Mrs. Joseph J. Sawaska, to

LAWRENCE B MEYER

"CAPS AWAY"

SEAMANSHIP AND NAVIGATION

ASCOLILLO, EDWARD L.	Roslindale	MEGONIGLE, CARL E	Manchester, Ct.
AYLMER, JOHN F.	Osterville	MEYER, LAWRENCE B	Edgartown
BROADBENT, CHARLES W.	Centerville	READEL, PETER F.	So. Walpole
BROWN, ROBERT D.	Orleans	REILLY, ROBERT E.	Sharon
DROHAN, DUANE E.	Dorchester	RILEY, ROBERT E.	Wallaston
HOGAN, DONALD F.	Medford	ROFFEY ROBERT C. JR.	Rockport
KEENAN, JOHN D, Jr.	Braintree	STRAUTMAN, ROBERT E.	So. Weymouth
GREER, RICHARD	Quincy	STICKNEY, ROBERT	Lynn

(Note: Both Greer and Stickney were omitted from the Graduation Program Reasons unknown)

LACAIRE, DAVID J	Spencer	SWEET, JOHN K. Jr.	West Andover
LACH, JOSEPH F	No. Dartmouth	TAYLOR, ROBERT K	So. Lancaster
LYNCH, JAMES J. III	Jamaica Plain	WEAVER, RICHARD G	Middleboro

MARINE AND ELECTRICAL ENGINEERING

ANDERSON, ROBERT N.	West Yarmouth	KOOPMAN,DEXTER H.	No. Weymouth
BILLINGS,HENRY C.	Mattapan	LOPAUS, ROY C. Jr.	No. Weymouth
BOLES, RICHARD J.	Brookline	MAHONEY, FRANCIS E.	Whitinsville
BUTHMANN,RICHARD A.	No. Andover	McCARTHY, JAMES J.	Dorchester
BUTLER, THOMAS F. Jr.	Hyannis	McCLUSKEY, JAMES M.	Dorchester
CHRISTIE, ARTHUR J	No. Scituate	McGRATH, JOHN J.	Concord
CIALDEA, GIULIO P .Jr	Newton	McKENNA, JAMES E.	Bridgewater
DUFFLEY, NEIL J.	Dorchester	MIRABELLO, EUGENE D.	Arlington
ELLIS, HERBERT, A. Jr	West Roxbury	O'CONNELL, JOHN R.	Brockton
FEE, JOSEPH, R	Hingham	PERSSON, RUSSELL H.	Oxford
FERGUSON, FREDERICK M.	Whitman	QUINLAN, THOMAS E.	Dover
FERRERA, JOHN J	Waltham	RUMNEY, ROBERT E.	New Bedford
FLAHERTY, JOHN F. Jr.	Brookline	SCARLATA, ANTHONY C.	Dedham
FREEMAN, DAVID V.	Dorchester	SOUTHWORTH, FRANK C.	Marblehead
GILLEN, JAMES F.	Hingham	SULLIVAN, PETER M.	West Roxbury
GRAHAM, FORBES	Gloucester	TASK, HAROLD L.	Dorchester
GRANT, KENNETH R.	Quincy	WALSH, JOSEPH F.	Dorchester

(Note: Both Grant and Walsh were inadvertently omitted in the first edition of "Letters to Lou)

KENDRIGAN, PETER M.	Wareham	YOUNG, ROBERT A.	Needham
KENNEDY, LINCOLN M	Walpole	YOUNG, WAYNE G.	Hingham

Note: Classmates Russell Manning, Joseph McCluskey, and William Reid Graduated with the Class of 1958.
I don't know if Donald Putignano and Mickey Spillane Graduated.   [Jim McCluskey June 2002]

After successfully passing the final examinations at the Academy we were allow to "sit" for the Third Mates (or Third Engineer) Examination. The exam was given at the Coast Guard Headquarters in Boston. It took more than five days to complete. Everything hinged on passing this exam. An unsuccessful candidate would not receive his degree from the Academy or a Commission as Ensign in the U. S. Navy. A certificate of three years attendance would be the only document issued by the Academy.

TYPICAL COAST GUARD LICENSE

The minimum passing grade for any one of nineteen examinations, except Navigation and Rules of the Road, was 60%; an average of 70% was necessary in order to pass the entire examination; and 90% was required in Navigation and Rules of the Road.

Letters to Lou…

August 12, 1957   It's a good thing you didn't waste your time and money coming up here for graduation…As I was walking into the hall, one of the kids showed me the program and my name was omitted from the graduating list. I looked up the officer in charge, only to find that the woman who had made up the graduation arrangements didn't put my name in. Consequently, I had no license, no degree, and no diploma. It would be unnecessary to tell you that I was quite worked up by the time I got to the Admiral. The Admiral told me that he was very sorry and sent to the office for the things I was missing. At the completion of the program he got the Commissioners together and had everything signed and presented to me. It will be an unforgettable event in my life, I promise you.

August 20, 1957   Dick Greer left yesterday for a round-the-world trip in the "Steel Navigator", a brand new ship. He is on as third and will make anywhere from 800 to 1,000 a month. I wish that I had followed his example and said the hell with the extra year also. It is hard to stay here and study and see all my classmates out in jobs like that or in the Navy having a ball.

August 22, 1957   A ship came up the canal last night sending flashing light. I went up to the bridge and took it. The message was from Bob Strautman, a classmate of mine, third officer on the African Pilot bound from Portland, Maine to Capetown, S. Africa. I wish that I was with him.

August 25, 1957   I had an unexpected guest at the ship Friday. Bo Taylor drove down to see me in his new red MG. Very impressive for a dashing young Naval officer. He has a DE out of Boston. A better arrangement couldn't be bought for love nor money. The worse thing of it is that he had put in for duty on the West Coast.

Classroom Building – 1997

MAY 18, 1958
ST. FRANCIS OF ASSISI CHURCH
MEDFORD, MASS

CLASSMATES
JAMES McCLUSKEY   WILLIAM REID
JOSEPH McCLUSKEY   JOSEPH WALSH

Quote..."Never marry an Irishman, a Catholic, or a Sailor"... Lou's Dad.

Oh well!!!

1957 U.S.T.S. Charleston Post Card

Whale Boat Crew
J. Piner, D. Greer, H. Billings, J. Aylmer, R. Brown - D. Hogan –
C. Megonigle, R. Riley, W. Young, H. Ellis, W. Reid

R. K. Reilly - E. Ascolillo

J. Lach - C. Megonigle

Jim Lynch - Ben Hogan – Bob (Red) Riley

C. Broadbent - J. Sweet

J.Alymer - getting a fix.

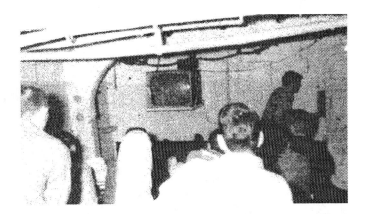

"Howdy Doody Time"

BIG PROP

"AFTERTHOUGHTS"

PART 4

A collection of Post Graduate Events, Alumni Bulletin Notes, Correspondence Newspaper Articles and Miscellaneous Other Stuff.

U.S.T.S. CHARLESTON
TRAINING SHIP OF THE MASSACHUSETTS MARITIME ACADEMY

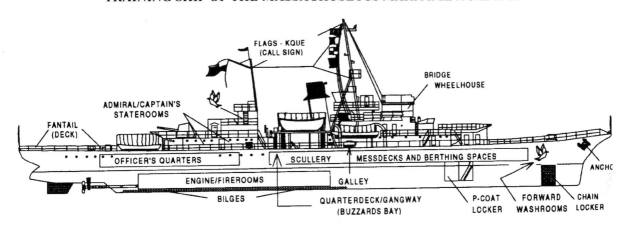

GLOSSARY

"86"	An alarm or warning, shouted loud and clear, when a person in authority approaches.
Anchor Pool	Money paid to an individual that holds a pre-assigned number based on the logbook entry of the exact minute of the ship's arrival. An illegal lottery run routinely by members of the upper-class that retain ten percent of the pool.
Anteen Raiders	A group of cadets that took advantage of an opportunity to purloin clothing items from temporary storage in the P-Coat locker room.
A.P.C.	All purpose capsule, aspirin.
Black Gang	Men that work in the engineering spaces of a ship.
Bogger	Born and raised around the cranberry bogs of the Cape.
Charlie Nobel	The name given to an exhaust pipe from the galley.
Century Club	100 demerits awarded for a single offense usually with the loss of liberty. 100 demerits = 10 weeks of restriction. All of the raiders became members of the 'Club'.
Cozy	Out of sight out of mind. Attempt to be invisible.
Deck Ape	The elite sailors and navigators of a ship. Also known as "deckies" and gentlemen.
Function	An assigned task or duty.
Fez	A small red cap with a tassel worn by men of distinction.
Hazing	Illegal abusive, humiliating stunts or ridicule directed at the freshman ("Youngie") class. A routine happening!
Gig	A special motorboat such as the "Captain's Gig."
Jobbed	Assigned a task, usually illegal, by an upperclassman.
Jumping ship	Leaving the ship, via various means, without permission.
Knot	A term used to indicated the speed of an object. Also a cute and clever arraignment of bends and terms in rope for a special purpose.
Liberty	Authorized freedom to leave the ship.
Messcook	A person assigned to a group responsible for food services, including set-ups and clean-ups, on the ship.
Muster	Attendance check or head count.

Posterior Drag	Harassment by a person in authority or others.
Punt	A small rectangular boat used to work on the sides of the ship.
Quarterdeck	Entrance/Exit to the ship.
Sea bag	A large canvas bag with a draw string used as a suitcase.
Scullery	A space used for washing food utensils-trays, dishes, etc.
Sick Bay	An area set aside for those with a prolonged illness or injury.
SPAM	A mid-watch delicacy sliced from long loafs.
Rack	Stretched canvas laced to a steel frame with a thin cotton mattress pad.

NOSTALGIA 1954 - 1957

President   Dwight Eisenhower
Vice President   Richard Nixon
AVERAGE INCOME $ 4,500.00
NEW CAR $ 2,000.00
NEW HOUSE $ 12,000.00
RCA TV BLACK/WHITE
FAMILY SIZE 14" $ 130.00
BIG SCREEN 17" $170.00
LOAF OF BREAD $ 15-.22
GALLON OF GAS $.12-.20
GALLON OF MILK $ .95
GOLD PER OUNCE $ 35.00
MINIMUM WAGE $ 1.00
DOW JONES AVERAGE   400 to 520
LIFE EXPECTANCY   70 YEARS
MAJOR NEWS EVENTS
        RUSSIA LAUNCHES FIRST MAN-MADE
        SATELLITE - "SPUTNIK"
        IKE INAUGURATED FOR SECOND TERM
        FIRST U.S. NUCLEAR POWER PLANT BEGINS
        OPERATION - SHIPPINGPORT, PA.
        THE KOREAN WAR ARMISTICE WAS SIGNED A
        YEAR BEFORE WE ENTERED THE ACADEMY
MOVIES - Academy Award Winners - 1957
        Best Picture - BRIDGE ON THE RIVER KWAI
        Best Actor   - ALEX GUINNESS - BRIDGE
        ON THE RIVER KWAI
        Best Actress - JOANNE WOODWARD
        THE THREE FACES OF EVE
    Winners 1954 - ON THE WATERFRONT MARLON BRANDO
             1955 - MARTY - ERNEST BORGNINE
             Others - SEVEN YEAR ITCH - MARILYN MONROE
             MISTER ROBERTS - JACK LEMMON
             1956 - AROUND THE WORLD IN 80 DAYS
             Others - THE KING AND I - YUL BRYNNER
MUSIC - 1957 SEVENTY SIX TROMBONES - YELLOW BIRD - CATCH A FALLING STAR
        1956 MY FAIR LADY DEBUTS ON BROADWAY
        ELVIS PRESLEY - ALL SHOOK UP - BLUE SUEDE SHOES - HEARTBREAK HOTEL
SPORTS- 1957
        BOSTON MARATHON - JOHN KELLEY, 2 HRS, 20 MINS, 5 SECS.
        NBA BASKETBALL - BOSTON CELTICS
        MOST VALUABLE PLAYER - BOB COUSY - BOSTON
        WORLD SERIES - MILWAUKEE BRAVES
        NATIONAL HOCKEY LEAGUE - MONTREAL CANADIANS
        PRO FOOTBALL - DETROIT
        INDIANAPOLIS 500 - SAM HANKS - 135 MPH
TRIVIA
        Fall of 1953 fifty percent of Americans owned a TV set. Three years later ninety percent of homes had one. Frozen
        TV dinners introduced followed quickly with TV-tray tables. Families planned in advance to watch Milton Berle,
        Lucille Ball, Ed Sullivan or Edward R. Murrow.
        Construction of personal Atomic Bomb Shelters continued.

VOL. 10 & 11   AUGUST - SEPTEMBER,1958   NO. 6-7

<u>Rear Adm. Julian D. Wilson, USN (Ret.)</u>

It is with deep regret that we announce the death of our beloved superintendent, Rear Admiral Julian D. Wilson, USN (Ret.), at the United States Naval Hospital in Boston, on September 1, 1958.

To Mrs. Wilson and family we extend, on behalf of the Massachusetts Maritime Academy Alumni Association, our deepest sympathy.

Admiral Wilson's passing is not only a great loss to our fine Academy, but also an even greater loss to our Alumni Association of which he was an honorary member. Without doubt, he, along with Mrs. Wilson, was the most ardent supporter of the Alumni, often going to great personal inconvenience and sacrifice to honor us with his presence and support.

Admiral Wilson came to us on January 11, 1949, after a long and illustrious career with the United States Navy, which began with his graduation from the Naval Academy in June, 1917, and continued with his serving in a multiplicity of Naval Assignments, some of which we mention here.

He served as Engineer officer and Executive Officer on destroyers during World War I, followed by one year as staff Commander of the U.S. Naval Forces in France. Admiral Wilson served also four years as instructor in Marine Engineering and Naval construction at the United States Naval Academy, was inspector of Ordinance, New York Shipbuilding Corporation, Camden, New Jersey, and was Executive Member of the staff of the Ship Characteristics Board Office of Chief of Naval Operations, Washington D.C.

Extensive sea duty saw him as turret officer on the battleship, ARIZONA in Pacific Operations, Commanding Officer of Navy Tanker, and Task Force Commander in the North Atlantic during World War II. During the battle of Okinawa Admiral Wilson commanded the battleship, U.S.S. MARYLAND, and he was awarded the Bronze Star for meritorious service I this operation.

Above all, Admiral Wilson was a real sailorman, personally commanding the U.S.T.S CHARLESTON and our BAY STATE on Annual Cruise. Admiral Wilson was a gentle man, beloved by all, and his policy of "fairness with firmness" has brought MMA through ten years of stormy seas, to its high position in the field of naval education. We will miss him.

"Afterthoughts"

SCUTTLEBUTT

Pete Readel '57, now living at 2117 Chestnut Avenue, Long Beach, California, is assigned to the U.S.S. Lucid and M.S.O. He and his lovely wife, Brooksie, whom he met on his last MMA Cruise, look forward to hearing from any of his old shipmates.

Harry Task '57 recently received his ensign's commission USNR and is sailing as Third Assistant for American Trading. Harry plans to be married in the very near future.

In a lengthy letter to the editor, **Chuck Broadbent '57** writes: "...have just received my copy of the BULLETIN, and needless to say, it was a pleasure. I am impressed with the compactness plus the abundance of information it produces, and if it so pleases the editor, I would like to make a small donation to help cover the expense of putting forth such a fine publication. Check for $10 enclosed." Chuck is aboard the U.S.S. NAVARRO, APA-215, out of Sasebo, Japan. Chuck, together with Jim Christy, on the APD-30, the U.S.S. COOK, had the pleasure of leading the first wave of ECUP's to the beach on the recent operation STRONGBACK, the largest amphibious operation of the Navy since World War II.

Tom Quinlan '55 recently visited the BULLETIN offices with his bride, Marie. Tom is sailing as Engineer Officer on the S.S. Independence.

Frank Mahoney '57, sailing as Third Assistant on the American Trader, recently received Naval Reserve Commission.

Dick Weaver '57 is serving aboard the U.S.S. WARBLER (MSC-206) out of Okinawa. Dick and his bride make their permanent home in Sasebo, Japan.

Linc Kennedy '57 is with the Navy on the U.S.S. NORTHAMPTON. Jimmy and a lovely lady-friend from Norfolk, Virginia, honored us with a visit recently.

Donald (Ben) Hogan '57 has recently been transferred from the USS GATLING DD 671 to Baltimore where he is ASW-CIC training Officer at the U.S. Naval Reserve Training Center. Don is also Commanding Officer of the U.S.S. HAMPTON (PCS-1386) and looks forward to seeing some of his old shipmates. Don is recently married and living with his bride at 100 Crain Highway (Southwest), Glen Burnie, Maryland.

Fred Ferguson '57 who, by the way, was recently married to Frank Flaherty's sister, Claire, is living in Norfolk, Virginia, attached to the U.S.S. RANDOLPH (CVA-15). Fred sailed September 8 for the 'Med', and he indicates that Paul McCarthy '53 is flying jets off his flight deck. Paul is a real hot pilot and graduated a few years back from Pensacola.

Irene and Hank Billings '57 announce the arrival of their daughter, Cathy Anne, on July 19, 1958. Hank is stationed aboard the U.S.S. VERMILLION (AKA-107) out of Norfolk, Virginia.

Dick Greer '57 is Third Officer on the U.S.M.S. WILLIAM O. DARBY. Dick was recently married.

Bob Stickney who graduated in 1957 as a deck officer returned to MMA and graduated in 1958, and he now holds licenses as Third Assistant Engineer and Third Mate. Bob has recently accepted a position with the Delta Line of Mobile Alabama as a Marine Engineer.

Robert Frimodig 58' announced he was married in his youngie year and is still going strong 42 years later. Congratulations for beating the system!

Sunday Morning Fall-About 20 years after graduation. I was sitting here in Arizona on my "sand ranch" watching the Lions just murder the Bears when a new car pulled up out front. Two guys got out _wearing suits and ties_, unheard of here in Amado. They vaulted the barbed wire fence, crossed the front yard and knocked on the door. I crawled out of my La Z Boy and answered. Then they flashed an aluminum wrapped twinkie and declared they were with the F.B.I. and wanted to talk to me. "Could they come in?" "Sure, come on in, sit down." "Do you like football?" "Ben, don't you know who we are?" "No!" "We're your snipe classmates **McCluskey** and **McCarthy!** Boy, had they changed! We had a great afternoon swapping stories with a few beers.

SCUTTLEBUTT (cont)

On June 20, 1958 the S. S. Gandia, Swedish merchant vessel, was forced to drop anchor in the Cape Cod Canal near the MMA Campus, to avoid collision with another vessel, in swinging with the tide her stern collided with the bow of our "Bay State."
[John Dalton '58']

Oh, and then there was this other accident ...

FILE DESCRIPTION: THE ACCIDENT REPORT

Dear Sir:

It was with regret and haste that I write this letter to you; regret that such a small misunderstanding could lead to the following circumstances, and haste in order that you will get this report before you form your own preconceived opinions from reports in the World Press, for I am sure that they will tend to over dramatize the affair.

We had just picked up the pilot, and the apprentice had returned from changing the "G" flag for the "H", and being his first trip was having difficulty in rolling the "G" flag up. I therefore proceeded to show him how, coming to the last part I told him to 'let go'. The lad, although willing, is not too bright, necessitating my having to repeat the order in a sharper tone.

At this moment, the Chief Officer appeared from the chartroom having been plotting the vessel's progress, and thinking that it was the anchors that were being referred to, repeated the 'let go' to the Third Officer on the forecastle. The port anchor, having been cleared away, but not walked out, was promptly let go. The effect of letting the anchor drop from the 'pipe' while the vessel was proceeding a full harbor speed proved too much for the windlass brake, and the entire length of the port cable was pulled out 'by the roots'. I fear that the damage to the chain locker may be extensive. The braking effect of the port anchor naturally caused the vessel to sheer in that direction, right towards the swing bridge that spans a tributary to the river up which we were proceeding.

The swing bridge operator showed great presence of mind by opening the bridge for my vessel. Unfortunately, he did not think to stop the vehicular traffic. The result being that the bridge partly opened and deposited a Volkswagen, two cyclists and a cattle truck on the foredeck. My ship's company are at present rounding up the contents of the latter, which from the noise I would say were pigs. In his efforts to stop the progress of the vessel the Third Officer dropped the starboard anchor, too late to be of practical use for it fell on the swing bridge operator's control cabin.

After the port anchor was let go and the vessel started to sheer I gave a double ring Full Astern on the Engine Room Telegraph, and personally rang the Engine Room to order maximum astern revolutions. I was informed that the temperature was 83 degrees, and was asked if there was a film tonight. My reply would not add constructively to this report.

Up to now I have confined my report to the activities at the forward end of my vessel. Down aft they were having their own problems. At the moment the port anchor was let go, the Second Officer was supervising the making fast of the aft tug, and was lowering the ship's towing spring down into the tug.

This sudden braking effect of the port anchor caused the tug to 'run in under' the stern of my vessel, just at the moment when the propeller was answering my double ring Full Astern. The prompt action of the Second Officer in securing the shipboard end of the towing spring delayed the sinking of the tug by some minutes thereby allowing the safe abandoning of that vessel.

It is strange, but at the very same moment of letting go the port anchor there was a power cut ashore. The fact that we were passing over a 'cable area' at that time may suggest that we may have touched something on the river bed. It is perhaps lucky that the high tension cables brought down by the foremast were not live, possibly being replaced by the underwater cable, but owing to the shore blackout it is impossible to say where the pylon fell.

It never fails to amaze me, the actions and behavior of foreigners during moments of minor crisis. The pilot, for instance, is at this moment huddled in the corner of my day cabin, alternately crooning to himself and crying after having consumed a bottle of gin in a time that is worthy of inclusion in the Guinness Book of World Records. The tug captain on the other hand reacted violently and had to forcibly be restrained by the Steward, who has him handcuffed in the ship's hospital while he is telling me to do impossible things with my ship and my person.

I am closing this preliminary report for I am finding it difficult to concentrate with the sound of police sirens and the flashing lights.

It is sad to think that had the apprentice realized that there is no need to fly pilot flags after dark, none of this would have happened.

Yours truly,   Master
[Bulletin Editor - 1998]

"Afterthoughts"

Maritime Academy Incidents

HAZING CADETS FACE DISMISSAL

BUZZARDS BAY -- Several midshipmen, reported to have subjected lower classmen at the Massachusetts Maritime Academy to severe hazing, face dismissal.

Academy Supt. Rear Adm. John W. Thompson, investigating a reported hunger strike at the academy, said today he has made the recommendation to the Academy's board of commissioners.

"Only a few are involved and I desire to remove these persons from the ranks if I can do so," Thompson said.

Upper classmen were reported to have gone on a hunger strike yesterday in protest against disciplinary measures invoked against them for hazing.

"There is no actual hunger strike," said Thompson. "I was told by the duty officer that some of the upper classmen didn't have supper last night or breakfast this morning.

"However, the canteen is doing a wholesale business. You don't call that a hunger strike."

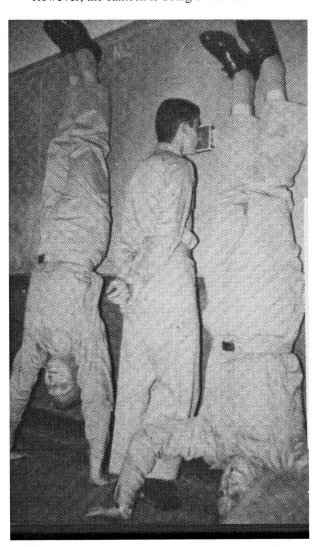

First and second classmen have been restricted to quarters pending investigation of charges that first-year cadets were given a severe hazing.

Smoking privileges also have been revoked and swimming periods eliminated. Instead of normal daily recreation activities, the midshipmen are being given close-order drill.

The investigation, Thompson said, began last week. "We have some facts, but we're not disclosing anything except to the commissioners until we get a full report."

The hazing, he explained, began when the senior class returned from leave Aug. 2 and started "raising the devil with the new boys who arrived July 23 for orientation."

"The exuberant group doing the hazing overstepped its bounds. Several of the new people quit."

"Hazing", he said, "is not new, but we'd like to get rid of it. They go too far when they make others quit."

"One mother of the uppers called today and said, 'My boy took it last year,' I answered 'I took it 50 years ago'."

The investigation is being conducted by the commanding officer, engineering officer and Thompson, in conjunction with the board of commissioners.

Chairman Arthur C. Sullivan of the Board of Commissioners confirmed reports of the hunger strike.

….AND THE BAND PLAYED ON!!!

THE BOSTON HERALD, SATURDAY, AUG. 11, 1962

MARITIME ACADEMY GETS TOUGH IN HUNGER STRIKE

150 Told Line Up Or Be Carried

BUZZARDS BAY -- Massachusetts Maritime Academy officials cracked the whip of discipline hard Friday night and served notice on 150 upper classmen on a "hunger strike" that they will be lined up at exercises Sunday "even if they have to be carried there."

The exercises will be for the graduation of 80 seniors who are in no manner involved in the incident that has broken out as a result of Rear Adm. John W. Thompson's determination to end hazing at the academy. The practice has got out of bounds the past two years and has plagued the academy with criticism for a number of years.

'They'll be There'

Adm. Thompson, superintendent of the school, said the 150 upper classmen, who are staging a boycott of the mess hall in retaliation for loss of privileges in the hazing crackdown, as well as about 75 new younger students who were the objects of such stunts that the parents of some complained to Gov. Volpe, will stand at attention Sunday when the senior class is commissioned as navigation and engineering officers in the presence of their families and state and Merchant Marine officials.

"They will be there," said Adm. Thompson tersely.

He added he wanted to emphasize that "the graduating class is apart from all this."

The superintendent and Frank B. Cook of Buzzards Bay, a member of the Maritime Academy Commission, declined to become concerned about the "hunger strike."

"What it amounts to is that they are staying away from the regular academy mess and eating chocolate bars in the canteen, which, incidentally, is doing a whale of a business," reported Cook. "When they get hungry and want a little red meat they will be back."

But both men stressed that the investigation by the superintendent's office and the full commission into all phases of hazing for the past several years would be continued. Some of the stunts have been forcing new boys to drink such concoctions as filter cigarettes steeped in vinegar.

Admiral Thompson indicated that he had tried to get it across to the students that hazing was a thing of the past.

"Hazing has not been condoned at the academy," he explained, "but as at all military schools, it has been going on for years, and when it gets out of hand we have to crack down."

The upper classmen protested they had been the victims of a misunderstanding, and were striving to win back their liberty privileges. They contended the forced consumption of cigarettes and vinegar occurred two years ago and that they, not the present new students, were the victims. They blamed the newcomers' lack of knowledge between "hazing and orientation" for the complaints to the Governor.

"A 17-year-old high school graduate can't come here and become adapted to our way of life in a couple of weeks," the upper classmen maintained. "It's not supposed to be easy **and takes some getting used to**."

July 1, *1958*

Dear Ben,

As you know I also have been at sea since graduation and my cousin is a Republican. My parents I won't discuss, but they can't work. They are totally dependent on my sisters who work in the area of the "Old Howard". My brothers, all nine, are in prison for all kinds of big bad things. I'm in love with a streetwalker who works Washington Street. She knows nothing about my background, including MMA, and says that she loves me. We intend to get married as soon as she gets out of jail. When I finally get to shore we plan to open a small "house" on the south end.

My problem, Ben, is this: (and please don't tell any of my snipe friends) In view of the fact that I intend to make this girl my WIFE, and bring her to prison visits with the family; should I ... or should I not ... tell her about my cousin who is a Republican???

———— Please reply A.S.A.P.

Regards,
Jim McCarthy

* · Note: All of the above was written in red crayon. ✏

December 15, *1987*

Dear Jim,

I've been agonizing over your problem for years. I'm finally prepared to advise you...since you seem to be clean and acceptable to the F.B.I., I think it's probably OK to tell her about your cousin.

Cheers,
Ben
COMSTUDLANT

P. S. I understand how this might be a rather personal and confidential matter so I've only sent a few copies to our reunion classmates.

cc: #1 of 53 copies

RICHARD J. BOLES
ATTORNEY AT LAW
DURHAM, NORTH CAROLINA 27705

January 4, *1988*

To: Jim McCluskey
North Weymouth, Mass. 02191
cc: Jim McCarthy
Milton, Mass. 02186

Gentlemen:

I am in receipt of your semi-literate letters to Ben Hogan dated June 31, 1958, and July 1, 1958, respectively, wherein you recite various calamities that were then occurring in your miserable lives, not the least of which was that you each had a cousin who was a Republican. Ben Hogan has forwarded to me his timely response (dated December 15, *1987*) to your combined drivel and requested a formal legal opinion as to whether or not you should divulge the fact that you have a cousin who is a Republican.

Have you two been *running in the sun too long again* or are you really that glassy eyed and silly as to think that revealing that there is a Republican in your family would not destroy what is left of your rotten reputations? Swapping stories for the last thirty years is no excuse for not exercising good judgment and protecting your reputations. Each of you would make a good poster boy for a *fence post.* Please wipe that silly look off your respective faces and realize that if you do not wish to embarrass your classmates, you should not reveal the Republican relationship in your families.

Sincerely,

Richard J. Boles

cc: Ben Hogan
        Amado, Arizona 85646

P. S. Ben, many thanks for the "picture" (Queenie and Dick in Surinam). God and I will get you for that (but not necessarily in that order). Big Dick

RICHARD J. BOLES
ATTORNEY AT LAW
DURHAM, NORTH CAROLINA 27705

177

September 23, 1996

Admiral John F. Aylmer
Centerville, MA 02632

Dear Jack:

As always, it was great to hear from you again. I think that the idea of an annual class reunion for these "old gray heads" is a super idea. The friendships that we made at the Academy have defined who and what we are today and should be carefully preserved and nurtured.

As to the proposal for sponsoring a scholarship, I offer the following thoughts:

1.   My own preference is to endow a chair for the faculty. If the faculty is strong, the academic program will excel and the students will come. If you help a student, you help one person. If you bring a great professor to the Academy, it is like dropping a pebble in a pond; you don't know where the ripples will stop and the lives he will influence;

2.   Whether it is a scholarship or a chair, I wonder how it will be funded. I have recently been involved with a client in establishing an annual scholarship (all expenses paid) for one student at Duke University. The endowment required to fund this scholarship is currently $500,000.00 and will increase every year due to inflation and growing operating costs. What dollar amount do we hope to provide a student each year? It seems to me, we need to ascertain this first and then work backwards to determine the size of the endowment required in today's dollars;

3.   Our class is probably too old to take advantage of the use of life insurance proceed to fund an endowment. I would urge the Academy to approach each graduating class and ask that each student take out a minimum $10,000.00 face amount policy payable to the Academy (or endowment). The policy could b designed to be paid up in a few years and if ownership of the policy is transferred to the Academy the insured is probably entitled to a tax deduction for the premium;

4.   Perhaps the Alumni association could establish a group term policy for the members. We could ask our classmates to participate in this program and to name the Academy or the endowment as the beneficiary; and

5.   Alternatively, at the next class reunion, we could single out some poor soul and heavily insure him. The premium being paid by donations from the rest of the class. Mysteriously, his body would be found washed up on the banks of the Cape Cod Canal a short while later (possibly only hours). We might have difficulty finding a volunteer for this program; however, if it is presented in a positive light I am sure several classmates will step forward and do the right thing.

For example, Ben (Don) Hogan is only the second generation in his family to walk upright. On the other hand, Hank Billings has spent his life fishing loose diaphragms out of swimming pool strainers; and Jimmie McCarthy and Jim McCluskey have been swapping spit in the shower for so long that we could probably insure the both of them for the price of one. Any of these gentlemen would make an excellent candidate. If they don't have the decency to do the right thing, then I propose that we single out some "youngie" under us and make him "our man".

Your Humble Servant
Richard J. Boles

cc: Ben Hogan, Hank Billings, Jimmie McCarthy, Jim McCluskey

Master R/V Knorr, 12:10 PM 10/21/97, Jack Sweet last cruise

Date: Tues, 21 Oct 1997 12:10:33 -0400 (EDT)
From: Master R/V Knorr
To: Wilson, Al <awilson@mma.mass.edu>
cc: Lauzon Shelley
Subject: Jack Sweet's Last Cruise

Captain Wilson,

This cruise, Knorr 154-II, from Ponta Delgada, Azores to Woods Hole, will be Jack's last cruise before retirement.

Jack graduated from MMA in 1957, and was a classmate of Bob Strautman. Jack was second mate on Knorr when I was a cadet here in 1977. He sails as Second Mate today, unparalleled!

I think Jack's career aboard Knorr is note worthy, it deserves mention in the MMA Bulletin, as well as the WHOI newsletter, put out by Shelley Lauzon, who I have cc'd on this letter.

"Afterthoughts"

The reason Jack's career is noteworthy is his influence on the vast number of licensed and unlicensed sailors who have "gone to school" on Jack's watch. He has in a real sense been the ships gyro compass giving direction and stability to many crewmembers.

As a young Captain I can best sum up my respect for the man by repeating the words I frequently say to Jack after a long day and evening on the bridge. I wait for the watch change at midnight, and the passing of watch information. I say " Good night Jack, call me if you need me." There is no more trustworthy or respected Mate I have ever sailed with.

The Knorr is scheduled to arrive in Woods Hole on 19 November. If you think it appropriate, it would be nice to see the MMA band on the dock when we arrive.

Sincerely,
A.D. Colburn

Captain A.D. Colburn
R/V Knorr
Woods Hole Oceanographic Institution
Woods Hole, MA. 02543

[Capt. Al Wilson via ADM Jack Aylmer]

Cape Cod Times
THE CAPE AND ISLANDS NEWSPAPER

No 17	30 Pages	Tuesday, January 20, 1998

Academy Officer Dies In Panama

By Mark Merchant Staff Writer

PANAMA CITY, Panama - One of the senior members aboard the Patriot State for the Massachusetts Maritime Academy's training ship died yesterday in a Panamanian hospital.

What should have been a joyous first day of liberty for the 450 cadets and 100 crew and faculty members quickly turned somber when Capt. Bushy announced the death of Cmdr. Robert Strautman shortly after 9 a.m.

"I know I've lost a friend...a person I loved to work and joke around with and the only person I would trust to suspend me in midair," Bushy, the Patriot State's master said.

Strautman died at Paitilla Hospital in Panama City early yesterday when his heart failed.

Strautman, 62, became ill a few days after the Patriot State sailed from Buzzards Bay on Jan, 10. He checked into the ship's sick bay and was under the constant care of the ship's doctor Anthony Capoblanco.

Strautman, who lives in Sandwich, had suffered a heart attack in the past.

Capoblanco was in daily contact with Strautman's physician and a Massachusetts hospital from the time Strautman checked into sick bay until the ship docked at Fort Rodman, Panama, Sunday.

Because Strautman's condition was stable, doctors decided not to airlift him off the boat or immediately put into port. He was taken to Paitilla Hospital immediately after arriving at Fort Rodman.

One of Strautman's son's, Robert, is serving aboard the Patriot State as a utility worker.

He will return to the United States today with his father's body.

The ship's flags were dropped to half-mast when the death was announced. At dusk last night, "Taps" was played by the school's honor guard. People otherwise happy to be in port became quiet and reflective.

"He was not a complex man. He was very dedicated to what he did. Teaching students is all he wanted to do," Joe Domingos, MMA's commandant of cadets said.

The athletic director aboard for the cruise, Paul Innis, said Strautman had a strong, stabilizing influence at the academy and aboard the ship. "That loss cannot be replaced."

Strautman had been considering retirement for the past few years. He was not originally assigned to this cruise, but when it looked like it might be short-staffed he volunteered to go.

"He was a seaman. When the ship was ready to go he just had the urge to go," Domingos said.

One student remembered Strautman as tough on the outside but caring within.

"When I first met him, I thought he was tough and was someone who didn't care about me. But I looked beneath all that and found I had a teacher who really cared for me a great deal." said Isais Chang, a 1989 MMA graduate said.

179

"Afterthoughts"

Strautman loved the sea and being a merchant mariner. He attended MMA and graduated in 1957. He served in the Navy, worked for private freight line and was a stevedore at the Port of Baltimore before joining the academy staff as a marine transportation teacher in 1973. "Everyone should remember Bob as truly dedicated to his family and to the training of cadets at MMA. They were his passion," Bushy said.

Memorial and funeral arrangements are still incomplete.   [Jack Alymer]

Email from Paul Dittman '91…23 January 1999…I was extremely saddened to hear about the passing of Mr. Strautman (Strauty, as he was called by the cadets). I had the pleasure of his tutelage from 1987 – 1991. All of us that had the benefit of his teaching learned where "Tokardi" is and how to make "boiler makers". We all listened intently to his many sea stories about the Baltimore longshoreman pushed into a cargo hold who turned around in midair and sot the guy that pushed him before landing in the square of the hatch. We heard about the Pakistani freight ship with the D-9 dozer sticking out of the 'tween deck shell plate. Mr. Strautman could be lecturing on brain surgery and he would start every lecture with "Very simply….you do this….that….the other thing, and there you have it." Know what…it always made sense.

Thank you Mr. Strautman, may God bless and keep you. You will live on through those of us you mentored so well…

Email from Veronica Recco '98…20 January 1999…I know the class of 98 will never forget that day.

I remember returning from leave only to discover that we had lost one of the best teachers I have ever known. My classmates and I went crazy trying to think of some way to honor him. The mate on watch told us we were not allowed to play taps because it wasn't navy protocol. We made threats and comments about not knowing the man. We talked amongst ourselves and came to the inevitable conclusion that there was no way he could stop us. As a Deckie CMDR, Strautman was our and we were going to decide what to do.

At sunset we lowered the flags to taps and thought about how much this man had been a part of our daily lives since we entered the academy. It was the end of an era.

Email from Al Wilson '59…19 January 1999…One year ago today, in the port of Balboa Panama, CDR. Robert Strautman passed away while aboard TS Patriot State. Bob passed away doing what he loved – going to sea and training cadets. He is sorely missed by all hands.

Captain Al Wilson Placement Officer

180

REPLIES TO "LETTERS TO LOU"

PART 5

This addition has been added to the original book for several reasons. The first is to put the book back in print, **forever**, using a print/publish-on demand computer system. The original 475 copies sold-out shortly after its release. It became a collector's item to many that attended or have an interest in the Massachusetts Maritime Academy. A second printing also allows those that were disappointed to finally get a copy. As before all proceeds will be donated ("give-back" money) to the MMA Emery Rice Scholarship Fund.

It also provides an opportunity to respond to questions asked and to share some of the numerous and sometimes very funny replies to the book.

The following are just a few of many, many replies. Note that excerpts are sometimes made for brevity and relevance

*Maurice Bresnahan 59' wrote...*Ben,
'LETTERS TO LOU' IS GREAT!! THANKS VERY MUCH FOR MY COPY. IT CERTAINLY BRINGS BACK THOSE THRILLING DAYS OF YESTERYEAR. DID WE REALLY LIVE THROUGH ALL THAT? MOSS

*October 2, 1998...*Ben,   THIS IS THE THIRD MESSAGE THAT I HAVE SENT TO YOU TO SAY WHAT A GRAND HIT "LETTERS TO LOU" WAS AT HOMECOMING. ALL RAVE NOTICES AND BIG SALES AT THE SHIP'S STORE. FULL RANGE OF EMOTIONS OBSERVED FROM READERS. I DETECTED SOME POST TRAUMATIC STRESS SYNDOME. MY PREVIOUS MESSAGES HAVE BEEN RETURNED AS BAD ADDRESSES. LET ME KNOW IF YOU DON'T GET THIS ONE. BEST REGARDS,   MOSS
*June 15. 1999...*ON BEHALF OF THE OLD SCHOOL, THANKS VERY MUCH...FOR THE DONATION AS WELL AS RECORDING HISTORY...WELL DONE DESERT DECKIE VERY WELL DONE.   MOSS

My reply...Many thanks for your messages! It's FUN TIME! I suggest a real "TALL- ONE" for your post traumatic stress. It's also nice to know that after writing the book that you and **Al Wilson** will still allow me back on campus   Cheers!!! Ben

It should be noted that **Rear Admiral Bresnahan**, President of the Academy, and **Captain Wilson**, Placement Officer, were both "our youngies" when we ruled as upper-jobs. We trained them well!!!

Email from Richard A. Volkin '63...18 June 1999   I want to thank you for the book "Letters to Lou". Although I am in the class of '63, it was so representative that it brought back great (and some not so great) memories.

I was reading the book on my way to Zurich, Switzerland, and people were looking at me as I constantly broke out laughing, even though it was 3:00 a.m. One man came up to me and asked me what was so funny. I tried to explain the book and the environment to him, but as you know, unless you have lived it, you don't understand it.

I will treasure this book in my library, and if I find the time, I many try my hand at a sequel "Letters to Karen". This potential book would pick up where you left off on the Bay State.

Please advise as how to start and how to proceed. Again, thanks for the memories.

My reply: Your reply, and others, makes the whole effort worthwhile! The book really hit an emotional nerve with many alumni! You wouldn't believe the number of replies, three big notebooks, we have received. Overwhelming to say the least! **Lou** agrees...if you didn't live it you'll probably not understand it...but it's ALL TRUE!!!

*Email from Kevin Seaver '79...30 July 1999...*Thank you for your generous contribution. I have tried to explain MMA to non-grads for years. What I should do in the future is have them read your book to get their feet wet. Everyone that has read the book has enjoyed the time spent. I will purchase a copy at the Outing and read it during my vacation upcoming.

Again, thanks for your kindness!

*Email from Rob Tryon,'99 Regimental Commander, MMA…17 December 1998…*Mr. Hogan, I received a copy of "Letters to Lou" from **Jay Schrage** '97. Great book – I let a couple of my shipmates read it as well. I will pass it on to next year's Regimental Commander. Thank you for the copy.

*Email from Stan Souza '85…13 May 1999…*I started reading the book on a flight home yesterday and so far it's great. It amazes me that even though we went to school 30 some odd years apart, there are so many things that were the same. Needless to say, it brought back a lot of fond memories.

> Thanks, Stan
> P.S. didn't I read that you didn't want to live in a 'hot/dry place'…Arizona??? Ha ha.

*Email from Peter L. Galanis '55…20 April 1999…*Tears of laughter have been rolling down my cheeks since I started reading it. Please send me another copy for my nephew, **Stephen Auger '81**.

*Email from Capt. Frank Johnston '59…24 February 1999…*Ben: Just finished "Letters to Lou". WHAT A BOOK! Dave Shannon, '58, presented it to me two days ago and I haven't done a stick of work since I cracked the first page. What memories. You may not remember but I was Bob Stickney's personal valet the first year at MMA. Black, strong coffee at his rack each and every day for the first year. That besides the shined shoes and the "extra" food from home when I wasn't on the 1-50 List. I would not give up one of those memories though at the time, I wished I was just a little bit taller than Bob and weighed more than 105 pounds. I often repeat the story of the extra day I served him coffee at 0530 and neglected to tell him of the whole package of EXLAX I had slipped into that very strong coffee. The resultant screams for anyone to find me were sheer pleasure. Anyway, Ben; a great job. Thank you.

"86"

In April 1999 I asked the following questions on the Internet to the alumni and received the following replies:

Does anyone know the origin of the alarm "86"? When was it first used? And why this particular number?

Re: "86" I suspect it's not an MMA invention. I remember old movies, Leo Gorcy & "The Dead End Kids", among others, using the term. Not always as an alarm either. Something in the back of my mind recalls phrases like, "he was 86'd." (not a good thing..) That would be a logical beginning of an alarm call about the threat of being 86'd. My guess would be it's a slang term from the 30's or 40's that survived in the smaller world of the MMA training ship/campus longer than it did "in the wild." **Bob Hillery 75'**

I don't know but it must have historical significance, it was in existence and going strong in my youngie year, 1951. **Peter Galanis 55'**

While watching "JAZZ" on PBS last night it was mentioned that "86" was used to warn patrons of a "speakeasy" that a raid was about to occur. The rear door was used as an exit. The number "86" was the number of the building's street address in New York (?).

I saw that show as well. I have never heard anything to the contrary. But it was interesting. So I guess your question is what came first, the chicken or the egg, and is it just a coincidence that that speakeasy is at an address of "86". **Tricia Kelly 94'**

I believe there was a radio code 86 that had to do something with warning. It will be interesting when you find out. **Richard (Dad) Phelan 54'**

Dear Dad, I checked my old copy of H.O. 87 under two letter signals, etc., but I found nothing regarding "86". One guy thinks that number was used because you could say it without moving your lips; another suggested that it is a police code for "gone"…10-86!

I know it was used in the 40's on the training ship in Long Island Sound? The real answer should come up soon. I wonder when it stopped being used?

See the passage about cadet life in "It Didn't Happen On My Watch" by MMA Alumni **George Murphy** ('43) for an explanation. A GREAT book by the way. What I recall him explaining is that "86" can be said out loud without moving the lips so as to give the "lookout" a way for sounding the alarm of an approaching Upper Job. **Ed Karle 79'**

Finally, from the Internet…"86" meaning to refuse to serve (an unwelcome customer) at a bar or restaurant. To throw away. Origin: Perhaps from Chumley's Bar and restaurant at 86 Bedford Street in Greenwich Village, NYC. Also…86'd to be thrown out of a bar!

*Email from Andrew A. Hodson '80…27 March 2001…*Here's a little Naval lore for your cold holiday enjoyment!

Every sailing ship had to have cannon for protection. Cannon of the times required round iron cannonballs. The master wanted to store the cannonballs such that they could be of instant use when needed, yet not roll around the gun deck. The solution was to stack them up in a square-based pyramid next to the cannon. The top level of the stack had one ball, the next level down had four, the next had nine, the next had sixteen, and so on. Four levels would provide a stack of 30 cannonballs. The only real problem was how to keep the bottom level from sliding out from under the weight of the higher levels. To do this, they devised a small brass plate ("brass monkey") with one rounded indentation for each cannonball in the bottom layer. Brass was used because the cannonballs wouldn't rust to the "brass monkey", but would rust to an iron one. When temperature falls, brass contracts in size faster than iron. As it got cold on the gun decks, the indentations in the brass monkey would get smaller than the iron cannonballs they were holding. If the temperature got cold enough, the bottom layer would pop out of the indentations spilling the entire pyramid over the deck. Thus it was, quite literally, "cold enough to freeze the balls off a brass monkey".

*Emails from Janice Walton…2 January 1999…*Reading MMA "The Bulletin" for the month of October 1998 on page 6 I saw "Letters to Lou". Does the journal about life at MMA tell about the staff at the Academy? My father, **Bing Crosby**, was an instructor there during that time frame in the engineering department.

"BING" Crosby, Instructor in class with "THE PINK BUBBLE"

The stories of the staff and the cadets at MMA were part of my life for twenty-five years. People like: Jobby Bobby, Hammering Hank, Lord Louie, "MO"…so many names and so many nick names…so many funny stories. Tragic stories, also.

…9 January 1999…
A top of the morning to you all. A Buzzards Bay winter's day here. Snow, sleet and lots of fog.

"Letters to Lou" came yesterday and the check shall be in the mail today.

I am with the "Charlie Tub" at the Boston Dry dock. If my mother only knew the number of holes in that old dame she would have Gray Taped the old man to his rocking chair in Buzzards Bay. The officers' wives would have raised holy hell about the old Swiss cheese love boat. God was truly looking after all of you men.

Shall write later when I have fully digested this "Mash Unit" of the high Seas. (This could be a good movie.)

I always enjoyed hearing the stories at exam time. Father would keep a phony exam in the ship safe in his room on the ship. He would then put grapes under his rug in his room the night before the exam. The next morning, he would find the grapes smashed under the rug…then he'd go to class and see "his boys" all happy as clams. He would sit there after the real exam was passed out and look at the expressions on all the faces. Like, "What the hell is going on here? This is not the exam that we stole last night." Score one for the instructor. Every day was a challenge to try and outsmart the kids. Some days he would win and many a day he would lose. But, that was life at the Merry Time Academy.

Bubble Head One and Bubble Head Two was a father and son act at the MMA when you were there. You had different names for them in the book. Can you figure out who they are?

My reply: Good Grief…Grapes!!! To even infer such a thing! You must be referring to the "Pink Bubble's" Class not mine! Never happen! However we did graduate with more demerits than any class since WW II (maybe in the history of the school), but…imagine…GRAPES!

*…10 January 1999…*Twenty pages to go and then I am done. Now, I know why I don't like red Jell-O and fruit cocktail. When I went to visit father during his over night watch, the big treat was to go to the Officer's Galley and have Jell-O. It always had this very thick crust on it and I would have to pile if off before I got to the rubbery part and then it would always taste like fish. It was free and I could eat ALL that I wanted with a very large silver spoon.

Just reading "Cape Cod Times on Line" and there are some very interesting stories about the MMA Cruise. I almost "ralphed" in a barrel when I read about a Teddy Bear had to go on the cruise with an MMA cadet. I thank God the ole Salts are gone, if they were to read about a Teddy Bear in a bunk the old sea words would sound like this #$$%(*)*. What is this Sea coming to?

My reply: First you mention "MASH", then **"teddy bears"**…sounds like a take off on "RADAR" in the TV series.

Excerpt from Cape Cod Times, January 10, 1999

Cherished belongings offer crew members a link to home   By Kevin Dennehy

ABOARD THE EMPIRE STATE – Sometimes even sailors need their teddy bear.

Cheryl Comeau, a sophomore at the Massachusetts Maritime Academy, won't leave home without hers. As she boarded the Empire State yesterday for her second training cruise with the school, her stuffed friend was by her side. She has slept with the bear since she was a baby, and there was no way she was leaving him behind.

"If I go away, it comes with me," said Comeau, a double major in marine engineering and marine safety environmental protection. "It's just special. I can't sleep without it anywhere."

Though space on the Empire State is scarce, many cadets brought along cherished belongings to remind them of home during the six-week training cruise.

Andrea Woelfel also brought her teddy bear. The doll reminds her that she still has a cozy and private bedroom waiting at home, she said.

Email from Carl Megonigle '57…27 September 1998… When you think about the Chun, and now that we are wise and older, that thing was in such bad shape, we should have just cruised the Charles River. It's a wonder we didn't go down at sea. I can remember opening hatches to tanks up forward and seeing blue water through the bottom of the hull.

Email from Don Flynn '52…19 August 2000… In regards to the youngies coming aboard, the greatest day of my life was standing on the quarter deck of the Chun at attention, my folks leaving with all visitors ashore and **Dickie Moore '50** saying "Say goodbye to mommy", and then the fun began!!

Letter from the "Pink Bubble" (received on PINK stationery).

PINK BUBBLE ENTERPRISES
A DIVISION OF THE REDNESS CORPORATION
3308 FAIRWAY OAK VILLA
FERNANDINA BEACH, FLORIDA 32034

LINES & DESIGNS\
P. O. BOX 726
AMADO, AZ 85645
AUGUST 24, 1998

YOUNG MAN

Your letter of July 1, 1998 with meaningless attachments was reviewed upon my recent return from New England and the Canadian maritime provinces. A copy of this correspondence has been forwarded to my attorney at the law firm of Dewey, Cheatum and Howe for further review of possible libelous content.

Regarding your request for an order for this "Letters to Lou." I will consider an order at such time as this publication is included in the New York Times best seller list … for fiction, of course.

You mention an incident where the "Pink Bubble" a.k.a. MR. BERRY, pushed his hand through a glass show case. I have no recollection of this incident but then again I cannot recall what I did last week.

The other incident where you deliberately splashed pink … excuse me, red lead on my shoes … if you are still overwhelmed by guilt for this dastardly deed, I presently wear size 10 ½ medium width footwear. Rockport walkers would be nice.

On a more serious note, your entry regarding the diving accident and death of **John Arnold** brought back the most devastating event of my four years at MMA. Good friend and probably the best seaman in our class. Of our graduation class of 51, we have lost 11 classmates. **Arnold, Callahan, Cueroni** [Note: He was found to be alive and living in Florida], **Kochanowicz, Moore, Weinfield, Smith, Flynn, Nickell, Green and Dan McLaughlin**. Looking forward to our 45th Reunion in the year 2000. Perhaps you and a few of your classmates would assist … we'll need people to mix and serve drinks, shine shoes, supply and light cigarettes and polish portholes.

One of my retirement hobbies is duplicate bridge and I run into **Harold Task** on a regular basis at the Jacksonville Bridge Club. Harold is an excellent bridge player … he told me so! Harold still works as a part time consultant to support his habit … restaurants!

In a vain attempt to garner some respect from you youngies … the "Pink Bubble" has amassed some interesting accomplishments in his career and his lack of modesty allows him to list them. First graduate of any federal or state maritime academy to graduate with both a Third Mate and Third Assistant Engineers license … a pilot's endorsement added later.

With all that nautical knowledge, it was only logical that I came ashore. 25 years with GTE Sylvania in manufacturing, sales and marketing with a reasonable amount of success allowed me to retire at age 52. Several years of managing an estate property in Marion … including two years of Culinary Arts at Johnson & Wales University … then a move to Amelia Island, Florida in 1992.

Underwhelming isn't it!

Still single … but it's very difficult to find women who like me who glow in the dark.

Tried to locate Amado but could not find it … is it a suburb of AJO?

I'm sure you live in a great home undoubtedly devoid of any painted surfaces. I do recall your ineptness in that media.

Returning to 1955 … my most prized accomplishment was the result of my active supervision of a third classman named **AYLMER**. I noticed you referred to him as Admiral … in whose navy?

Seriously, I am proud of **Jack Aylmer**'s success which I strongly feel are related to his proper training and indoctrination as a young man.

Your 1997 reunion was enjoyable … I had an opportunity to talk to many of your classmates … was amazed at how many of them actually graduated and secured employment …but maybe I was too hasty in my earlier appraisal of the Class of '57. The homecoming weekend at the Cape Cod College of Nautical Knowledge has become an annual event for me and I will see my upper jobs … 1953 … this year. Can't wait til 2000 or 2002!!!!!!

After reviewing your drafts and assessing your writing skills …don't give up your day job!

Glowingly yours,
Paul F. Berry

My reply (on pale BLUE paper):

Thank you for your most enthusiastic reply and book endorsement. You are probably aware that it was selected as the "book of the month" by the barflies at the Cow Palace here in downtown Amado

I'd also like to thank you for the check. It was deposited this morning. Don't hold your breath waiting for a book! It may be my final and ultimate posterior drag.

Add that to your frivolous legal action. Your letter has been forwarded to my attorney listed below.

Here I am about to make you world famous and you're gonna sue me? You realize that one must have a character before it can be assassinated.

If you were upset by the meaningless attachments I sent you … you ain't seen nothing yet! I sent you the nice stuff!

Congratulations, Paul, you are about to become infamous!!!

Oh, about duplicate bridge. I've built a few and even flown under one but I never had a chance to play with one. The ones I built were never duplicated since they were all washed away by floods.

I hope the above does not burst your bubble. Your letter is a classic! I'll have it framed and hung on the doghouse wall.

Cheers from cactus country …Ben

Cc: Mr. **Richard Boles**,'57
Attorney at Law
Durham, North Carolina 27705

PS: About the paint … normally you don't paint adobe walls.

*Email responses regarding the Pink Bubble6…December 2001…*Forty-four years after graduation and three years after the release of "Letters to Lou"… This message was left on my answering machine from the notorious "Pink Bubble".

… Please leave a message after the beep…

I hope that voice is Ben Hogan. To refresh your memory this is Mister Berry calling (with a loud and angry voice). I knew before I died that you or one of your classmates would try to poison me. You didn't get me but you did get my computer with your virus! Thanks a lot! But Ha-Ha-Ha-Ha, I made a simple fix with Norton's. Give me a call when you get a chance. That's an order! Do it!

Later that night I did call him back … COLLECT … and recommended penicillin and bed rest.

*Letter from Lee Cueroni '55.5…23 November 1998…*I must finish this note and mail it soon. It's taken me as long to complete this letter, as it used to take you (Ben) to get a midnight cigarette for me.

It was great hearing from you and a few others from that time of the century. Throughout the years, I had worked with **Dave Callahan** (U.S. Lines & Vietnam), **Bob Collis** (Ismian (sp??) Lines, U.S. Lines), **Carl Megonigal** (sp?? Pensacola Flight Training, Vietnam). MMA was well known throughout the full spectrum of the maritime industry. I hope that it still is, but I feel that when it acquired the "college" status it lost its uniqueness. I have visited it once in the last 43 years.

I haven't perused your most unique odyssey as yet, but rest assured I will. I'm not sure if you remember that I, among others in my class, did not graduate with the group. We were a part of that July 16th **Wikander** fiasco [re: "Letters to Lou", Part I.] (very complicated). As I recall, 12 of us were expelled on July 20th, but held persona non grata in the 2nd deck after chart room. We were deleted from graduation ceremonies, etc., etc., but we dubbed ourselves Class of 55.5. I feel that we should have gotten some help from the class leaders. We lived, slept, ate, and were assigned daily punishment for about 3 weeks (I think it was 3 weeks). **Bob Collis**, myself, **Dave Sheehy** built the infamous garbage battery, and the quonset huts. One night Rounds sent Mo, the cook, up and told us we could go. That was it. About 3 weeks later we got our degrees and mates papers in the mail. I went with U.S. Lines as a Jr. 3rd on the American Scientist and Pioneer Minx for about 2 yrs., then to the SS America for about a year, then into USN. Retired as an 05 (commander) in '79, was a beltway bandit for 11 years, retired again and came here.

       I wouldn't change much if I had a chance to do everything over again. I'd be a bit smarter in some areas, but I'd take the same wife and son, and family (I'm sure you would also).

Email from Alumni Talk…3 March 1999…
The Midshipman's Cadet Prayer

Now I lay me down to sleep.
I pray the Lord my gear to keep.
Grant that no other cadet shall take
My shoes or socks before I wake.

Lord, please guard me in my slumber.
Keep my hammock on its number.
Make no clew of footrope break.
Nor let me down before I wake.

Keep me safely in thy sight.
Grant no fire drills late at night.
And in the morning, let me wake
Breathing scents of sirloin steak.

God protect me in my dreams
And make life better than it seems.
Grant that time shall swiftly fly
Til these 18 months are safely by.

I long for a snowy feather bed
On which to rest my weary head.
Far away from all these scenes
And the smell of half-steamed beans.

Take me back into the land
Where they don't scrub things down with sand.
Where no demon typhoon blows
And the women wash the clothes.

God, knowest all my woes.
Help me in my dying throes.
Take me back, I'll promise thee
Never more to go to sea.

Email from George Stewart '56…27 September 1998… I just finished reading "Letters to Lou" and I thought it was great. It took me about half way through the book to discover that the "Dirty old Man" was the "Bum". I would have thought it was Sid. [Actually the moniker was used for both. Ben]

       I will have to admit that you deckies had it rougher than us Engineers. During our first week in the school, our four striper (1954), **Bob Shepherd** gave us a rundown on the various instructors we had to watch out for. He mentioned Rounds,

Woodland, Connors, and Hop, among others. Afterward, we asked him about the engineering instructors. He said, almost as an afterthought "don't worry about them, all they want to do is teach you engineering". I guess that resulted in our receiving a little less character development than the deckies.

Anyway, thanks for a great effort.   GWS

PS If anyone is interested, you will find my 2 cents worth in the attached file.

Massachusetts Maritime Academy (MMA) first opened in 1891. Prior to World War II it consisted of a training ship which was berthed at a pier in the North End of Boston. The school had a succession of training ships. From 1909 to 1940, the schoolship was the USS Ranger, renamed "Nantucket", a sailing vessel with an auxiliary steam engine which dated back almost to civil war days. In 1942, the school was moved to the campus of the State Teachers College in Hyannis, Mass. After World War II, the federal government provided the USS Charleston (PG51), a patrol gunboat. It had been built in 1934 and had served in the Pacific during the war.

The water at Hyannis was not deep enough to accommodate the Charleston, so it was berthed at the State Pier on Taylor's Point at Buzzards Bay, Mass. The pier is located at the Western entrance to the Cape Cod Canal. It soon became apparent that bussing students between Hyannis and the Charleston was impractical. The solution was to move all of the students aboard the training ship. Facilities were very rudimentary. The school consisted entirely of the Charleston and a modest size classroom building on the pier. There were no dormitories, athletic fields, or a library. There were no modern expressways leading to Cape Cod. The only methods for getting back and forth were to take the train, obtain a ride from a classmate, or to hitch hike.

The school was three years in length, with no summer vacations. There was a three month cruise every winter. There were only two choices of a major, Deck and Engineering. Graduation led to a Merchant Marine license as Third Mate (Deck) or Third Assistant Engineer, a commission as an Ensign, US Naval Reserve, and a Bachelor of Science degree in either Marine Transportation or Marine Engineering. (It took me until 1961 to discover that the school did not have accreditation). I chose the Engineering Curriculum because it seemed to offer more opportunities for a shore side career, if I wanted one. The school was not particularly expensive, as it was heavily subsidized by the federal government. The greatest expense was in the purchase of uniforms. My parents actually got a rebate of part of the tuition when I graduated. There had been some disquieting news in the papers about a hazing scandal at the academy during the previous year, but we assumed that these problems had all been cleared up. Accordingly, in August 1953, I packed my sea bag and put on my wash khaki uniforms (We had not yet received our dress uniforms) and my parents put me on the train in Brockton. There were three or four other new cadets on the train with me. At Buzzards Bay, we disembarked and proceeded out on the road to Taylor's Point. It was a bright summer day. The Charleston was plainly visible in the distance. We proceeded up the finger pier and crossed the gangway. We were promptly sent back by the cadet officer of the deck, after a short lecture on how to properly salute the colors. Waiting for us was a rather dirty looking, very pale skinned, pimply-faced upper classman with a sinister look on his face. It was **Don Sinclair** (1954 Version), "Donster the Monster" the bane of my existence during my first year at MMA. The "Donster" proceeded to line us up in ranks and gave us our initial introduction to the school. He always sounded very dramatic when he spoke. Essentially it went as follows " Henceforth you are to be referred to as a "Young Man" I am a first classman. All first classmen are to be addressed as "Sir" and are to be obeyed without question. Do you understand?" After we all responded with a "Yes Sir," he announced,

George Stewart

"We will now lay below and I will direct you to your bunks and lockers". I had a somewhat sinking feeling that I had gotten myself into something I had not bargained for, but there was no turning back at this point.

Replies to "Letters To Lou"

Understanding life at MMA required learning a whole new language, so I have included a glossary of terms:

Upper Job - A First Classman. Except when there was an officer around, an Upper Job was lord of all that he surveyed. Always to be addressed as "Mr." or "Sir" and to be treated with great respect. All orders from an Upper Job had to be instantly obeyed, legal or not.

Young Man, or Youngie - A Third Classman. The lowest form of life at MMA. A youngie's only purpose in life was to take direction from and provide entertainment for the Upper Jobs. Essentially a lackey or slave.

Second Job - A Second Classman. A Second Job was expected to run work details but did not have hazing privileges. A Second Job was always frustrated because he was not yet an upper job, having to wait for the next set of youngies. Relations between the Upper Jobs and Second Jobs were always tenuous, at best. A youngie was never to call a Second Job " Mr." or " Sir "or he would get in trouble with the Upper Jobs.

Getting Jobbed - Having to run an errand for an Upper Job.

Hazing - Definitely illegal at MMA but....

Personal Servitude - The same.

Ass Dragging - Making another midshipman as miserable as possible, within the limits of one's authority.

Eighty-Six - The universal code that an officer was present and that all illegal activities had to immediately cease.

Eighty-Six Watch - A youngie, strategically placed in such a manner as to provide a warning to the upper jobs if an officer or the Master-at-Arms was in the area. Woe be to any youngie who allowed an Upper Job to be caught.

Zapped - Being placed on report and having to go to captain's mast. Going to mast meant getting demerits and missing out on precious weekend liberty.

Job Suit - Our dress uniforms. To be worn when going on or off the ship. However never get caught wearing one at home on a weekend or you would never hear the end of it. I found this out after I wore mine to a Boston Celtics basketball game on a Saturday

Hurricane - When a group of Upper Jobs would come back from liberty after an evening on the town and decide to entertain themselves by turning a fire hose on in a berthing compartment.

Mississippi - A stainless steel trough which served as the community sanitary facility. Seawater entered at one end and flowed through in river like fashion to the other end where it drained overboard. The users had to sit on boards which bridged the Mississippi and formed the vague outline of a toilet seat.

Jumping Ship - A privilege reserved for the Upper Jobs during the week (depending on who the duty officer was). The only time we were allowed to leave the ship legally was on weekends.

Shit Faced - Having had too much to drink.

Anna Banana - A legendary young woman who regularly provided entertainment for the Upper Jobs out in the parking lot during the week.

College - A favorite saying by an Upper Job was "What do you think this is, college?"

Chun - The USS Charleston (PG 51), our schoolship. It was one of a class of two Patrol Gunboats built in 1934. The ship was 327 feet long and displaced 2216 tons. It gave the general appearance of a small cruiser. It was propelled by geared steam turbines driving twin screws and developing 6200 horsepower. The ship could make 20 knots. Originally it had been intended for use as a flagship in the Caribbean, but it had spent most of World War II in the Aleutians. In the Navy, it had sported 6-inch guns and a variety of other weapons. In 1948, it had been donated to MMA for use as a schoolship. All armament had been removed, with the exception of the after 6-inch gun mount. It later formed the model for the 327 foot Campbell class coast guard cutters.

Deckies - Deck Cadets - Our natural rivals throughout our school days. It was a known fact that all deckies were "Chicken Shit ." Our relation with Deckies was always a bit strained because they were "Chicken Shit."

Snipes - Engineering Cadets. The good guys. The term "snipe" originated in the British navy when, after his first visit to an engine room aboard a steamship, a senior naval officer was heard to remark that it resembled a snipe marsh.

Stripers - Cadet officers. There was one "Four Striper", a "Three Striper", and "Two and One Stripers " for each division. The "Four Striper" actually ran most of the daily activities of the midshipmen and he was answerable directly to Commander Rounds, the Executive Officer. The stripers were expected to maintain order and they generally kept themselves above the hazing process. The previous Four and Three stripers had lost their stripes, when things got out of hand.

Jobbing the Line - Jumping into the messline ahead of others. A privilege reserved for the Upper Jobs.

IMC - The general announcing system.

Most of the Upper Jobs were off the ship on liberty and there was only a skeleton crew on board during the first week, so things were relatively quiet. There was probably some degree of apprehension on the part of the Upper Jobs as to just how much the officers would let them get away with, in view of the problems during the previous year.

The "Donster" showed us where our bunks and lockers were and told us to report to the storeroom to draw the remainder of our clothing. After standing in line for about 1/2 hour, I faced the School Supply Officer Lt. "Honest **Al**" **Anteen** who scowled (he always scowled) and asked me what sizes I wore. I had expected to be measured and was quite unprepared, so I timidly told him that I did not know. He stared at me for a moment and then barked at me " You had better find out", and sent me to the rear of the line. I was not sure exactly what to do, but I finally picked out one of my new classmates who appeared to be about my size and asked him what he wore. He looked at me rather strangely, but I learned enough to at least mumble out some answers when I had to face Honest Al again. This time he scowled some more but finally decided to throw me a pile of clothes and books. Most of the clothes did not really fit me but I learned to make do. Our next exercise was to mark our names on all of our new supplies with a " Stencil Pencil." Being caught wearing another midshipman's clothes was a "Zappable" offense. My bunk and locker were situated fairly conveniently in the engineer's berthing compartment. However, I was warned that I would have to give them up and find another location, as they would most certainly be taken over by an upper classman, for use as a second locker. My locker assignment only lasted for a week, but I did manage to keep the bunk until the cruise.

The first day went by fairly quickly and I do not remember very much about it. I can vaguely remember my first meal on the messdeck, presided over by a rather strange looking old man wearing dirty looking "khaki's and puffing on a pipe. In the evening, I was introduced to my cleaning station, in the Auxiliary Machinery Room where I was given a wire brush and a rag and told to shine up the deck plates, and coat them lightly with diesel oil. The deck plates aboard the Chun were kept cleaner than on any ship that I have ever been aboard since. They were always scrubbed three times per day, whether they needed it or not. I guess this was to keep the youngies busy. I smelled of diesel oil for my entire youngie year. The hazing routine had not really begun in earnest as yet, because the majority of the upper classmen were off the ship until the next Monday. I can vaguely remember crawling into my bunk after a very long day and hearing taps announced over the IMC. It was not very comfortable, but I had no difficulty getting to sleep.

The next thing that I heard was a voice announcing reveille over the IMC. At first, nobody stirred. After a few minutes I heard someone banging on the lockers and shouting up a barely intelligible announcement. It sounded like " Abiyde, out of your bunks, make em up, abiyide. Roll out and grab a sock, abiyide". I doubt that these were really the correct words. They came out rather slurred, but this litany became burned into my brain, forever. It was the old man who had been presiding over the messdeck on the previous evening,

Sid Sanford, the Master-at-Arms, was to become a very familiar figure over the next three years. He had been a chief petty officer in the navy in the early part of the century. Sid lived on board and he almost never left the ship. I do not remember him ever missing a day, except on weekends.

In the next few paragraphs, I will try to describe a typical day. On paper, the routine would probably not appear much different from the routine at the Naval Academy. In practice, it was another story. The best way to describe it would be as a corruption of the Naval Academy system.

At 6:15, the IMC blared out again for us to lay to the pier for check muster. At check muster, the four striper read the roll call in the presence of the duty officer while each midshipman answered in turn with a "Here sir." In the winter, this could be a rather unpleasant evolution, especially with a Westerly wind blowing off the Cape Cod Canal. If the duty officer was considered to be an easy mark, many of the Upper Jobs chose to forego this evolution. Instead they would assign a youngie to answer up for them when their name was called. In fact, most of the Upper Jobs would immediately return to their bunks as soon as a youngie had been posted as an 86 watch in a strategic position looking up the passageway to the messdeck. At 6:30 Sid would return to wake up the authorized late sleepers from the midnight to 4 AM watch. As soon as the 86 watch caught sight of Sid, he was supposed to frantically run around the compartment yelling 86. In the process he had to make sure that each and every upper classman was up before Sid arrived. Sid always obliged by walking very slowly down the passageway so as to give the 86 watch enough time to perform his assignment. As soon as he left, about half of the Upper Jobs would return to their bunks. This ritual was repeated everyday.

On completion of check muster we would return to the ship and shower and shave prior to breakfast. At least that was the way it was supposed to work. Actually it was impossible for a youngie, as he would have to wait for all of the upper classmen to finish before he could get a space in the crew's head. At first, the idea of shaving and showering every day was rather foreign to me, but the Upper Jobs soon convinced me of its necessity. Actually, this operation was not as simple as it sounds. The Chun lacked a hot water system. Hot water in the showers was obtained by mixing steam and cold water in a small jacket at each shower.

If the water pressure was lost for any reason, you got a shot of live steam and had to scurry out of the way. To heat water for washing or shaving, it was necessary to fill a hand washbasin with cold water and then place it under a live steam jet. A loud crackling noise would then ensue it was necessary to test the water with your finger until the temperature felt right. At this time, I began to develop some survival skills. In order to avoid being assigned as an 86 watch, I found a way to avoid the engineer's compartment entirely and I began showering and shaving in the forward crew's head, while all of the upper class deckies were eating breakfast.

By the time that we mustered on the pier at 7:45 for daily personnel inspection in our khaki's, I was as ready for the day as possible. I still had a tendency to miss spots while shaving and my uniforms were not always the best. But I got by.

Classes ran from 8 to 12 AM. The first year consisted mostly of basic academic subjects such as English, Math, Physics, etc. They were not taught on a very high academic level and none of my classmates took them very seriously. It was just as well that the classes were easy, as the daily routine allowed little time for serious study. I did not find the work very interesting and really did not put forth much of an effort during the first year. I think that I finished about 20th in my class, out of 38 students.

At noon we would return to the ship for lunch. It was necessary to get into line and pick up a rather spotty looking tray and some silverware. Regardless of your place in line, an Upper Job could always job the line, so a youngie might have a long wait. The food was no great shakes, but it was usually adequate. It was necessary to request permission from an Upper Job prior to sitting at a mess deck table and, if there was any decent desert on the menu, you always ran the risk of being jobbed by an Upper Job to go back through the line and get him a second portion. Rather than run the risk of being noticed by Sid, it was easier to give up your own portion.

The next step was to change back into dungarees for a 1 PM Muster. The hours between 1 and 4 PM were devoted to practical work aboard ship. We were organized into four Watches which were actually similar to divisions on a navy ship. Watch IV, to which I was assigned, was nominally the Auxiliary Division, however we rotated between the Boiler, Engineroom, Electrical, and Auxiliary Divisions on a weekly basis. For youngies, one week per month was spent as a messcook. This involved setting up the messdeck prior to meals and cleaning up afterwards. I always volunteered for scullery duty (Called Scullery Maids), in order to avoid being jobbed to steal second portions of desert for an Upper Job. Actually, after a fairly short time, the Upper Jobs gave up on jobbing me to steal food for them, as I was absolutely incompetent when it came to thievery and they realized that they ran the risk of being caught by Sid if they tried giving me this assignment.

At 4 PM, we knocked off ship work and reported to our cleaning stations. This involved the omnipresent task of scrubbing down the deck plates in the engineering spaces or in some cases, steel wooling the deck in the berthing compartment. The worst assignment was head cleaning. The Mississippi all had to be flushed and shined up with steel wool daily. Most of the upper jobs took naps, so it was relatively quiet during this time. Evening meal began at 5 PM. It was essentially a repeat of lunch.

At 7 PM we were back into our khakis for evening study hall. This was actually a misnomer as little or no studying was done. Essentially the hours from 7 to 9 PM were nothing but a hazing session where the Upper Jobs amused themselves at the expense of the youngies. There was no place to hide and the best way to survive these sessions was to remain as inconspicuous as possible. Promptly at 8 PM, the duty officer would come over the gangway and slowly walk across the pier for his inspection. The 86 watch would come running through the building to warn of his approach. By the time he arrived for his very brief tour, the building was a model of decorum. As soon as he left the building and the 86 watch gave the all clear signal, the building returned to havoc and chaos. Of course, we all were convinced at the time that the duty officers were all unaware of what was really going on. This ridiculous charade went on every evening.

At 9 PM we returned to the ship for one more shot at cleaning stations and more hazing. In some cases, an Upper Job would give us a pair of his shoes to shine. Again, in my case, the Upper Jobs soon gave up on giving me this assignment as I was a terrible shoe shiner. Taps was announced at 10 PM but whether or not this meant anything depended totally upon what officer had the duty that evening. As often as not, the lights stayed on and the Upper Jobs continued amusing themselves at the expense of the youngies. Sometimes a contingent of Upper Jobs would create a lot of noise after returning late after an unauthorized evening on the town (Usually spent imbibing a few beers at the Knotty Pine Tavern out in town). Of course, there was always the threat of a hurricane, but none ever occurred while I was at the school.

Upper Jobs actually fitted into several categories. As I previously mentioned, the stripers normally stayed above the process. Some were just having fun. One upper Job named **Herb Jones** liked to line us up in the aisle next to his bunk and sing us a chorus called "Herba is our leader, he will never fail us". I did not mind people such as Herba. However there were some others who had gained a taste of authority for the first time and they could be outright mean. My friend **Don Sinclair** fell into this category. He had undergone a good deal of torment at the hands of the upper class himself and was doing his best to pay it back in kind. Being a very quiet and innocent fellow, I became an obvious target and I therefore did my best to avoid him wherever possible. The most chilling words that I could here were "Stooart, come here." My classmate, **Walter Piotti** (later a Vice Admiral) had the misfortune to bunk directly below the "Donster." Walter had an outstanding talent for shining shoes and he essentially became Sinclair's lackey. When Don could not think of anything else to do, he would sometimes just give an order to Piotti such as "Frown" or "Amuse me". The "Donster" could always be recognized walking up the pier by his long strides. One of my classmates described him as walking like Hopalong Cassidy.

Life at MMA was made bearable by weekend liberty. We had two long weekends (off on Friday), one short weekend (noon Saturday), and one duty weekend (no liberty) each month. It was about 50 miles to Braintree. I did not do very much exciting on weekend liberty during my first two years, but they did provide a temporary escape from the routine. During my second class year, my parents bought their first TV set, and I became an avid watcher. Of course, there was always the dreaded limit of 10 PM on Sunday evening, when we had to be back to the ship for check muster.

On my first weekend at home, I described some of the routine to my parents. This caused my mother to become greatly upset at what her baby had gotten himself into and she began to cry. But as far as I was concerned, there could be no turning back. I had no other place to go.

Of course, all of my classmates were going through something the same routine so we were all in the same boat. I did start to make a few friends among the others in my watch section, but I was not really very close to any of my classmates, although this situation did improve greatly by my second year. I was still very shy, however and was probably the most innocent person in the school. By now, most of my class had acquired nicknames. Some memorable ones were: Goldfish, Cow, Muff, Sick Bay, Suction, Fog, Abdullah the Camel Driver, Punt, Tinker, White Germ, Genius, Ollie Bitchmore, Bumble, Dumbo, Swish, Alec the Egg Man, Negroid, and Pink Bubble. I was called the Duck. Any time that anyone came into a classroom late, you could count on a chorus of Quacks, Moos, Slurps, etc. For "Sick Bay" there would be agonized groans. We took out our frustrations at being youngies by tormenting each other.

Of course, most of my classmates had proclaimed themselves to be sexual athletes with a succession of conquests and I wondered why I was so backward. Naturally, I felt very inferior. One upper job assigned one of my classmates, **Jack Fitzgerald** to fix me up on a double date. I was scared green and did not acquit myself very well.

It sounds like the school was total chaos, but that was not really the case. Nearly all of the instructors were graduates of the school from the 1920's and 30's, and they had probably been subjected to even worse conditions than we had during their days aboard the "Nantucket". One reason that the school was unaccredited was that few, if any of the instructors had advanced degrees and some had no degrees at all. They did, however, have a firm grasp of nautical subjects. I can truthfully say that I have found some use for virtually everything that I ever learned at the school. I still have most of my MMA textbooks in the office at work. The faculty allowed a certain degree of tolerance to the conditions that I have just described. However there was never any doubt as to who exerted ultimate control. There were many memorable characters on the staff and, of course, we had assigned nicknames to all of them:

Vitamin - Rear Admiral USN (Ret.) Julian D. Wilson, the superintendent. He was a rather thin, ascetic man and we had very little direct contact with him. During the War he had been Commanding Officer of the Battleship Maryland.

Stupid - Captain Jack Thompson, MMA Class of 1912. The captain of the Charleston. His name came from his rather wooden manner. Our only contact with him was on the occasions when we had been Zapped and had to go to Captain's Mast. He was not very quick witted and one upper job claimed to have avoided punishment for being late by telling him that "The bridge was up".

Stupid Junior - Captain Thompson's son, a rather scruffy looking character who drove the academy garbage truck.

Rounds – Cdr. Dick Rounds, the Executive Officer. He was a little round-faced man with a very imperious manner who always wore a frown. He always came across as very cold and calculating, however nobody ever questioned his competence. We all lived in fear of him. As far as we were concerned, he was the person who really ran the school.

The Bird (Woody) – Cdr. Louis Woodland. The Navigator on the Chun. A short man with a close-cropped mustache.

The Bum - Cdr Bill Connors, who taught deck seamanship. His name came from his pock marked face and somewhat seedy manner. He was the undisputed lord of the Deckies. He made no secret of his disdain for snipes. He had a very strong command presence and was not somebody you wanted to trifle around with. There was no jumping ship and lights always went out on time when he had the duty. If a Deckie wanted to be a striper, he had to be on the good side of The Bum. Of course, Rounds, Woody, and the Bum were Chicken Shit.

Honest Al, Armpits Al, - Al Anteen, the Supply Officer, who I already mentioned. A thoroughly nasty man at all times.

Sid - Sid Sanford, the Master at Arms, I already described him. Surprisingly, he did not really bother me very much. At least he represented some degree of order. However, I never could really understand the words in his wakeup call. Sid's teeth did not fit very well and his speech was very slurred. I understood that at one time he had been a chief boiler tender in the Pre-World War I Navy.

Hop - Lt Lee Harrington, the registrar, athletic coach, and sometimes math teacher (when he showed up for his classes). Hop was a very intense, combative individual who always seemed to be about to boil over. His temper was legendary and we were told that he had, at one time, thrown a chair at a student who had fallen asleep in his class. He was a member of a famous Massachusetts political family and this helped him become the superintendent in the 1970's. Hop always recruited just enough athletes (mostly from Dorchester) to enable the school to field teams in football, basketball, and baseball. Although none of the teams were very good. I remember one time I came under his wrath when he decided to inspect our fingernails at morning muster. Naturally, I failed.

The Gander - Lt. Fred (Wickie) Wickander. This was Wickie's first year at the school. He was a very shy man who was totally out of place at the Academy. He was unable to exert any kind of authority. His English classes were total havoc and chaos. Conversations went on in the classroom as if he wasn't there and there were at least 1 or 2 book fights that I can remember. On several occasions, other instructors had to come into the room to maintain order. The youngies loved him, because he was the only person in the school that they could walk over. Wickie was gone by the end of our second job year.

Jim Murray - Cdr. Jim Murray was the head of the engineering department and chief engineer of the Chun. He was all business, controlled his classes well, and was a very capable instructor. He was the closest thing that I could find to a role model at the school, although he could be somewhat petty at times. He was known for babying his machinery. The ship normally cruised at 10 or 12 knots, however the speed always seemed to creep up a few knots during the last few nights of the cruise. One evening when the increased vibration from the screws became too noticeable, he appeared suddenly in the Engineroom and uttered his best-known quote, "What do you think this is, a speedboat?"

Hammering Hank - Cdr Bill Hemmerly, who taught electrical engineering. His classes could be very dry and we all thought of him as a terrible instructor. However I ended up learning quite a lot in his classes.

"Bing" – LCDR James Crosby. He bore a slight resemblance to John Belushi. He told many funny sea stories in class and everyone loved him.

Doc Boyle - The ship's doctor, who only came aboard for the cruises. A scrawny little man with glasses and a mustache who appeared to have drank too much alcohol during his life. Like Al Anteen, he was cranky, irascible, and generally nasty to everyone. We all thought of him as a quack.

MO - A giant Filipino cook. He was invariably hostile and surly. Our favorite quote from him was "You want sheet, I geeve you sheet." This was not an entirely inaccurate description of his culinary efforts.

There were others, but these were the most memorable ones.

About my third or fourth week at the school, I was assigned to my first watch in the fireroom. The ship had two 325PSI "A" type main boilers. In port, we periodically would fire up one boiler and raise the steam pressure up to safety valve setting. The steam was used for quarters heating, hot water, dishwashing, etc. The boiler was oil fired and was lighted by a hand torch. The watch consisted of one second job and one youngie. Other than driving a car, firing up the boiler was the first practical thing that I had ever learned to do in my life and I was very proud of myself when I mastered it. I immediately became interested in learning all phases of operation of the Chun's engineering plant. This was to pay great dividends later. Besides, it was quiet down in the machinery spaces and it was the best way to avoid harassment by the Upper Jobs. I found a quiet spot on top of the Chun's distilling plants where I would not be noticed by the Upper Jobs.

The year moved along fairly swiftly and before I knew it, it was time for the 1954 cruise. Up to this time, I had never seen the engines fired up or the Chun underway. In mid January, we sailed up to Boston for a brief period in the East Boston Shipyard, prior to departure for 10 weeks in the sunny Caribbean. I was surprised and a bit ill at ease when I went up on deck for the first time underway and saw that we were out of sight of land.

After a short dry-dock period and our annual Coast Guard inspection, we were ready to sail. On departure, my parents gave me $50, which was supposed to last for the entire 10 weeks. It did not even last for half of the cruise. As I left home to return to the ship, my mother started to cry. Her baby was going off for the first time.

Finally, on 5 February 1954, we were underway, heading Southward. As soon as we passed Cape Cod the weather got bad, and it was to remain so for the next four or five days. The Chun began to roll and pound alarmingly. Since nearly all of its topside armament from its Navy days had been removed, the ship was, if anything, too stable. It rolled with a very violent whipping motion. I have never seen this motion duplicated on any ship that I have ever been to sea on since. The ship was ringed with portholes, which were only a few feet above the water line, and many of them proved to leak. The result was a fair amount of water sloshing around in the berthing compartments. On top of this, the majority of midshipmen and a fair amount of the instructors became seasick. The combination of the ship's motion and the stench of vomit was overpowering. In the middle of this bedlam, a pair of messcooks spilled a large tray of ravioli onto the messdeck as they were trying to carry it down the ladder from the galley. Sid's remedy was to scoop up as much of the ravioli as possible and then throw down some bags of sawdust on top of the remnants. Of course, my reaction to this bedlam was to become violently seasick for about 4 days. I found that the best thing to do was to get as low as possible in the ship. The possibility entered my mind that the ship might roll over and sink or break in half, but I was too seasick to really care.

It was a big relief to finally see some good weather as we passed the Bahamas. The sunshine and fresh air looked very good to me. Our first stop was to be Ciudad Trujillo in the Dominican Republic. It was my first look at a foreign country and I was quite excited.

I was a bit disappointed when I discovered that most of my classmates were more interested in visiting bars and whorehouses than absorbing the local culture. At the time, I had never even tasted a beer and I was to hold out until the middle of the cruise. The second day in port, **Doc Boyle** assembled us on the pier and indicated that he had issued nearly 100 packages of prophylactics on the previous day. He further announced that there would be no more prophylactics issued on the ship and that anyone who contracted a case of venereal disease would be restricted for the remainder of the cruise. Also he indicated that a letter would be sent to the parents of anyone who had to be placed on the VD list.

We usually stayed in each port for 4 days, with a four or five day transit between ports. Liberty hours were from 1 to 10 PM. There was no overnight liberty. The ports we were scheduled to visit were Barbados, Trinidad, La Guira in Venezuela, Coco Solo (Canal Zone), Havana, Houston, Nassau, Fort Lauderdale, Charleston, S.C., and back to Boston.

The machinery space ventilation did not work very well and temperatures of 120 to 130 were not uncommon. But I really did not mind the underway time as I was learning a lot. When the Chun was underway, all watch stations, except for the Officer of the Deck and the Engineering Officer of the watch, were manned by midshipmen. The watch assignments for the youngies tended to be rather menial. Virtually every automatic control device in the machinery spaces were either inoperative or had been disabled. Youngies were assigned to some rather dreary tasks such as taking pressure and temperature readings, maintaining water levels or regulating some pressure or temperature. I guess it was necessary to find something for us to do. The Upper Jobs had let up quite a bit by this time and many of them were actually trying to teach us something useful.

In La Guira, I had been ashore, but had decided to return to the ship early. Three second jobs asked me if I would take their swimming gear back to the ship. I was walking down the pier, when I decided to stop and look at a Venezuelan ship. All of a sudden, I heard some alarm bells ringing on the Chun, followed by an announcement that the gangway was closed. The cadet officer of the deck came out on the pier and placed me under arrest. I was immediately taken up to see the Bum. He demanded to know what I had in the bag. I guess he thought that I was trying to smuggle some drugs or alcohol on board. When I showed him that the bag contained nothing but a mass of smelly swimming trunks, he look confused, and then decided to take me up to see Cdr. Rounds. Rounds demanded to know whom the trunks belonged to. I told him that a group of second classmen had asked me to bring their gear back to the ship. The Bum promptly gave me a withering stare and said, " Asked you to or told you to?" I said, emphatically that they had asked me to. He then said, why did you stop when you were coming down the pier. I said that I had stopped to look at the Venusian (I was a bit rattled) ship. By now, Rounds looked very perplexed and all he could think of to say was "This is rather unusual," and told me to lay below. Some Upper Jobs later told me that I was lucky that the gear belonged to second jobs, or I would have been in trouble for failure to report hazing.

Replies to "Letters To Lou"

In Coco Solo, I had my first beer. We went out to a strip joint and the only way that the waiter would let me stay was to buy a beer. I sipped it very slowly and did not like it very much. I was to develop more of a taste for it later.

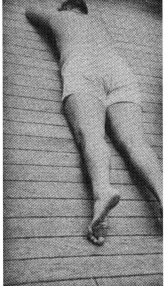

Typical Deck Sleeper

By the time we got to Havana, I was essentially broke. In addition, I had lost most of my clothing in the ship's laundry and was barely able to keep myself dressed. By now, I had been kicked out of my bunk by an upper job and had taken to sleeping up on deck. This was not as bad as it sounds. It was really very pleasant up there with the ship gently rolling under clear tropical skies at night. If it rained, I slept on the deck in the pea coat locker, down in the bowels of the ship.

My grandmother had a brother and sister in Houston. I called up my mother's cousin, Thurban Barker, and we had a very pleasant visit. I met an aunt and uncle that I never knew that I had. I also took advantage of their phone to call my mother and requested more money. She sent another $25 which I received In Fort Lauderdale. It did not help me very much, because I owed about $15 of it to classmates who had previously lent me money. By the time we got to Charleston, I was broke again and I could not afford to go ashore. I was very happy to return to Boston on April 15 and my parents were very glad to see me. By then, I was completely broke and I did not have any underwear.

The rest of the year went by fairly fast. The time spent in the engineering spaces was beginning to pay off and I had managed to teach myself how to operate most of the on deck equipment. By the end of the year, I was more knowledgeable than most of the second jobs.

A big weight was lifted off my shoulders when the upper Jobs were last seen going over the gangway. A few of them have stuck in my memory. Our Company Commander (4 Striper), **Bob Shephard** had provided us with much of our basic indoctrination. He was an outstanding role model in all respects. The Company Adjutant (3 Striper), **Sanford Williams** was very impressive looking, but he was a complete blockhead. We got to know **Bob Doonan** much later in the early 1970's in Virginia Beach, VA. He and his wife have both since passed on. **Tom Kelleher** died when he fell while being lowered onto the deck of a naval vessel from a helicopter. It occurred while he was accompanying the Propulsion Examining Board on an inspection in 1975. I was nearby in the Virginia Capes operating areas at the time and heard it described as it occurred over the voice radio. **Bill Kelley** later became president of the Navy League. **Malcom MacLeod** is now the president of Moran Towing and Transportation, the same company that my Uncle Harry used to work for. **John (Noble) Fiske** was a Harvard dropout, complete with accent.. He seemed totally out of place at MMA. **Frank Burger** has a high level position at Litton Industries in Pascagoula, Miss. I saw him during the acceptance trial of USS Vincennes, the ship that later shot down the Iranian Airbus. **Paul McCarthy** became a Vice Admiral and served as Commander Seventh Fleet in the Pacific. **Don Sinclair** and **Herb Jones** have already been described. **"Red" Russell** had made a career out of being an Upper Job. He started out in the class of 1952 and ended up in my class. I am not sure if he ever graduated.

In reflection, I bear no ill will toward the majority of the class of 1954. There was a contingent of football players who had escaped much of the hazing when they were youngies, but were enthusiastic participants as Upper Jobs. I do have some lingering resentment toward these people. Many of the First Classmen had just tasted authority for the first time and did not really know how to handle it. The graduates who have been the most successful in life were generally not obnoxious as Upper Jobs.

Unfortunately, I wasn't quite where I should have been yet. There was a small active duty Naval Science detachment at the school consisting of three officers and two chief petty officers who were responsible for our basic naval indoctrination. Our first year's course in Naval Orientation had consisted largely of Victory at Sea movies. Toward the end of the year, our instructor Lt John (Blackjack) Smith decided (with some good reason) that my reliability and military bearing was not up to standards and that I was not officer material. My relief at seeing the Upper Jobs depart was tempered by the fact that it appeared that I had lost my shot at a naval commission. I was no star academically, having finished 13th out of 37 students in the first term and 20th in the second term. I did not appear to have a very bright future. But I had become a firm believer in the axiom "One day at a time", even at age 17.

Even though all students were required to attend graduation, I decided to skip it and accept a captain's mast. I was determined to get up to Maine to see my friends and relatives. I had a cold feeling in the pit of my stomach about losing my navy commission, but I did not tell a soul about my difficulties.

By now, I did not really have very much to show for my life. I had managed to make it through my youngie year, but my academic performance had been mediocre, I was in trouble with the Naval Science department, and I was facing captain's mast. What next?

When I returned to the school, a lot had changed. There was a new set of youngies and I was a second job. That took away a lot of the pressure. But I still had two hurdles to face. At captain's mast, I was given 20 demerits. That meant the loss of two weekend's liberty. I accepted that it was my own fault and decided to get on with it. Soon afterward, I was called in for an interview with Blackjack Smith (who we all considered to be "Gung Ho") and his department head, Lieutenant Commander Simone (Who was a complete zero). Blackjack told me that he had given me the lowest ranking in the class for military aptitude, but that after careful consideration, they had decided to retain me in their program. I breathed a big sigh of relief.

Looking backward, this was a good character-building lesson. But I have mixed feelings about it, because it was sprung on me all at once. There was little or no counseling beforehand. My grades in Naval Science had been fairly good. But I cannot say that Blackjack was really unjustified in his opinion of me.

As a side note, Blackjack later became the driving force in the establishment of the Propulsion Examining Boards, in which I was to play a major part. In 1973 I called on him in his office in Washington. By then I was a Commander. He was quite bowled over and somewhat embarrassed to see me. Ironically, he retired from the navy after he failed to screen for major command as a Captain. I actually ended up going farther in the navy than he did.

The most memorable event of that fall was when we were hit directly by a hurricane. It was while I was serving one of my weekend restrictions. It was quite spectacular. We were quite safe aboard ship, but we lost electricity from shore and had to start generating our own power. Taylor's Point was flooded to a depth of several feet. Most of the summer cottages that covered the point were washed away into Buzzard's Bay. Most of my classmate's cars, which were in the parking lot, were submerged and some were washed completely off the pier. They are probably still rusting away at the bottom of the Cape Cod Canal. My classmates all blamed Rounds for not letting them move their vehicles to higher ground. Whenever anything bad occurred at the school, we always blamed Rounds.

By now all of the major hurdles had been overcome and it was time to get into the school year. From here on, things began to change dramatically. The class work was mostly professional marine engineering subjects. The extra work that I had done down in the engineering spaces began to pay off. For the first time in my life, I had found something that I was not only interested in but I was good at. (It did not hurt that we now actually could use study periods for studying.) This took some getting used to. Up to that time, I had always assumed that I was always going to fail at everything. My grades began to shoot upwards. I told my parents that they could expect to see a better report card than they had become used to seeing. They were a bit dubious, in view of my previous performances. When the returns were in, I was second in my class. I'm sure that they breathed a giant sigh of relief. My self-confidence had improved greatly. In the space of just four months, everything had changed. But the change was not complete. My social skills were still atrocious.

Of course, it soon became time for my second class cruise to the Caribbean. This time, I was much better prepared. I made sure that I had enough clothes and, to play it absolutely safe, I took a part time job in the ship s laundry to make sure that I would not lose anything. My parents gave me the princely sum of $150, which I promptly turned over to Honest Al for safekeeping. We left Boston on 17 January 1955 and headed South.

The weather was basically a rerun of the previous year, but this time I was only briefly seasick. On the second or third night out, we were rolling heavily and I could not sleep, so I got up and walked around a bit during the mid watch. We were wallowing along making about 10 knots through the water. In the engine room, just about the entire watch section was out of action, due to seasickness. The only exception was the Engineering Officer of the Watch, **George Custer**, a retired navy Chief Machinist's Mate. He was standing under a supply vent looking totally miserable. In the fire room, the only person that I could find was a youngie **(Lewis)**, He was smoking a big cigar and he was very happily firing the only boiler that we had on the line. It was his first day at sea and he had never fired a boiler underway before. However, at that moment, he was all that was standing between us and the mercies of the sea.

QUARTERDECK MAINTENANCE

"BOBBY JOBBIE" IN THE SHIP'S STORE

Our ports of call on this cruise were to be St. Thomas, Martinique, Paramaribo (Surinam), Trinidad (again), Curacao, Cartagena, Colombia, Port Au Prince, Vera Cruz, New Orleans, Jacksonville, Philadelphia, and back to Boston.

This cruise was a lot more fun. By now I had developed some fairly close friends among my classmates, primarily those in Watch IV, like myself. My closest associates were **Jim Travers, Alan "Tinker" Thorpe, John Blazewicz, Steve Soule**, and **Morgan Ryan**. Morgan's father had at one time been the Registrar of Motor Vehicles in the State of Massachusetts and he had connections to all of the states political bigwigs. One year he came to the annual ring dance with the governor's daughter. Morgan was (or appeared to be) very world wise and he was generally considered to be the most witty and sophisticated member of our class. My mother was quite impressed that I had such close contact with greatness and did not hesitate to tell her friends and relatives that Morgan was my best friend (Although Morgan was a great guy, this was a slight exaggeration).

I usually rode back and forth on weekends with **John Blazewicz**. He lived in Brockton, which was close to Braintree. John's car left a good bit to be desired. The brakes were not very good and he had to pump them frantically in order to get the car stopped. Sometimes at stoplights, we had to open the doors and complete the braking action by dragging the soles of our shoes on the road. I guess God sometimes is known to protect fools and knaves. But we did not give this a second thought.

Not too much exciting happened during this cruise. The high point was probably in Vera Cruz when we threw a dance aboard ship. Many of the local girls showed up with their dueñas (chaperones). I had volunteered for galley duty in order to avoid participation. My relationships with the opposite sex were still almost non-existent. My greatest vice was an occasional beer during the cruise. I never have smoked a cigarette. Drugs were totally unknown at the school.

In Port Au Prince, I attended my first Catholic Mass. This was because all of the people that I usually went ashore with were Catholic. The mass was in Latin and I could not understand anything that was going on.

Doc Boyle was still looking out for the health, well being, and moral character of the midshipmen. One day during the cruise, he decided to conduct a "Short Arm Inspection". The Doc sat on the anchor windlass up on the forecastle and we all had to line up on the Starboard side of the main deck. One by one we had to go to the forecastle and respond to the Doc's command to unzip and "Peel Back." He carefully inspected us for signs of venereal disease while his assistant, **Tony Tassinari** checked us off on the muster list. On completion of the Doc's inspection, we zipped back up and proceeded back down the port side. In my case, there was not much to worry about, as I knew that life would no longer be worth living if my parents received notification that I was on the VD list. All of the unfortunates who made the list were required to use the after crew's head in the engineer's compartment (a thoroughly foul and dismal place) and were restricted for the rest of the cruise.

We returned to Boston on 30 March 1955. Compared to my youngie cruise, this one had been a rousing success. I was making progress.

My grades continued to be good. At the end of the next term, I finished No. 3 in the class. My mother carefully recalculated my scores and discovered that the calculation of my overall score was incorrect. She wrote a letter to the school pointing out the error. A recalculation showed that I had actually finished first.

By this time, several of my classmates had become determined to remedy my greatest failing. It was announced that I had been fixed up with a date for a class beach party in Cohassett, Mass. I went along with it, but I was scared to death. The evening went well enough and I had another date with the same girl, but then she abruptly dropped me. With my low level of confidence, this seemed to be a deathblow.

Now it was time for the Class of 1955 to depart. There was a slight diversion on the last evening of the school year when the Bum decided to hold a surprise check muster. A number of the graduating class were discovered to be off the ship, on unauthorized liberty. The unfortunate few did not graduate on time. The story was that the Bum had set them up by giving a hint that he would be turning a blind eye to these activities. I don't know if this was really true.

There are a few members of this class worth mentioning. **Gerry Scannell**, the 4 Striper, became head of the Occupational Health and Safety Administration (OSHA). **Ed Ducharme**, one of the unfortunates who were caught in the Bum's net, became Chief Engineer of another ship in my first Destroyer Division.

198

U.S.T.S CHARLESTON ARRIVING WILLEMSTAD, CURACAO, FEBRUARY 1955

Lee Cueroni, who was basically a wild man, lived across the street from us in Navy housing in Newport, R.I. in 1963. **Bob (Bogger) Collis** was in this class (everyone from Cape Cod was always called "Bogger"). We became close friends with his younger brother, Dave (Class of 1958) and his wife Marge. The Bogger was a bit of an adventurer, but Dave was a very straight arrow. Dave was to die tragically in 1980, of cancer.

John Arnold was killed during the cruise, when he broke his back while diving into shallow water during a beach party in Curacao. I had some vicarious pleasure when one of the more self-righteous members of this class was placed on report during the cruise for chilling a can of orange juice with a CO2 fire extinguisher.

Normally, a person with my academic standing would have been considered for two stripes during the first class year. But three of my closest friends were chosen ahead of me, and I was passed over. It is perfectly obvious to me now that I was viewed as less mature than my classmates. But 19 year olds are not very good at self-assessment.

On my return to the school two things had changed. For one thing, I was belatedly appointed as a Cadet Ensign (1 stripe) and was reassigned to the boiler division. I was the assistant to **Carl Trapp**, the Cadet Lieutenant (two striper) for the division. Now I was an Upper Job myself. A new set of youngies had reported in. Gradually, I worked my way out of my funk and got on with the school year.

I made no effort to exert the authority I had newly acquired as an Upper Job. I just did not see any point in hazing and I left that up to other members of my class.

I continued to excel academically. I remained on top of my class for the fall term. For the first two years, I had volunteered for the duty during the weekend of the annual ring dance. For my first class year, my classmate, **Alan "Tinker" Thorpe** insisted that I go with him on a double date. That evening did not go especially well either, and I had just about given up on the whole thing.

Of course, there were no girls at the school, unless you wanted to count Anna Banana. But sex was a constant source of discussion. Many of my classmates' analyses of the subject resembled those of "Beavis and Butthead." Since I firmly believed that all of my classmates were more accomplished than me, I continued to feel deeply inferior.

Finally, my classmates decided that something absolutely had to be done about my situation and a group of them had a council of war. **Tom "Pincho" McLaughlin** indicated that he had a sister, which was a total surprise to all of us. This time it worked out and I dated his sister, Anne on a fairly steady basis until graduation when I went out to the West Coast. However, we never had a firm commitment and I was not yet ready to make one.

The year went by pretty fast and suddenly, it was time for our Upper Job cruise. This one was to the Mediterranean. We left Boston on 5 March 1956. The weather was more co-operative this time. Our scheduled ports were Bermuda, Gibraltar, Marseilles, Barcelona, Genoa, Tangier, Madeira, Santa Cruz de Tenerife (Canary Islands), San Juan (Puerto Rico), Baltimore, and back to Boston.

In Bermuda, we had to stay a few extra days in order to repair a hole in the side of the ship, which was causing us to leak fuel. The cause was a furrow of rust in the side of the ship caused by prolonged runoff from one of the officer's washbasins. Of course, Gibraltar was a very interesting place to visit. In Marseilles, I found out that I had retained much of my high school French. Much to my surprise, I was able to read signs and make myself understood.

We were in Barcelona on Easter, 1956. A few of us attempted to find a Protestant church to attend. Since this was Franco Spain that proved to be rather difficult. There were only two small churches in the city located unobtrusively in back alleys. I had the 20 to 24 (8 to 12 PM) watch in the Engineroom on my duty night. One of my classmates informed me that one of the local ladies of the night had set herself up in business in the chart room. There was a line formed outside the door on the starboard side of the O-2 level. The chart room was directly over Cdr. Round's cabin, but I guess he must have been a sound sleeper. She left happily at midnight with a full purse. I am afraid that I was not ready for this kind of activity. I never forgot about the dreaded VD list.

In Genoa, we were actually allowed two overnights liberty. Originally we were scheduled for a tour of Rome, but when the tour guide failed to show, we opted for a trip to Florence. I still have pleasant memories of it. When we returned to the Chun, a large, elegant passenger liner had moored directly across the pier. It was the Andrea Doria, which was to meet a tragic end in a collision just a few months later.

Just as we were about to lift the gangway prior to getting underway, my classmate, **Bob Cashman** suddenly came running down the pier in his wash khaki uniform. He had observed an extended nights liberty. Bob had the reputation of hard steaming while on liberty. His most prominent physical features were tattoos of dripping faucets over each breast labeled "Sweet" and "Sour" Bob also had twin propellers tattooed on his rear end. He was promptly suspended when we got back to Boston. I do not know if he ever went back and graduated.

Tangier was my only visit to an Arabic country. Our activities there are not fit for publishing in this narrative. However I stayed out of trouble.

Madeira, Santa Cruz de Tenerife, and San Juan seemed like afterthoughts. Our last stop was Baltimore. The waterfront consisted of decaying steamboat wharves and rat infested warehouses. This was true of all East Coast ports in the 1950's. The city has certainly done an amazing job on cleaning up this area since then. The principal activity in town seemed to be strip joints up on Baltimore Street. I was still too young to legally purchase a beer.

On return to Boston, we were really on the home stretch. The last few months went by rapidly. Before we knew it, it was time to take our Coast Guard license exams. Cdr. Murray had boasted that no midshipman within memory had ever failed the exams. The reason turned out to be that the Coast Guard examiner for many years had been a graduate of MMA. Unfortunately he had retired and his replacement was an ex-Coast Guard enlisted man who had little use for maritime graduates. Several of my classmates failed to pass the exam. Since this was a graduation requirement, these people only received blank slips of paper at graduation. Most of them eventually re-took and passed the exams, but at least one class member never did.

Another disquieting piece of news was the status of our naval reserve (USNR) commissions. The legislation which covered our program had expired after our youngie year and it had become necessary to find us another program. The solution was to enlist us as Officer Candidate, Seaman Apprentice, (OCSA) USNR. The advantage of this was that we got to collect two extra years of longevity for pay purposes. This adds to my retirement pay (a corresponding Naval Academy graduate did not get longevity). The disadvantage was that we were required to serve three years on active duty, immediately upon graduation. I had never been particularly motivated toward naval service, but now I had no choice. My class was the only one ever affected by this ruling.

The next thing we knew, it was time for graduation. My parents, Uncle Harry, Aunt Mildred, Maybelle, and Esther all attended. Overall, I had finished number two in my class and I won several awards, in the process making my relatives quite proud.

Looking back, there were both positives and negatives to attending the academy. The positives were that I had gotten out of my shell and developed a great deal as a person. But I still had a long way to go. I had learned some practical (and survival) skills which were to really help me later on in life. I honestly can say that I have made some use or another of most of what I learned at the school. Some subjects, such as Reciprocating Steam Engines and Scotch Marine Boilers were already out of date in 1956. The negative side was that the academic level was quite low. The curriculum could not be considered as equivalent to a college level engineering course. We had led a very closed existence without much exposure to the world around us. When I graduated, I had no idea who Elvis Presley really was. However, if somebody today asked me if I had to do it all over again would I have gone to MMA, the answer would be a resounding YES!!

The next week was spent in limbo. We were waiting to see what the navy intended for us. There had been an incident at Kings Point earlier in the year, when it was discovered belatedly that one of the graduate's mother was a member of the Communist Party. Because of this, it had been decided not to hand out our commissions at graduation. After a few days wait, I received a phone call from a secretary at the Boston Office of Naval Officer Procurement (ONOP). My parents had hoped that I would be sent to Newport, Rhode Island, but she informed me that I would be going to San Francisco for further transportation to a destroyer which was based in San Diego, California. I was directed to come in to be sworn into the navy and pick up my orders.

The next day, I reported to the Boston ONOP. A grizzled Chief Petty Officer told me to get into line for processing. I quickly discovered that the line was for people who were applying to enter MMA. I went back over to the Chief and explained that that was not what I was there for. He looked at me rather puzzled and said "You are too young to have a commission." I can't blame him for this impression. I was still a few weeks short of my 21st birthday and I looked very young. Finally, I was taken in to see the Officer in Charge, who swore me in as an Ensign, USNR, and issued me my orders.

The next step was to figure out how to get to San Francisco. This was not so easy in 1956. The only air connections that I could get were by Northeast Airlines to New York, American to Los Angeles, and Western to San Francisco. The trip would require about 12 hours. All planes were propeller driven. Jets would not come until 3 years later. I had never been on an airplane before. Neither had any of my relatives.

It finally became time for departure. I put on my uniform and packed my bags. My parents took me to Logan Airport. I said good-bye to my parents and very nervously boarded the DC3 which was waiting at the ramp. The plane looked huge to me at the time. There is one just like it hanging from the roof of the Air and Space Museum at the Smithsonian and it looks tiny to me now.

After what seemed like an interminable wait, the engines came to life, and we taxied out to the end of the runway. I had no idea what the future held and I was too nervous about the takeoff to give it much thought Finally we roared down the runway, lifted into the evening sky, and headed for New York. The next chapter in my life was about to begin.

Email excerpts on the USS Doyen: APA-1 later renamed Bay State

Email from Carl Megonigle '57...16 October 1998...How are things going? I have been meaning to send you an Email to ask questions about the Doyen. I have been trying, for the last couple of months, to remember something. I got called in by ADM Wilson and was given a pile of money to go get the SS Doyen with eleven other midshipmen. The first question, I can't remember who went? We took the train to New York, stayed at the "Y" at Brooklyn as usual, took two subways down to the Bowery to meet the Bum and an Engineering Officer, but I don't remember who? We were carrying all kinds of gear so we could sleep on the ship. We arrived at the tug boat on time, but of course, the Bum came out of his cage and screamed at us, but I don't remember what for? We rode the tug up the Hudson and pulled the Doyen out and went to the yard in New Jersey, Hoboken, to get the hull cleaned. I think we slept on the ship in the yard, but of course we had no lights and no water and no bathrooms. Real first class Mass Maritime operation. We went to the supermarket and bought bread, cookies, Spam, and soda for the trip to the Cape. The Bum went crazy because I bought Spam, and got a whole run down on how much Spam he ate during the war. Of course, we had no refrigeration, so that's why I got Spam. I don't think the Bum rode with us up the Cape, because it was too quiet. We slept on the Bridge and stood watches on the tug line. It was dark and eerie. That's my memory. Anybody add anything? I spent all the money on food, train tickets, and other necessities. Big Al Anteen called me in and wanted all my receipts and a complete breakdown of my expenditures. He went crazy when I didn't have anything and wanted to know why I didn't understand the Massachusetts accounting and travel regulations. I don't remember much about the meeting, because we were in a closed room and I passed out from the odor. Ha!

*...17 October 1998...*The Doyen: This has become a real itch with me. The more I think about it, because everything went so well, meaning nobody gave me a hard time, and everybody was where they were supposed to be, which leads me to believe that the eleven other people were second job deckies. I don't think there were any snipes, I don't remember any oil spills. The work we did was all deck work. Pulling the ship out of the pack, going in and out of dry dock, and being towed to the Cape. The reason I don't remember any names is because second job deckies had no names. The only one that gave me a hard time was the Bum. The more I think about it, he rode the tug down the Hudson and I don't think he rode the ship to the Cape, which is why I don't understand why he rose hell about the Spam since he wasn't going to eat it. I'll bet while we were sleeping on the ship and eating in the Nedics Orange Room in Hoboken, he was probably in the Plaza in New York. I am going to eventually work this all out. Any input would be helpful. Email from **Pete Kendrigan '57**...02 November 1998...***If the Doyen became the Bay State which we transported "dead ship" from NY in '57, then I was on board but have little recollection except that it was cold and dark.***

*Email from Peter Readel '57...17 December 2001...*I thought that more than **Carl Megonigle** went down for the Doyen from our class, but I cannot think who it would have been. **Roffey – Meyer – Sweet** or some combination? I would have thought that Carl would have remembered. I do remember tales of excursions thru the shipyard and "jobbing" hawsers, wire mooring lines, etc., and the complete cooperation of the stevedores in getting them aboard. Also remember the usual fiasco of mooring her alongside the canal when she finally arrived. I think it was Hurst that tried to write me up for "abandoning my post" when I was standing a 12-4 AM watch and I went over to check the lines. He came on deck and went "ape" because I was not there. Connors and Rounds talked him out of it, both said that I had shown "initiative and responsibility" as a ship had just gone by and the surge that woke Hurst up warranted my going and checking. Actually I was at the far end of the building, enjoying the company of a female!!! Had forgotten all about that until just now!!! Real impression that girl made!

    The following comments were taken from letters written by **Robert L. Stickney** to **Jane F. Smith**, his future wife who lived in New Orleans, Louisiana. They cover the period from September 8, 1957 to July 24, 1958. Comments prior to this were included in Donald "Ben" Hogan's book, "Letters to Lou".

    During this time **Bob Stickney**, who graduated from Massachusetts Maritime Academy in August, 1957 and received a third mate's license, was completing post-graduate work in engineering. He received that degree in 1958.

    The DOYEN had been transformed into the BAY STATE.

    Unless otherwise noted, the letter can be assumed to have been sent from Buzzards Bay, MA to New Orleans, LA. Normally the date shown will indicate the date the letter was written. Undated letters are listed by the postmark date. Only portions related to the DOYEN/BAY STATE have been excerpted.

DOYEN/BAY STATE – BUZZARDS BAY CAMPUS

8 September 1957 I am leaving in the morning for New York for a period from one to six weeks. I don't know how long we will be there. We are supposed to work on the Bay State, take her on the trials and then take her back to Buzzards Bay. It will be interesting and very educational, for the whole engine room is torn apart. If you should like to mail your letters to me, the address is:

*Robert L. Stickney
O'Brien Brother's Shipyard
200 Edgewater Street
Staten Island 5, New York*

14 September 1957 (Staten Island, NY) We have been busy 24 hours a day around here, and it looks like we will be here for at least three weeks.

The living conditions have not been good at all. The lights are few and far between, and [there is] no hot water. The rooms are too hot to sleep comfortably in because all the blowers are apart. The engines are in a thousand and one pieces, and I doubt if they will ever be put back together again properly.

I am writing from the fantail and have to stop every few minutes to watch a passing ship and dream. I have a beautiful view of New York harbor and all the activity. I believe that there are more ships coming in and out of New York in one day than there are in Boston in one week.

20 September 1957 (Staten Island, NY) I was working in the forward engine room today, and I thought I would get killed. As soon as I would put steam into a line, the place would burst into steam from any number of leaks which were sure to be there. If this ship is in good working order in a year, it will be by the grace of God. It is another poor example of how the Navy knows little of what they are doing but are sure to spend a lot of the taxpayers' money.

25 September 1957 (Staten Island, NY) I believe that we shall be here in the shipyard for at least another two weeks. It seems as though there is always something wrong. As a matter of fact, the man who brought your letter had to use a flashlight to find me. We had lost the plant, and there wasn't a light on the ship. At first it used to upset me, but it has happened so often now that I am used to it.

We were working on the main engines today and found that the thrust and pedestal bearings were receiving no lubrication at all. A few yardmen and myself took them apart and found the trouble. I can't believe that the Navy used the ship like that. If so, they must have replaced a bearing every few hours. But, as I have told you, the Navy has a strange way of doing things.

10 October 1957 (New York) The "Bay State" is little by little starting to look like a ship. It has been a long and tedious grind, but I believe that it will prove its worth. It is at least of a size and construction comparable to that which the graduates will work on as officers. If they, the powers that be, stay away from the Navy side of the picture it shall be a fine training ship.

I have missed quite a few classes since I have been here in New York and have done little if any studying on my own. I shall have to make up for this in the next few weeks.

20 October 1957 (New York) I found out this morning that we will not leave here this week after all. I believe that it has been postponed until a week from Thursday. I am back in my old spirits again, my love. This morning I got into another verbal battle with Mr. C[onnors]. His attitude will never change.

21 October 1957 (New York) It is now expected that we will leave here on Thursday as was previously planned. However, I don't believe that we will. There is always something to do, and then there is the wait for the outfitters to do the job. The people who run this outfit are penny wise and pound foolish...The ship has put out over $250,000 for what $150,000 would have paid for the job had it been handled correctly. However, I am learning by their mistakes, and I am storing these little facts away for future use.

I feel very badly today, for last night I inadvertently harmed one of the cadets. It seems that as I shut off the ship's water to fill some empty tanks, our friend was in the shower. As soon as the water stopped, he got hit on the back with live steam. He was taken to the hospital last night and came back after they had dressed the burn, which was quite a relief for me.

It is getting colder and colder around here, Jane. Last night I nearly froze to death. Of course, when they wrote the specifications for the repair, no one had thought about the heating system. Consequently we are without heat. That is one of the reasons for so many of the boys going down to the hospital with the flu.

28 October 1957 (New York) *We were to leave New York at 0800 Thursday but did not get out of there until after noon. First there was a steam leak in the admiral's quarters and then some broken equipment on the evaporators. We were out for half an hour or so when we had trouble with one of the boilers. It was a pain in the neck and took us several hours to find the trouble. After that we tried to blow the soot from the generating tube, but instead of going up the stack it blew into the forward engine room and made a hell of a mess. Shortly thereafter we had trouble with one of the main engines in the forward room and had to shut the plant down. So we limped back to Buzzards Bay with only one screw.*

8 December 1957 (New York) *There is talk of going to Boston either this week or next, but I don't know if it will come about or not...It is rumored that the ship has never had a stability test and that we must get one before we are able to put to sea.*

15 December 1957 (Boston, MA) *We are now swinging on the hook in Boston harbor and shall go in with the morning tide. After fueling we will proceed to the shipyard for a stability test and then back to the Bay.*

7 January 1958 *Today the Coast Guard was aboard, and they, as usual, found a million and one things which didn't conform with the rules and regs. When and if we ever come up to the specs, it will cost well over one hundred thousand – so I think. We shall get the old political bailout and seek a waiver.*

Today I had the misfortune to be around when we had an oil spill and 4,000 gallons of fuel oil came spilling out all over the mess deck. No one had any idea of where or why it was coming out. After about an hour we found that one of the fill lines had given way, and the oil was going into a _ _ _ _ (illegible) which had an open hand hole.

15 January 1958 *I have been making an exhaust blower for the forward engine rooms. The blower is high in the fidley (stack), and there are many BTU's present. Well...it was quite unpleasant to work there. I figured that I would save time if I didn't go down to the switch box and pull the fuse. Of course with the fuse on the current is still in the machine, and of all the wires to hit, I brushed the live one as I was putting some service in. I thought that my hair was standing on end. I hope you never have to feel 220 volts. The second time was the same thing, only it happened when the drill I was using shorted out.*

The picture of the ship, of course, is foreign, but it is quite common. It is similar to the American C-2. A five-hold ship, capacity about 10,000 gross tons. (100 cu. ft. to the ton.) This type of ship, however, is being replaced quite rapidly by the Mariner Class, which is a bigger and faster ship.

26 January 1958 (San Juan, PR) *We will put into port early in the morning and drop the hook for four days work and drill. The ship is a day late because of bad weather and numerous breakdowns...I honestly believe that each and every piece of equipment that we have has broken down at least once during this short trip. One day in particular we had a lot of trouble, and for the day's run we logged about fifty miles...I have worked on the main fuel pump so much that I can take it apart and put it back together again in my sleep.*

27 January 1958 (San Juan, PR) *As you can see from the postmark on my last letter, we are in San Juan, not in St. Thomas. We had to put in here for emergency repairs, and we will be here from three to ten days.*

29 January 1958 (San Juan, PR) *At the present time we are tied up to the Army pier and have been getting a lot of "in place" work done. Tomorrow we will shift piers and tie up in the shipyard. I don't think we shall come out of the water, but [that] remains to be seen...It seems like everything that is in the hardest place to get at or that we have no parts for is going completely out of order.*

7 February 1958 (Ciudad Trujillo, DR) *We fueled before we left, and a good percentage of that went on the deck. The fuel line that was used was old and rusty so the boilers went out because we couldn't keep a fire going in them. After an hour's run out of San Juan, the condensate pump came apart in a thousand and one pieces. After that one of the force draft blowers kicked out and so far has stayed out of order. The fuel pumps are shot to hell; we have only one out of four left. The main engines have a terrible rumble in them, which at first appeared at 10 rpms and stays until 30 rpms. So, all in all, we will be damn lucky if we don't have to send for a cutter to tow us in.*

20 February 1958 (Postmark: Merida, Yucatan, Mexico) *We just got over the bar [Mississippi River] and into the Gulf when the brand new force draft blower kicked out. And it is out for a good long time. It has a burned out armature. The after three burners are not in such good shape, either.*

Replies to "Letters To Lou"

22 February 1958 (Postmark: Merida, Yucatan, Mexico) It seems that the Admiral decided that he wanted to go to Progreso but forgot to check the charts. Now we are anchored five miles offshore and can't get in any further because the water is only 15 feet deep. We can't use a small boat for it is a 1-½ hour ride, at least, not to mention the wind and current. The pilot boat was kind enough to bring the mail out to us.

28 February 1958 (Havana, Cuba) We tried to get into the dock when we arrived here this morning, but after eighty-six engine orders we are still on the hook. This has been the only time that this ship has needed a tug, and it is the only time that we didn't get one. We made two do or die trips for the dock and several other runs, but all came to no avail. The wind was blowing quite hard, and on the first pass we nearly took the dock down. An emergency "full astern" saved us. After that, we called for the tugs, but we were in it up to our necks, and they did us little or no good.

4 March 1958 (Corpus Christi, TX) We may be in Texas longer than planned. It seems that the repair work will wait no longer. At least two of the fore [four] draft blowers are out of it completely. A couple of pumps need bushings and bearings badly, and the roar of the main engines is getting noisier by the day.

8 March 1958 (Corpus Christi, TX) The people in Corpus Christi did a job of welcoming the Bay State. We pulled alongside to the music of a fine brass band. After that a ...baton drill team from Del Mar performed...

The blowers went out today to be repaired and are supposed to be back before Sunday...According to the Admiral, we will leave Sunday.

(No date, but apparently Saturday) (Postmark: Jacksonville, FL; written: Corpus Christi, TX) If we leave here on time tomorrow, I will be quite surprised. The motors were due back today, but as of yet they are still being expected. To remove one of the motors from the engine room, a hole had to be cut in the bulkhead. This was done in San Juan and not welded back in place. It was done again here, but they are taking no chances in the future, for I see where they have drilled holes in order to bolt the plate back instead of a permanent welding job.

13 March 1958 (Tampa, FL) We now have a fuel pump, which I spent the day on, and a main engine out of order. The pump could be fixed if we had a hydraulic press aboard – which we do not – so that will have to go to the shipyard. I worked on it all day with Mr. Crosby, but with few tools and Norwegian steam, there is little that can be done. The main engine has a thrust and a pedestal bearing that have burned out.

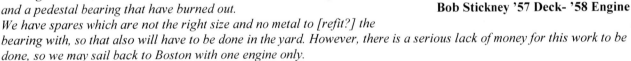

Bob Stickney '57 Deck- '58 Engine

We have spares which are not the right size and no metal to [refit?] the bearing with, so that also will have to be done in the yard. However, there is a serious lack of money for this work to be done, so we may sail back to Boston with one engine only.

14 March 1958 (Tampa, FL) I am sorry to report that we shall be at Tampa a good deal longer than we expected to. It is either that or lack a shaft and make our way back to Boston on one engine. The forward main engine has had the course. It couldn't move a foot if it had to.

16 March 1958 (Tampa, FL) Tomorrow is the day we will find out how long we are going to be here or if we stay at this yard at all. The engine casing will be lifted off, and if there is trouble with the [blading] we will have to go to a different yard.

17 March 1958 (Tampa, FL) We are leaving here on the morning tide this Wednesday. ...We are having a big drive to get as much done as is possible before we leave the yard. The yard made a bid on the work, but it would have cost too much and would have taken too long to do. I think it was around $60,000 and five weeks. It has taken all the money the school has to get the port shaft bolted in place so that no further damage will be done to the engine. With only one engine, which gives us a speed of six or seven knots, we will have had the course if we hit any weather at all. The next stop will be Jacksonville and then Boston.

22 March 1958 (Jacksonville, FL) We had a very slow and uneventful trip around the Keys. The ship moved along at a clipping four knots until we hit the Gulf Stream, which pushed us up to a smashing seven and one-half knots. It is not hard for anyone to tell that the Captain is not used to a single screw ship. It took us a good hour and three tugs to come alongside the dock.

24 March 1958 (Jacksonville, FL) There has been very little that has happened since I wrote yesterday, except things that are wrong with the ship, and I imagine that you are tired of hearing about them. All that I will say is that we are taking a slow boat to Boston and won't get there until next Sunday or Monday – that is if the weather holds good the whole trip.

8 April 1958 The ship arrived in Boston a little ahead of time. The trip was not bad except for some bad weather around the Carolinas. In Boston both of the main engines were taken out to be worked on. They will be back to us down here on the Cape.

25 April 1958 Today I had the pleasure of showing 50 Cub Scouts around the ship. It was a group from the Admiral's hometown, and he personally shook hands with each of them. I believe that the Admiral got more out of it than the kids did.

22 May 1958 Today, as you know, is Maritime Day, and this place was jammed with people who had come down to check out the big boat. The supply officer had sandwiches and coffee for them on the mess deck.

15 June 1958 I don't know what is going to happen…here we have about five weeks to go to school, and the ship is about to go into dry dock again. We don't know where we will go or for how long, but we shall leave either this week or next. The kids are out now, and we will more than likely end up in New York or in Baltimore. It will make a fine thing for the license exams! …I think graduation is to be postponed.

18 June 1958 The people around here are all upset for the word is out that we shall go to the shipyard early next week.

20 June 1958 Today was a very exciting day around here, indeed. The good ship Bay State got into its first accident. A tow was coming up the canal and suddenly lost its steering gear. As the current was running with it at about six knots, the tow quickly caught up with and smashed into the tug. In order to prevent its possible capsizing, the tug cut across the canal.

However, it failed to notice that a Swedish freighter was coming down the canal, also. The freighter pulled out as much as he could and then dropped the anchor. This was a positive action to be sure, but with the speed of the ship combined with the speed of the current, it was not enough. Realizing this, the Swedish captain started to back down full and pivot on his starboard anchor. This almost worked out, but the current carried him along a little too far and right into the bow of the Bay State he went. There was a lot of noise and little damage – thank God for that. I must say that the captain of the Swedish ship did a fine job considering the circumstances of the case.

23 June 1958 We leave here on Wednesday morning for the Ordell [note: Ardell?] Marine Corp. in Brooklyn, NY. It is estimated that we shall be there until the 25th of July. I, however, have my own idea on that, and I will give us until at least the first of August…The second and third classes will go on a leave period while we are down there, but the first classmen shall not. The reason is that they intend to hold special classes for the graduating class while we are in the shipyard.

29 June 1958 (Postmark: Brooklyn, NY) The weather is very hot, and it does not cool down a bit even at night. This makes for very uncomfortable living, for the ship is steel and gets red hot in the sun. Not only that, but most of the blowers are out of the ship to be repaired.

5 July 1958 (Brooklyn, NY) It is a shame the way this school is run. All the time that we are putting into ship repairs is for naught. The work is not being done properly – why, I don't know, but that is the way it is. The other day they found the low-pressure turbine to be out of balance. The damn fools, instead of fixing it, are going to put it back together in the same manner as they found it. The reason they gave is that it would cost too much to fix it. However, they seem to lose sight of the fact that when they put the high-pressure turbine back, they will still have only half of an engine that is working properly. And it will not take long for the l.p. to foul up the h.p., and the ship will have to come back into the yard. Perhaps now you can see how I got so angry with the people around this place. It makes me sick to see useless things as this going on when, with little or no effort, the job could be done properly in the first place.

9 July 1958 (Brooklyn, NY) We are trying to hold classes while the ship is here so that we might be able to get out of school on time. It is almost a waste of time, for the heat is sweltering, the subjects boring, and the noise from the fabricators much too loud.

I have a very sore head. The decks and the ship have been covered with an insulating material. It has added about an inch to an inch and a half to the deck. As I am quickly learning, I now must duck for things I never had to [duck for] before and duck lower for the things that I already do duck for. A few more bumps and cuts and I should have the pattern figured out pretty good. [Note: Bob was 6'4 1/2" tall.]

14 July 1958 (Brooklyn, NY) There is talk of getting out of here by this Friday night, but unless these yard people can do wonders, I don't believe that we shall make it.

16 July 1958 (Brooklyn, NY) [Note: They are taking exams while on the ship.]

19 July 1958 Today we had a four-hour dock trial, and on Monday we will have an eight-hour sea trial. We will go out around the lightship and run her at full speed for at least four hours. After returning to the shipyard on Monday evening we will have to pull the turbine and check it all over again.

21 July 1958 (Brooklyn, NY) The ship has been completed satisfactorily, and we shall sail tomorrow at 8:30 which will bring us back into the Bay around seven on Wednesday.

24 July 1958 (Buzzards Bay) I have just come from the briny deep. It is my last night at the academy, and all my fine friends thought that I should go for a swim. It took me as a surprise, as I came aboard a group formed around me and, in about two seconds, over the side I went. The water was cold, really cold.

[Note: At this point Bob left the ship, and it was not mentioned, to my knowledge, in subsequent letters. Jane S. Stickney]

1958 FIRST CRUISE OF THE BAY STATE ITINERARY

ARRIVE	PORT	LEAVE	DISTANCE	IN PORT	AT SEA
	Buzzards Bay	20 Jan Mon	1550		7
24 Jan Mon	San Juan, PR	7 Feb Fri	250	11	1
8 Feb Sat	C. Trujillo, DR	10 Feb Mon	1565	2	6
16 Feb Sun	New Orleans, LA	19 Feb Wed	556	3	2
21 Feb Fri	Progreso, Mex	25 Feb Tues	4204	2	
27 Feb Thurs	Havana, Cuba	3 March Mon	860	4	3
6 Mar Thurs	Corpus Christi, TX	9 March Sun	810	3	3
12 Mar Wed	Tampa, FL	15 March Sat	610	3	2
17 Mar Mon	Nassau, Bahamas	20 March Thurs	410	3	2
22 Mar Sat	Jacksonville, FL	25 March Tues	750	3	3
28 Mar Fri	Philadelphia, PA	31 March Mon.	419	3	2
2 April Wed	Boston, MA	5 April Sat	54		1
5 April Sat	Buzzards Bay		7854 Total		

*[Note: Copy of the itinerary, which had been revised Feb. 15th after the ship's initial mechanical troubles. You can tell from the dates of the letters that it was not followed. **Jane Stickney**]*

REGARDING THE ACQUISITION OF THE CHARLESTON

Email from Capt. Neil A. Daboul '88…28 September 1998…I found a documentary biography on the SS American Mariner by Herbert Paul Hahn some time ago. The ship has a very interesting history. There is an entire chapter devoted to the 1948 cruise where the Charleston was picked up in Florida and brought back to MMA. The author includes many photos of memos to the Dept. of State. What was the deal with that cruise anyway? You guys in the '48 cruise were scheduled to go on the American Sailor but he mentions a ship called the Yankee States as a training ship also? I would love to see some details on that period.

Email from Capt. Robert E. Vaughn '49…28 September 1998…The cruise of 1948 is well documented in the Muster for 1949. Our class departed Buzzards Bay in January 1948, with Maine Maritime cadets, in the USTS American Sailor. That ship was a Hog Island freighter with a one screw wet water wheel turbine plant.

Many years later, when I was on a sea trial with Rickover, I commented on the fact that our newest submarines were using a steam plant that had it genesis in the 20's. He did not take kindly to my remarks. Our first port of call was at Tampa. We lived in the Sailor while we cleaned and prepared the USTS American Mariner for the next leg of our cruise. The Mariner was a liberty ship with a reciprocating engine. All of the engineers learned about drawing a "D slide valve" from memory, as that was purportedly a big question on the license exam. Now, I don't recall if it was or not.

We sailed through the Panama Canal to San Francisco where we picked up the Charleston. That made our trip infinitely more interesting than if we had picked up the Charleston at Tampa, as you imply in your e-mail. The Maine cadets returned to Tampa in the Mariner. We picked them up in Charleston and took them to Castine before our cruise ended with a port stop in Boston.

Hope this helps to broaden your base of knowledge about the 48 cruise. I thought it was grand. One of my room mates was caught, at Long Beach, trying to jump ship through the Mariner's fueling port!!

The USTS American Sailor, a Hog Island freighter, with a water wheel turbine plant that I next went to sea with 17 years later in a nuclear powered submarine, for passage to Tampa. We prepared the American Mariner, a Liberty ship, reciprocating engine, for the trip to San Francisco via the Panama Canal, Acapulco, and Long Beach. Three very different ships made for a good education for us snipes. My personal contribution to the cruise was a profound statement about shaft alleys, "When you've seen one, you've seen them all."

William J. Connors (the Bum), Louis A. Woodland ("Lord Louie") and James M. Murray all made the cruise with us. Murray was embarrassed when we laid dead in the water for a day before we could get into Acapulco. I don't recall what happened to the plant. It may have been the main engine because I recall we lights all the time we were wallowing around.

*Email from Don Leach '49...*Hi: Read your offering and the comments you have received and decided I had better get on board. I was with the class of 49 and made the trip to the West Coast to retrieve the gray ghost at Hunters Point Naval Shipyard, also history now. I have a picture I found on the ship during final cleaning that showed the ship on China Station, guns evident, probably prior to WW II. Also have a cut down brass shell casing, Japanese origin, probably a souvenir that someone put away and forgot. I found this in the engine room bilge when as a "deckie" I was being introduced to the engineering department. Great memories.

CHARLESTON BOILER ROOM

Email from Paul Driscoll '62 thru '65...October 2001...Paul attended MMA for three years until he was dismissed for unceremoniously dumping Stupid Junior's maintenance truck in the canal. History sometimes repeats itself. His father, the Captain, lost his car to the canal during the hurricane of September 1954 about 11 years earlier.

Oh hi it's me. I have this half hour ordered the book, "Letters to Lou". I ordered it through Barnes and Nobel. God love them. It had a review done by **Anthony Scarlata**, one of your classmates, I'm assuming these are letters to his mother or his girl friend. It must have been something doing cruises on the Charleston. I have done some quick and cursory look sees into the "Chung". It was referred to as a "Banana Battleship" because it spent so much time in the Caribbean, as part of the Special Service Squadron. It and the Erie had Seaplanes stowed aft of the Stack. They were also the first ships to have installed the "NEW" 47 Caliber 6" guns. I have a question; one of the stories about the Chung was that the something or other Maru was traversing the canal. Some guys were bored out of their skulls or had made some shine or got some beer, or all of the above. They climbed into the turret and followed the Watchamacallit Maru with the 6" 47. The Japanese took a dim view,, wrote letters to the Navy, and that which we all know the existence of, grew in shape and immediately rolled down hill at a high rate of speed.

That was one of the stories that was told to us, as the reason we could not receive weapons training to enhance our Naval Reserve Midshipmen's status.

I have stories at all levels of my involvement in MMA. Before, During and After. A whole lot after. And that reminds me of a story. I'm out on 128, as a Massachusetts State Trooper, going south on Rt. 128. I see a kid in uniform. I'm on patrol. Cruiser 268. 460 cu. in. engine. I stop. Get in! Where are you headed? "Sir, I'm enroute to Buzzards Bay. I'm going to school there." Really? I say. It was like 5:00 PM. What time are you due back? Kid says, "My liberty is over at 1800 hours, Sir." I'm heading south, from the HJ's in Newton. I'm asking him questions about the ship, the courses. He doesn't know whether I'm going to lock him up or what.

He's not paying attention to the area. I make a couple of radio transmissions about going off the clock and enroute to home. He asks me if he could get a ride to Route 24, he would be most appreciative. We had already blazed by the ramp to 24. He was sitting in the back wondering why all the people on the highway were driving so slow cause we were passing them like they were going backwards. We are chatting about all kinds of stuff, what he wants to be when he grows up and what he wants to do when he graduates, etc., etc., etc. It dawns on him that we are on 25 approaching Wareham. I pull through the gate, and the kid climbs the gangway at about 1750. Totally bewildered. Newton to the Gulch in 45 minutes. Who knew? It was practice! And so much fun!

My reply: You talk about memory flashbacks...WOW!! Your story about delivering a cadet to the ship in a cruiser rang my bell! I "bummed" my way to and from MMA many times with a seabag full of laundry and food for the upper jobs (Tuna fish, etc.).

His reply: The story of me driving that kid of Mass. Maritime was one of those stupid things I did while I was out on patrol. I was constantly doing stuff like that cause I could fast forward and say to myself, "Will this kid by talking about this until he's 80?.....Yeah!" So off I went. The date of that little episode of nonsense was around the end of October of the beginning of November 1974. The Doyen was long gone, the Chief Engineer was **Oscar Forand** and one of the other engineers was **Gerry Miante**, both my former classmates '65. The ship they had was a cruise liner of some kind. I remember standing with Gerry and Oscar chatting about the Doyen and the school et al. Then I headed for my home in Duxbury. The cruiser was a 1973 Ford Custom, 460 cu. in. engine. It was a jet plane. 110 mph in that thing was a snooze. Cr. 268 was the number. I had that number for 3 years. It was my Nom de Plum of sorts. That was an amazing car. I had so many adventures in that Ford, it was really something.

Andover was a circus. I had black heads on my knees from doing deck plates until June of '68. Trying to explain what deck plates were was harder than Chinese Algebra. The most common question, "Why would you do that?" I just laughed. My stint at the Gulch, I had an instant answer for everything. Drove the Sergeants crazy. They couldn't understand how I always had an answer. The Corporals gave up after about 2 months.

Serious flashbacks. The cruises to me were more than time away from the snow and the gulch. They were an absolute adventure.

9 November 2001...This is so incredible. Cripes, this is like unreal. Was **Buz Schofield** a 2nd job when you graduated? He had something to do with the Lobster Festival in Marshfield 1963 and '64. Me and **John Borden** escorted a couple of the beauty queens. The first year, '63, the graduating class of '64 escorted the contestants and wore their whites.

In '64 they needed more escorts so they used 2nd jobs and we wore Summer Dress. What a circus! The local car dealers let us drive the girls with new cars. 1964. What do you suppose the Ford dealer let me and Bordoons drive? You guessed it. Mustangs!!! After we dropped the girls off, John and I drove out onto Route 3, SBL. We had the Lobster Festival Grand Prix. The engines were all carboned up for about a mile, then Zoooom. Cripes, we drove back to the Marshfield Ford and turned our cars in. Well, John did. I had mine for the rest of the day. I drove John back to Swansea. Why do I remember this?

Take care and stay happy. I'm getting rope burns from my Rosary Beads for the Diamondbacks. They deserve it.

I just thought of one. Did you guys ever bob for oranges in chocolate pudding? One Halloween we had the Witch Games. One kid was bobbing for oranges. He got one and blew his nose – there was enough for a Hershey Bar. We were laughing so hard somebody slipped in or was set in the chocolate pudding. That required a shower in the clothes on your back. That one just came to me. Oh, God, what other tidbits of foolishness and teenage deprivation lie just below the surface of my psycheeee?!!

Well, here they are…The big one was the inside liner of the cover of the 1964 yearbook. The '64 class was a really good class. Not only was it a good class, it had a lot of classy guys. They worked really hard at having a yearbook to be proud of. As near as I can figure this photo was taken by a man named **Melvin Howard**. I tried to get the son-in-law to look through his files to see if he could find the roll this photo was taken on. If he bracketed his shots, one of them may have shown more of Taylor Point. That would have been Taylor Point with all the houses. The places we used to march every Friday during NavSki drill. The upper jobs would smoke and yuck it up and basically made the youngies' lives hellish, unless the youngies were into making fools of themselves. NavSki drill was two clicks away from being the stupidest thing we would ever do in a group. Some of that stuff was so incredible, it was like the basis of the funny, stupid shit that has followed me for all of my like. Talk about being dipped in Stupid Sauce. That was the beginning. As **Capt. Bill Owen** used to say about the trainees in the State Police Academy, "Departments around the country would suck up our rejects". It was like the same thing at the "Gulch". Guys that couldn't follow a line of popcorn that they left for the return trip would end up being hired for stuff that would scare you. 2 funny! I tried for several years to get that picture of the Point, because every time we tell the story about how cut off we were, being surrounded by barbwire that faced in. We had to access the Point by the Black Iron Railroad Bridge that was condemned in the '70's. Wow! Who knew?

The other reason was, compared to the Academy of today, the average person could never imagine how the Academy started. The school was the ship and the ship was us. We were so different; we never realized how different until we came in contact with people that thought you never used anything else (Bunny Bread) for napkins. Hahahahaha!

And cockroaches were beings to be feared, not just a minor annoyance unless they got to the jelly first.

When you were going through the "Gulch" there was an Engineering Watch, 24 hours a day. There was an Engineering Watch right up until November of 1962. They installed a switching building to convert AC current to DC current for the ship. The only thing they needed the boilers for was hot water and heat. If you look behind the forward stack of the Bay State you can see the roof of the switching building. There were 3 lines that went on board the ship from the dock. We used to use them to jump ship and then go to the Blue Flame in Onset. Weren't we something? Jumping ship in the '60's. Who knew?

One time we jumped ship and **FL Dixon Yard** had the duty. He was on the Flying Bridge and turned on the signal/search lights and, POW, there are all these bodies on the Soccer Field. We all jumped up and ran back on board the ship. We made the ship before he could get to the 01 deck. Whew!! Talk about close! The stuff I remember about that place sometimes scares the crap out of me. Ever have one of those times, some smell or sound makes your brain go.zzzzzz zzzzzzstmmm boing!! And you start thinking about something and you can't remember when it was. But you think it was some out of body experience. I have those all the time. I usually laugh and say must have been back in my **Bobby Jobby** days. When else could that stuff have happened??

The picture, as near as I can figure, was taken probably in the early fall of 1963. The trees have leaves, the soccer field is there, but the lines are faded. The roof of the AC/DC building is there, and the ship is looking good. Every year when we came home the ship looked good cause that's all we did on Field Days, was paint and chip and chip and paint and paint some more. I could never imagine that I could get that much experience in 3 years of my life being in one place. But, surprise, surprise, it's only a movie. I wish they had taken a picture like this of the Charleston. What a picture that would be.

The current of the canal where the Doyen is docked can run as much as five knots. On a couple of occasions we tied a piece of plywood with a handle to the dock and we would aquaplane on the current. On one Sunday we were doing this and the current was strong enough that it looked real. Well, I was waving to the yachts as they went by. All went well until one guy freaked out and called the Coast Guard and tells them, "Some kid is water skiing in the canal and his boat ran into the dock at the school ship and he doesn't even know it he was still waving when we went by!"

Who was mad at us? Would you believe the Coast Guard, the Corps of Engineers, the Officer of the Day? Take your pick. They were all sore, but people on the other side of the canal got a big laugh out of it.

Tucked in behind the bow were two pulling boats twenty-eight feet long. We would have six to ten guys row over to Buttermilk Bay and dock on the north side of Route Six. The guy with the best phony I-D card would run across to the package store and for six bucks American we would buy two cases of Reading Beer (just the thought of consuming that stuff makes my bladder wanna run away from home!). About four beers apiece was our limit. Of course, a few guys refused to drink the beer because to them it tasted EVIL!

We would then row around Buttermilk Bay saying "Hi" to the pretty girls and their Moms. Occasionally we would throw everybody overboard and have ABANDON SHIP DRILLS plus REPEL ALL BORDERS which scared everybody on shore - so much so that once they called the police.

One Saturday after we had cavorted in Buttermilk Bay, we tried to take the boat out under the railroad bridge and found that the tide had come in. What to do? If we left the boat and walked back to the Academy it would have meant Captains Mast for all of us. So we ended up getting a couple of buckets and filled the boat with enough water to sink us to the point where we would just make it under the pipes that hung below the base of the bridge. We worked like coolies sinking the boat and pulling it under the pipes. Midway through one of the guys actually started crying, "What are we going to do if we sink?"

"Don't worry!" says I.

Another guy says, "We always do," and a third says, "We spend more time in the shit with Driscoll than a toilet bowl brush." We all laughed and then worked ourselves deaf, dumb and stupid getting the boat through. Then we had to bail it out. Any buzz we had from the beer was long gone and we felt awful.

We finally made it back to the ship. During the whole afternoon Commander Page, the O.O.D., had been watching us from the Bridge of the Bay State. He was getting such a laugh out of it he could barely control himself. We got it tied up, the oars stowed and the boat completely bailed. We had to help each other up to the dock, even though it was only a few feet. We were moaning and whimpering when from the ship above our heads Commander Page says, "Everything stowed away?"

"Yes, SIR!" we said in unison. What an afternoon. A few of the guys vowed they would never get in a boat with me and John Bowden again. We laughed. From 1962 to 1965 it was a never-ending string of situations and encounters, but we always had the good sense to get back to the ship.

Email from Tony Scarlata '57...10 November 2001...

Comments made in the year 1957...

"I'll tell you one thing, if things keep going the way they are, it's going to be impossible to buy a week's groceries for $20."

"Have you seen the new cars coming out next year? It won't be long before $5000 will only buy a used one."

"If cigarettes keep going up in price, I'm going to quit. A quarter a pack is ridiculous..."

"Did you hear the post office is thinking about charging a dime just to mail a letter?"

"If they raise the minimum wage to $1, nobody will be able to hire outside help at the store."

"When I first started driving, who would have thought gas would someday cost 29 cents a gallon. Guess we'd be better off leaving the car in the garage."

"Kids today are impossible. Those duck tail hair cuts make it impossible to stay groomed. Next thing you know, boys will be wearing their hair as long as the girls."

"I'm afraid to send my kids to the movies any more...ever since they let Clark Cable get by with saying "damn" in "Gone With The Wind", it seems every new movies has either "hell" or "damn" in it.

"I read the other day where some scientist thinks it's possible to put a man on the moon by the end of the century. They even have some fellows they call astronauts preparing for it down in Texas."

"Did you see where some baseball player just signed a contract for $75,000 a year just to play ball? It wouldn't surprise me if someday they'll be making more than the president."

"I never thought I'd see the day all our kitchen appliances would be electric. They are even making electric typewriters now."

"It's too bad things are so tough nowadays. I see where a few married women are having to work to make ends meet."

"It won't be long before young couples are going to have to hire someone to watch their kids so they can both work."

"Marriage doesn't mean a thing any more; those Hollywood stars seem to be getting divorced at the drop of a hat."

"I'm just afraid the Volkswagen car is going to open the door to a whole lot of foreign business."

"Thank goodness I won't live to see the day when the Government takes half our income in taxes. I sometimes wonder if we are electing the best people to Congress."

"The drive-in restaurant is convenient in nice weather, but I seriously doubt they will ever catch on."

"There is no sense going to Lincoln or Omaha anymore for a weekend. It costs nearly $15 a night to stay in a hotel."

"No one can afford to be sick any more; $35 a day in the hospital is too rich for my blood."
"If they think I'll pay 50 cents for a hair cut, forget it."

Email from Mat Cleary '94...18 February 2000...Got this off the marine list from a Capt. Shelton and thought it good enough to pass on...How to Simulate Shipboard Life – For Ex-Sailors Who Really Miss "The Good Old Days"

1. Sleep on the shelf of your hall closet.
2. Replace the closet door with a curtain.
3. 6 hours after you go to sleep, have your wife whip open the curtain, shine a flashlight in your eyes, and mumble: "Whoops, sorry wrong rack".
4. Build a wall down the middle of your bathtub, and lower the showerhead to chest level.
5. While showering, turn off the water while soaping.
6. Put "lube oil" in your humidifier, and turn it on "high".
7. On TV, watch only old movies in the middle of the night, have your family vote on a movie to watch, then show a different one.
8. (for Snipes) Leave the lawn mower running in your living room for 24 hours.
9. Have the paperboy give you a haircut.
10. Once a week blow compressed air up your chimney, watch the soot land on your neighbor's car, and laugh while he curses you.
11. Buy a trash compactor, but only use it once a week. Until then, store the trash in the other half of the bathtub.
12. Wake up at midnight and have peanut butter on stale bread.
13. Make up your family menu for a month in advance without any regard for the inventory of food on hand.
14. Set alarms to go off at random times. When they go off, run into your yard, grab the garden hose and wet down your house.
15. Once a month take every appliance apart (whether they need it or not) and put them back together; hoping you do it right.
16. Invite about 85 people that you don't really like to stay with you for about 2 months.
17. Install a 6" fluorescent light under your coffee table, and then lie under it to read a book.
18. Lockwire the lug nuts on your car.
19. Once a week, throw the cat in the pool and shout, "man overboard". Then run into the kitchen, sweep all the dishes off the table, and yell at your wife for not having the place "stowed for sea".
20. Use 17 scoops of coffee for 8 cups of water, let it stand for 6 hours with the grounds still in the pot, and then drink it.

Email from Jack. A. Butler '47...18 February 2000...To that list, I'd add:

16a. Wonder which of the guests lifted your wallet while you were showering.
21. When the breeze comes up take your tablecloth directly out of the washer and spread it damp on the kitchen table where you can then eat your dinner comforted that your plates won't slide off to the floor.
22. When your laundry bag is full to bursting, have your wife start fixing the washer then hand you a bucket, scrub brush and bar of soap to tide you over. String the clean stuff to dry around your shelf in the closet
23. (Deck Apes) Just before sacking in, arrange to have someone take that 24-hour lawn mower and run it by your window in short passages for several hours to remove the cargo of grass. It helps if they turn it off for very short periods until you fall asleep.
24. The day you've cashed your paycheck and come home from the bank with cash have friends drop by to see if you want to continue your membership in the union, or need life insurance, toothpaste or condoms.
25. Collect old magazines from your Jiffi-Lube dealer to read in a few months when you get bored.

Email from Larry Marsden – Author of "Gemini Ship"...21 May 2002...Jim Finch, author of **"Desert Sailor"**, forwarded this tome. As I told him in my reply, "He may not have been a Browning or a Keats, but he was able to bring tears to the eyes of this old sailor." Hope you like it. Larry

Just A Simple Sailor

He was getting old and paunchy and his hair was falling fast
And he hung out with his buddies telling stories of the past,
Of a war that he had fought in, and the deeds that he had done
In his exploits with his buddies; they were heroes, every one.

And 'tho sometimes to his neighbors, his tales became a joke
All his buddies listened, for they knew whereof he spoke
But we'll hear his tales no longer, for old Nick has passed away
And the world's a little poorer, for a sailor died today.

No, he won't be mourned by many, just his children and his wife,
For he lived an ordinary, very quiet sort of life,
He held a job, and raised a family, simply going on his way;
And the world won't note his passing, 'tho a sailor died today.

When politicians leave this earth, their bodies lie in state,
While thousands note their passing and proclaim that they were great,
Papers tell of their life stories from the time that they were young,
But the passing of a sailor goes unnoticed, and unsung.

Is the greatest contribution to the welfare of our land
Some politician who breaks promises and cons his fellow man?
Or the ordinary fellow who in times of war and strife
Goes off to serve his country and offers up his life?

The politician's stipend and the style in which he lives
Are sometimes disappropriate to the services he gives,
While the ordinary sailor, who offered up his all,
Is paid off with a medal, and perhaps a pension small.

It's so easy to forget them, for it was so long ago
That our Nicks and Jims and Johnnys went to battle – but we know
It was not the politicians, with their promises and ploys,
Who won for us the freedom that our country now enjoys.

Should you find yourself in danger with your enemies at hand
Would you want some politician with his ever-waffling stand?
Or would you want a sailor who has stepped up to defend
His home, his kin, and country, and would fight until the end?

He was just a common sailor and his ranks are growing thin
But his presence should remind us, we may need his like again.
For when countries are in conflict, it's the unsung hero's part
To clean up all the troubles that the politicians start.

If we cannot do him honor while he's here to hear the praise,
Then at least let's give him homage at the ending of his days.
Perhaps a simple headline in the paper that might say,
OUR COUNTRY IS IN MOURNING, FOR A SAILOR DIED TODAY.

Written by an unknown sailor aboard USS Lexington (CV-2)

In Keeping With Tradition
MMA Alumni-Talk Page

*Email from David Anderson '91…10 December 2001…*Article from the "Cape Cod Times" today…
31 youths arrested after police disperse party
SANDWICH – Police arrested 31 young people, mostly cadets from the Massachusetts Maritime Academy in Buzzards Bay, at a party in East Sandwich late Friday night. Officers were called to a rented house on North Shore Boulevard at 10:08 p.m. after receiving a complaint that young men were urinating along the road.

Each person arrested was charged with being a minor in possession of alcohol. Nearly all were 18 or 19 years old, according to police, along with one 16-year-old female and a 20-year-old male.

One of those arrested, an 18-year-old MMA cadet, had apparently rented the house.

No damage was reported to the house or neighboring properties, police said, and those arrested cooperated with police.

All were released on personal recognizance later that night. With the exception of the juvenile, those arrested are scheduled to be arraigned in Barnstable District Court tomorrow. The juvenile will be arraigned on a separate date, police said.

*Email from Chuck Sweet '59...11 December 2001...*More likely that MMA's punishment is worse than the State's. Some people will be spending a lot of time in their Chambrays this cruise...

*Email from Josh Hill 2001...11 December 2001...*Hi there...just thought you may be interested...from a "leak" at MMA. 23 cadets, all charges dropped. The cadet whose family rented the cottage are getting a $600 fine. I guess they were partying and no water in the house. Neighbors did not appreciate all the urinating in the outdoors.

Now the bad news...all cadets are getting three Class II tap sheets. I guess underage drinking in the state of Massachusetts is allowed now!

AND MORE TRADITION

*Email from Al Wilson '59...04 December 2001...***Mass Maritime Academy Cadets Ship Out to Train and to Support the United States Armed Forces**

Twenty-eight MMA Cadets will be forming up this Christmas Eve morning on the Academy's parade field. They will then board a military bus and spend the next two months on Military Sealift Command ships throughout the world.

Most college Juniors are preparing to spend the holidays with their families, exchanging gifts and going to parties. Not so at Mass Maritime Academy. Approximately 80 Cadets have chosen to do their winter training at sea, Military Sealift Command ships and other American Flagged vessels.

On the morning of December 24th, 28 cadets will be packing their sea bags at their home and saying their good-bye's to Mom, Dad, brothers, sisters, relatives and loved ones. They will report to Mass Maritime Academy at 0700 for a breakfast, sponsored and paid for by the Academy Alumni Foundation and MMA Alumni Association.

At 0900 the Cadets will say their farewells and board the Military bus for Norfolk, Virginia. All well-wishers are welcome to see the Cadets off at this time. (Bring a flag to show your support.)

The Cadets will spend Christmas Day together in Norfolk, VA and will begin processing on the 26th. After this has happened, the Cadets will receive their orders and will be sent to their assigned ships.

This is an assignment each Cadet feels strongly about. This is what they have been trained for in support of our national goals. It is a tradition for the U.S. Merchant Mariners and Cadets to serve when needed.

Hats off to the Cadets and Mariners who are serving during this holiday season.

"LET'S ROLL"

God Bless America

About The Author

Upon graduation I was assigned to the USS Gatling (DD-671), a year later transferred to the Baltimore Training Center and Officer In Charge of the USS Hampton (PCS-1386), then to the USS O'Hare (DDR-889), and finally was allowed to resign in 1963. I loved the Navy…but I hated the long Mediterranean cruises and being away from my family.

The highlight of my Naval career occurred October 1962 while as Operations Officer on the USS Charles S. Sperry (DD-697) we located and surfaced a Russian submarine during the blockade of Cuba. The recent movie "13 Days" accurately portrayed the country's struggle to prevent nuclear war and brought back many memories. Ironically, thirty-nine years later the Academy's schoolship and forty-five cadets were used for this film.

I retired in 1994 from the Smithsonian Astrophysical Observatory. For thirty-one years I was privileged to work for some outstanding people and on a number of fascinating projects. A knowledge of navigation started my Satellite Tracking career working in Florida, New Mexico, and in Shiraz Iran (2 years). In 1967 I was fortunate to be selected to conduct "seeing tests" on Mt. Hopkins, near Amado, AZ, for the future Fred L. Whipple Observatory. In the subsequent years, I installed and worked on various telescopes and on the observatory's development. I retired as the Support Supervisor/Mountain Manager of the Fred W. Whipple Observatory.

Since retirement in 1994 I've operated a part time, home based, computer drafting and graphics business.

Lou and I are still happily married with three children, five grandchildren, and living in Southern Arizona.

Ben and Lou 1998